HISTORICAL ATLAS OF RELIGION IN AMERICA

HISTORICAL ATLAS OF RELIGION IN AMERICA

Edwin Scott Gaustad

HARPER & ROW, PUBLISHERS, NEW YORK AND EVANSTON

To Norma McEachron Gaustad

Contents

List of Figures

Maps are indicated in this list by the use of boldface type. For additional information on the statistical and geographical sources used in the preparation of maps, charts, and graphs, consult the Sources following each chapter and "A Note on the Sources," pages 165-166.

Color Map: **Religion in America: 1950** *endpaper pocket*

Preface

Late in the eighteenth century, the Reverend Thomas Bacon wrote from Maryland to his sponsoring mission society in England: "Religion among us seems to wear the face of the country; part moderately cultivated, the greater part, wild and savage." Bacon's suggestion that piety may be related to geography is not wholly unwarranted. While it is not the purpose of this work to create a "geotheology," environment did palpably influence the nature and the progress of that institutional religion which either withered or flourished on the American vine.

For the first time in its hoary history, Christianity entered a fresh and empty continent to explore, to settle, to redeem. No central authority directed the effort; no master plan supplied the details. Parish lines and political boundaries were yet to be hacked through the forests, flung across the mountains, pushed into the plains. Ecclesiastical overlords and political princes were 3,000 miles away in space and even further away in time. Here, in a boundless new world, one could improvise or experiment; one could become fearful or one could become brave. The form of modification or of revolution was often fixed by the shape of the land—by a land that "was ours before we were the land's." To this beckoning wilderness, men came on a grand errand. And while some chafed or scoffed or betrayed or fled, most found a continent worthy of their sacrifice and of their seed. They therefore gave themselves to the land "and forthwith found salvation in surrender."

There are at least six characteristics of American religion which owe their force to the milieu in which the churches and synagogues made their way: (1) *individualism,* evident not only along the frontier but also in the colonial assembly, market place, and church; (2) *experimentalism,* producing new revelations, new denominations, and a host of new interpretations; (3) *atavism,* in the sense of an effort to return across the centuries to the original, the primitive, the natural, to the Old Testament and the New; (4) *nativism,* in the broadest sense, involving the pride in and sense of superiority concerning that which was "American"; (5) *probabilism,* meaning that men, questioning the force and certainty of restrictions on their actions, repeatedly chose the path of greater liberty; and (6) *denominationalism,* in the sense of ecclesiastical organization which made no claim to be the Church Universal, but only a portion thereof, and further made no effort to direct or control all of the life of the communicant, but only a segment thereof.

To represent the religious history of America statistically and geographically is to generalize dangerously and to court disaster openly. All statistics have their deceptions, their ambiguities, their non sequiturs. Far from being exceptions in this regard, religious statistics may be considered the prime example. The criteria of membership vary, not only from group to group but also from age to age; the definition, to say nothing of the location, of a church changes; the reliability of records leaves almost everything to be desired. A work of this sort, accepting the risk of generalization, is almost certain to err, to omit, or—less pardonably—to distort. The reader's indulgence and his correction are sought.

In Part I, denominational growth has been judged principally in terms of the increase in churches. In the period covered in this section (1650–1800), membership statistics proved to be too spotty, too ambiguous, and too elusive to permit valid comparisons. To be sure, even the word "church" has its ambiguities. A church may be a chapel of ease, a preaching station, a body of like-minded worshipers, an imposing edifice. The general principle followed throughout this *Atlas* has been one of inclusiveness: i.e., all missions, chapels and the like, where identified, have been counted as churches. Figures 3 through 7, which provide denominational comparisons on the basis of the number of churches, are therefore to be understood only as approximate measures of strength, for "church" is not a standard, fixed quantity, but rather a fluid entity varying in size, import, and nature from one denomination to another, from one location to another.

Part II, spanning the period from 1800 to 1960, offers comparisons based both on number of churches and membership. Religious statistics in this later period acquire a firmer foundation, though even at best, significant uncertainties remain. (For a discussion of the sources available, see the statistical section of the Note on Sources, p. 165.) At first glance, membership appears to be a far more accurate index to denominational size than the number of churches. But "member," like "church," is a word of many interpretations. A member may be a contributor, a baptized infant, a communicant in good standing. Again, the principle of inclusiveness has been followed: i.e., if a report indicates 30 "communicants" and 60 "members," the latter figure has been regularly used. It is recognized, of course, that religious bodies vary in their inclusiveness when reporting membership. Some will never count as members those who have not communed, others will always count the baptized infant, still others will change their method of tabulation from time to time. Some report heads of families only; others, free persons only; and others, "born-again Christians" only. There appears to be no really acurate way to balance all these factors. To invent a mathematical formula of reduction (or of expansion) is to appear scientific, but the precision is false and therefore misleading. In general it must be kept in mind that there are qualitative differences in the statistics of members as well as of churches. For example, 100 Baptist churches will not be the equivalent of 100 Roman Catholic churches, but of something a good deal less (since one Catholic church normally serves a great many more communicants than one Baptist church). On the other hand, 100 Baptist members will not be the equivalent of 100 Roman Catholic members, but of something more (since Baptists count only "baptized believers"—adults—as members, while Catholics include the entire baptized family—infants and adults).

By comparing denominations in both ways (number of churches and size of membership), some balance of the variables described above is obtained. Thus, Figures 42 and 43 offer comparisons based on the number of churches, while Figures 40, 41, 95, and 96 offer comparisons based on membership. Again, the summary chart, Figure 127, is based on the number of churches, while the large color map is based on membership.

Part II continues the history and expansion of the eight religious bodies discussed in Part I. On the basis of their numerical strength, three other groups are added to the colonial fellowships: (1) the Disciples of Christ, (2) the Methodists, and (3) the Mormons, or the Church of Jesus Christ of the Latter-day Saints. In Part III certain other groups, most of which are of comparatively recent origin, are surveyed. Part IV abandons the denominational treatment to consider special aspects of American religion.

At the end of each section of the text, the reader will find full bibliographic information on the sources which have been quoted in the body of the text. The concluding bibliography ("A Note on Sources," pp. 165-166) is therefore limited to works which have been drawn on for the book as a whole. An Index to Authors and Titles is included to facilitate ready reference to any work cited or quoted in the *Atlas*.

In expressing appreciation to the many who made this book possible, a word of thanks must first be offered to the American Council of Learned Societies which in 1952-1953 granted a fellowship that provided for a protracted period of uninterrupted research. Brown University, with its accustomed generosity, extended the full privileges of the John Hay and the John Carter Brown Libraries during that period. More recently, members of the University of Redlands Library staff have endured with patience the trials set before them.

Any venture in book writing requires the close cooperation of publisher and author. But this has been particularly and acutely true in a work of this nature, involving as it does the sympathetic collaboration of many departments, persons, and skills. I am particularly grateful for the cartographic skill of John Tremblay, who gave final form to all but a few of the maps.

The courtesy of correspondents, the helpfulness of pastors, the graciousness of colleagues, the assistance of students—these acts of kindness are too numerous to mention but not too numerous to recall with warmest gratitude. Special acknowledgment must be made to two persons: Professor Robert T. Handy of Union Theological Seminary for an informed, critical reading of the text; and to my wife, without whom was not anything done that was done.

E. S. G.

A Note to the Reader

Following each quotation in the text, an abbreviated reference designates the author and page number of a work cited; full bibliographical information appears in the "Sources" listed alphabetically at the end of every chapter. For sources used in the preparation of maps, charts, and graphs, the List of Figures beginning on page vii and "A Note on the Sources," pages 165-166, should be consulted. The Appendices on pages 167-169 provide precise numerical summaries to supplement the key maps showing denominational distribution in 1650, 1750, 1850, and 1950. The color map contained in the endpaper pocket is discussed in detail on pages 159-162.

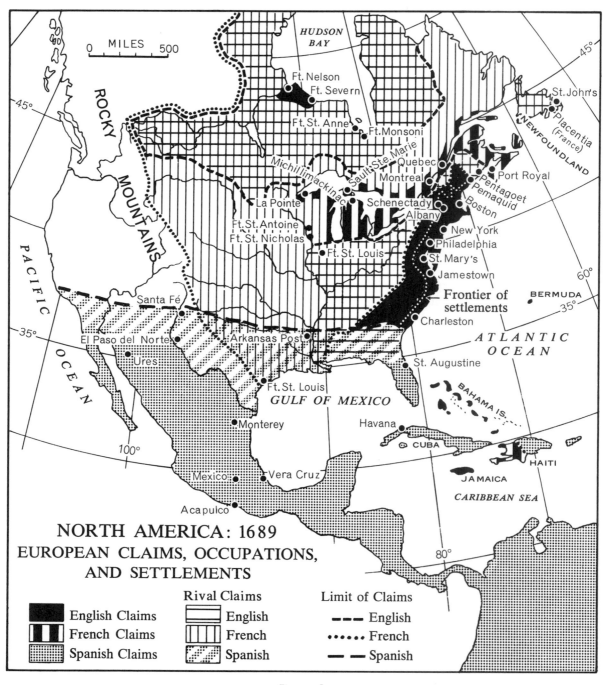

Figure 1

PART I

Religion in America, *1650–1800*

1. INTRODUCTION

It is difficult to believe that serious attempts have been made to describe the history of America's colonization in such a way as to ignore the role of religion. These attempts have, understandably, largely given way to more balanced accounts. For while it is hardly necessary to treat each colonist as though he were a flaming evangelist to the New World, only the most incautious and unskilled of surgeons would cut away that which more often than not gave direction and spirit to the body social. What follows here is, of course, in its own way an unbalanced treatment of colonial history. For the eye of the reader is kept upon the religious settlement and progress of the colonies, to the virtual exclusion of the thoroughly relevant areas of commerce and government, war and exploration. To a full understanding of America's colonial history, the story of religion contributes; but there is no suggestion that this is the whole story. The growth in the number of churches is here described (1) by the three major areas of settlement (New England, the Middle Colonies, the Southern Colonies), and in more detail (2) by the eight principal religious families.

New England. Because the story of the Pilgrim Fathers is so familiar, a detailed retelling of the events of the 1620's is unnecessary. Out of several colonizing efforts, Connecticut and Massachusetts emerged as the prime representatives of Congregationalism. The settlers were predominantly English, and religious homogeneity was more nearly achieved here than anywhere else in colonial America. Churches "of the Congregationall Way" received state sanction and support until well into the nineteenth century—a more enduring establishment than anywhere else in America. Neither the homogeneity nor the establishment was maintained without strenuous effort, and the history of both colonies is replete with litigation concerning unlawful assemblies, unauthorized preachers, intolerable opinions, improper promiscuity, and unthinkable tithe-evasion.

Yet, as early as 1670, the colonial records of Connecticut bear witness to a diversity distressing to the establishment. "Our people, in this colony, are some of them strict congregational men, others more large congregational men, and some moderate presbyterians. The congregational men, of both sorts, are the greatest part of the people in the colony. There are four or five seventh day men, and about so many more quakers" (Trumbull, I, 397). At this time the colony had 21 churches and a settled minister in each of the 26 towns "except in two . . . newly begun."

One element of heterogeneity not so negligible in quantity as the Sabbatarians and Quakers was the Indians. But the Congregationalists set to work almost immediately to convert these heathen, and the first Bible to be printed in America (and the only one in the seventeenth century) was John Eliot's translation of the scriptures into a phonetic approximation of the Algonquin's spoken language. In Massachusetts, churches of baptized Indians were established at Martha's Vineyard (1642), Sandwich (1658), Natick (1660), Middleborough (1665), Mashpee (1670) and West Tisbury (1680) (see Fig. 12). By the end of the seventeenth century, Cotton Mather, judging that the "Indians on the Islands of Martha's Vineyard and Nantucket, might justly bear the denomination of Christians," placed the number of adult converts there at 3,000 (I, 87).

Rhode Island was altogether another matter: establishment and religious homogeneity were far from its ken. Founded by Roger Williams in 1636, the colony "of Rhode Island and Providence Plantations" became a haven for all types of dissenters and malcontents. But "haven" is not the word the seventeenth-century observer was likely to choose; "stink-hole" seemed far more appropriate. When two Dutch Reformed ministers in New York bade an unreluctant farewell to some Quakers in 1657, they observed, "The following morning early they hoisted anchor and sailed eastward, towards Hellgate, as we call it, in the direction of New England. We suppose they went to Rhode Island; for that is the receptacle of all sorts of riff-raff people, and is nothing else than the sewer (latrina) of New England" (Hastings, I, 399 f.). There, all were tolerated; none was favored. In such clime, diversity and even novelty was to be expected, and there is no evidence of any disappointment on these counts.

New Hampshire and Maine reflected more the character of Massachusetts and Connecticut than of Rhode Island. Indeed, Maine was a part of Massachusetts throughout the colonial period, and New Hampshire was under its strong influence. Settlement of Vermont began only near the end of the period under discussion; and of that state Jedidiah Morse wrote in 1790, "As to the character, the manners, the customs, the laws, the policy and the religion of the people in Vermont, it is sufficient to say they are New Englandmen" (p. 471).

Middle Colonies. New York was first New Amsterdam,

1

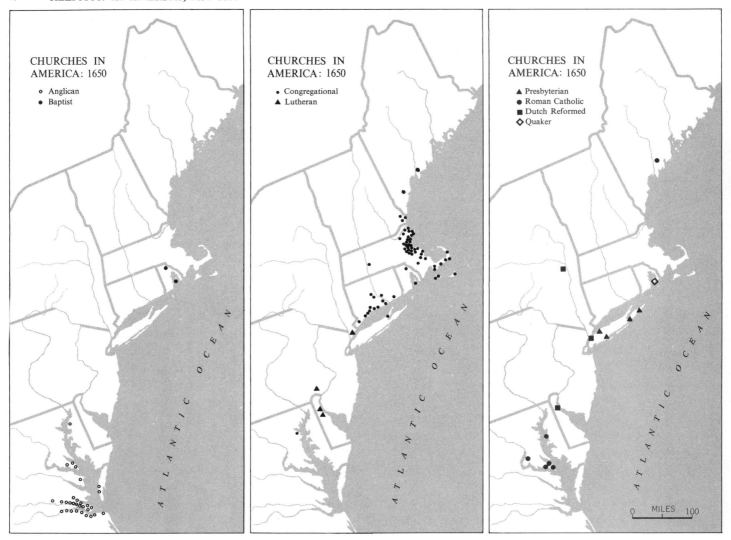

Figure 2

For location and date of each church, see Appendix A.

and the story of the Dutch Reformed in the early settlement of Long Island and along the banks of the Hudson River is a study in frustration. Every difficulty haunted and hobbled this early ambitious settlement until the British seized the land in the name of the Crown in 1664. Ten years later, English rule had to be reaffirmed, but thereafter it remained constant. The evidence of Dutch Reformed influence is still apparent, however, to the present-day tourist of Manhattan's churches. And in New York along with New Jersey, much of the strength of this denomination continues.

The Dutch Reformed ministers were, almost from the beginning, harassed by the problem of religious diversity. The English governor, Edmund Andros, found the situation in New York no better when he took over in 1686. The whole business of vital statistics broke down either because ministers were too perverse or too few. "Noe account," he wrote the British Board of Trade, "can be given of childrens births or christenings. . . . There are Religions of all sorts, one Church of England, severall Presbiterians and Independents, Quakers and Anabaptists of severall sects, some Jews. . . ." It was a discouraging prospect for the census taker.

In New Jersey the work of the Dutch had been severely limited by Indian hostility. At the time of the English conquest, there were only a few compact settlements, all in and around Bergen County. Some Swedish Lutherans along the Delaware River formed their first church at Wilmington in 1638; then they too came under English rule in 1664. With the extension of British influence over this area, many inhabitants of New England migrated into New Jersey, sometimes after a few years' pause on Long Island. One historian speaks of the "Connecticut zone covering the original Essex and Middlesex Counties, and the Rhode Island zone in Monmouth" (Tanner, 26). West Jersey was largely in the hands of the Quakers, and when it was divided into smaller proprietorships, the majority of these went to the Quakers. Most of the settlers in West Jersey, moreover, "were of English middle class, substantial artisans, tradesmen and small farmers," the very class, as Tanner notes, which the Friends themselves represented.

In Pennsylvania the Quakers achieved a dominance sufficient to assure the continued association of their name with that state long after numerical superiority had been lost. Like Rhode Island, Pennsylvania made a virtue out of what was to most a vice: freedom of religion. William

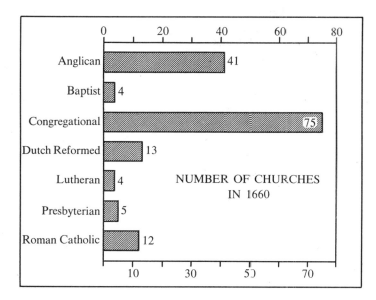

Figure 3

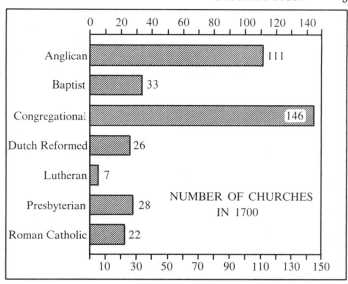

Figure 4

Penn's "holy experiment" began with the founding of Philadelphia in 1682, and before the end of the century, Mennonites, Keithites (a Quaker faction), and "some Independents, but neither many, nor much bigotted" (Bray, *Memorial*, 11) were in the land. The Church of England, too, had managed to erect "a very fine' building in Philadelphia by 1695. To a contemporary observer, Gabriel Thomas, the Swedes had the advantage of at least being religiously uniform: they were all Lutherans. But the English had no less than "four sorts of Assemblies here"—Anglican, Anabaptist, Presbyterian, and Quaker. In the next century Pennsylvania was to present a picture of even more remarkable diversification, largely as a result of the great influx of German immigrants. As Charles Woodmason wrote in 1766, "Africk never more abounded with New Monsters, than Pennsylvania does with New Sects, who are continually sending out their Emissaries abroad."

Southern Colonies. To one degree or another, the Southern Colonies had an official establishment of religion in accordance with the regulations and rubrics of the Church of England. But rarely has the official fallen so far short of the actual. Only in Virginia did Anglican establishment leave a permanent stamp, and even there the necessary compromises, the inevitable diversities, the insufficient ministries were clearly apparent. South Carolina in the seventeenth century was, from an Anglican point of view, almost respectable; but if one wandered very far from Charleston, he would likely find himself in a nest of Quakers or Huguenots or Anabaptists or "Persons careless of all Religion." There were also Indians and Negroes among whom there was for the most part no vigorous evangelizing effort.

Georgia and North Carolina, both slow in being settled, never felt to any appreciable degree the bane or blessing of Anglican establishment. And, at least through the seventeenth century, the Church of England minister had all that he could handle and more within Virginia and South Carolina. It seemed, indeed, as though one might be pushing Providence too far to seek out deliberately such an area as Currituck, North Carolina, which was "a very incommodius Place for damp Colds in Winter, and muschatoes in Summer" (Humphreys, ch. 6). The 839 souls there in 1702 simply had to struggle along a few more years without mission or missionary. Despite the earnest efforts of agents of the newly established Society for the Propagation of the Gospel (S.P.G.), North Carolina seemed to harbor, if it did not engender, everything but God-fearing churchmen. William Gordon wrote the S.P.G. in 1709 concerning the area of Perquimans: "The Quakers in this precinct are very numerous, extremely ignorant, insufferably proud and ambitious, and consequently ungovernable" (Hawks, *History of North Carolina*, II, 307). And even such Anglicans as could be found were hardly the sort to advance the cause of their church. The twelve vestrymen of Perquimans, Gordon reported, are "loose in their lives, and unconcerned as to religion. . . . Their ill example, and the want of ministers and good books, have occasioned many who were better disposed, through ignorance, to join with the Quakers; being willing to embrace any thing that looks like a religion, rather than have none at all." Others observed that North Carolina had many inhabitants destitute of all religion and "would be Quakers, if by that they were not obliged to lead a more moral life then they are willing to comply to" (Hawks, *Contributions*, II, 296).

The eighteenth century saw no improvement in North Carolina so far as Anglican proprieties were concerned. The irrepressibly indignant Charles Woodmason wrote in 1766:

As to North Carolina, the State of Religion therein is greatly to be lamented—If it can be said, that there is any Religion, or a Religious Person in it. . . . The manners of the North Carolinians in General are Vile and Corrupt. The whole Country is in a Stage of Debauchery, Dissoluteness and Corruption—and how can it be otherwise? The People are compos'd of the Out Casts of all the other

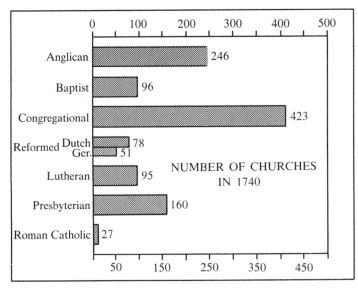

Figure 5

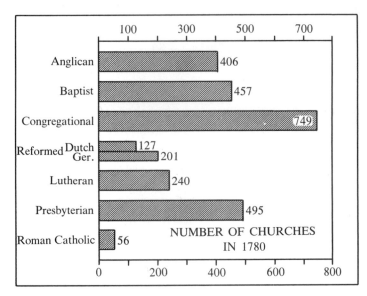

Figure 6

Colonies who take Refuge there . . . Marriages (thro' want of Clergy) are perform'd by ev'ry ordinary Magistrate.—Polygamy is very common—Celibacy, much more—Bastardy, no Disrepute—Concubinage General—When will this Augean Stable be cleans'd!

When Mr. Woodmason later considered the situation in Georgia, he noted that while it was "greatly below" South Carolina, it was "much superior in all respects to North Carolina." The valley of humiliation was never so completely humiliated as by this irate Englishman.

Virginia, a land where good books were not altogether absent, presented a more positive picture of religious progress. As its development so closely paralleled the development of Anglicanism itself, this growth is considered in the following section of the text (Part I:2).

Maryland was settled in 1634 under the auspices of the English Roman Catholic, Lord Baltimore, and the first church for English Catholics was established in 1640 at St. Mary's City. In Maryland as in New Amsterdam, there was pressure to encourage all respectable settlers in the new land. Whatever privilege the Catholic population may have sought or welcomed was lost, therefore, in the midst of a rapidly diversifying citizenry and a shifting governmental authority. Though the Roman Church continued to be strong in Maryland, it enjoyed no special privilege; indeed, before the end of the century it saw the colony of Maryland also become a royal province and the Church of England by 1703 the legal religion. While Maryland in the seventeenth century did, to a degree, become an asylum of dissent, it provided for the Catholics themselves no particular refuge from the Protestant suspicions and insults to which they were subject throughout the colonies. One contemporary complained bitterly that not until the eighteenth century was the populace of Maryland rescued from "the Roman Priests Cunning and the Quakers Bigotry" (Oldmixon, 333).

With the end of the colonial period, full religious liberty was the rule to which only New England Congre-gationalism was the exception. Church of England establishments dissolved rather soon after the king of that England was defeated. No other religious body—whether by position or preference—was a serious contender for federal patronage. In 1777 the State of New York repealed all laws or acts which "may be construed to establish or maintain any particular denomination of Christians or their ministers . . . [Furthermore] the free exercise and enjoyment of religious profession and worship without discrimination or preference shall forever hereafter be allowed within this State to all mankind" (Hastings, VI, 4300 f.). And a newborn nation, "conceived in liberty," turned toward its own holy experiment in religion and the free exercise thereof.

SOURCES. GENERAL. Thomas Bray, *Memorial representing the Present State of Religion on the Continent of North America* [London, 1700] (Thomas Bray Club, no date). Jedidiah Morse, *American Geography, or A View of the Present Situation of the United States of America* . . . (London [second edition], 1792). John Oldmixon, *The British Empire in America* . . . Vol. I (London [second edition], 1741). Charles O. Paullin, *Atlas of the Historical Geography of the United States* (Carnegie Institute of Washington and American Geographical Society of New York, 1932). Frederick Lewis Weis, *The Colonial Clergy and the Colonial Churches of New England* (Lancaster [Mass.], 1936); *The Colonial Churches and the Colonial Clergy of the Middle and Southern Colonies 1607-1776* (Lancaster [Mass.], 1938); *The Colonial Clergy of Maryland, Delaware & Georgia* (Lancaster [Mass.], 1950); and *The Colonial Clergy of Virginia, North Carolina and South Carolina* (Boston, 1955).

Population estimates for the colonial period may be found in Evarts B. Greene and Virginia D. Harrington, *American Population Before the Federal Census of 1790* (New York, 1932); W. S. Rossiter, *A Century of Population Growth* (Washington, 1909); and Herman R. Friis, "A Series of Population Maps of the Colonies and the United States 1625-1790" [American Geographical Society Mimeographed Publication #3] (New York, 1940).

NEW ENGLAND. John Callendar, *An Historical Discourse on the Civil and Religious Affairs of the colony of Rhode-Island* (Providence, 1739). Joseph B. Felt, *The Ecclesiastical History of New England* . . . 2 vols. (Boston, 1862). Jonathan Greenleaf, *Sketches of the Ecclesiastical History of the State of Maine* (Portsmouth, 1821). Robert F. Lawrence, *The New Hampshire*

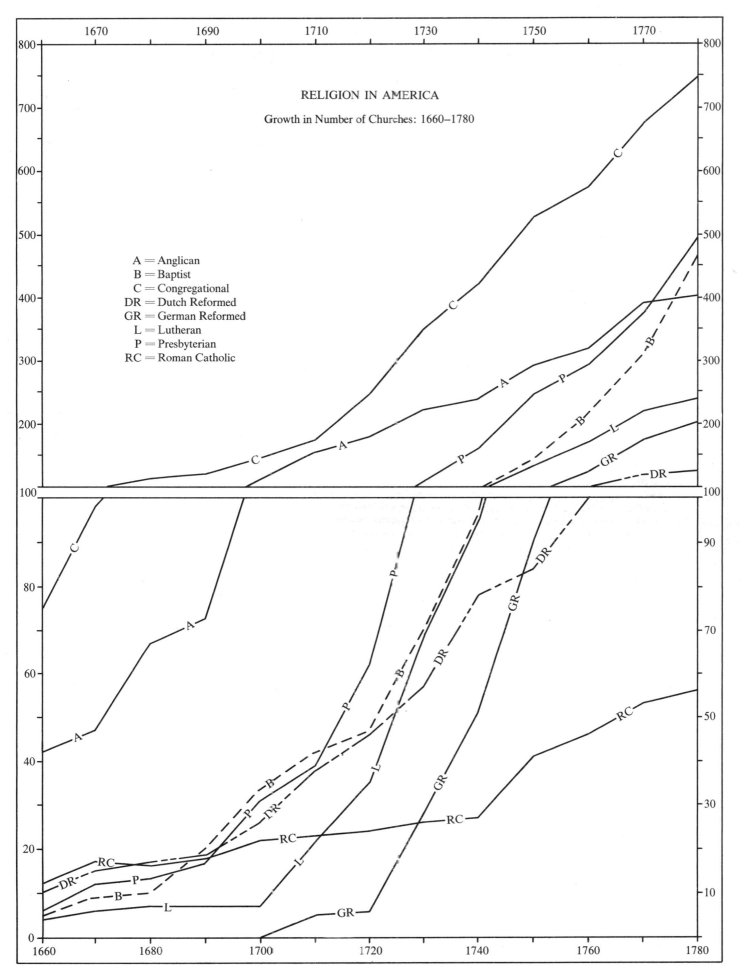

RELIGION IN AMERICA

Growth in Number of Churches: 1660–1780

A = Anglican
B = Baptist
C = Congregational
DR = Dutch Reformed
GR = German Reformed
L = Lutheran
P = Presbyterian
RC = Roman Catholic

Figure 7

Churches: comprising histories of the Congregational and Presbyterian Churches in the State, with notices of other denominations . . . (Claremont [New Hampshire], 1856). Cotton Mather, Magnalia Christi Americana . . . (Hartford [reprinted], 1855). Daniel Neal, The History of New-England Containing An Impartial Account of the Civil and Ecclesiastical Affairs of the Country To the Year of our Lord, 1700, 2 vols. (London, 1720). Benjamin Trumbull, A Complete History of Connecticut Civil and Ecclesiastical, 2 vols. (New London, 1898).

THE MIDDLE COLONIES. Thomas F. Gordon, The History of Pennsylvania . . . (Philadelphia, 1829). Hugh Hastings (ed.), Ecclesiastical Records. State of New York, 7 vols. (Albany, 1901-1916). Francis B. Lee, New Jersey as a Colony and as a State, 4 vols. (New York, 1902). Robert Proud, The History of Pennsylvania . . . 2 vols. (Philadelphia, 1797-1798). Samuel Smith, The History of the Colony of Nòva-Caesaria, or New-Jersey . . . (Burlington, 1765). Edwin P. Tanner, The Province of New Jersey (Columbia University Studies in History, Economics and Public Law, Vol. XXX) (New York, 1908). Gabriel Thomas, An Historical and Geographical Account of the Province and Country of Pennsilvania and of West New-Jersey in America (London, 1698; reprinted Cleveland, 1903).

THE SOUTHERN COLONIES. Samuel Ashe, History of North Carolina, 2 vols. [map following p. 376 shows settlements and races to 1776] (Greensboro, 1908). Robert Beverly, History of Virginia . . . (London [second edition], 1722). John L. Bozman, The History of Maryland from . . . 1633 to . . . 1660 . . . 2 vols. (Baltimore, 1837). Philip A. Bruce, Institutional History of Virginia in the Seventeenth Century, 2 vols. (New York, 1910). Charles Campbell, Introduction to the History of . . . Virginia (Richmond, 1847). B. R. Carroll, Historical Collections of South Carolina . . . 2 vols. [frontispiece map shows location of chapels and churches] (New York, 1936). William H. Foote, Sketches of North Carolina . . . (New York, 1846). Francis L. Hawks, History of North Carolina: with maps and illustrations, 2 vols. [very useful map, following p. 570, vol. II, showing precincts and settlements] (Fayetteville, 1858). Arthur H. Hirsch, The Huguenots of Colonial South Carolina [a parish map of the state around 1700 is contained herein, p. 14] (Durham, 1928). Robert R. Howison, A History of Virginia . . . 2 vols. (Richmond, 1848). David Humphreys, An Historical Account of the Incorporated Society for the Propagation of the Gospel in Foreign Parts (London, 1730). William Meade, Old Churches, Ministers and Families of Virginia, 2 vols. (Philadelphia, 1878). William J. Rivers, A Sketch of the History of South Carolina to . . . 1719 (Charleston, 1856). Stephen B. Weeks, The Religious Development in the Province of North Carolina (Johns Hopkins University Studies in Historical and Political Science, Tenth Series, V-VI) (Baltimore, 1892). Charles Woodmason, "Account of South Carolina, North Carolina, Georgia, &c" (manuscript in Library of Congress, dated 1766); also available in Richard J. Hooker, The Carolina Backcountry on the Eve of the Revolution . . . (Chapel Hill, 1953). Lawrence C. Wroth, "The First Sixty Years of the Church of England in Maryland, 1632 to 1692," Maryland Historical Magazine, XI: 1 (1-41).

2. ANGLICANS*

The first Anglican church in America was established at Jamestown in 1607. From that point in time and space, Anglicanism moved to the north and south and, at a slower pace, to the west following the rivers' courses (see Figs. 2 and 8). The Church of England was formally established (that is, received government sanction and support) in 1619 when the Virginia legislature made some financial provisions for the maintenance of an Anglican

* The term "Anglican" is used in the colonial period (Part I), the term "Episcopalian" in the national period (Part II).

ministry. There were at this time only five ministers of the Church in the colony (Hawks, Contributions, I, 35 f.). Legislative aid, however, could not forestall the Indians, who in a bloody massacre in 1622 reduced a population of about 3,000 to little more than one-half that number. Nor did establishment succeed in preventing a less bloody invasion of Massachusetts Congregationalists who, early in the 1640's, set up their worship in Nansemond County, Virginia.

There were quite enough internal problems, moreover, to keep the struggling Anglican enterprise anxious. Parishes were too large, transportation too awkward, and ministers too few. A Perfect Description of Virginia, published in London in 1649, noted that there were 20 churches in the colony for a population of about 15,000 English and "of Negroes brought thither, three hundred good servants." All the ministers observed "the Doctrine and Orders after the Church of England" and enjoyed livings "worth at least £100 per annum"—paid in tobacco and corn. The author's concluding observation on religion in Virginia, viz., that the inhabitants "all live in peace and love," places the document within that sizable category of apologia for the New World.

It was so far from being a "peace and love" situation that persons on the spot were close to desperation. In 1660 Virginia, possessing 35 of the 41 Anglican parishes in all America, would seem to have been in a superior position. But then one notes the condition of many of those parishes: without meeting house, glebes, parish house, or even a chapel of ease. The parish might be a legislative division and little more. Why? Well, the difficulties were many. A pamphlet printed in London in 1662 charged that the greatest curse hanging over Virginia was its neglect of public worship. The reasons given for this were two: (1) "scatter'd Planting," and (2) ministerial shortage. Concerning the first, the author's description of the "dispers'd Seating" of the inhabitants is impressive. There are, he writes,

about Fifty Parishes, the Families whereof are dispersedly and scatteringly seated upon the sides of Rivers; some of which running very far into the Country, bear the English Plantations above a hundred Miles, and being very broad, cause the Inhabitants of either side to be listed in several Parishes. Every such Parish is extended many miles in length upon the Rivers side, and usually not a mile in Breadth backward from the River . . . The Families of such Parishes being seated after this manner, at such distances from each other, many of them are very remote from the House of God, though placed in the middest of them. Many Parishes as yet want both Churches and Gleabes, and I think not above a fifth part of them are supplyed with ministers; where there are Ministers the People meet together Weekly, but once upon the Lords day, and sometimes not at all, being hindered by Extremities of Wind and Weather: and divers of the more remote families being discouraged, by the length or tediousnesse of the way, through extremities of heat in Summer, frost and Snow in Winter, and tempestuous weather in both, do very seldome repair thither (Force, ed., III, Virginia's Cure, 4).

The "cure" for this deplorable situation, the author declared, was to form "societies and towns" in which all the English would live, the plantations being run by the servants who themselves would "repair to their Houses in the Town, and there remain with their Masters until the publick Worship and Service of the Lords Day be ended" (p. 10).

For the second problem—the lack of clergy—the proposed cure was to establish "Virginia Fellowships." One of these would finance a promising young man through seven years of education at either Oxford or Cambridge, in return for which the candidate, following ordination, would agree to serve seven years in Virginia. That the problem was genuinely acute is evident from a legislative act of 1656 which offered a bounty of £20 sterling to anyone who succeeded in transporting "a sufficient minister" into the colony. But, as Francis Hawks observes, "the country was not in the best repute, and but few clergymen of merit were found willing to make it their permanent home. Clergymen emigrated, indeed, but so far as the colony was concerned, better had it been had they remained at home" (*Contributions*, I, 64 f.). Neither of the "cures" was adopted, and Virginia's difficulties only increased.

There was no sympathy "back home" and no uniformity of worship in the new land. When, late in the seventeenth century, Anglican leaders appealed to the mother country for money with which to build a college because they, like the New Englanders, had souls to be saved, the famous remark of an impatient Lord Seymour was evoked: "Damn your souls! Make tobacco!" Money, nonetheless, was raised and the College of William and Mary was chartered in 1693. When the legislature tried to encourage and provide the proper kind of worship for all there were those "schismatical persons" who "out of the new-fangled conceits of their own heretical inventions did refuse to have their children baptized." For such misguided souls, the legislature thoughtfully provided a fine of 2,000 [!] pounds of tobacco, one-half to go to the parish and the other half to the informer (Hawks, *Contributions*, I, 68).

Anglicanism elsewhere was, if anything, under even greater stress. In South Carolina at the beginning of the eighteenth century, there was only one Anglican clergyman outside of the city of Charleston, and this solitary soul had as his parish all the people settled along the three branches of the Cooper River. The white population of the colony was at this time about 5,000; of these, the Anglican cleric in Charleston wrote, the dissenters were "the soberest, most numerous, and richest people of the province" (Rivers, 216 f.). However, the inception of the Society for the Propagation of the Gospel in 1701 strengthened the position of the Church of England during the next several decades both in South Carolina and elsewhere. David Humphreys remarked in 1730 that "tho' there was scarce any Face of the Church of England in this Province, when this Society was first established, there have been

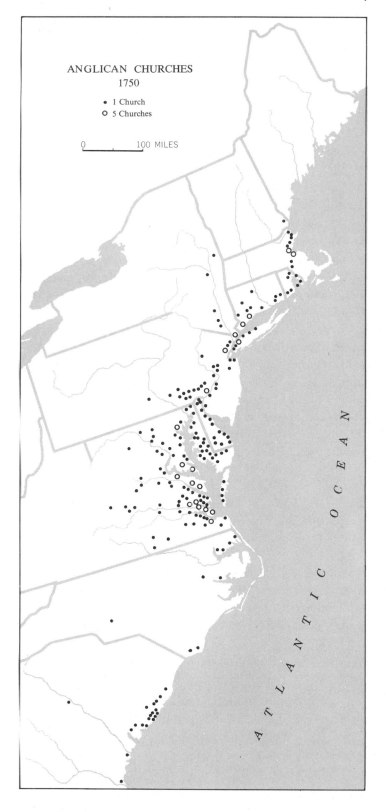

Figure 8

13 Churches, and 4 Chapels of Ease since built . . ." (p. 127). And, a generation later, Charles Woodmason, describing in detail some of the leading Anglican churches in South Carolina, made the situation attractive enough to entice any Oxford student of theology. St. Phillips of Charleston "is allow'd to be the most elegant Religious Edifice in British America." A brick building, it housed a Great Organ with sixteen stops. And, as one might well expect,

"Divine Service is perform'd here with Great Decency & Order; both on Holidays & Week Days." Then there was Prince William Church, which "is beautifully pew'd and Ornamented"; St. George's, "a very handsome Brick Church"; St. James', on Goose Creek, "one of the best Country churches in the province." The only trouble with St. James' was that the parsonage was so close to the "Bridge over which is the Greatest Flux & Reflux of People" that the minister "is daily & hourly pester'd with Travelers calling for Lodging or Entertainment." All things considered, however, Woodmason believed that Anglicanism in South Carolina was in so fine a condition that it was "almost a Sin for any of the parochial Clergy longer to receive the Mission Money . . . This money could be better employ'd in Georgia."

Georgia had a late start. John Wesley, the first Anglican clergyman to preach on Georgia soil, sailed in 1735 at the behest of Governor Oglethorpe. Results were disappointingly meager, and in a very short time Wesley went back home. The youthful and bold evangelist, George Whitefield, was next on the scene, and though he founded an orphanage in Bethesda, his greatest successes were elsewhere. Wesley and Whitefield, said Woodmason, have "thrown a Damp on all Religious Matters in this colony: They strain'd the Cord, till it broke." There was, in other words, too much Methodism in their madness. A missionary to Savannah was appointed by the S.P.G. in 1740 and one in 1750 to Augusta where there were only 8 communicants. In 1758 the Assembly showed more interest in supporting the Anglican ministry, but by the end of the colonial period there were probably no more than 200 Anglicans in the whole of Georgia (White, 95 f.).

North Carolina, as has been pointed out, was the despair of its more respectable neighbors to the north and south. William Byrd of Westover, Virginia, a not unbiased reporter, described North Carolina in the 1730's in this way:

One thing may be said for the Inhabitants of that Province, that they are not troubled with any Religious Fumes, and have the least Superstition of any People living. They do not know Sunday from any other day, any more than Robinson Crusoe did, which would give them a great Advantage were they given to be industrious. But they keep so many Sabbaths every week, that their disregard of the Seventh Day has no manner of cruelty in it, either to Servants or Cattle . . .

Sometimes the Society for propagating the Gospel has had the Charity to send over Missionaries to this Country; but unfortunately the Priest has been too Lewd for the people, or, which often happens, they too Lewd for the Priest. For these Reasons these Reverend Gentlemen have always left their Flocks as arrant Heathen as they found them (Lefler, 56 f.).

Though Byrd's words are more intemperate than most, the sentiment of Anglicans ran heavily against North Carolina.

Maryland, founded by Roman Catholics, became a royal province in 1691, and by 1703 Anglicanism was fully established there. The 10 counties were divided into 25 parishes, each of which was to be "endowed with a competent Main-

tenance for a Minister." This action was not taken with seriousness until 1694 when Sir Francis Nicholson became governor and "with an indefatigable Industry and Zeal" revived the legislative enactment, adding other laws to it. Provisions were made for church buildings and parsonages, and for a "free-school" in each county, the primary purpose of which was the "Fitting such as are dispos'd to Study Divinity to be further Educated at His Majesty's College Royal in Virginia . . ." (Bray, *Proposals*, 12 f.). Seven Anglican churches existed in Maryland before it became a royal province, but progress was rapid after the turn of the century—the only serious competition coming from Roman Catholics and Quakers, "for the presbyterians were few in number, and exhibited no acts of hostility." But Thomas Bray, the tireless evangel and founder of the S.P.G., found that many of the parishes of Maryland were, like those of Virginia, so gigantic "that the far greatest part of the Heads of Families, I am sure, are seldom able to come to Church; and the Poor, who have not Horses, as also the Children and Servants, scarcely ever" (*Circular Letters*, 40). Again, as in Virginia, the shortage of ministers meant that "not only many Dayly fall away either to Popery, Quakerisme, or Phanatacisme, but alsoe the lord's day is prophaned, Religion despised, & all notorious vices committed soe that it is become a Sodom of uncleaness & Pest house of iniquity. . . ." (Wroth, 1). It could not have been quite that desperate, however, for Maryland and Virginia were the only 2 colonies to which the S.P.G. did not send missionaries and support. Yet the settled clergy provided their share of the scandals that harassed colonial Anglicanism.

In the Middle Colonies there was virtually no Anglican worship before the eighteenth century. In New York and Pennsylvania there were only 4 churches prior to 1700 (New York City, 2; Philadelphia, 1; Chester 1: see Fig. 8) and in New Jersey there was none before that date. After the S.P.G. got under way, however, the tempo of church building and missionary activity increased significantly. By 1710 there were 11 Anglican churches in New York, 8 in New Jersey, and 8 in Pennsylvania. In the absence of government assistance, churches in Pennsylvania were built by private subscription, and by 1730 there were 15 "very decent Structures for Celebrating Publick Divine Worship" (Humphreys, ch. 7). In New Jersey the proprietors of Perth Amboy seated that colony's first Anglican minister, donating the church building themselves. A spectacular conversion/apostasy in the person of the Quaker, George Keith, gave Anglicanism an effective approach to many Quakers. Keith, a leader in Pennsylvania Quakerism (see p. 25), returned to England to take orders in the Church of England, then became a missionary for the S.P.G. in the Middle Colonies.

In New York a measure of government aid did exist. Although the dissenters were by far the majority of the populace, a law passed the Assembly in 1693 which provided that "there should be called, inducted, and established, a good sufficient Protestant minister." Though the law did *not* stipulate that he be a Church of England Minister, Governor Fletcher chose to interpret it so (Hastings, II, 1073-1115). This financial boost plus, once more, an active program by the S.P.G. soon brought ministers into New York City, New Rochelle, Rye, Albany, Staten Island, and Long Island. William Vesey, rector of Trinity Church (established in 1697) in New York City, had high hopes for the conversion of all inhabitants of the colony. The Independents of Suffolk County, even though "upheld in their separation by New England Emissaries," were "already well affected to the Church." And the Dutch Reformed of Ulster County—at the time lacking a minister of their own—were being served by an Anglican; so there were "good hopes of bringing the Dutch to a conformity." But two S.P.G. missionaries, William Urquhart and John Thomas, more realistically observed that most of the Long Island Independents were "averse to the discipline of our holy mother, the Church of England & enraged to see her ministry established among them." There were suggestions, indeed, that the animosity aroused by government patronage had in New York done the church far more harm than good, and that "in the Jersies and Pennsylvania where there is no Act in her favor, there is four times the number of Churchmen than there is in this province of New York, and they are so much of them on principle" (Hastings, III, 1553-1589; see also 1899-1915).

New England was the least hospitable area in all the colonies to the ministrations of the Church of England. The area was "well-churched"; it was prepared both legally and intellectually to repel invasion. But the wall was broken. The first break, and not a particularly serious one, was political. King's Chapel in Boston was opened in 1689 as the "first Place where the Church of England Worship was exercised in New-England." The Anglican governor, Edmund Andros, was responsible for the move, but the resentment it aroused reflected to the disadvantage of this communion in Massachusetts. In Connecticut the growth was more subtle and a great deal more enduring—despite the "abundance of odd kinds of laws" that Connecticut citizens have "to prevent any dissenting from their Church, and endeavor to keep the people in as much blindness and unacquaintedness with any other religion as possible . . ." (Hastings, III, 1612). In Stratford the first Anglican church of Connecticut was built; it opened for services on Christmas day, 1724. The rector of the Stratford church traveled throughout much of Connecticut, and the next year opened a church in Fairfield. In 1732 a church in New London was built, with the elder Samuel Seabury serving as minister. By 1736 there were 4 missionaries in the colony, 6 meeting houses, and about 700 Anglican families (Beardsley, I, 60-105). More spectacular than the conversion of the Pennsylvania Quaker, George Keith, was the shift to Anglicanism in 1722 of several outstanding Connecticut clergymen, including Timothy Cutler, president of Yale, and Samuel Johnson, formerly tutor at Yale.

The gain in prestige for the Church of England was considerable, and the gain in numbers under the later leadership of Bishop Samuel Seabury, son of the New London rector, was steady. A report of 1774 reckoned 1 out of every 13 citizens of Connecticut to be an Anglican.

Rhode Island received its first S.P.G. missionary in 1704, and within two decades a church was built in Providence and one in Narragansett. In 1726 "the most beautiful Timber Structure in America" was built in Newport—

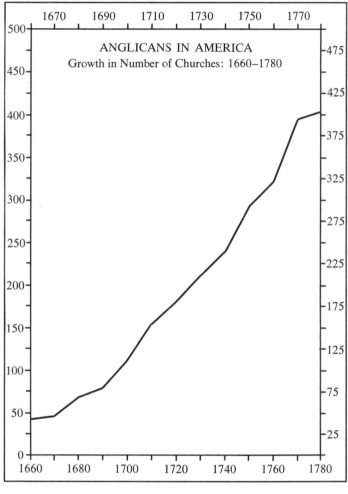

Figure 9

Trinity Church. By the end of the colonial period, there were 7 Anglican churches in Rhode Island, 2 in New Hampshire, and 3 in Maine. (There had been 1 in Maine and 1 in New Hampshire early in the seventeenth century, but neither had survived.) Massachusetts had 22, and Connecticut the largest number, 37 (see Fig. 8).

The effect of the American Revolution upon the Church of England was harsh. A majority of the clergy was Tory, and virtually all were assumed to be. In Virginia there were, at the beginning of the war, 95 parishes and 9 clergymen. After the war, over one-third of the parishes were "extinct or forsaken." Of the 91 clergymen, only 28 remained. Of these, "fifteen only had been enabled to continue in the churches which they supplied prior to the . . . hostilities; and thirteen had been driven from their cures by violence or want . . ." (Hawks, *Contributions*, I, 153 f.).

The Reverend Charles Inglis of Trinity Church in New York City affords ample testimony of not only his own unswerving Loyalist sentiments but of those of many colleagues. Denouncing the "present rebellion" as "certainly one of the most causeless, unprovoked, and unnatural that ever disgraced any country," he reported joyfully to the S.P.G. that every one of its missionaries both in New England and in the Middle Colonies "have proved themselves faithful, loyal subjects in these trying times; and have to the utmost of their power opposed the spirit of disaffection and rebellion." Among the other Anglican clergy, not missionaries, in these two areas, the same line of conduct had been followed. "And although their joint efforts could not wholly prevent the rebellion, yet they checked it considerably for some time, and prevented many thousands from plunging into it who otherwise would certainly have done so." Of the Southern Colonies, however, Inglis was not so confident. He had heard that some clerics there were conducting services in which the collects for the king were omitted. This was most distressing, but "I never expected much good of those clergy . . ." For his own part, he would not only refuse to alter the service, he would shut up his church and advise others to do likewise. With his own church locked tight, Inglis sat and waited for the day when "his Majesty's arms will be successful, and finally crush this unnatural rebellion." While waiting, Inglis was appealed to by the revolutionary chaplains for permission to use the locked church for services for the soldiers. ". . . with these requisitions I peremptorily refused to comply, and let them know that, 'if they would use the churches, they must break the gates and doors to get in' " (Hastings, VI, 4292-4300). Repeated requests were followed by repeated refusals. No doors were broken.

In addition to the odium attached to an institution that was English as now distinct from American, there was the jolt of disestablishment, which for Anglicanism, unlike Congregationalism, came swiftly. The case of Virginia is typical. In 1776 all dissenters were exempted from contributions of any sort to the Church of England. A proposal to have a general assessment for the support of all religion was defeated in 1779, largely through dogged Baptist opposition. In 1786, following a memorial presented by James Madison, the declaration of religious freedom drawn up by Thomas Jefferson was passed. But the dissenters were still not at ease. The Church of England continued to hold a great deal of property not used for worship, granted in much earlier days. Thus, in 1802, the "legislature passed the law, by virtue of which the glebes of Virginia were ordered to be sold for the benefit of the public. The warfare begun by the Baptists seven-and-twenty years before, was now finished; the church was in ruins, and the Triumph of her enemies was complete"

(Hawks, *Contributions*, I, 232). One can hear the writer muttering, "Curse those Baptists!"

To whom we now turn.

SOURCES. E. E. Beardsley, *The History of the Episcopal Church in Connecticut . . .* 2 vols. (Boston [fourth edition], 1883). Thomas Bray, *Proposals for the Encouragement and Promoting of Religion and Learning in Foreign Plantations . . .* [1697] (Thomas Bray Club, no date); *Several Circular Letters to the Clergy of Mary-land* [1701] (Thomas Bray Club, no date). Philip A. Bruce, *Institutional History of Virginia In the Seventeenth Century,* 2 vols. [excellent description of growth of the parishes] (New York, 1910). George M. Brydon, *Virginia's Mother Church . . .* 2 vols (Richmond, 1947; Philadelphia, 1952). Charles Campbell, *Introduction to the History of Virginia* (Richmond, 1847). E. C. Chorley, *Men and Movements in the American Episcopal Church* (New York, 1946). Peter Force (ed.), *Tracts and Other Papers relating principally to the Origin, Settlement, and Progress of the Colonies in North America . . .* 4 vols. (New York [reprint], 1947); Volume III of this series contains R[oger?] G[reen?], *Virginia's Cure: or An Advisive Narrative Concerning Virginia. Discovering The true Ground of that Churches Unhappiness, and the only true Remedy* [London, 1662]. Hugh Hastings (ed.), *Ecclesiastical Records. State of New York,* 7 vols. (Albany, 1901-1916). Francis L. Hawks, *Contributions to the Ecclesiastical History of the United States of America,* 2 vols. (New York, 1836; 1839); and, *History of North Carolina . . .* 2 vols. (Fayetteville, 1858). David Humphreys, *An Historical Account of the Incorporated Society for the Propagation of the Gospel in Foreign Parts* [maps] (London, 1830); [transcripts of the correspondence of missionaries of the S.P.G. may be found in the Library of Congress]. Hugh F. Lefler (ed.), *North Carolina History Told by Contemporaries* (Chapel Hill, 1934). William S. Perry, *A Handbook of the General Convention of the Protestant Episcopal Church . . .* [valuable statistics in Appendix I, p. 341 ff.] (New York, 1881). William J. Rivers, *A Sketch of the History of South Carolina to . . . 1719 . . .* (Charleston, 1856). George White, *Statistics of the State of Georgia . . .* (Savannah, 1849). Samuel Wilberforce, *History of the Protestant Episcopal Church in America* [contains a diocesan map and list of all Protestant Episcopal clergy by states for the year 1848] (London, 1849). Charles Woodmason, "Account of South Carolina, North Carolina, Georgia &c" (manuscript [1766] in Library of Congress). Lawrence C. Wroth, "The First Sixty Years of the Church of England in Maryland, 1632 to 1692," *Maryland Historical Magazine* XI:1 (1-41). See also the excellent bibliography by Niels H. Sonne in *Religion in Life,* XXV:3.

3. BAPTISTS

Baptist growth in the seventeenth century was exceedingly slow. In 1660 there were only 4 Baptist churches in the colonies, and they were in Rhode Island: 2 in Providence and 2 in Newport. By the end of the century there were slightly over a score, with Massachusetts and Rhode Island accounting for well over half that number.

The first Baptist church in America was founded in Providence in 1639 under the temporary leadership of Roger Williams. The second was established in Newport soon after by John Clarke, who contributed much more direct leadership to the young denomination than did his better-known colleague (see Fig. 2). These Baptists, as was true of virtually all who settled in New England, were of English origin, the immigration of German Baptists occurring in the eighteenth century. But English Baptists provided enough diversity in the earlier period: Seventh-Day Baptists from England first settled in America in 1671 at Newport; Six-Principle Baptists, whose chief distinction was the requirement of "laying on of hands" for all baptized members (Hebrews 6:1,2), founded a church in Newport in 1654; about the same time the Providence church split on this issue of the imposition of hands. Then too, the theological orientation of many of these earlier Baptists was Arminian, with Calvinism rising to eminence only in the next century. After Rhode Island, Massachusetts was numerically the leading colony for Baptist churches: there were 6 before 1700. No permanent Baptist meeting was held in Connecticut in the seventeenth century, the first church being established in Groton by Valentine Wightman in 1706. And for twenty years there was not another one in that colony.

While the early growth of Baptist churches was concentrated in New England, the first effective organization of these churches was in the Middle Colonies: the Philadelphia Association, founded in 1707. For almost half a century it was the only such group in the colonies. Baptists began settling in Pennsylvania in 1684 when a "Mr. Dongan, from Rhode Island, gathered a church of baptists, at Cold Spring, above Bristol, in the county of Bucks." Two years later, Baptist immigrants from Wales (Radnorshire) and Ireland (Killarney) settled northeast of Philadelphia on Pennypack Creek, where they established a church. An English convert from the group was elected in 1698 as pastor of a Philadelphia church "composed of nine persons only" (Gordon, 571). At the time of the organization of the Philadelphia Association, there were only 3 Baptist churches in Pennsylvania, 6 in New Jersey, and none in New York. From this Association came the major thrust for Baptists during most of the remaining colonial period. A confession of faith was adopted, ministers were ordained, discipline was enforced, and missionaries were sent out.

In the Southern Colonies, the earliest church was in South Carolina (1696), but the greatest growth was in Virginia. Robert Semple, an eighteenth-century Virginia Baptist, wrote that there were three sources for these dissenters in Virginia. "The first were emigrants from England, who about the year 1714, settled in the southeast parts of the state. About 1743, another party came from Maryland, and formed a settlement in the northwest." But neither of these contributed as much as the third group from New England who "acted the most distinguished part . . ." (p. 1). Particularly after the middle of the century, Baptists grew rapidly in Virginia. One local factor which helped them "to shake the faith of many who belonged to the [Anglican] Church" was a lawsuit on behalf of the established clergy seeking certain salary adjustments. Anticlericalism in Virginia rose and Baptists profited, even though it was true that "No dissenters in Virginia experienced . . . harsher treatment than did the

BAPTIST CHURCHES
1750

• 1 Church
○ 5 Churches

0 _____ 100 MILES

ATLANTIC OCEAN

Figure 10

Baptists" (Hawks, *Contributions*, I, 121). By 1790 John Leland reported that "There are in Virginia, at this time, about one hundred and fifty ordained preachers of the Baptist denomination, and a number besides who exercise a public gift." And, after reviewing in detail the growth of churches and members, this Baptist itinerant pointed out that "the number of communicants compose but a small part of those who commonly attend Baptist worship. It will not appear extravagant to those who are generally acquainted in the state, to say that, taking one part of the state with another, there are more people who attend the Baptist worship, than any other kind of worship in the state" (Greene, ed., 116 f.).

In that woeful state of North Carolina, the Baptists also experienced their greatest expansion in the latter part of the eighteenth century, even though a church had been established at Chowan as early as 1727. The sensitive soul

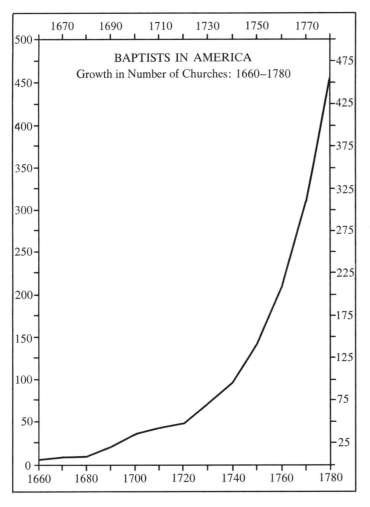

BAPTISTS IN AMERICA
Growth in Number of Churches: 1660–1780

Figure 11

of Charles Woodmason was sorely aggrieved by the rise of these "Anabaptists"—the most "zealous among the Sects, to propagate their Notions." Indeed, in the fact that the Baptists were building churches in the interior, he saw a truly sinister plot—a plot akin to France's chain of forts from Canada to Louisiana. "If they could not *suppress*, they would *cramp* the progress of the Liturgy and the Church Establish'd." This the Presbyterians had first tried to do, but the Baptists had (before 1766) "by their Address & Assiduity . . . worm'd the Presbyterians out of all their strong Holds . . ." The Baptists were now the threat, being "the most numerous and formidable Body of people the Church has to encounter with, in the Interior and Back parts of the Province. . . ." But Woodmason had hope for his Church. That hope lay in the

intense antipathy which he believed existed between the Presbyterians and the Baptists. "A Presbyterian would sooner marry ten of his children to members of the Church of England than one to a Baptist. . . . Their Rancour is surprizing—But the Church reaps great Good by it." In a soberer second thought, Woodmason admitted that "these Baptists have great prevalence and footing in North Carolina, and have taken such deep Root there that it will require long Time and Pains to grub up their Layers." Their footing was sure, indeed; by the end of the colonial period, there were in North Carolina some 55 Baptist churches as compared with 23 Anglican ones.

In South Carolina, too, the denomination's activity was intensified in the latter half of the eighteenth century. The second Baptist association to be formed in the colonies was at Charleston in 1751. Before that date there were only 5 Baptist churches in the colony. Between that date and 1780, 30 were established. (See map in Leah Townsend, *South Carolina Baptists 1670-1805*, Florence [South Carolina], 1935). In Georgia the denomination only got its foot in the door in the colonial period, having but 5 churches there by 1780. The real conquest of that area came in the nineteenth century.

So far as the colonies as a whole were concerned, the last decades of the eighteenth century were years of phenomenal growth for the Baptists (see Fig. 11). Jedidiah Morse noted in 1790 that the "Baptists are the most numerous religious sect in Kentucky. In 1787 they had sixteen churches established, besides several congregations where churches were not constituted" (p. 406). But the familiar story of expansion on the frontier should not obscure the fact that expansion was likewise tremendous in the settled eastern areas. In the single decade 1770–1780, 67 Baptist churches were formed in Virginia alone; and 37 were established in Massachusetts from 1760 to 1780. In 1780 there were only 12 associations in the colonies; by 1790 there were 35! In the single year 1791, Baptists in America grew by 1,500 members and 30 churches. By the end of that year, there were in all 564 Baptist clergy, 748 churches, and 60,970 members (Rippon, 73).

How does one account for this spurt of activity after a rather lackadaisical seventeenth century and an equally sluggish first half of the eighteenth? In 1794 a Congregational clergyman, Noah Worcester, thought it time to raise that question; he did so by way of *Impartial Inquiries concerning the Progress of the Baptist Denomination*. Mr. Worcester posed two queries: (1) "Whether the increase of the baptist denomination is any certain evidence of the rectitude of their peculiar sentiments?" and (2) "Whether other probable causes of the prevalence of their sentiments, or increase of their numbers, may not be assigned?" It did not take the author long to dispose of the first question, for if numbers proved religious truth, then consider what this would declare about "the peculiar sentiments of Mahomet," the "Papists," and others. But the second inquiry took more time. Among the reasons Worcester offered for Baptist growth were these: the coldness of the ministry and of "private professors" in other denominations; the persecution which Baptists had endured; their taking advantage of revivals and "divisions in societies"; their "confident manner, and affecting tone, with which they address the passions of their hearers"—together with an abundant use of irrelevant Scripture; the desire of some persons to flee the "gospel-discipline, in [of] pedo-baptist churches"; and, finally, "the want of qualifications, in some baptist teachers." In expounding his last point, the author observed:

Many people are so ignorant, as to be charmed with sound than sense. And to them, the want of knowledge in a teacher . . . may easily be made up, and overbalanced, by great zeal, an affecting tone of voice, and a perpetual motion of the tongue. If a speaker can keep his tongue running, in an unremitting manner . . . and can quote memoriter a large number of texts from within the covers of the Bible, it matters not, to many of his hearers, whether he speaks sense or nonsense (pp. 19 f.).

Some of Noah Worcester's analysis is familiar and probably correct; some is myopic and unfair (e.g., there is no evidence that "gospel-discipline" was more strict in the "pedo-baptist churches," and the contrary may well have been true). The appeal to emotion and the itinerant, unlearned ministry were certainly factors in the growth of the denomination, though more so in the great westward expansion than in the original states. But revivals and "divisions in societies" hit close to Worcester's home. For the Great Awakening in New England had split the established churches into Old Light and New Light wings. From the latter, and particularly from the Separatist New Lights, the Baptists reaped much gain. Apart from church divisions and "disaffection to settled ministers," the waves of revivalism in all the colonies directly or indirectly augmented this religious body. This need not mean, and often did not mean, that the revivals were held under Baptist auspices. Any evangelistic emphasis appeared to assist their cause.

Worcester's mention of the persecution of Baptists suggests a further factor: the spirit of freedom, the love of liberty, manifest in and engendered by the American Revolution. Baptists, from New England to the Carolinas, took an active part in the crusade for religious freedom, and those who resisted or resented that crusade were, after 1776, often cast in the contrasting role of the villain. Isaac Backus of Massachusetts wrote frequently and fervently on this theme, presenting under one title or another *An Appeal to the Public for Religious Liberty, against the Oppressions of the Present Day* . . . (Boston, 1773). The Baptists of Virginia were singled out by both Jefferson and Washington for their contribution to freedom of conscience, and it is in a letter of Jefferson's to the Danbury Association of Connecticut that the famous "wall of separation" phrase occurs. The martyr whose position is

vindicated occupies a rather formidable position. Before long, Baptists had taken so deep a root all over America that it might well stagger the imagination to reflect on what "long Time and Pains" would be necessary "to grub up their Layers."

SOURCES. John Asplund, *The Annual Register of the Baptist Denomination, in North-America* . . . (n. p., 1791). Isaac Backus, *Church History of New England* . . . Vol. III (Boston, 1796). David Benedict, *An Abridgement of the General History of the Baptist Denomination* . . . (Boston, 1820). John Callendar, *An Historical Discourse in the Civil and Religious Affairs of the Colony of Rhode-Island* (Providence, 1739). Thomas F. Gordon, *The History of Pennsylvania to . . . 1776* (Philadelphia, 1829). L. F. Greene (ed.), *The Writings of the Late Elder John Leland* . . . (New York, 1845). Francis L. Hawks, *Contributions to the Ecclesiastical History of the United States of America*, 2 vols. (New York, 1836; 1839). Jedidiah Morse, *American Geography* . . . (London [second edition], 1792). Lemuel Moss, *The Baptists and the National Centenary* . . . (Philadelphia, 1876). John Rippon, *The Baptist Annual Register* . . . (London, 1793 [?]). Robert B. Semple, *A History of the Rise and Progress of the Baptists in Virginia* (Richmond, 1810). Charles Woodmason, "Account of South Carolina, North Carolina, Georgia &c" (manuscript [1766], Library of Congress). Noah Worcester, *Impartial Inquiries concerning the Progress of the Baptist Denomination* (Worcester, 1794). See also the valuable bibliography by Leo T. Crimson in *Religion in Life*, XXV: 1.

4. CONGREGATIONALISTS

As was noted in the Introduction to Part I, the early history of New England and of Congregationalism was largely one—even as the early history of Virginia and of Anglicanism was largely one. Unlike Virginia, however, New England (Rhode Island always excepted) succeeded in creating and maintaining an established church that rested on a broad base of popular support. Congregationalism was the religion of the people. The covenant which bound them together as a church was as much their own creation as the Mayflower Compact. And while legislature and court in every way extended aid and comfort to the establishment, they did so as the voice of a people in covenant with God.

The first Congregational church in the New World was formed at Plymouth, Massachusetts, in 1620, its founders being from John Robinson's congregation-in-exile in Leyden. These Puritans had already separated from the Church of England and were engaged, in the familiar phrase, in a program of "reformation without tarrying for anie." The major stream of New England Congregational life flows, however, from the immigrations a few dozen miles farther north: Boston and Salem. Here, under the direction of the Massachusetts Bay Company, in the late 1620's and more heavily in the 1630's, came large numbers of sons and daughters of England. These sought, not a religious liberty for all, but a liberty which would permit them to build up a true church of God, a true church of the New Testament, a true "Church of England." That church was soon to receive the distinguishing name of Congregational (pointing,

CONGREGATIONAL CHURCHES
1750

- 1 Church
○ 5 Churches
● 25 Churches

0   100 MILES

A T L A N T I C   O C E A N

Figure 12

of course, to a type of church government that was *not* episcopal; church rule was by a body of believers, not.by bishops).

Despite the severities of nature and the hostilities of Indians (neither of which factors should be minimized), the growth of Congregationalism in New England was steady and, comparatively speaking, swift (see Fig. 7). By 1640 there were 29 churches "of the Congregationall Way" in Massachusetts alone. (In Virginia, which had an earlier start, there were in the same year only 14 Anglican churches.) In 1635 Thomas Hooker led some families west to the banks of the Connecticut River, founding the colony of Connecticut with settlements at Windsor and Hartford. By the middle of the century, only a decade and a half later, a dozen churches had been formed (see Fig. 2). The manner of their organization is faithfully described by Benjamin Trumbull:

The churches of New-Haven, Milford, and Guilford, were formed first, by the choice of seven persons, from among the brethren, who were termed the pillars. A confession of faith was drawn up, to which they all assented, as preparatory to their covenanting together in church estate. They then entered into covenant, first with God, to be his people in Christ, and then with each other, to walk together in the strict and conscientious practice of all Christian duties, and in the enjoyment of all the ordinances and privileges of a church of Christ (I, 236).

After the Long Parliament of England began in 1640, the more favorable attitude toward and treatment of the Puritans brought an end to the great colonial emigration of the previous decade. Those earlier years, however, had brought persons in sufficient number and of sufficient stature to ensure to New England a relatively stable future. The land could be held; it could be cultivated; it could be redeemed. By the end of the century there were 77 Congregational churches in Massachusetts, 35 in Connecticut, 6 in New Hampshire, and 2 in Maine.

Outside of New England some ventures had been made; numerically, however, there was little strength south of Fairfield County, Connecticut. There had been early migrations across the Sound to Long Island and even some penetration into New York City while the Dutch were still in control. The minutes of the New Netherland Council, June 6, 1641, reveal that "a good number of respectable English people with their preacher have petitioned for permission to settle here and live among us" (Hastings, I, 137). About the same time a Puritan congregation from Massachusetts settled in Virginia (Nansemond County) and by 1648 was reported to have a membership of 118 persons. Although Governor Winthrop tried to intercede on their behalf, Governor William Berkeley was in no mood for tolerating this invasion. Under governmental pressure, therefore, a portion of the group was soon forced to flee. Virginia for Maryland, settling near the present site of Annapolis, which they named Providence. Other Puritan migrations into Maryland led by 1654 to the breakdown of Roman Catholic power in that colony. "From this period they [Roman Catholics] never afterwards could regain their just and due influence in the province, although for many years they continued to form the majority of the inhabitants thereof" (Bozman, II, 495). Near the end of the seventeenth century, a group of Puritans from Dorchester, Massachusetts, settled in and around Charleston, South Carolina, forming a new Dorchester. A group of these Carolina Dorchesters migrated to Georgia in 1752, establishing at Midway (Liberty) the only colonial Congregational church in that colony.

In this period a close kinship was established between the Presbyterians and the Congregationalists. As the former became entrenched in the Middle Colonies, an intimate working relationship developed between them and the Congregationalists of New England—the clearest and most significant example of sectarian cooperation in the colonial period. Despite theoretical differences in ecclesiastical polity, the practice of the New Englanders (particularly in Connecticut after the adoption of the Saybrook Platform in 1708) approximated that of the Presbyterians in many details. On the other hand, many Presbyterians were moving toward a more Congregational polity. John Leland, near the end of the eighteenth century, described the ministers of Connecticut as "Presbyterial, Congregational and Consociated preachers." Pulpits were freely exchanged; the Westminster Confession was commonly revered; episcopacy (not to speak of papacy) was mutually feared. Jonathan Edwards, the prominent Congregational theologian, became the third president of the Presbyterian College of New Jersey (Princeton); on the other side, the list of invited preachers to Connecticut's Yale is liberally sprinkled with New York and New Jersey Presbyterians. This does not mean that the harmony was without beginning or end. Samuel Finley, fifth president of Princeton, was ridden out of Connecticut—not on a rail, to be sure, but in a manner no less injurious to pride and brotherly love. And in the nineteenth century, as we shall observe in Part II, the harmony suffered major disruptions. During much of the eighteenth century, however, the clearest distinction between Presbyterians and Congregationalists was geographical.

The surge of revivalism in that century, usually styled the Great Awakening, promoted this harmony between the two groups even while it evoked schisms within each denomination. Gilbert Tennent, a leading New Jersey Presbyterian, toured New England in the winter of 1740-41, preaching wherever he had an invitation from those favorably disposed to this type of evangelism. Thomas Prince of Boston characterized his preaching as being "as searching and rousing as ever I heard," adding that the man "seemed to have as deep an acquaintance with the experimental part of religion as any I have conversed with" (p. 12). Similarly, New England preachers traveling into New York and New Jersey also carried a message of experimental religion. The pro-revivalists of both groups ("New Light" for the Congregationalists and "New Side" for the Presbyterians) felt an especially strong bond, the fruit of which was to manifest itself in significant ways.

Prior to the Great Awakening, Massachusetts and Connecticut had, by and large, maintained a considerable degree of religious homogeneity. In 1700 there were in Massachusetts 2 Baptist churches, 1 Anglican, and 1 Quaker; in Connecticut there were no churches other than Congregational. Shortly after the turn of the century, the Society for the Propagation of the Gospel (Anglican)

introduced its missionaries into New England, threatening this homogeneity and infuriating the Congregationalists. Daniel Neal was perplexed and perturbed: "How this can so properly be called Propagating the Gospel, when the Christian Religion was planted in those Parts long before the Societies Missionaries settled in them, I don't understand; unless we will say, that the New-English Ministers don't preach the Christian Doctrine, or, that the Gospel can't subsist without the English Liturgy and Discipline

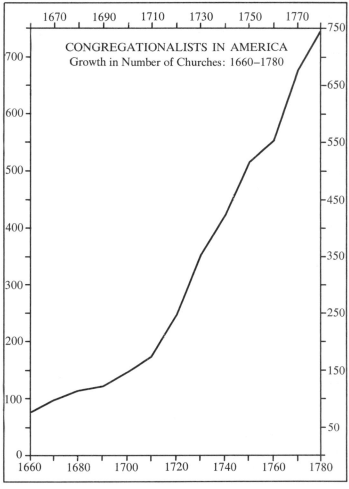

Figure 13

. . ." (II, 609). And Jonathan Mayhew made a major crusade out of his trenchant criticism of the *Character and Conduct of the Society For the Propagation of the Gospel in Foreign Parts . . .* (Boston, 1763). It did appear that the New Englanders had a point in suggesting that the Society was more interested in propagating Anglicanism than the gospel. For in 1761, while there were only 9 of the Society's missionaries in Pennsylvania, 10 in New Jersey, and 16 in New York, there were 30 in New England.

But the Society did its work well, and Anglicanism became a significant force in New England, particularly in western Connecticut. By 1750 there were nearly 20 of its churches in that colony (see Fig. 8). Baptists also increased outside of Rhode Island, slowly before the Awakening and rapidly after. The third major "dissenting" group were the Quakers who, likewise emanating largely from Rhode Island and to a lesser extent from New York, infiltrated southern Massachusetts, the Piscataqua area of New Hampshire and Maine, and scattered towns in Connecticut. Ezra Stiles, in 1760, estimated the number of Anglicans in all New England to be 12,600; the number of Quakers, 16,000; and the number of Baptists, 22,000 (p. 143).

The growth of these extralegal bodies did not, however, adversely affect the growth of Congregationalism itself. The years 1720 to 1750 were exceedingly productive for Congregational churches (see Fig. 13). In each of the three decades, about 90 new churches were added. Indeed, it is quite possible that the Great Awakening is as much an effect of church growth as it is a cause. This is particularly likely in view of the fact that many of the new members in this period were being received under the terms of the "Half-Way Covenant." That is, they could become members without a personal testimony to their own experience of salvation, without that deep acquaintance with the "experimental part of religion" of which Thomas Prince spoke. Such a field was ripe for the revival's harvest.

Following the wave of revivalism, there was continued growth, but much of it now took the form of church schisms. Many New Lights became Separatists, and the latter sometimes returned to the Congregational fold, sometimes became Baptists or, later, Methodists. As one may observe in Figure 13, however, the growth was steady to the end of the colonial period. Ezra Stiles, when giving the estimates of dissenters noted above, placed the number of Congregationalists in 1760 at 60,000 to 70,000 (though at one point he subtracts the estimated number of dissenters from the total population of New England, concluding that everybody left is Congregationalist; by that bit of arithmetic legerdemain, the number is 440,000!).

The American Revolution worked no hardship on the prestige and popularity of Congregationalism. Quite the contrary. A large number of the clergy took a conspicuous part in the agitation, and leading ministers who were finding aspects of the covenant theology galling gave the full power of their pens and pulpits to the colonists' cause. While enjoying legal privilege and establishment, Congregationalism suffered at this juncture no great political censure because it was clearly not an *English* establishment. Ecclesiastical criticism, however, the dissenters provided in full measure. To meet the religious unrest, even Connecticut felt obliged to moderate its position, passing a Toleration Act in 1784 that did much to soften resentment though it did not remove all irritation. Complete disestablishment did not come until 1818 and then Lyman Beecher—who had so long resisted the move—overcame his fears to rejoice that all "occasion of animosity between us and the minor sects was removed." Massachusetts, deep in a Unitarian turmoil (see Part III, 5), postponed disestablishment for another fifteen years.

Toward the end of this period the New England church was most severely limited, not by the growth of dissent or by the threat of disestablishment, but by the influx of rationalism. Beginning as a cloud no bigger than a man's hand, it mushroomed into a dark storm that washed away many of the supports of the establishment. Revelation was ignored or deliberately rejected, and reason became, in John Adams' words, "a revelation from its maker, which can never be disputed or doubted." An anti-institutional rationalism, often joined by an anti-institutional pietism, reduced Congregationalism in influence and power, even though it did not immediately reduce its numerical superiority. As will be noted, however, Congregationalism continued to exhibit great vitality in the next century as it established schools, founded missions, and wrestled with a sinful society. In so doing, its role gradually altered from that of a dominant, sometimes persecuting, majority to that of a sensitive, sometimes leavening, minority.

SOURCES. Leonard Bacon, *Genesis of the New England Churches* (New York, 1874). Lyman Beecher, *Autobiography, correspondence, etc.* . . . Vol. I (New York, 1864). John L. Bozman, *The History of Maryland* . . . 2 vols. (Baltimore, 1837). Joseph S. Clark, *A Historical Sketch of the Congregational Churches in Massachusetts* . . . (Boston, 1858). *Contributions to the Ecclesiastical History of Connecticut* . . . [includes sketch of each Congregational church up to 1860] (New Haven, 1861). Edwin S. Gaustad, *The Great Awakening in New England* (New York, 1957). Hugh Hastings (ed.), *Ecclesiastical Records. State of New York*, 7 vols. (Albany, 1901-1916). Jedidiah Morse, *American Geography* . . . [includes a breakdown by counties of all Congregational churches in Massachusetts and Maine] (London [second edition], 1792). Daniel Neal, *The History of New England Containing An Impartial Account of the Civil and Ecclesiastical Affairs of the Country to the Year of our Lord, 1700*, 2 vols. (London, 1720). Thomas Prince, *An Account of the Revival of Religion in Boston* . . . (Boston [reprint], 1823). Ezra Stiles, *A Discourse on Christian Union* . . . *1760* (Brookfield [Mass.], 1799). Benjamin Trumbull, *A Complete History of Connecticut* . . . 2 vols. (New London, 1898). George Leon Walker, *Some Aspects of the Religious Life in New England* (Boston, 1897). And see the bibliographies by H. M. Dexter, *Collections toward a bibliography of Congregationalism* (New York, 1880); and Verne D. Morey in *Church History* XXI:4.

5. LUTHERANS

Lutheranism entered the colonial life of America on the waters of the Delaware River; here Swedish colonists met as a congregation at Wilmington in 1638. Although earlier groups of Dutch and German Lutherans had settled a little farther north in New Netherland, there was no congregational organization among them until 1648. By that time, there were about 500 people in New Sweden, and a second church had been formed at Chester, Pennsylvania (see Fig. 2). Eyed with suspicion by the Dutch Reformed to the north, this Swedish Lutheran settlement was conquered by Peter Stuyvesant in 1655. Weakened in morale and in numbers, Swedish Lutheranism virtually came to an end in the seventeenth century; in the nineteenth century, however, it was to enjoy a powerful resurgence.

The Dutch Reformed, whether along the Delaware or the Hudson, were not inclined to deal sympathetically with the Lutherans. As was so often the case in the colonies, the folks back home looked at things rather differently from the colonists themselves. The Dutch West India Company could see some virtue in a measure of religious toleration; the Dutch inhabitants of New Netherland could not. And—as was also the case from Massachusetts to Virginia—those who were on the spot could determine which orders they wished to obey and which they preferred to "misunderstand." When Stuyvesant placed some Lutherans in jail in 1656, the Directors of the Company protested that "it has always been our intention to treat them quietly and leniently . . . Hereafter you will . . . let them have free religious exercises in their houses." That last phrase sounded as though a modest congregation might gather in a private home. But Stuyvesant did not so interpret it; for him it meant only "that every one must have the freedom to serve God quietly within his own dwelling . . . without instituting any public gatherings or conventicles. When this interpretation is recognized, our complaints [to the Directors] will cease." The Classis of Amsterdam agreed with Stuyvesant against the weakening Directors, and by 1659 it could be proudly reported that the Lutheran pastor "Goetwasser had been thrown into jail" and "that the Lutheran conventicles had thereby been stopped . . . the Lutherans now again come to the meetings of the Reformed." The matter continued to be tossed back and forth across the Atlantic, however, during the remaining years of Dutch rule—the Directors ever hopeful that they might find a few young preachers of "peaceable and moderate temperament" who would "not be infected with scruples about unnecessary forms" (Hastings, I, 322-381, 478).

However infected the English were about such matters on their home ground, they granted toleration to the Lutherans in 1664 when New Netherland became New York. A pastor finally reached these Lutherans in 1668, a church being organized in New York City and another in Albany. The numbers involved were not large; at this time there were 80 to 100 Lutheran families at Albany and 150 to 200 on Manhattan and Long Island. The Lutheran settlements were small because there was, after the conquest of the Swedish settlements along the Delaware, "no other *group* of Lutheran settlers . . . till after the turn of the century. There were sporadic cases of German and Scandinavian settlers, explorers and adventurers . . . but they formed no definite groups and they organized no churches" (Qualben, 148). The great influx of Lutheranism into colonial America was German, not Swedish, and it came in the eighteenth century, not the seventeenth. One may note, therefore, on the accompanying graph (Fig. 15) that Lutheranism was in the seventeenth century virtually at a standstill and in some areas (e.g., Albany) it had entered a sharp decline (Kreider, 50).

Figure 14

One church also on St. Simon's Island, Georgia

In the early decades of the eighteenth century, however, the Middle Colonies' "great migration" began. The Palatinate refugees (a great many of whom were Reformed rather than Lutheran) moved up the Hudson in 1708-10, and Lutheran churches appeared on both banks of the river, as far north as the Mohawk River. In New Jersey a church was established at Hackensack in 1704; at Raritan in 1714; and at Remaboeck (Mahwah) the following year. At this time 347 Palatine families had settled along the Hudson, about one-fourth of "these poor people" being Lutherans. By the middle of the eighteenth century there were 26 Lutheran congregations in New York and 19 in New Jersey (see Fig. 14).

In Pennsylvania, meanwhile, both the German immigration and Lutheran church-building had moved ahead at an astounding rate. The greatest immigration was

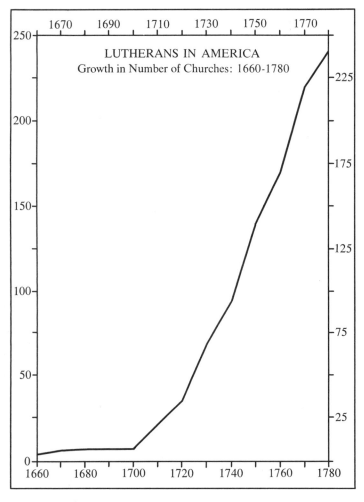

LUTHERANS IN AMERICA
Growth in Number of Churches: 1660-1780

Figure 15

from 1730 to 1745; by 1750 there were more than 60,000 Lutherans in Pennsylvania alone. In a single year, 1730, 21 Lutheran churches were established in this colony— more than New York had all together! Unlike the Swedish Lutherans, who had settled along the coast, the Germans settled in the interior counties of Bucks, Lancaster, and Lebanon. Pennsylvania became the focal center of colonial Lutheranism, and when Henry Muhlenberg arrived from Halle in 1742, he made Philadelphia his principal base of operations. By 1748 he had organized the first permanent Lutheran synod in America: the Evangelical Lutheran Ministerium of Pennsylvania.

From Pennsylvania came much of the Lutheranism in the Southern Colonies. Muhlenberg himself traveled all the way to Charleston (which had been his initial point of debarkation in the colonies) and made more frequent trips

to Delaware and Maryland. In Maryland there were 3 Lutheran churches by 1750 and 10 more by the end of the colonial period. In Virginia and West Virginia there were 9 such churches by 1780, chiefly in the counties of Shenandoah, Berkeley, and Frederick. In 1771, a contemporary reports, in North Carolina (in the counties of Rowan, Orange, Mecklenburg, and Tryon), there were "already settled near three thousand German protestant families, and being very fruitful in that healthy climate, are beside, vastly increasing by numbers of German protestants almost weekly arriving from Pennsylvania, and other provinces of America . . ." (Lefler, 69).

In the southernmost colonies of South Carolina and Georgia, the Lutherans arrived directly from Europe rather than by migration from Pennsylvania down the Appalachian valleys. There were Lutheran settlements in and near Charleston, South Carolina, by 1734, though the first church was organized at Orangeburg in 1735. In Georgia some 91 Lutherans together with 2 clergymen arrived in Savannah in 1734 from Salzburg, Austria. In gratitude they named their first settlement Ebenezer; by 1740 the community had been increased by other immigrations to the point where it numbered 1,200. In New England a small German colony was formed at Waldoborough, Maine, in 1739; augmented by other immigrants in 1740, it was the only representation of Lutheranism in that area during the colonial period.

Lutheranism was neither greatly forwarded nor retarded by the Revolution. Very probably most of the Lutherans were sympathetic with the American cause; there were certainly no ties of loyalty or blood with England. However, the political sentiments of the valley dwellers, Lutheran or otherwise, were sometimes clouded by resentments toward wealthier citizens along the coast, and Tory-Whig alignments varied from colony to colony. One of Henry Muhlenberg's sons, a minister, became an officer in the Continental army in 1775 and by 1783 had risen to the rank of major general. Another son, also a minister, took an active role in the political affairs of New York and of the young nation. Some Lutherans of New York and New Jersey did migrate to Canada following the Revolution, but again the motives were probably mixed. In any event, Lutherans as a whole were placed under no cloud so far as their political loyalty was concerned, and the severance of ties with England constituted no barrier to their progress.

Lutheranism's chief difficulties were internal. The continued use of the German (or other European) language manifestly limited the denomination's proselyting activities. Muhlenberg had to master—and preach in—three languages, but few were equal to that demand. And a particular church, in any case, could conduct its service in only one language, thereby limiting its appeal to a special cultural group. The denomination was torn by those who, on the one hand, would boldly adopt English in order to win America, and those who, on the other hand, feared to embrace English lest they be lost in America. It was a struggle that has had many counterparts in the history of man, but it postponed the days of Lutheranism's great progress for at least one hundred years.

The Lutheran churches were also weakened by the rationalism which had left its mark on the German universities in the eighteenth century. Creeds were softened and confessions often omitted. Particularly in New York, the tendency was strong to substitute what was acceptable and polite for what had been traditional and required. Related to the inroad of rationalism was the growth of a kind of ecumenicity that sprang partly from charity and partly from a lack of Lutheran esprit de corps. In New York there was serious discussion of union with the Protestant Episcopal Church, and negotiations for an organic union were actually begun. In Pennsylvania and North Carolina there was great similarity and cooperation between the Lutherans and the German Reformed. Often they migrated into the same counties and cooperatively built a single church in which the two groups alternately met. Occasionally, even common hymnbooks and catechisms were used. In such a situation, the Lutheran churches were frequently engaged in merely a holding action, and sometimes they did not even hold. Divided ethnically, theologically, and linguistically, the Lutheran churches had great difficulty believing in their own unity, much less making it an effective evangelizing force. Such problems continued to press upon them well into the twentieth century. It is, then, no small tribute to tenacity and ecclesiastical loyalty that Lutheranism is today the third largest body in American Protestantism.

SOURCES: Benjamin Ferris, *A History of the Original Settlements on the Delaware . . .* (Wilmington, 1846). Sydney G. Fisher, *The Making of Pennsylvania* (Philadelphia, 1896). Hugh Hastings (ed.), *Ecclesiastical Records. State of New York,* 7 vols. (Albany, 1901-1916). Amandus Johnson, *The Swedish Settlements on the Delaware . . . 1638-1664,* 2 vols. (Philadelphia, 1911). Henry J. Kreider, *Lutheranism in Colonial New York* (New York, 1942). Hugh T. Lefler (ed.), *North Carolina History Told by Contemporaries* (Chapel Hill, 1934). Henry M. Muhlenberg, *The Journals of Henry Melchior Muhlenberg,* 3 vols. (Philadelphia, 1942-5). Lars P. Qualben, *The Lutheran Church in Colonial America* (New York, 1940). Charles W. Schaeffer, *Early History of the Lutheran Church in America . . .* (Philadelphia, 1857). Theodore E. Schmauk, *The Lutheran Church in Pennsylvania (1638-1800)* (Lancaster, 1902). P. A. Strobel, *The Salzburghers and Their Descendants* (Baltimore, 1855; Athens [Ga.], 1953). Abdel Ross Wentz, *A Basic History of Lutheranism in America* (Philadelphia, 1955). And see the useful bibliography by J. G. Morris in *Lutheran Church Review,* XIV.

6. PRESBYTERIANS

As is apparent on the accompanying graph (Fig. 17), Presbyterianism, like Lutheranism, was a rather limited enterprise in the seventeenth century. But in the following century its growth was so rapid that by the end of the colonial period the Presbyterians had overtaken all except the Congregationalists (see Fig. 7). And with the latter, as previously noted, a harmonious cooperation had been established. (The name "Presbyterian" refers to a church rule by "presbyters" or "elders," clerical and lay, who in the local session, the larger presbytery, or the still larger synod, govern the affairs of the members.)

A determination of which was the "first Presbyterian church" in the colonies rests upon a principle of classification. The churches of Long Island, established by emigrants from New England around the middle of the seventeenth century, may be considered as Congregational or Presbyterian or as "Congregational-Presbyterian." Theologically, these churches were indistinguishable from the established churches of Connecticut and Massachusetts; in polity, the former, pending the formation of a presbytery and a synod, were also closely related to the latter. These New England Puritans affiliated readily, however, with the "Scotch Independents" of the Middle Colonies and contributed significantly to the later organization of American Presbyterianism. For these reasons, the Puritan churches formed in New York and New Jersey between 1640 and the end of the century are counted as Presbyterian. They include the congregations at Southampton (1640), Newton (1642), Hempstead (1643), East Hampton (1648), Huntington (1658), Jamaica (1661), Setauket (1665), Smithtown (1677), and Bridgehampton (1695). Between 1670 and 1680, Scottish Presbyterians settled on the eastern fork of the Elizabeth River, near Norfolk, Virginia. For a time they were served by a minister from Ireland "until the Lord was pleased to remove him by death" in 1683. On the eastern shore of Maryland there was a sufficient number of Ulster Scots to lay a petition in December of 1680 before a presbytery in Ireland, requesting that a minister be sent to them. At least by 1683, there was an unambiguously Presbyterian church in Rehoboth, Maryland.

The moving spirit in the early period of American Presbyterian history was Francis Makemie. From New York to the Carolinas, he ministered effectively through the last two decades of the seventeenth century and the early years of the eighteenth. He maintained contacts in old England and New, being praised by Cotton Mather as a "reverend and judicious minister." In 1706 he participated in the formation of the first American presbytery, this important step being taken, probably at Philadelphia, on the eve of large-scale emigration from Ulster to America.

By 1716 there were enough churches to justify the formation of the Synod of Philadelphia, with 4 subsidiary presbyteries. In the next fifty years something like 200,000 "Scotch-Irish" made the voyage to America, the majority of these debarking at Philadelphia, to migrate thence to western Pennsylvania, and down the valleys into Maryland, Virginia, and the Carolinas.

Many of these newcomers (such as the Tennents) were to become the strength of colonial Presbyterianism; others, "poor, land-hungry, boisterous and contentious," would be

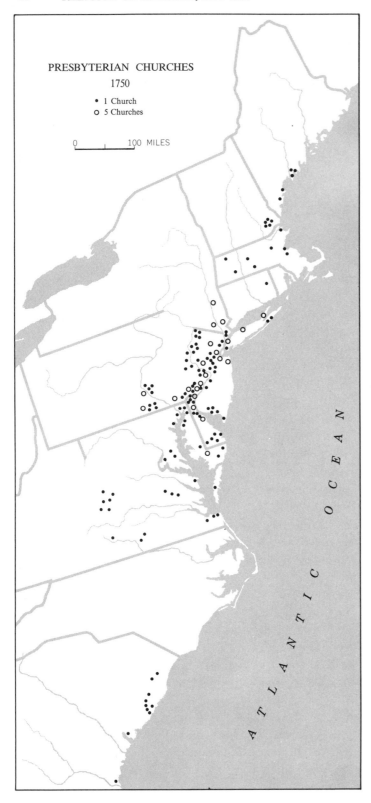

PRESBYTERIAN CHURCHES
1750

• 1 Church
o 5 Churches

0 _____ 100 MILES

ATLANTIC OCEAN

Figure 16

its bane. A letter of 1723 from a Pennsylvania clergyman to a fellow Presbyterian in Ireland testifies to the presence of the latter element among the divines themselves:

[Although the clergy] and congregation be multiplied with us; yet alas, there is little of the power and life of Religion with either: The Lord disappoint my fears. There are not above thirty ministers and Probationer preachers in our Synod, and yet six of the said number have been grossly scandalous; Suspension for four Sabbaths

hath been the greatest censure inflicted as yet (Armstrong *et al.,* 21 f.).

The records of the local Sessions show that the sheep were no better than the shepherd; trials dealt with drunkenness, Sabbath-breaking, swearing, lying, adultery, and, occasionally, even witchcraft.

The period of the Great Awakening was one of enormous stimulation to American Presbyterianism, though here, as among the Congregationalists, the immediate effect was rancor and schism within the fold. From the "Log College" of the Reverend William Tennent, Sr., there came a group of young ministers, including the sons of the elder Tennent, vitally concerned about a personal piety, an experiential religious faith. These evangels were not only sympathetic with the ecumenical, ebullient, irregular preaching of George Whitefield; they set about imitating it. Gilbert Tennent, as noted above (p. 15), spent three months touring New England in 1741, being received with joyful acclaim by the pro-revivalists and with contemptuous disdain by the anti-revivalists. The same dichotomy prevailed in the Middle Colonies, with the Old Side anti-revivalists expressing grave concern over "enthusiasm," inadequate education, "censoriousness," and ecclesiastical disorders. The New Side, for their part, supported the Awakening out of a concern over spiritual deadness, "the letter-learned," Pharisaic formalism, and "hiding the glorious Work of divine Grace."

In 1741 the New Side men were expelled from the Synod of Philadelphia for, among other reasons, their "heterodox and anarchical principles," "their irregular irruptions upon the congregations to which they have no immediate relation," "their rash judging and condemning," and their "so industriously working on the passions and affections of weak minds . . ." (Armstrong *et al.,* 47 f.). This exiled group in 1745 formed its own Synod of New York. In 1758, after animosities had cooled, a plan was offered which brought the two groups back together under the name of the Synod of New York and Philadelphia.

Meanwhile, another disturbance had occurred in 1742 with the formation of the "Covenanters" or Reformed Presbyterians on the basis of strong opposition to British rule. These Scots, under the leadership of Alexander Craighead, issued their views at Middle Octoraro, Pennsylvania, under the title of "The Declaration, Protestation, and Testimony of a Suffering Remnant of the Anti-Popish, Anti-Lutheran, Anti-Prelatick, Anti-Erastian, Anti-Latitudinarian, Anti-Sectarian, True Presbyterian Church of Christ in America"; and the statement, decrying King George I as an "outlandish Lutheran," proceeded in similar voice. The Covenanters had only three clergymen at the time of the American Revolution, and their number did not greatly increase in later times.

In the second half of the eighteenth century the Synod of New York and Philadelphia made notable strides. Around 1760 a Pennsylvania historian noted that the Presbyterians were more numerous in that colony "than any other particular society, taking in the Dutch, or German Calvinists; several of the back countries being principally peopled by them; they have flowed in, of late years, from the north of Ireland, in very great numbers, besides their great internal increase and still greater industry, than that of many others, to make proselytes" (Proud, II, 340; see Fig. 16). Prior to the Revolution there were at least 30 Presbyterian churches in the Virginia back country, particularly in the counties of Berkeley, Rockingham, Augusta, and Rockbridge. In the single year 1774, 18 Presbyterian churches were established in Virginia. In this same Virginia valley there were 7 more churches in what was to become West Virginia. A decade earlier there had been a similar "bumper crop" in North Carolina, with 11 churches formed in 1765 alone. In South Carolina a presbytery was organized in 1784, though there were 6 clergymen in the colony as early as 1775.

The period of the Revolution found divided sentiments among the Presbyterians as well as among the colonists generally. The Presbyterians of western Pennsylvania, who were busy fending off the Indians, found the pacifism of the wealthier Quakers to the east difficult to understand. The Scotch-Irish of the Carolinas bitterly resented the easterners' political monopoly and high taxation policies; thus, by reaction, some were initially loyalist in opposition to the wealthier patriots. The Virginia back country, however, was clearly patriotic. Probably the great majority of all Presbyterians were patriots, following the forceful example of Princeton's president, the only clergyman signer of the Declaration of Independence, John Witherspoon. Charles Inglis, the outspoken Anglican loyalist of New York's Trinity Church, reported with disgust that he did not know of a single Presbyterian minister "nor have I been able after strict inquiry, to hear of any, who did not, by preaching and every effort in their power, promote all the efforts of the congress, however extravagant" (Hastings, VI, 4293). Such testimonies help explain why the War of Independence has sometimes been described as a "Presbyterian Rebellion."

Even before the Revolution the Presbyterians were pushing out the western frontier. After the conflict that movement was accelerated. Thus, Presbyterians joined with Baptists and newly arrived Methodists in traversing the mountains and fording the streams, settling in Tennessee, Kentucky, and the Ohio Valley even before the eighteenth century came to a close. The Presbytery of Redstone was formed in western Pennsylvania in 1781 with congregations worshiping among the trees in the summer and wherever there was sufficient warmth in the winter. To meet the challenge of the West, the denomination strengthened its organization, convening in 1789 the first General Assembly of American Presbyterianism. The country was there divided among four synods (the Synod of New York and New Jersey, the Synod of Philadelphia, the Synod of Virginia, the Synod of the Carolinas) and when

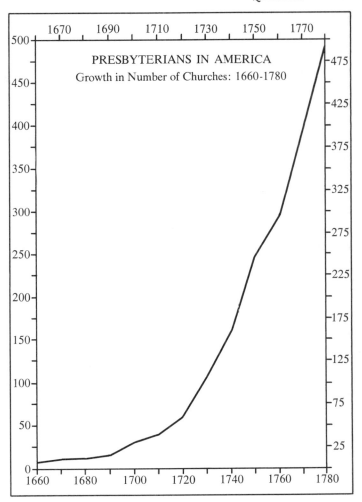

Figure 17

the dawn of the new century arrived, the "Presbyterian Enterprise" was well on its way.

SOURCES. Archibald Alexander, *Biographical Sketches of the . . . Principal Alumni of Log College* (Princeton, 1845). Maurice W. Armstrong *et al.* (eds.), *The Presbyterian Enterprise: Sources of American Presbyterian History* (Philadelphia, 1956). Charles A. Briggs, *American Presbyterianism. Its Origin and Early History* [map of "Presbyterian Colonies at the Close of the 17th Century," frontispiece] (New York, 1885). Samuel Davies, *Letters from the Rev. Samuel Davies, &c. Shewing the State of Religion in Virginia* (London [second edition], 1757). E. H. Gillett, *History of the Presbyterian Church in the United States of America*, 2 vols. (Philadelphia, 1864). F. H. Hart, *The Valley of Virginia in the American Revolution 1763-1789* (Chapel Hill, 1942). Hugh Hastings (ed.), *Ecclesiastical Records: State of New York*, 7 vols. (Albany, 1901-1916). Charles Hodge, *The Constitutional History of the Presbyterian Church in the U. S. A.* (Philadelphia, 1839-40). Guy S. Klett, *Presbyterians in Colonial Pennsylvania* (Philadelphia, 1947). Robert Proud, *The History of Pennsylvania . . .* 2 vols. (Philadelphia, 1797-1798). L. J. Trinterud, *The Forming of An American Tradition: A Reexamination of Colonial Presbyterianism* (Philadelphia, 1949). Richard Webster, *A History of the Presbyterian Church in America . . . until the year 1760 . . .* (Philadelphia, 1857).

7. QUAKERS

The well-ordered society preserves its stable position by keeping the lines of authority completely untangled and firmly in hand. If ultimate authority resides in God, then the rulers of society must be God's authentic spokesmen; if the authority is the Bible, they must be its legitimate interpreters; if the authority is power, the control of that power must be wholly theirs.

To any such neat boxing and compassing of the social order, the Quakers were a fearsome threat. If God be supreme, the Quaker was His messenger; if the Bible be authoritative, the Quaker was its interpreter; if power be the final appeal, the Quaker was a veritable spiritual dynamo. The Quaker—so named for his trembling in the presence of God—trembled in the presence of no other. For within his own being there burned an Inner Light, there dwelt a Christ within, redeeming the Quaker and marking him as an instrument of redemption to all men. But to the ecclesiastical and political authorities, the Friend seemed more the instrument of Satan than of God, more demon-possessed than Spirit-led.

Howard Brinton, in dividing the history of Quakerism into four periods, speaks of the years 1650 to 1700 as the apostolic or heroic years. Neither term exaggerates. The seventeenth-century Quaker was as conscious of being blessed by the Spirit as was the first-century Christian. Charismatic gifts were the only kind he knew, and suffering for Christ's sake and the gospel's was a common experience. Heroism, or perversity, brought four Quakers back to Massachusetts to meet their promised martyrdom on Boston Common: two in 1659, one in 1660, and the fourth in 1661. Unusual punishments and impossible fines demanded stern stuff of Quakers everywhere from New England to the Carolinas.

In the case of each religious body thus far described, expansion occurred as a small knot of dogged settlers battled mosquitoes, Indians, snow, and disease in order to claim a precious parcel of land. While this was to be the case also with the Quakers, it was not the way in which the doctrines of George Fox first fought their way onto colonial soil. Missionaries, young and old, male and female, sober and ecstatic, were sent over not merely "to spy out the land" but, if possible, to take it. Two Quaker women debarked in Boston in 1656, only to be imprisoned, then exiled. With other Quakers soon arriving, Massachusetts felt impelled to pass stern laws against these dangerous deluders, against any ship captain who transported them, and against any householder who harbored them. As soon as a Quaker was discovered in the colony, he was to be arrested, whipped, imprisoned, then banished. A law of 1657 provided that if a banished Quaker returned to Massachusetts, he would have his ear cropped; a second return and the second ear would be cropped; a third return would bring a hot iron to the tongue, until a hole had been burned through. When it became clear that these severe measures were insufficient deterrent, the authorities the next year imposed the death penalty upon any exiles who dared to return. It was under this law of 1658 that the four martyrdoms occurred (Jones, I, ch. 4).

Connecticut, happily free of "sectaries," endeavored to keep its land pure by passing harsh measures in 1656 against "any Quakers, Ranters, Adamites, or such like notorious heretics" who might, misguidedly, seek haven in that colony. At the most, such persons might be endured for a limit of two weeks, then prison or exile awaited them. In such hostile environment, Quakers turned to nearby Rhode Island, where the sword of state was not wielded against them. Here they thrived, even in the earlier years, making converts of men of influence and making men of influence of their converts. In 1661 the first Quaker Yearly Meeting ever held gathered in Newport. Strengthened in Rhode Island (and elsewhere) by the timely visit of George Fox in 1672, Quakerism grew to dominate this tiny colony—despite formidable opposition in the earnest polemic of the aging Roger Williams.

Quaker evangelists also roamed the preserves of the Dutch Reformed, on Long Island and around New Amsterdam. Governor Stuyvesant, who had already endeavored to prevent the Lutherans from adulterating pure worship, was in no mood to abide this English rabble. Hardly needing the prodding he received from Massachusetts, the governor levied fines, banned private conventicles, exiled and harassed the Quakers in a manner of which John Endicott would certainly have approved. Once more, however, the directors of the Dutch West Indian Company, recognizing the needs of their business venture, ordered a course of greater moderation; and the roots of New York Quakerism went ever deeper (Hastings, I, 399 f., 415, 530; see Fig. 18).

In the same year that the first Quaker women sailed into—and out of—Boston harbor (1656), another prophetess, Elizabeth Harris of London, arrived in Virginia. In her one-year stay, chiefly in Maryland, she made many converts, a success enlarged upon by two men who arrived the following year: Josiah Cole and Thomas Thurston. Such was their cumulative effect that the Virginia legislature in 1658 ordered the banishment of all Quakers from Virginia. In York County the Quaker influence was thought to be so strong as to provoke "the disturbance of the country's peace and the country's government." And for Governor Berkeley that "pestilential sect" deserved whatever fines, floggings or incarcerations he could impose (Bruce, I, 228 f.).

For a time the Quakers had North Carolina virtually to themselves. In that uncultivated and unchurched land, the exponents of the Inner Light were not proselyting from established churches but were preaching to the spiritually homeless. Prior to the end of the seventeenth century, the Anglican Church had made no penetration of North Carolina. No places of worship had been built, no tithes had been levied, no parishes had even been marked off. In such fertile fields, Quakerism was firmly planted. As early as 1676 considerable organization had been developed; and for the next quarter of a century the Quakers were the only organized religious body in the

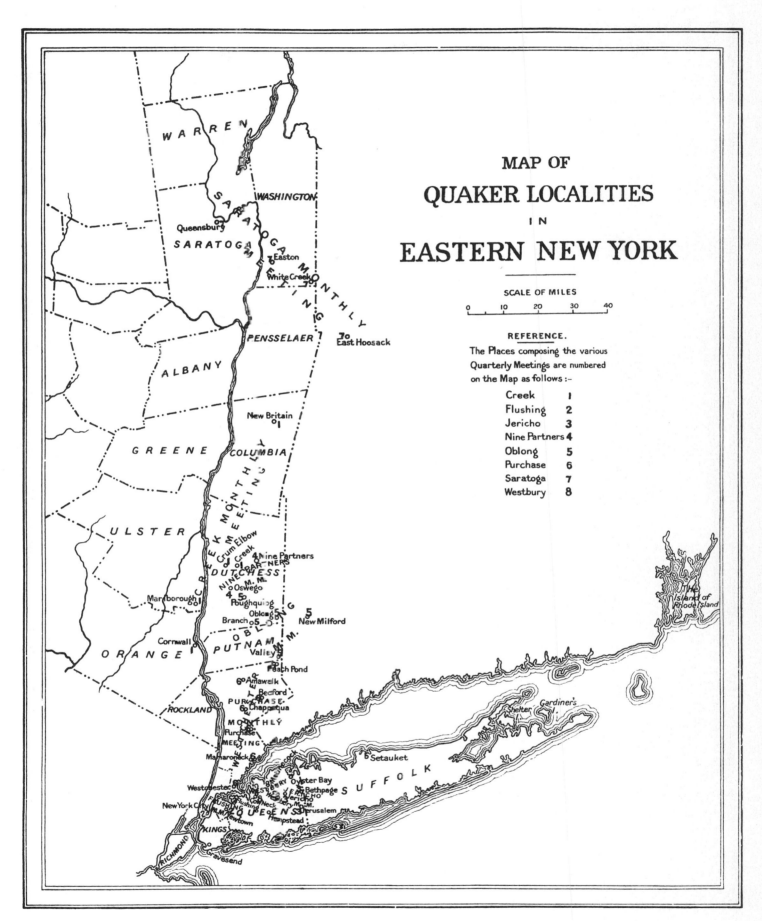

Figure 18

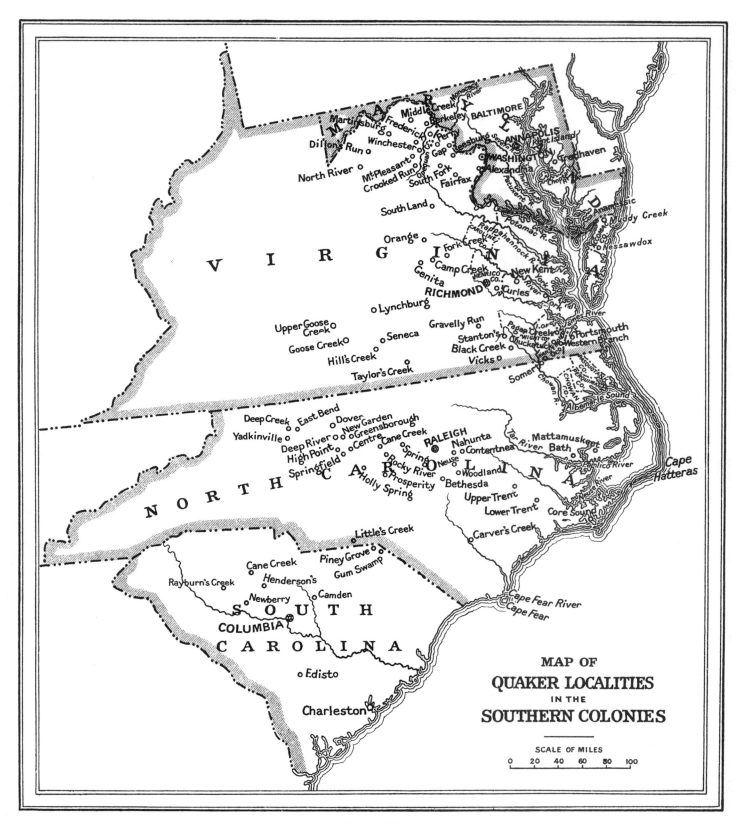

Figure 19

colony. In 1681 George Fox advised his followers in North Carolina to join with the Quakers of South Carolina in a Yearly Meeting, and by 1689 North Carolina's own Quarterly Meeting was begun. The last decade of the century saw the Carolina Quakers gaining so greatly in numbers and in influence that one might indeed have a care for "the country's peace."

But in 1700 a zealous Anglican, Henderson Walker, assumed the office of deputy governor and immediately launched a drive to make the Church of England the official and effective religion of North Carolina. Parishes were laid out, churches built, ministers called. Against this swift succession of events, Quakers and other dissenters protested, and they had sufficient strength to return a majority of their own numbers to the Assembly in 1703. Walker in haste and alarm wrote the Lord Bishop of London that something must be done, and that quickly, about these multiplying Quakers:

If your Lordship . . . doth not put a stop to their growth, we shall the most part, especially the children born here, become heathens. I humbly entreat your lordship to send some worthy, good men amongst us to regain the flock. . . and put a stop to the pernicious growing principles of the Quakers (Hawks, *Contributions*, II, 294).

Renewed efforts in 1704 to establish the Church of England and in 1705 to apply England's Test Act met not only with political reverse but also with open revolt. While the Quakers were certainly in the minority in North Carolina (one contemporary estimate—probably too low—declares they were "not the seventh part of the inhabitants"), there were enough others of the "anti-Church party" to join them in forcing the government's hand. A report in 1708 to the Society for the Propagation of the Gospel complained that the Quakers "have in a manner the sole management of the country in their hands, and of late years have at their pleasure procured a revolution of government as often as he that sat at the helm seemed to favor our church, or endeavored to make any provision for a ministry." The Quakers, together with the Presbyterians, were riding hard " and instead of our making proselytes, we shall, I am afraid, be hardly able to keep what we have from being perverted and seduced in this place of so great ignorance and enthusiasm" (Hawks, *Contributions*, II, 299 f.).

Despite the urgency of the warning, the Anglican cause was scarcely strengthened. A generation later the North Carolina governor noted not only that the Quakers "in this Government are considerable for their numbers and substance," but even worse, they had become respectable; indeed, the "regularity of their lives, hospitality to strangers and kind offices to new settlers" enhanced both their membership and their reputation (Lefler, 65 f.; see Fig. 19).

This far, and no word of William Penn. But this omission must not be extended. For it is in New Jersey and in Pennsylvania that we at last find a Quaker analogy to the accounts of Anglican settlers along the Virginia tidewater, Baptist families in Newport, and Congregational communities in New England. A decade after the British took over New Netherland in 1664, influential Quakers in England succeeded in purchasing portions of the huge land grants made to the Duke of York at the time of the English conquest. New Jersey, which until 1702 was separated into "East" and "West" Jersey, was first to be the scene of significant Quaker immigration. William Penn was personally involved in the settlement of West Jersey and in the framing of its liberal constitution. In 1675, and again the next year, a London ship of Quaker colonists made its way to the coast and up the Delaware River. By 1681, when Penn was negotiating for

the sale of that much larger block of land which was to bear his name, approximately 1,400 Quakers had settled in West Jersey. In the same year East Jersey was purchased by a group of 24 proprietors, the majority of whom were Quakers. In both Jerseys, then, Quakerism grew, not as an evangelistic phase, but as a colonizing development. Before the end of the century there were regular Monthly Meetings in Shrewsbury, Salem, Rahway, Burlington, Gloucester, and Newark.

Pennsylvania was, of course, the great prize for colonial Quakerism. Because of Penn's influence in the royal court and because of a £16,000 claim of his father's estate against the Crown, this far-sighted, noble-spirited man was able in 1681 to obtain the munificent grant of Pennsylvania. As governor, legislator, and sole proprietor, Penn arrived at New Castle, Delaware, on October 27, 1682. Because land was plentiful, government democratic, and religion free, colonists came in great numbers. By the end of 1682, 23 ships had sailed up the Delaware, depositing about 2,000 colonists, of whom the greater part were Quakers (Jones, Book V).

Major Quaker settlements were formed in the counties of Philadelphia, Chester and Bucks. "I need not tell you," wrote an Anglican cleric of Chester in 1712, "that Quakerism is generally preferred in Pennsylvania, and in no county of the province does the haughty tribe appear more rampant than where I reside, there being by a modest computation 20 Quakers . . . to one true Churchman" (Jones, 524).

The divine could take some comfort, however, in that schism of Quakerism which had directly aided the progress of the Church of England: the rupture led by George Keith, a learned Scottish Quaker. Believing that many of his co-religionists so emphasized the Inner Light as to minimize or ignore the demands of Scripture and of the historical Jesus, this "contentious apostate" (in the words of Thomas Story) organized in 1692 a group of his own, the Christian Quakers. Keith carried his controversy to England, where he seems to have had little success, and where he soon became an Anglican. As a newly appointed missionary of the Society for the Propagation of the Gospel, he returned to the colonies in 1702 to ply his trade especially in the Quaker meetings, creating deep resentment and fostering bitter reaction. How great the number of "Keithians" became it is impossible to say, but every indication is that the number was small. By the time of Keith's death in 1716, the major part of colonial Quakerism had closed ranks against him, presenting a united front which was not to be shattered for more than a century.

Because of the circumstances of its founding and the diligence of its colonists, Pennsylvania afforded genuine security. Men in high places politically and economically insured Quakerism a stability which elsewhere in the colonies it had not known. And even when numerical superiority began to slip away from the Quakers, as it did before the colonial period ended, they were still "esteemed among the wealthiest, and most substantial of the inhabitants" (Proud, II, 339). By 1770 there were more than 60 Quaker meetinghouses in Pennsylvania alone, and the Philadelphia Yearly Meeting had an estimated 30,000 members.

It is difficult to measure with precision the strength of colonial Quakerism. Ezra Stiles estimated that in 1760 there were sixteen thousand Quakers in all of New England. In the Southern Colonies at the time of the Revolution there were, according to the judgment of Rufus Jones, between 11,000 and 13,000 Quakers. While early settlements such as those of North Carolina and Rhode Island continued as vital Quaker centers, these sections could not keep pace with the Middle Colonies, where the great strength of Quakerism lay. With a total of something over 200 meetinghouses in 1800, Quaker institutional life was strongest in Pennsylvania (60 to 70 meetinghouses), followed next by New Jersey (41) and New York (20). At the end of the eighteenth century, there were approximately 50,000 Quakers in all the colonies (see Fig. 83).

In the colonial period the Quakers held their own numerically, being outstripped only by the Anglicans, Congregationalists, and Presbyterians (see Fig. 127). In 1750, for example, the Quakers had about the same number of churches as the Lutherans and the Baptists, while they enjoyed a sizable lead over the Reformed bodies, as well as over the Roman Catholics. Although, as the Republic grew, Quakers continued to exercise an influence far greater than their size would appear to warrant, they began to lose numerical standing. Numbers and denominational growth never mattered much, however, to those whose "great business," in the words of the beloved John Woolman, was "to labour for an establishment in Divine love, where the mind is disentangled from the power of darkness."

SOURCES. James Bowden, *The History of the Society of Friends in America*, 2 vols. (London, 1850). Howard Brinton, *Friends for 300 Years* (New York, 1952). Philip A. Bruce, *Institutional History of Virginia in the Seventeenth Century*, 2 vols. (New York, 1910). George Fox, *The Journal of George Fox*, 2 vols. (Cambridge, 1911). Hugh Hastings (ed.), *Ecclesiastical Records. State of New York*, 7 vols. (Albany, 1901-1916). Rufus M. Jones, *The Quakers in the American Colonies* (London, 1923). Hugh T. Lefler, (ed.), *North Carolina History Told by Contemporaries* (Chapel Hill, 1934). Ezra Michener, *A Retrospect of Early Quakerism . . .* (Philadelphia, 1860). Robert Proud, *The History of Pennsylvania . . .* 2 vols., (Philadelphia, 1797-1798). Stephen B. Weeks, *Southern Quakers and Slavery* [contains useful map of Quaker communities in the southern states] (Baltimore, 1896). John Woolman, *The Journal of John Woolman* (Chicago, 1950).

8. REFORMED

In contrast to "congregational," "presbyterian," and "episcopal," the name "reformed" is theological rather than political. The churches which followed in the tradition of Calvin were styled "reformed," while those in the Lutheran heritage were often called "evangelical." Colonial America was heavily "reformed" in this theological sense. Indeed, it would be possible—though not particularly useful—to describe the Congregationalists as "English Reformed" and the Presbyterians as "Scottish Reformed," for the Calvinist orientation of each is unmistakable. Also, as earlier noted, Calvinism became the major theological tradition among Baptists in the eighteenth century. Of the colonial religious bodies, only the Quakers and Roman Catholics stood distinctly outside the Reformed tradition.

Our attention here, however, is focused on Reformed groups other than those just mentioned; namely, the Dutch Reformed and the German Reformed. There was a third and much smaller group, the French Reformed, who in the earliest days of settlement in the New World exhibited incomparable courage and heroism. From the sixteenth-century efforts of Admiral Coligny to colonize Florida and Nova Scotia to the somewhat more successful seventeenth-century settlements around Boston, New York, and Charleston, the Huguenot story is a gripping one. As their numbers remained small, however, and diminished rather than increased after 1700, the graph (Fig. 21) does not include their progress. There were about 15 French Reformed churches in 1700, and approximately one-half that number at the end of the colonial period.

Dutch Reformed. The ambitious program of exploration and colonization carried on by Holland in the seventeenth century led to settlements in the Hudson River area shortly after 1614. Under the Dutch West India Company, citizens of Holland emigrated to this New Netherland, establishing their first church at New Amsterdam in 1628. Their second church, founded at Fort Orange (Albany) in 1642, marked the northern end of the settlement for the remainder of the century. The churches that followed these two were scattered over the southern half of Long Island, southern New York, and northern New Jersey; by 1700 there were 26 Dutch Reformed churches in the colonies.

The beginnings were slow and painful. Although there were 2 churches in 1650 (see Fig. 2), there was but a single clergyman. The plea went out that orders "be given forthwith for the immediate calling and support of at least three preachers; one to attend to Divine Service at Renselaer's Colonies; the second in and about the city of New Amsterdam, and the third in the distant places . . ." (Hastings, I, 270). By 1660 there were 6 Dutch ministers, so the Company apparently had heeded the petition. In Brooklyn—that is, Breuckelen—there were 24 members of the Dutch Reformed Church; and the Bowery, "a place of relaxation and pleasure," was regularly the scene of the Sunday evening worship service "whither people go from the Manhattans." Resistance to the toleration of any other form of worship was high, with Lutherans constituting the immediate threat. Two Reformed ministers urged the governor not to grant permission for the settlement of a Lutheran minister for "This would tend to the injury of our church, the diminution of hearers of the Word of God, and the increase of dissensions, of which we have had a sufficiency for years past." And if Lutherans were to be tolerated, soon "our place would become a receptacle for all sorts of heretics and fanatics' (Hastings, I, 317).

The issue was, before long, academic. In 1664, when the English took over New York, the question was whether the Dutch Reformed should be tolerated. They were. The inhabitants retained their rights and their property, and the Church enjoyed a privileged status: charters were granted to the two *national* Churches, the Church of England and the Church of Holland; to no others was legal sanction given, and not until 1777 was proscriptive and punitive legislation regarding dissenters repealed. Though chafing somewhat under British rule, the Dutch Reformed Church held its position for the remainder of the century. A report to the Classis of Amsterdam offers the following statistics of membership for 1681: Long Island, 360; New York, about 500; Bergen, about 110; Staten Island, about 50; Esopus [Kingstown], about 200; Albany, 375; and "at Schoonechtede [Schenectady] one hundred; so that we have here together about seventeen hundred members, Dutch and French" (Hastings, II, 795).

Governor Thomas Dongan, somewhat dismayed by the religious diversity of New York in 1687, acknowledged that "the most prevailing opinion is that of the Dutch Calvinists." In New York City, the Anglican and the Dutch shared the original Reformed church edifice within the Fort; Dongan found this "very inconvenient; therefore I desire that there may be an order for their building another. . . ." The "another" was Trinity Church, completed in 1697, which enabled the Anglicans to worship, so to speak, on their own ground and not as though they were in "a conquered Foreign Province held by the terrour of a Garrison" (Hastings, II, 878 f.; 1311). At Albany and Schenectady there was, upon the death of a Reformed cleric in 1710, no ministry available to the Dutch except an S.P.G. missionary, Thomas Barclay. Hoping to win the inhabitants over to the Church of England, Barclay reported that there were about 100 Dutch families in Schenectady and that most of Albany's population of 3,000 was Dutch. In other parts of New York (e.g., Orange County), 3 or 4 Dutch churches without ministerial leadership pooled their resources in an effort to offer an attractive salary, with "land enough to pasture two horses and two cows" thrown in.

Although several Dutch Reformed churches were established in New Jersey in the latter decades of the seventeenth century, it was not until about 1720 that this colony moved more fully under their influence. This came about through the dynamic leadership of Theodorus Jacobus Frelinghuysen, who left Holland in response to

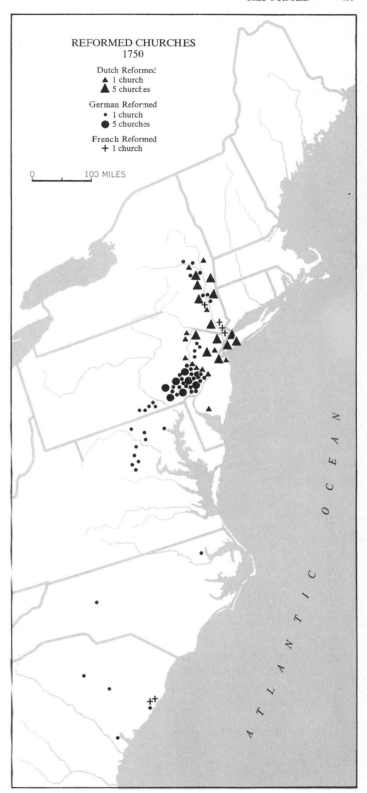

Figure 20

the invitation of several Dutch inhabitants of Somerset, Middlesex, and Hunterdon counties. Frelinghuysen, like the Presbyterian New Sides and the Congregational New Lights, placed much emphasis on warm, personalized, emotional, earnest, evangelical preaching. He trained young men for the Reformed ministry; he saw the need for the establishment of a college comparable to the Presbyterians' Princeton and the Congregationalists' Yale;

finally, he took steps that led (after his death) to an independent Reformed Church in America, severed from the rule of the Amsterdam Classis. By 1765 the number of ministers in East New Jersey alone was 14 or 15 "and each of them do for the most part supply two or three different congregations" (Smith, 492 f.).

In urging the need for a Dutch Reformed college, Frelinghuysen in 1746 wrote the ruling Classis: "Our Reformed Church, numerous as it is in membership is in a

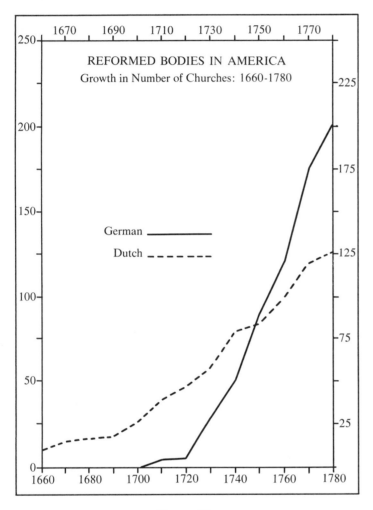

Figure 21

desolate condition. It has neither Classis nor Synod, nor any money for instructing those who would give themselves to the study of the learned languages, the sciences and arts, and especially Sacred Theology. Many churches without pastors do not know how or whence they may obtain help. They will be obliged to go and seek in other denominations what they cannot find among ourselves." Urging that an American Classis be promoted instead of resisted, Frelinghuysen respectfully adds, "The time has now come, Rev. Fathers, for our eyes to be opened somewhat . . ." (Hastings, V, 3648 f). Out of this appeal there ultimately came Rutgers University (Queens College) in 1766. Out of the appeal for an American Classis came the first step toward separation from Amsterdam in 1771; and the Synod of New York and New Jersey, emboldened

by the success of the War of Independence, became in 1789 the Reformed Dutch Church of North America.

German Reformed. Although the first German Reformed church in America was not founded until 1710, by 1750 this group had already overtaken their Dutch brethren. The great German immigration of the third and fourth decades gave this Reformed body a depth which the trickles of Dutch from abroad could never match. While at the beginning of the eighteenth century there was no German Reformed church, at the end of the colonial period there were approximately twice as many German as there were Dutch churches (see Figs. 4 and 6).

The first wave of immigration was that of the Palatinate refugees from 1708 to 1710. The Board of Trade in 1709 informed the Council of New York that the Queen has "thought fit to order the sending of some three thousand of the poor Palatines to New York." The Council was instructed to take the proper measures in providing for these refugees upon their arrival, "both as to lodging and provisions." As noted in the discussion of Lutheranism, the chosen settlements were on both banks of the Hudson and in the Mohawk River Valley. With an eye to the constant need for naval stores, the Board of Trade pointed out that in these areas were "very great numbers of Pines fit for production of Turpentine and Tarr, out of which Rozin and Pitch are made" (Hastings, III, 1808-1812).

The greater influx, of course, was in Pennsylvania in the 1730's and following (see Fig. 21). When the German Reformed were first getting under way in this colony, the members of the small and isolated churches felt a faith-testing insecurity "living among all sorts of errorists, as Independents, Puritans, Anabaptists, the New-born, the Saturday-folks . . . yea, as living among some of the most dreadful heretics" (Hastings, IV, 2429). Nor did the fact that most of their civil magistrates were Quakers in any way alleviate the strain. But by 1750 there were 64 German Reformed churches in Pennsylvania and this strength brought considerable comfort (see Fig. 20). Like the Lutherans, the Reformed settled inland, notably in the counties of Montgomery, Lehigh, Northampton, Lancaster, Berks, and York. Pennsylvania was their principal dwelling place, not only in the eighteenth century but also in the nineteenth and twentieth.

While the German Reformed group readily outdistanced the Dutch (not to mention the French), this increase was a function wholly of immigration, not of relative success in proselyting or in becoming "Americanized." In the latter kind of expansion, neither group achieved great success in the colonial period. Both were hampered by organizational problems and subservience to the Dutch Church abroad. For even though composed of Germans (and some Swiss), the German Reformed were under the jurisdiction of the Amsterdam Classis until 1793, when they took the name of the German Reformed Church. Moreover, the language limitation hobbled both of the Reformed bodies. Some of these German-speaking congregations felt that the surrender of their distinctive tongue could only lead to a coalition with the English Presbyterians, and that they would lose their identity completely. Even so, notes an observer in 1754, "it is generally feared that the very next generation will scarce furnish one person in this city [Philadelphia], except their clergy, well-acquainted with the tongue." While that fear was not everywhere realized, the principal point was made: that the "too long continued use" of German or Dutch was a tether restraining the Churches' movement and growth (Hastings, V, 3459 f.).

The concern for linguistic and theological purity was maintained with greater success and determination in the Dutch Reformed than in the German Reformed Church. The latter, in succeeding generations, manifested an active interest in ecumenical overtures, in an open-minded experimentation in Methodist-type revivalism and, by contrast, in Catholic-type liturgy. Philip Schaff, the noted German Reformed Church historian, was to popularize the dictum: "In essentials unity; in doubtful points freedom; in all things love." With this spirit the German Reformed Church entered the larger stream of American Christianity, yielding its own separate identity to the cause of a united and strengthened witness.

SOURCES. Edward T. Corwin, *A Manual of the Reformed Church in America 1628-1902* [a rich mine of information] (New York [fourth edition], 1902); *A History of the Reformed Church, Dutch* (American Church History Series, VIII) (New York, 1895). David D. Demarest, *History and Characteristics of the Reformed Protestant Dutch Church* (New York, 1856). *Deutscher Kulturatlas*, 5 vols. (Berlin and Leipzig, 1928-38). Joseph H. Dubbs, *A History of the Reformed Church, German* (American Church History Series, VIII) (New York, 1895). Sydney G. Fisher, *The Making of Pennsylvania*, (Philadelphia, 1896). Thomas F. Gordon, *The History of Pennsylvania, from its discovery by Europeans to the Declaration of Independence in 1776* (Philadelphia, 1829). Hugh Hastings (ed.), *Ecclesiastical Records. State of New York*, 7 vols. (Albany, 1901-1916). Arthur H. Hirsch, *The Huguenots of Colonial South Carolina* (Durham, 1928). Albert C. Myers (ed.), *Narratives of Early Pennsylvania, West New Jersey and Delaware 1630-1707* (New York, 1912). Samuel Smith, *The History of the Colony of Nova-Caesaria, or New Jersey . . .* (Trenton [second edition], 1877).

9. ROMAN CATHOLICS

Spanish Missions. Many Americans mark the beginning of the religious history of their country at a point not far from a small gray rock on the coast of Massachusetts. Others, however, have been bold to assert that God did not arrive on the *Mayflower,* but that His Good News had been heard in the land at least a century earlier. Priests probably accompanied the Spanish colonizers into Florida in 1521; in 1526, near Cape Fear, mass was offered by two Dominicans who were joined to Vasquez de Ayllon's 600-man expeditionary force. Within a year, however, all that remained of this latter settlement along the Chesapeake were the more than 400 dead left behind.

The Spanish Crown was hardly less fervent than the Spanish Church in making diligent and repeated efforts to penetrate the land north of the Gulf of Mexico. In accordance with established policy, the Church and the state were to work in the closest of unions. Pope Alexander VI, in his declaration of 1493, had drawn 100 leagues west of the Azores the famous line of demarcation. West of it he did "give, grant, and assign to you and to your heirs and successors, kings of Castille and Leon, forever . . . all islands and mainlands found and to be found . . ." (Ellis, *Documents,* 2). It was a generous offer; though later it had to be somewhat modified in favor of Portugal, Spain could regard herself for the most part as the appointed messenger of Roman Catholicism to the new continents.

This union of throne and altar, though it suggests a harmonious identity of purpose and tactic, was nevertheless beset by sharp differences and deep distrust. Not even the humanitarian plea of Pope Paul III that under no circumstances were the Indians "to be deprived of their liberty or the possession of their property, even though they be outside the faith of Jesus Christ . . ." could pass uncontested (Ellis, *Documents,* 9). So vigorous was the church-state controversy that the papacy found it necessary in 1538 to retract its earlier pronouncements, consenting to a lesser role in the formulation of colonial policy.

Missionaries of the major religious orders, nonetheless, maintained a heroic struggle against insuperable odds in the forays of sixteenth-century Spanish explorers. One year after the collapse of Ayllon's efforts along the Chesapeake, Narvaez anchored in Tampa Bay. Diocesan clergy as well as religious accompanied him, but neither found much opportunity for evangelizing among any but the wounded and the dying—both Indian and European. Brutal, bloody skirmishes ceased only with the retreat of the intruders who, finding no ships to return them to Cuba, hastily constructed vessels only partially seaworthy. The sea was without mercy, and only five men—among them Cabeza de Vaca—finally escaped its grasp. De Vaca, after spending some time with the Indians, made his way back to Mexico, having traversed the whole of the southern plains to the Gulf of California. In Mexico, in 1540, his tales inspired two well-known adventurers: De Soto and Coronado. However prodigious the marches and gallant the efforts of these two men, their effect on the religious history of America was not great. De Soto died in 1542, one year after his discovery of the Mississippi River, and Coronado returned home without having found gold or anything else that seemed to justify the Crown's efforts. When Coronado turned back from the central plains, however, he left behind—at their own insistence—three Franciscan friars who hoped to sow the seeds of the gospel in greater depth and in the patience of hope. Of the three, the fate of only one is documented; Juan de Padilla was killed by Indians, probably in southern Kansas, in 1542. This is the first record of Christian martyrdom on American soil.

Later in the same decade, a further Dominican attempt

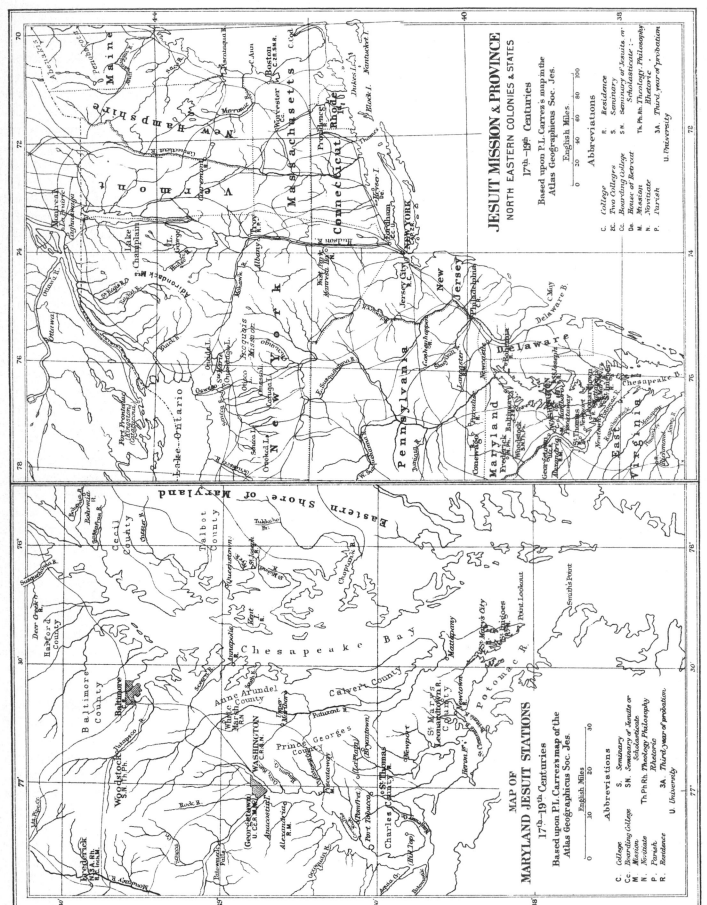

Figure 22

was made to win converts among the Florida Indians; still another was made in 1559. Both were abortive, halted either by the death of the friars or by the withdrawal of Spanish forces. By 1561 Philip II had decided to give up the plan to colonize Florida. The one permanent settlement, St. Augustine, was established at the expense not of hostile Indians but of Huguenot Frenchmen. Under the direction of Admiral Coligny, French Protestants had come to Florida's east coast in 1562-68 to find, if possible, a refuge from the massacres of their homeland. At the hands of the Spanish colonizer, Pedro Menendez, however, they died as had many of their brethren on the Continent; thus was Florida "saved for Spain and the Church" (Maynard, 29).

At this juncture, members of the Society of Jesus took up the evangelizing efforts in Florida, extending their labors as far north as Virginia. But the obstacles had in no way grown smaller, and after six heroic years and six martyred Jesuits, the General of the Society in 1571 decided that "not only is it not fitting to keep the Company in that land, but it must not be done . . ." (Ellis, *Documents*, 16). The hostility of native and of nature was as evident in these Spanish beginnings as it was in the English beginning with the ill-fated colony of Roanoke.

Greater success was enjoyed and far greater impact was made in the Southwest. The missions of New Mexico and California maintained a program of social and religious reformation which was to leave its permanent stamp on American culture. As early as 1630 the Franciscan superior in New Mexico reported that 35,000 Christian Indians were nurtured by the 25 Roman Catholic missions (see Fig. 116). In the last decade of the seventeenth century, Father Eusebio Francisco Kino (1645-1711) labored in what is now northern Sonora and southern Arizona—"the heart of all this North America," in his words—establishing missions, defending the Indians against unjust accusation, writing fervent pleas for more priests, and drawing valuable maps. In all, this hardy Jesuit made 14 major trips into Arizona (see the excellent map of his journeys in *Arizona Highways*, XXXVII:3 [March, 1961], pp. 12-13).

The chain of missions along the coast of California began in San Diego with the establishment of the San Diego de Alcala mission in 1769 and ended with the dedication of the San Francisco de Solano (Sonoma) mission on July 4, 1823. The original Franciscan genius of this mighty effort was Father Junípero Serra (1713-1784), who in his final report of 1784 placed the number of confirmations among the California Indians at 5,307 (Ellis, *Documents*, 45).

In Texas, the first high mass was sung on May 16, 1675, following an expedition across the Rio Grande to a branch of the Nueces River. Nearly 1,200 Indians were instructed and baptized on this occasion (Ellis, *Documents*, 24). The scholarly writings and the careful maps of Herbert E. Bolton make clear the extent and the depth of Spanish Catholicism in the Southwest; there is yet ample "unexplored territory" here for the student of American civilization.

French Missions. The development of Roman Catholic missions under the aegis of France is a tale extraordinary both in its determination and its documentation. Concerning the latter, the members of the Society of Jesus had the happy habit of providing written reports for their superiors, who in turn transmitted or compiled the same for the General of the Order. These "Jesuit relations," as they appear in Reuben Gold Thwaites' 73-volume edition (*The Jesuit Relations and Allied Documents*, Cleveland, 1896-1901), constitute an invaluable, irreplaceable source of knowledge regarding the entry of Catholicism into the northern and central parts of America.

With regular visits being paid by French ships to the fishing grounds off Newfoundland, French contacts with the New World in the sixteenth century grew both in frequency and in intensity. Initial efforts at colonization, however, were abortive. The importing of inmates from French prisons did not constitute the most auspicious beginning, and the results justified whatever somber prophecies may have been made.

Not until the seventeenth century was there a more hopeful effort by the French to colonize the New World. And this effort was, curiously, both Protestant and Catholic. With royal approval the Sieur de Monts, a wealthy French Calvinist, was given a trade monopoly in North America of all the territory between the fortieth and forty-sixth parallels. De Monts was also expected to establish an agricultural settlement. Many of the harried Huguenots were willing to settle under the leadership of a fellow Protestant, and with the explicit guarantee of religious freedom. But the royal directive had made it clear that while Huguenot ministers could accompany the colonizer in order to minister to their own faithful, Roman Catholic priests must be taken along in order to convert the savages to the way of Rome.

Some settlement was made in 1604 in Nova Scotia, with a portion of the group moving south to Ste. Croix Island where priests celebrated the "first mass on New England soil." Despite a promising beginning, however, the colony did not prosper; the southernmost group retreated to Port Royal, Nova Scotia, where survival proved to be the chief occupation. Under prodding from Europe, some mission work was carried on among the Abenaki Indians.

In 1610 Champlain succeeded in establishing a permanent hold on Quebec, though this boon was overbalanced by his unfortunate alienation of the Iroquois—a fact which augured ill for French missions along the St. Lawrence. In 1611 two Jesuit fathers arrived in Port Royal and began the incredible task of mastering Indian languages. Two years later they were put to flight (and a lay brother was killed) during an English attack led by

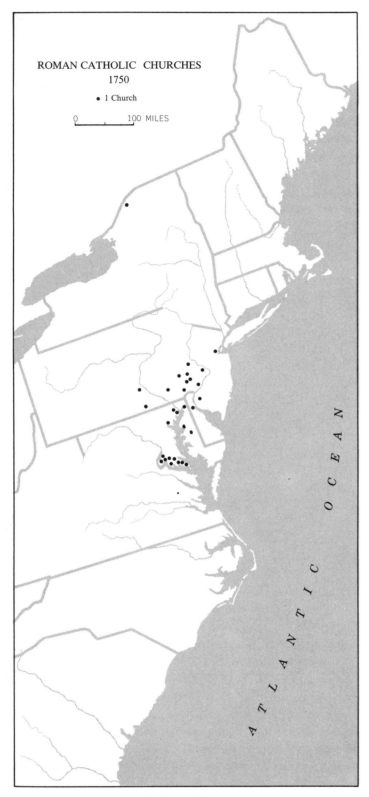

ROMAN CATHOLIC CHURCHES
1750

• 1 Church

0 _____ 100 MILES

ATLANTIC OCEAN

Figure 23

the resurgence of English power over the continent in 1629, driving all French from their newly settled lands. With the terms of peace, however, Canada was returned to France, and by 1632 the Jesuit missions were once more under way. The members of this order had specific charge of the new missions field, and their renewed labors began in earnest. In the words of Reuben Thwaites, "The mission of the French Jesuits to these widely-scattered hordes of savages forms one of the most thrilling chapters in human history" (Kenton, ed., xxvii).

So far as the territory of the present United States is concerned, five of the missions of the French Jesuits are of particular interest: those among the Abenaki, the Huron, the Iroquois, the Ottawa, and along the Mississippi River.

The Abenakis, as noted above, were ministered to as early as 1610 by missionaries based in Port Royal. Franciscans, working the area of this tribe's wandering, established missions in the seventeenth century along the Penobscot and the Kennebec Rivers (see Fig. 23). At Sillery and St. Francis de Sales (both in the area of Quebec), missions set up around 1650 proved more than once to be welcome places of strength and of refuge. Some of the missions in Maine were maintained until the downfall of New France in 1763, though the English-French tension was nowhere so constantly in evidence, so inevitably irritating to both sides.

Among the Hurons, concentrated to the east and south of the lake that bears their name, missionary efforts antedated the fall of Canada to England in 1629. The Franciscans whom Champlain had encouraged roamed far from the safety of Quebec to preach to a tribe that was comparatively peaceful. But treachery and hardship cost the lives of some, and efforts to get this hunting tribe to settle in villages were resisted by the French commercial interests. Under Jesuit direction the Huron missions were reopened in 1634, with significant centers being created in Michigan, Wisconsin, and Minnesota. By 1640, however, despite years of cold courage and warm affection on the part of the missionaries, there were only 100 converts, many of whom were among the aged and infirm, and often died shortly after baptism—a fact that understandably aggravated the Indians' suspicions.

The concern of the missionary to avoid everything that would hamper his evangelistic effort is fully, even poignantly, revealed in the instructions of Brébeuf to other Jesuits new in the work. First, and clearly above all else, "You must have sincere affection for the Savages,— looking upon them as ransomed by the blood of the son of God, and as our brethren with whom we are to pass the rest of our lives." The practical detail, however, did not escape the monk's attention. "Be careful not to annoy any one in the canoe with your hat; it would be better to take your nightcap. There is no impropriety among the Savages." One should take care, moreover, not to get his gown wet, for thus he brings sand and water into the

Samuel Argall. Champlain, deciding by 1615 to attempt some mission work among the Indians in the area of Quebec, brought four Franciscans (Recollects) to his western outpost. After a decade of stoic labor, these friars invited the stronger Jesuit order to assist them. Three wearers of the black gown came, among them Jean de Brébeuf, who for pertinacity and fidelity to duty was to establish a record that was notable and probably inimitable. But the making of that record was delayed by

canoe. A tinderbox or burning mirror will enable the priest to start the campfire for the Indians in the evenings, and "these little services win their hearts." The food that is offered must be eaten, no matter how dirty or repugnant. "As to the numerous other things which may be unpleasant, they must be endured for the love of God, without saying anything or appearing to notice them" (Ellis, *Documents*, 51 f.).

Even with such conscientious concern, the Huron missions did not succeed. A large measure of their failure is explained by the ferocious hostility of the Iroquois, whose repeated attacks decimated the Huron tribes and resulted in five Jesuits, including Brébeuf, being put to death. The incredible torture to which Brébeuf was subjected and the even more incredible strength with which he endured it were enough to make Francis Parkman declare this founder of the Huron mission to be "its truest hero, and its greatest martyr" (Parkman, 491).

The failure of the Huron mission forced the Jesuits to consider a direct approach to the Iroquois. These tribes had been the Jesuits' greatest and seemingly intractable enemy, but shortly after the middle of the seventeenth century, the politically astute Iroquois, threatened from other quarters, found it expedient to present a more conciliatory face to the French. Quickly seizing the unexpected opportunity, Jesuits began opening missions in upper New York State (Onondaga and Cayuga), and by 1668 there were Roman Catholic preaching posts among all five of the Iroquois nations. But within two decades the increase in English power in the area brought an end to this activity.

As early as 1639 Jesuits worked among the Chippewas, establishing a mission at Sault Ste. Marie. Also the Miami, the Illinois, and others of the Ottawa group were faithfully cultivated throughout the century. For nearly thirty years the Jesuit Allouez worked with the Ottawa, erecting La Pointe Mission in northwest Wisconsin in 1665. It was from this mission that the famous Marquette went forth, forming other centers in the north central area of America. St. Ignace, founded on the northern Michigan peninsula in 1670, became the largest mission of the region. And in 1673 Marquette joined Joliet in the well-known expedition on the Mississippi River. While it is not possible to follow in any detail the number of Ottawa conversions, there appears to have been a steady, if sometimes slow, success among the tribes of this group. Hostility, not from the Iroquois, but from the Sioux, on occasion required retrenchment by both the Ottawas and their Christian evangels. But Jesuit brothers were present until their suppression in the late eighteenth century, and even to some extent thereafter. French settlements grew around the missions, intermarriages took place, and the influence remained (Kenton, ed., xliii-xlvi).

The Marquette-Joliet expedition down the Mississippi River in 1673 opened the way for French claims to the territory of that great valley, and therefore opened the

way subsequently for French missionary activity. Marquette himself established no mission in the lower Louisiana Territory, but in the early 1680's some instruction was given to the Indians by a Sulpician and a Franciscan. (La Salle was not overly fond of the Jesuits.) Moreover, seculars were operating in the area out of their seminary base in Quebec, from which episcopal see Bishop Laval presided—technically at least—over all French possessions in North America. In 1698 seculars established a mission

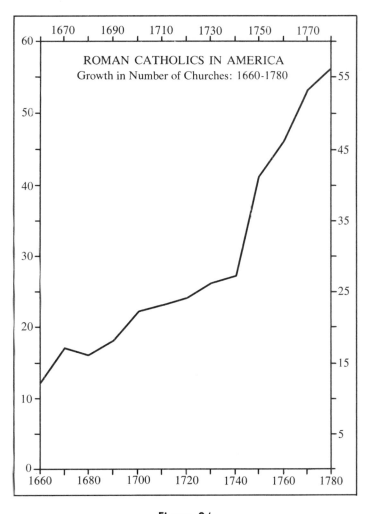

Figure 24

Includes only those missions located in the thirteen colonies.

on the Yazoo River among the Natchez. Others from the seminary presided over "the first canonically erected parish in the western country," Fort Louis, established in 1703 on the site of the present city of Mobile, Alabama. The Jesuits, however, continued to look upon much of this Indian territory as their peculiar responsibility and, operating out of a house established near New Orleans, they maintained missions among the Arkansas, Yazoo, Choctaws, and Alibamons. Their work was restricted to the "savages," with the secular priests taking over regular parish work. Although in 1762 the Jesuit order was suppressed in France, the Jesuit mission in New France was not completely closed until 1770. The Superior of the Jesuits in the Illinois country, describing in detail their conformity to the order to evacuate, had no reply for the remark of fellow Frenchmen that "this (command) was only to be expected from the open enemies of the Catholic religion," and hardly from officers within the Church (Ellis, *Documents,* 92). It was a harsh blow, not alone to the Society of Jesus, but to French Catholicism in the New World. However, the influence of the total effort throughout the Mississippi Valley remained, and Louisiana in particular continues to witness to the work of Franciscan, Jesuit, and other earnest laborers in an unfriendly wilderness.

English Colonies. When the *Ark* and the *Dove* sailed up the Potomac River in March of 1634 to establish Maryland's first permanent settlement at St. Mary's City, among the passengers were two Jesuit missionaries: Andrew White and John Altham. On March 25 Father White offered the first mass—a divine service "never before performed in this part of the world," wrote White—on St. Clement's Island in the Potomac. The missionaries and the Catholic passengers (many were non-Catholic) then cut "a great cross out of a tree . . . took it on our shoulder, and going in procession to the place selected . . . we erected it as a trophy to Christ our Saviour, after reciting humbly on our knees, with feelings of profound emotion, the Litany of the Holy Cross" (Hughes, Text I, 324). White's house in St. Mary's City served for a time as a chapel, and the first church was established in that city in 1640. Thus began the first and only one of the colonies successfully launched by a Roman Catholic proprietor.

But the Crown was still Protestant, and by the middle of the century, Catholic power was reduced to a minimum and Catholic population to a minority. Before that occurred, however, an ordinance passed in 1639 guaranteed to all inhabitants of the colony "all their rights and liberties according to the great Charter of England" (Hanley, 4, 122 *et passim*). A decade later, through the sponsorship of both Protestants and Catholics, Maryland's Act of Toleration was passed. It was repealed five years later —to the immediate and tragic disadvantage of the Catholics. Jesuit houses were plundered, priests were forced to flee the colony, and four Catholics were put to death (Ellis, *American Catholicism,* 27).

These radical changes in Maryland resulted primarily from Cromwell's coup in the mother country and Lord Baltimore's concurrent loss of power. By making appropriate arrangements with the new political authorities, Baltimore managed by 1657 to be restored to his former position as proprietor of Maryland. But by that time Maryland was no longer, in any meaningful sense, a Catholic colony. When, in 1677, there was a move to grant special privileges to the Church of England, Lord Baltimore objected, not on the grounds that many Roman Catholics would resent such a move, but on the grounds that three-fourths of the inhabitants "doe consist of Proesbiterians, Independents, Anabaptists and Quakers." It would be a

most difficult task, he noted further, "to draw such persons to consent unto a Law, which shall compel them to maintain Ministers of a contrary persuasion to themselves, they having already an assurance by that Act for Religion that they shall have all freedom in point of Religion and Divine Worship . . ." (Wroth, 22). The protest held Anglican establishment off for a time, but with the appointment of the first royal governor in 1692 the process got under way. By the end of the century, Thomas Bray was pleased to note that "the Papists in this Province appear to me to be not above a twelfth Part of the Inhabitants" (*Memorial,* 8); and by 1703 the establishment of the Church of England was complete.

Notwithstanding the harassing, and worse, endured by the Catholics in Maryland, that colony continued to serve as a vital center for the Roman Church (see Fig. 22). Protestant governors expressed grave concern about those "Popish priests and zealous Papists" who "seduce, delude and persuade diverse of his Majesty's good Protestant subjects to the Romish faith," while Protestant clergymen suggested that there should be laws preventing Jesuits from ministering to persons when they were "dying and phranticke" (Hughes, Text II, 446 f.). The number and tone of such testimonies, as well as the variety of legal restrictions passed (including making Irish Catholics dutiable by imposing in 1704 a tax of 20 shillings on each such immigrant), give evidence that Catholicism was not dead. If the abundant evidence is taken too seriously, however, it could lead to the erroneous conclusion that the "Jesuites and other felons" (to use Governor John Seymour's phrase) were making Catholics out of virtually all the inhabitants. Such was not the case. In 1708, out of a population of 33,883, only 2,974 were Catholics (Hughes, Text II, 463). And by 1750, there were three times more Anglican than Catholic churches. The Catholic minority remained a minority, but it proved to be a powerful one in teaching, training and, above all, in inspiring other Catholics (see the map of Maryland mission centers, Fig. 22).

And inspiration was a useful ingredient in a day when men banded together to prevent the growth of popery. Even when popular sentiment brought about a measure of religious toleration, Roman Catholics were generally made the conspicuous exception. In New England, Rhode Island soon withdrew its promise of full religious freedom, denying the franchise to Roman Catholics possibly as early as 1664. Connecticut and Massachusetts, of course, maintained their zeal for religious purity with peculiar intensity against the Romanists. In the seventeenth century their protective wall appeared impenetrable; in the eighteenth century holes began to appear in the dike; in the nineteenth century the flood came. In 1732 Timothy Cutler. reported to the S. P. G. that "some few Papists" were known to be in New England, but "the most . . . of them are concealed." A careful inquiry in Boston at this time revealed that perhaps two dozen Catholics resided there. Governor Belcher regarded this threat as sufficient to require the following order "to the sheriff of Suffolk county" on March 5, 1732:

Whereas it has been represented unto me that there are a considerable number of Papists now residing within the Town of Boston or elsewhere in sd County who have Joyned with their Priest or do speedily design to Assemble together in order to say their Popish prayers or Celebrate Masses and to use other of the Romish Ceremonies and Rites of Worship, and derive their Power or Jurisdiction from the Pope of Rome and are harboured or Entertained by the Inhabitants within the sd County Contrary to the good and wholesome Laws of the Province.

These are therefore to will and require you and each of you respectively in His Majesty's Name forthwith to make diligent Enquiry after and search for the said Popish Priest and other Papists of his Faith and Perswasion and (if need be) in order to apprehend them or any of them you are Directed and Impowered to break open any Dwelling houses shops or other Places or appartments where you shall suspect they or any of them are kept concealed and them or any of them having found you are to Convent before lawful Authority in order to their being secured and proceeded against as to Law and Justice appertains. Hereof fail not at your Peril . . . (Riley, app. F).

Most of these improper Bostonians were Irish, for with the eighteenth-century immigration of Presbyterian "Scotch-Irish," there was, said William Douglass, "an intermixture of wild Irish Roman Catholicks" (Riley, 264). But soon after the middle of the century French Acadians migrated from Nova Scotia into New England. Between November of 1755 and the following August, over 3,000 Acadians landed in Massachusetts. In the next decade, having endured much hardship, many made their way south, ultimately to Louisiana. Others returned to Canada, and still others remained in New England. It is estimated that there were about 600 Catholics in New England in 1785, but their freedom to worship was steadily denied until after the American Revolution. Their first church was erected in Boston in 1788; the second, in Maine (Damariscotta) in 1808.

England's anti-Roman Test Act (1673) was not applied in New York until 1691, when all public officials were required to deny transubstantiation as well as to declare that the mass and the adoration of Mary "or any other saint" were "superstitious and idolatrous" actions. In the same year a Bill of Rights was passed but amended to make clear that the clause concerning liberty of conscience did not apply to "any persons of the Romish religion." And, in 1700, the Council of New York gave "Jesuits and popish priests" until the first of November (the decree was issued in August) of that year to leave the colony upon pain of "perpetuall Imprisonm't"; if one should escape from such imprisonment and be recaptured, "he shall Suffer such paines of Death penalties and forfeitures as in the Cases of felony" (Hastings, II, 1368-1370).

All of this was in marked contrast to the toleration which had prevailed in the first generation of British rule of New York. In 1683 Thomas Dongan, a Roman Catholic,

was appointed governor; his "Charter of Libertys and Privileges" reinforced the earlier instruction of the Duke of York to leave everyone in peace and quiet on the subject of religion. Dongan brought with him the first English Jesuit missionary to New York: Father Thomas Harvey. The Provincial of the Jesuit order was so encouraged by these developments that he proposed that New York become the center of the Society's mission to America, and that a college be established there (Hughes, Text II, 142 f.). But the bright and hopeful promises of the seventeenth century grew dark and foreboding as the eighteenth century drew near. (For further details of this "penal age," see Sister M. Augustina Ray's *American Opinion of Roman Catholicism in the Eighteenth Century* [New York, 1936].)

After Maryland, the colony of Pennsylvania provided the most fertile soil for colonial Catholicism, soil carefully cultivated, once more, by the Jesuits in the middle decades of the eighteenth century. In 1733 the Jesuit Joseph Greaton opened a small chapel in Philadelphia for about 40 Catholics, most of whom were of German extraction. Opposition to the presence of a popish chapel was suppressed by an appeal to the colonial charter of Pennsylvania; the way was thus opened for an expansion of the Catholic missionary enterprise. To that end, two German Jesuits, Theodore Schneider and William Wappeler, crossed the Atlantic to establish mission stations at Goshenhoppen and Conewago. Other Jesuits developed a significant work in the town of Lancaster, and this urban center, together with the two rural areas mentioned above, continued to serve as major propaganda stations (see Fig. 22). The actual number of Catholic communicants was, however, minute. In 1757 a Pennsylvania militia act called for an indication of religion by all those enrolled. The number of adult Catholic communicants indicated there was as follows: Philadelphia, 378; and, by county: York, 189; Berks, 205; Northampton, 159; Bucks, 26; Chester, 120; Lancaster, 251; and Cumberland, 12 (Marie, 240 f.). In 1765, when the colony had a population of about 200,000, there were an estimated 6,000 Catholics, children and adults, in Pennsylvania, or about 3% of the populace; in Maryland, Catholics at this time accounted for more than 10% of the total number of inhabitants (Hughes, Text II, 502). In Pennsylvania the communicants were principally of German extraction, with some Irish also present. As may be noted in Figure 23, by 1750 Pennsylvania was second only to Maryland in the number of Roman Catholic churches.

The period of the War of Independence was not an easy time for America's Catholics. The Sons of Liberty made "No Popery" part of their battle cry (Hastings, III, 1449), and the Quebec Act, opening the door for Roman Catholicism in Canada, opened at the same time a door to recurrent colonial fears that some sinister plot was afoot to make America Catholic by force. It is not at all surprising that some Catholics were loyalists—more surprising that many were not. Concerning the patriots, the Irish were often willing to have another go at the English; and the French, once the alliance was made, had motive for support of the American cause. Catholic planters and merchants, like their Protestant counterparts, found the acorn of resentment against British economic policies growing into a mighty oak of defense on behalf of personal and constitutional liberty. Charles Carroll of Carrollton rendered most conspicuous service to the Revolutionary cause. Well trained in the principles of both natural and English law, and tempered in his legalism by flames from the Enlightenment, Carroll's defense of liberty was eloquent and persuasive. To a friend he wrote that the English constitution granted to all Englishmen the "invaluable privilege . . . of being taxed with their own consent." He added that "the definition of freedom is being governed by laws to which we have given our consent, as the definition of slavery is the very reverse" (Nuesse, 66). The expression of such sentiments, and the service of such Pennsylvania Catholics as, for example, Colonels Moylan and Doyle, Captains Barry and McGuire, helped diminish anti-Catholic feeling—an important, even though not a permanent, shift. The military support rendered by the French dictated a policy of at least restraint in high places; and, when the Constitution's first ten amendments were drawn up, no exception to liberty was made for those belonging to the "Romish religion." By 1800 the Roman Catholic Church in America was in truth ready for a "New Start."

In 1785 Bishop John Carroll of Baltimore, reporting on the "State of Religion in the United States of America," described the Catholic community in these words:

There are in Maryland about 15,800 Catholics; of these there are about 9,000 freemen, adults or twelve years of age; children under that age, about 3,000; and above that number of slaves of all ages of African origin, called negroes. There are in Pennsylvania about 7,000, very few of whom are negroes, and the Catholics are less scattered and live nearer to each other. There are not more than 200 in Virginia who are visited four or five times a year by a priest. Many other Catholics are said to be scattered in that and other States, who are utterly deprived of all religious ministry. In the State of New York I hear there are at least 1,500 (Ellis, *Documents*, 152).

This total of 24,500 was approximately doubled by the end of the century.

The problems of organization, assimilation, language and internal discord lay, for the most part, ahead of Roman Catholicism. In the nineteenth and twentieth centuries, rather than in the colonial period, these demons of the night would be wrestled with and a genuine catholicity would be won.

SOURCES. Herbert E. Bolton, *Spanish Exploration in the Southwest 1542-1706* (New York, 1916); and, *Wider Horizons of American History* (New York, 1939). Thomas Bray, *A Memorial representing the Present State of Religion on the Continent of North America* [London, 1700] (Thomas Bray Club, no date). John Tracy Ellis, *American Catholicism* (Chicago, 1956); and, as editor, *Documents of American Catholic History* (Milwaukee, 1956). Thomas O'Brien Hanley, *Their Rights & Liberties* (Westminster [Md.], 1959). Hugh Hastings (ed.), *Ecclesiastical Records. State of New York*, 7 vols. (Albany, 1901-1916). Thomas Hughes, *History of the Society of Jesus in North America* . . . Text I (London, 1908 [reissue; includes three maps]); Text II (London, 1917 [includes six maps]). J. H. Kennedy, *Jesuit and Savage in New France* (New Haven, 1950). Edna Kenton (ed.), *The Jesuit Relations and Allied Documents* [a one-volume abridgement of Reuben Gold Thwaites' massive work] (New York, 1925). William L. Lucey, *The Catholic Church in Maine* (Francestown [N. H.], 1957). Blanche Marie, "The Catholic Church in Colonial Pennsylvania," *Pennsylvania History*, III:4 (October, 1936), 240-258. Theodore Maynard, *The Story of American Catholicism* (New York, 1943). C. J. Nuesse, *The Social Thought of American Catholics 1634-1829* (Westminster [Md.], 1945). Francis Parkman, *The Jesuits in North America* . . . (Boston, 1906). Arthur J. Riley, *Catholicism in New England to 1788* (Washington, 1936). John Gilmary Shea, *History of the Catholic Missions among the Indian Tribes* . . . (New York, 1855); and, *History of the Catholic Church in the United States*, 4 vols. (New York, 1886-1892). Reuben Gold Thwaites, *The American Nation*, Vol. VII [France in America 1497-1763] (New York, 1905). George M. Wrong, *The Rise and Fall of New France* (New York, 1928). Lawrence C. Wroth, "The First Sixty Years of the Church of England in Maryland, 1632 to 1692," *Maryland Historical Magazine*, XI:1 (March, 1916), 1-41. For exhaustive bibliographies, see John Tracy Ellis, *A Guide to American Catholic History* (Milwaukee, 1959); and Edward R. Vollmar, *The Catholic Church in America: An Historical Bibliography* (New Brunswick, 1956).

PART II

Religion in America, *1800–1960:*
Colonial and Larger Noncolonial Bodies

1. INTRODUCTION

From 1800 to 1960, American religion presents for the most part a picture of ruddy health: confident, vigorous, prolific, and on the move. The expansion, both numerical and geographical, is dramatic; it is epic. Five factors in that burgeoning growth may be noted.

(1) The most obvious and the most heroic factor is an oft-told tale: *the conquest of the West* (see Figs. 26, 27). That conquest began even before 1800, but in the first decades of the nineteenth century it became the national occupation. Whether or not one is fully persuaded by the familiar Turner thesis that "to study this advance, the men who grew up under these [frontier] conditions, and the political, economic, and social results of it, is to study the really American part of our history" (Turner, 4), the facts of the expansion themselves are well worthy of attention. The first great natural barrier was the Allegheny Mountains. Once this was crossed or circumvented, population spread rather quickly to the Mississippi River, where it paused for less than a generation, then made the rush to the Far West. Later, the great empty plain began, more slowly, to fill up.

By 1800 the Ohio Valley, especially on the Kentucky side, had already received several thousand settlers. Ten years later, land was being cleared in southern Ohio, Indiana, and Tennessee. By 1830 the entire area east of the Mississippi was generally, if sparsely, populated (with the exceptions of northern Illinois and Indiana, Michigan and Wisconsin, northern Alabama and most of Florida). At mid-century, Louisiana, Arkansas, and Missouri had been colonized, along with the eastern portions of Texas and Iowa. And by 1900 there were at least two inhabitants per square mile throughout the United States except for the western plains and deserts.

The churches followed and occasionally led this steady migration. They did not always come, in John Steinbeck's inelegant phrase, "prancing like brewery mules," but often were the cohesive and sustaining force in an otherwise scattered, fearful community. As in the colonial days, the ministry was scarce and that which was to be found was not always above censure. Eastern denominational leadership often could not meet the frontier's needs, and almost as often was unaware of its needs. As a result, those groups less dependent upon such leadership enjoyed a

tactical advantage which was fully exploited. Preaching was vivid, theology was simple, worship was eclectic.

While descriptions of the churches of the frontier are myriad and far from consistent, religion in the West does seem to have had some general characteristics. Novelty was no sin, tradition no burden. Improvisation was the rule in doctrine, in polity, and in morality—not to mention architecture and hymnology. Logically, the ultimate in improvisation was the creation of new denominations. Related to the acceptance of and indulgence in novelty was the loss of authority; the latter, indeed, is the obverse of

Figure 25

the former. Recognizing no ecclesiastical, creedal or political authority, the frontiersman—churchman or no—proudly asserted, even flaunted, the liberty which was for him a daily experience. James O. Pattie of Kentucky, having visited Mexico in the late 1820's, could upon his return speak of little else but that country's lack of freedom, liberty and "the collision of rival minds." His pride

37

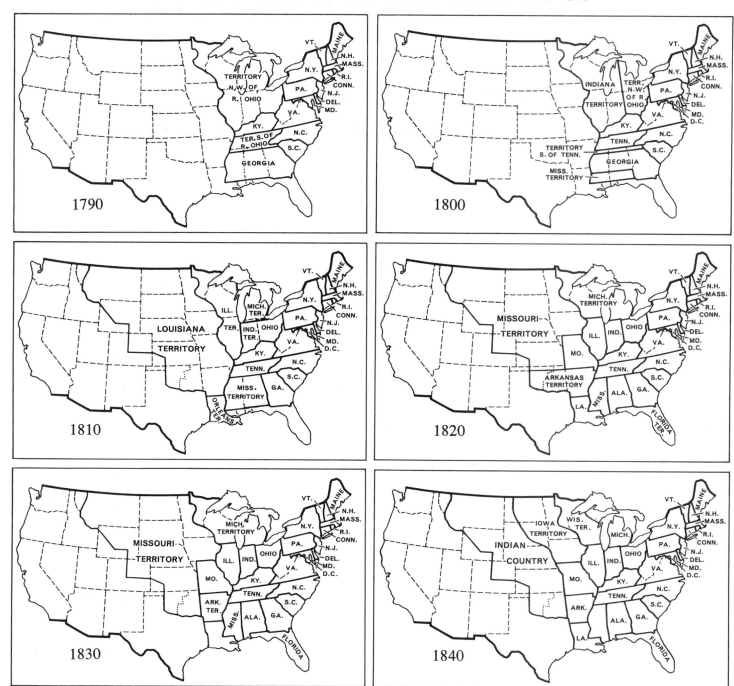

Figure 26

in the freest sort of institutional religion, such as he knew in Kentucky, is unmistakable. There,

the mind need not feel itself shut up between two adamantine walls; where no one need fear to think because a stupid doctor of divinity assures him he will be damned, if he dares to think. Give us freedom, with all its appendant drawbacks. Deliver us from the abominations of a dominant church establishment. Deliver us from a submission, and a cringing conformity, which is not enjoined by the voluntary movement of a free mind, but which is extorted by a creed maker, armed with a little brief and bad authority. . . . We would not be understood to object to the Catholic church, as such. We believe it at present among the most tolerant and liberal churches; and they are wretchedly mistaken, who think, that bigotry belongs exclusively to that profession. It is a cheering consideration in our country, that the bigotry of one denomination

neutralizes that of another; so that 'all nature's discord makes all nature's peace.' Heaven defend us from a dominant religion, or a worship enforced by law! (*Early Western Travels*, XVIII, 344 f.)

The sense of freedom could have its drawbacks, not only in obvious disorganization and diversity, but also in a hungering insecurity. Authority must be found somewhere. Frequently it was found in the New Testament, and found in such a way as to require a Gargantuan leap over eighteen hundred years of intervening history. The New Testament could speak to every man, however encrusted by ignorance or sin, without the media of clergy, creed, or even church. Such individualism could readily evolve into the fearful antinomianism of Anne Hutchinson, the extravagant enthusiasm of James Davenport, the

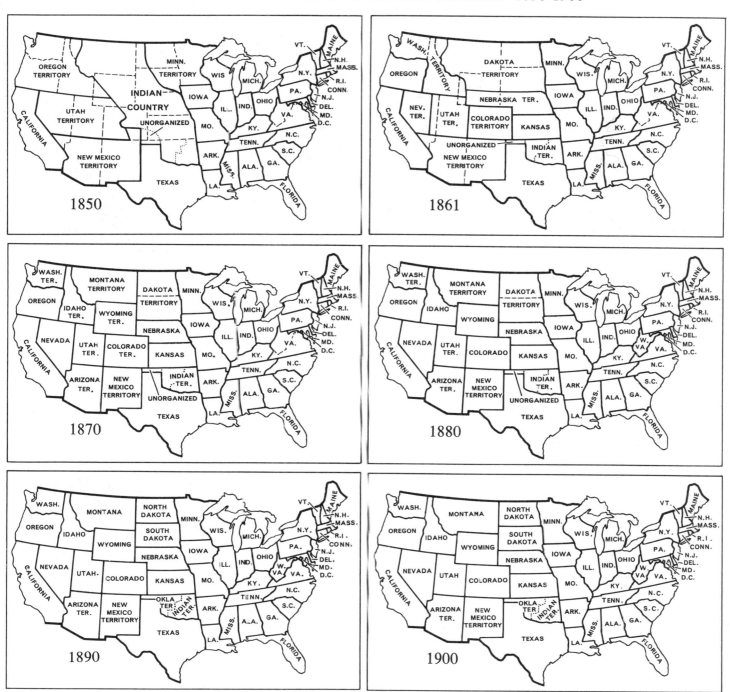

Figure 27

unpredictable mysticism of Henry Antes. "Religious mania," said Henry Caswell in 1839, is "the prevailing form of insanity in the United States" (p. 325).

Denominational generalship, in so far as such existed, tried to cope with the situation, though some groups were still occupied with the problems of survival in the East. The important Plan of Union drawn up in 1801 by the Presbyterians and Congregationalists was a bold effort to pool the "home mission" resources of the two largest colonial Churches. While it later became an object of bitter contention, it offered for a time effective support—personal, moral, and financial—in providing churches and schools for the West. Out of this "Plan" came the organization of the American Home Mission Society in 1826.

Concurrently, tract, Bible and Sunday School societies were formed to aid in the missionizing of America no less than of the "foreign field." The lives of such men as John Mason Peck, Benedict Joseph Flaget, Sheldon Jackson, James Lloyd Breck, Francis Asbury, Jonathan Going and others deserve to be better known for their vital roles in Christianizing those who settled between the Appalachians and the Pacific.

One aspect of this migration, worthy of special attention, is the founding of church academies and colleges. While it is true that most of these did not survive, enough did to testify to the concern of many a frontier evangelical for the development of the mind. This was true not only among groups which required a formally educated minis-

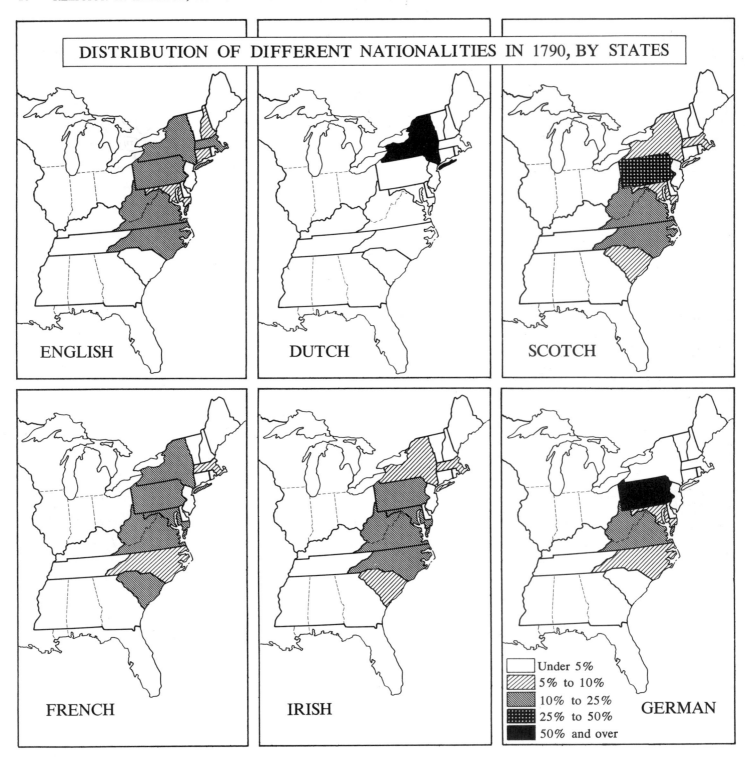

Figure 28

Percentages apply to the United States total for a given nationality, not to the total population of an individual state. Data was not available for the states of New Jersey, Delaware, Vermont, or Maine.

try but even among those who did not. There were, for example, 6 times as many Methodist colleges as Episcopal colleges in 1850. And the Baptist John Peck is as good an example as any of the driving effort expended in getting Christian schools and colleges under way. In 1850, there were 231 colleges in the United States; of these, less than 30 received any tax support whatsoever, while the remainder were supported by one or more religious groups. The denominational colleges in 1850 which survived the century were as follows: Baptist, 24; Congregational, 11; Congregational and Presbyterian (jointly), 9; Disciples, 3; Episcopal, 4; Lutheran, 7; Methodist, 25; Presbyterian, 29; Quaker, 3; Reformed, 5; and Roman Catholic, 18. Most of the schools were designed, like their colonial predecessors, to be promoters of piety, training centers for the clergy, recruitment pools for the church. Each denomination carefully nurtured and supported its schools, quickly placing its graduating young men into the church's service. Annual reports were made on the number of ministers being trained, the number of "pious students," the spiritual state of the faculty, and so on. While widespread concessions on the frontier were made regarding the educational standards for ministers, there was neither a disdain for learning nor a deliberate embrace of obscurantism.

The impression of a people plunged into emotionalism and ignorance probably comes chiefly from outsiders' descriptions of camp meetings. But even these gatherings could be a time of instruction and learning. The following description of a frontier meeting by a contemporary historian, Timothy Flint, is singular for having attained at least a degree of objectivity; neither attacking nor apologizing, his account explains the nature and effectiveness of this sort of evangelism and is therefore worth reproducing here in some detail:

There are stationary preachers in the towns, particularly in Ohio. But in the rural congregations through the western country beyond Ohio, it is seldom that a minister is stationary for more than two months. A ministry of a year in one place may be considered beyond the common duration. Nine tenths of the religious instruction of the country is given by people, who itinerate, and who are, with very few exceptions, notwithstanding all that has been said to the contrary, men of great zeal and sanctity. These earnest men, who have little to expect from pecuniary support, and less from the prescribed reverence and influence, which can only appertain to a stated ministry, find, at once, that everything depends upon the cultivation of popular talents. Zeal for the great cause, mixed, perhaps, imperceptibly, with a spice of earthly ambition . . . and other motives . . . goad them on to study all the means and arts of winning the people. Travelling from month to month through dark forests, with such ample time and range for deep thought . . . the men naturally acquire a pensive and romantic turn of thought and expression, as we think, favorable to eloquence. Hence the preaching is of a highly popular cast, and its first aim is to excite the feelings.—Hence, too, excitements, or in religious parlance 'awakenings,' are common in all this region. Living remote, and consigned the greater part of the time, to the musing loneliness of their condition in the square clearing of the forest, or the prairie; when they congregate on these exciting occasions, society itself is a novelty, and an excitement. The people are naturally more sensitive and enthusiastic, than in the older countries. A man of rude, boisterous, but native eloquence, rises among these children of the forest and simple nature, with his voice pitched upon the tones, and his utterance thrilling with that awful theme, to which each string of the human heart everywhere responds; and while the woods echo his vehement declamations, his audience is alternately dissolved in tears, awed to profound feeling, or falling in spasms. The country opens a boundless theatre for strong, earnest and unlettered eloquence; and the preacher seldom has extensive influence, or usefulness who does not possess some touch of this power.

None, but one who has seen, can imagine the interest, excited in a district of country perhaps fifty miles in extent, by the awaited approach of the time for a camp meeting; and none, but one who has seen, can imagine how profoundly the preachers have understood what produces effect, and how well they have practised upon it. Suppose the scene to be, where the most extensive excitements and

the most frequent camp meetings have been, during the two past years, in one of the beautiful and fertile valleys among the mountains of Tennessee. The notice has been circulated for two or three months. On the appointed day, coaches, chaises, wagons, carts, people on horseback, and multitudes travelling from a distance on foot, wagons with provisions, mattresses, tents, and arrangements for the stay of a week, are seen hurrying from every point towards the central spot. It is in the midst of a grove of those beautiful and lofty trees, natural to the vallies [sic] of Tennessee, in its deepest verdure, and beside a spring branch, for the requisite supply of water.

The ambitious and wealthy are there, because in this region opinion is all-powerful; and they are there, either to extend their influence, or that their absence may not be noted, to diminish it. Aspirants for office are there, to electioneer, and gain popularity. Vast numbers are there from simple curiosity, and merely to enjoy the spectacle. The young and the beautiful are there, with mixed motives, which it were best not severely to scrutinize. Children are there, their young eyes glistening with the intense interest of eager curiosity. The middle aged fathers and mothers of families are there, with the sober views of people, whose plans in life are fixed, and waiting calmly to hear. Men and women of hoary hairs are there, with such thoughts, it may be hoped, as their years invite.—Such is the congregation consisting of thousands.

A host of preachers of different denominations are there, some in the earnest vigor and aspiring desires of youth, waiting an opportunity for display; others, who have proclaimed the gospel, as pilgrims of the cross, from the remotest north of our vast country to the shores of the Mexican gulf, and ready to utter the words, the feelings

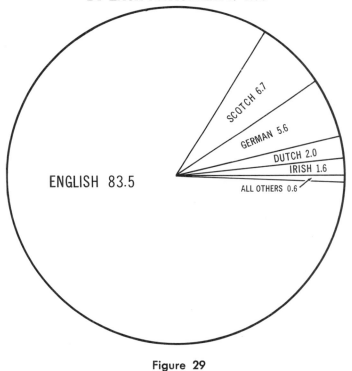

PERCENTAGE OF TOTAL POPULATION FORMED
BY EACH NATIONALITY: 1790

SCOTCH 6.7
GERMAN 5.6
DUTCH 2.0
IRISH 1.6
ALL OTHERS 0.6
ENGLISH 83.5

Figure 29

and the experience, which they have treasured up in a travelling ministry of fifty years, and whose accents, trembling with age, still more impressively than their words, announce, that they will soon travel, and preach no more on the earth, are there. Such are the preachers.

The line of tents is pitched; and the religious city grows up in a few hours under the trees, beside the stream.

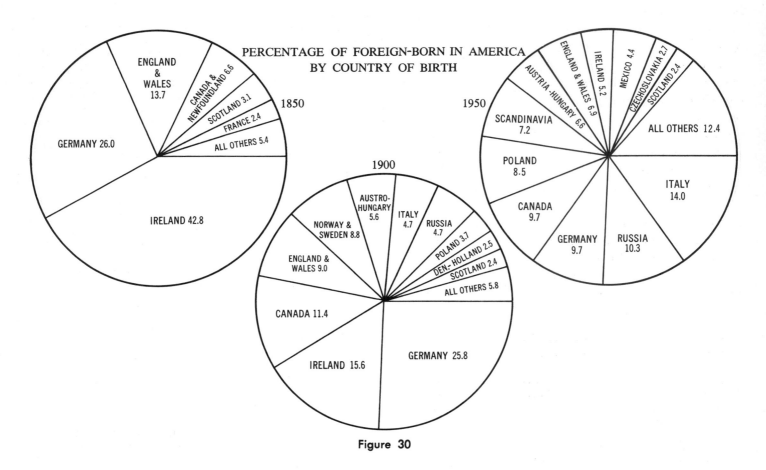

PERCENTAGE OF FOREIGN-BORN IN AMERICA
BY COUNTRY OF BIRTH

Figure 30

Lamps are hung in lines among the branches; and the effect of their glare upon the surrounding forest is, as of magic. The scenery of the most brilliant theatre in the world is a painting only for children, compared with it. Meantime the multitudes, with the highest excitement of social feeling added to the general enthusiasm of expectation, pass from tent to tent, and interchange apostolic greetings and embraces, and talk of the coming solemnities. Their coffee and tea are prepared, and their supper is finished. By this time the moon, for they take thought, to appoint the meeting at the proper time of the moon, begins to show its disc above the dark summits of the mountains; and a few stars are seen glimmering through the intervals of the branches. The whole constitutes a temple worthy of the grandeur of God (Flint, 143-145).

It cannot be denied that this instrument assisted the growth of religion in the westward march, and those groups who shunned it competed on unequal ground for the allegiance of the western settler.

(2) A second factor in the growth of institutional religion was *the reconquest of the East.* In the urbanization and industrialization of the original colonies, church loyalties were often lost or never found. The French Revolution had had a detrimental effect upon institutional ties, and disestablishment was disruptive. Yale's president, Timothy Dwight, complained in 1809 that religion had become, in the minds of many, on the one hand "a vision of dotards and nurses, and on the other a system of fraud and trick, imposed by priestcraft for base purposes upon the ignorant multitude." Revelation was groundless and "moral obligation a cobweb, which might entangle flies, but by which creatures of a stronger wing nobly disdained

to be confined" (IV, 376). There were souls to be saved even in Boston. And to an appreciable extent, the saving was to be done in the East by those same groups that were succeeding in the West—and by methods not wholly dissimilar (see Figs. 31-33). It is a serious mistake to attribute the growth of the pietistic, revivalistic, free-church denominations wholly to their success with log cabin dwellers. In many of the original colonies, their growth was as great as it was across the mountains. In mid-twentieth century, there were over 10 times as many Methodists in Calvert County, Maryland, as there were Roman Catholics; in King George County, Virginia, there were 12 times as many Baptists as Episcopalians. In Kent County, Delaware, there were 12,000 Methodists, but only 411 Lutherans.

Churches accustomed to being despised, dispossessed, and disestablished had some advantage in the early days of the Constitutional guarantees of religious freedom. Most of the others caught up, however, finding in their new insecurity and nakedness a kind of self-respect and self-reliance that made for good health. Churches had to prove themselves, support themselves, propagate themselves. No longer accepted as being as inevitable as taxes, the propaganda and recruitment centers must manifest zeal and vitality—or die. The churches of Connecticut, said Lyman Beecher after the disestablishment there in 1818, were thrown "wholly on their own resources and on God." And contrary to all expectation, the ministers had not lost in influence, but gained. "By voluntary efforts,

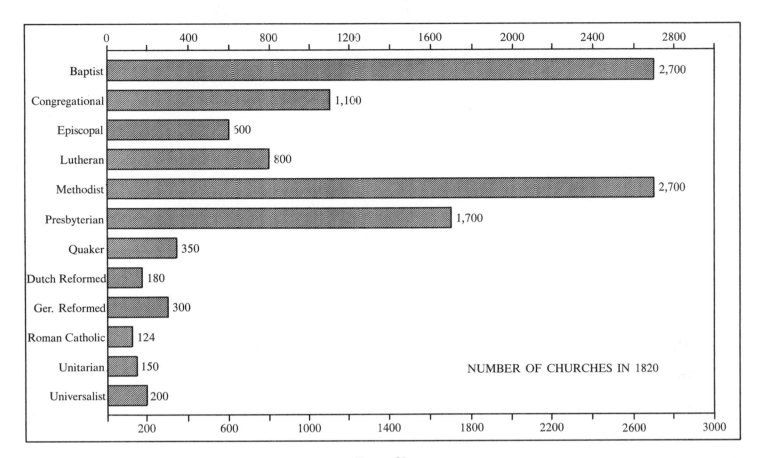

Figure 31

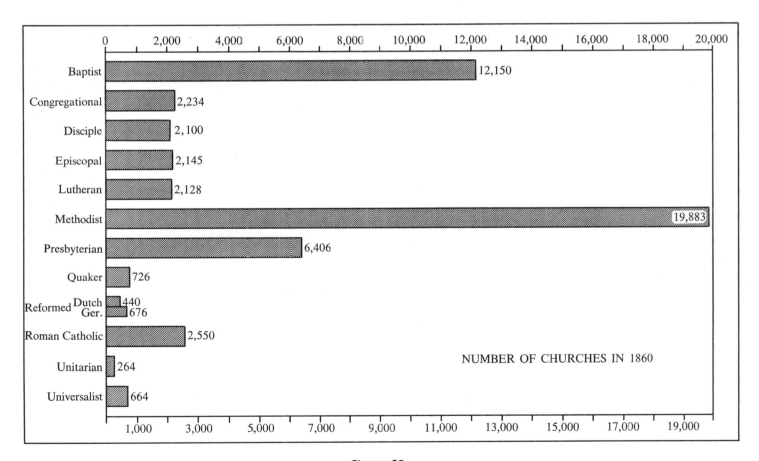

Figure 32

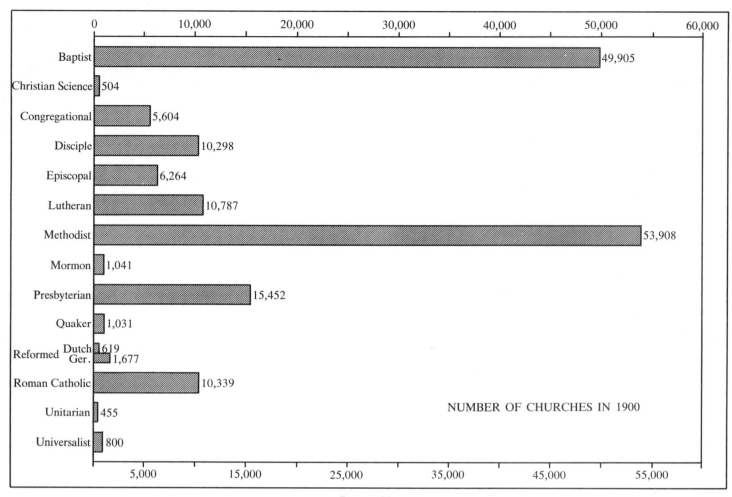

Figure 33

societies, missions, and revivals, they exert a deeper influence than ever they could by queues, and shoe-buckles, and cocked hats, and gold-headed canes" (I, 344).

The "reconquest" also moved on the waves of revivalism, sometimes more restrained than that on the frontier, but often not. The "Second Great Awakening" in New England was generally kept in bounds, but the "new measures" of Charles G. Finney seemed to many to be well out of bounds. Though Finney was first a Presbyterian and later a Congregationalist, his theology was much closer to that of the Methodists. However, revivalism—East or West—did its best to be nondenominational in character, to show men the way to heaven without asking the name of the "hotel" in which they were staying. "If you love the Lord Jesus, give me your hand." The "frothy food" of theological or ecclesiastical nicety was scorned; the solid substance of regeneration was sought. This has been equally true of the successors to Finney, from Dwight L. Moody to Billy Graham.

The progress through eastern revivalism was only partly offset by the active opposition it aroused. As in the previous century there were anti-revivalist parties who feared the excesses and doubted the validity of revivals. Presbyterians, Congregationalists, Lutherans, and even Quakers were torn by the issue. Joseph John Gurney led one branch of the Quakers in 1828 in the direction of revival-

ism; Elias Hicks led a large group away from it. The Presbyterians split in 1837, reuniting just before a more enduring division developed over slavery. Congregationalists, who had lost many New Lights in the eighteenth century and the Unitarians in the nineteenth, managed under Lyman Beecher's generalship to avoid actual schism. But schools, societies, and friendships were rent in twain. Lutherans were pulled in the direction of informal, nonconfessional pietism by Samuel Simon Schmucker and in the opposite direction by Charles Porterfield Krauth. Though it was the occasion of much ecclesiastical strife, revivalism, often supported by the laity in opposition to the clergy, added numbers daily to the church.

In addition to the urban centers, eastern revivals were also regularly held on the college campuses, with the number of "hopeful converts" being duly reported. The *Eighth Annual Report of the Directors of the American Education Society* (Boston, 1823) shows the pervasiveness of revivalism on the collegiate scene. In the course of their "last revival," there were 17 converts at Dartmouth, 27 at Amherst, 40 at Yale, and 10 at Colgate. Princeton had had its most recent revival in 1821; Hampton Sydney in 1822; Williams in 1819; and Brown in 1820. Only Harvard indicated with dignified nonchalance that the year of its last revival was 1740—the early days of the first "Great Awakening."

The agencies which came into existence partly as an arm of the home mission effort also assisted in the reconquest of the East. There were voluntary societies for everything. Orestes Brownson complained that "matters have come to such a pass, that a peaceable man can hardly venture to eat or drink, to go to bed or get up, to correct his children or kiss his wife" without the sanction and direction of some society (Persons, 160). The new institution of Sunday School, which like revivals was nondenominational, spread with amazing rapidity. In the latter half of the nineteenth century and the first quarter of the twentieth, Sunday Schools tended to displace revivals as the prime instrument of recruitment. Temperance unions and organizations for benevolence or reform were at once arms of and recruiters for the churches. Missionary and Bible societies, said John Bristed in 1818, "have already considerably diminished the ignorance, poverty and vice of our larger cities. Many of our most respectable families . . . gratuitously engage in the labour of teaching the Sunday scholars, black and white, old and young. Their exertions have caused the Sabbath to be respected by the poor, the idle, and the profligate; and have quickened the growth of piety, order, industry, and cleanliness . . ." (p. 415). The East as well as the West was being newly churched, intensively churched; and the proportion of church members to the total population began its growth from approximately 10% in 1800 to well over 60% by 1960.

(3) A third factor in America's religious growth, and one fully as obvious as the westward move, was *immigration*. In particular, the period from around 1840 to World War I was one of tremendous influx of Irish, Germans, Scandinavians, and southern Europeans (see Fig. 30). At the time of the first census (1790), the percentage of English in America was 83.5, of Scottish 6.7, of Germans 5.6, of Dutch 2, and of Irish 1.6 (see Fig. 29). Never again would a single ethnic stock account for more than four-fifths of America's population. In 1850 the newcomers in the United States were primarily from Germany (26% of foreign-born total), Ireland (43%), England and Wales (14%). By 1900 immigration from Ireland had dropped below 16% and from England to 9%; Germany held its own; that from the Scandinavian countries now had increased to 10%; and newcomers from Austria, Hungary, Italy, Russia, and Poland—who made up less than 1% in 1850—were, in 1900, 19% of the foreign-born population. In 1850 a majority of the Irish-born lived in the middle states (New York, New Jersey, Pennsylvania, Delaware) and in 1900 only slightly less than a majority (45%) lived there. Likewise, in both periods, about one-third of the German-born were concentrated in the middle states, but the remaining two-thirds had moved across the mountains into the upper Mississippi Valley. Over 80% of all Scandinavian immigrants, both in 1850 and 1900, had moved westward, settling by the latter date most heavily in the Dakotas. About one-half of the Italians emigra-

ting in the early nineteenth century left the coastal region, but in the later influx, three-fourths settled in the area of the original colonies. In 1850 there was a foreign-born population of 2¼ million in America; by 1900, there were more than 10 million. Of those in the East, the greatest number settled in the middle states and the fewest in the southern states (only 2.4% in 1900). About half of the nineteenth-century immigrants became part of America's pioneering force in the West (see Figs. 34-39).

Not all of the immigration was via the Atlantic, and not all European immigrants landed in Eastern ports. The days of the "Yellow Peril," after 1850, saw many impoverished and exploitable Chinese brought into California to play their hard part in the completion of the transcontinental railroad. A great proportion of the Europeans who debarked at Pacific ports were Mormons, particularly from England, Germany, and the Scandinavian countries. Indeed, much of Mormon growth around the middle of the nineteenth century was due to large-scale, Church-sponsored immigration that is without parallel in American history.

Another element among the foreign-born, but separately classified in the censuses, were the many slaves forcibly brought to the United States. At the beginning of the nineteenth century there were fewer than 1 million slaves in America, but by 1860 there were nearly 4 million. Even so, the concurrent immigration of Europeans reduced the proportion of blacks to whites from 22 per 100 in 1790 to 16 per 100 in 1850. In the latter year, there were no slaves in New England and only 2,500 in the middle states. All of the remainder, therefore, were to be found in the original southern states and in the newer territory nearer the Mississippi.

The effect of immigration upon the growth of American religion cannot be measured by numbers alone, particularly if one proceeds on the assumption of a 1-to-10 ratio of church membership to population. For the immigrant tended to hold on to the security that he knew in his religious life, or to seek a moderately adapted (or in the case of the Negro, eclectic) "American" institutional expression. In the words of Oscar Handlin, to whose rewarding studies the reader is referred, "As his stable place in a whole universe slipped away from under him, the peasant come to America grasped convulsively at the familiar supports, pulled along with him the traditional bulwarks of his security." And despite difficulties that must have appeared insurmountable, the nineteenth-century immigrant, like the seventeenth-century colonist, immediately set about building his churches in a world still new, still niggardly. The arduous process of replanting religion, to quote Professor Handlin once more, "left each of the newer religions a painful history writ not so much in the blood of martyrs as in the sweat of loyal laborers" (chap. V).

(4) *The rise of new religious groups* in America constitutes a fourth factor in the numerical expansion during

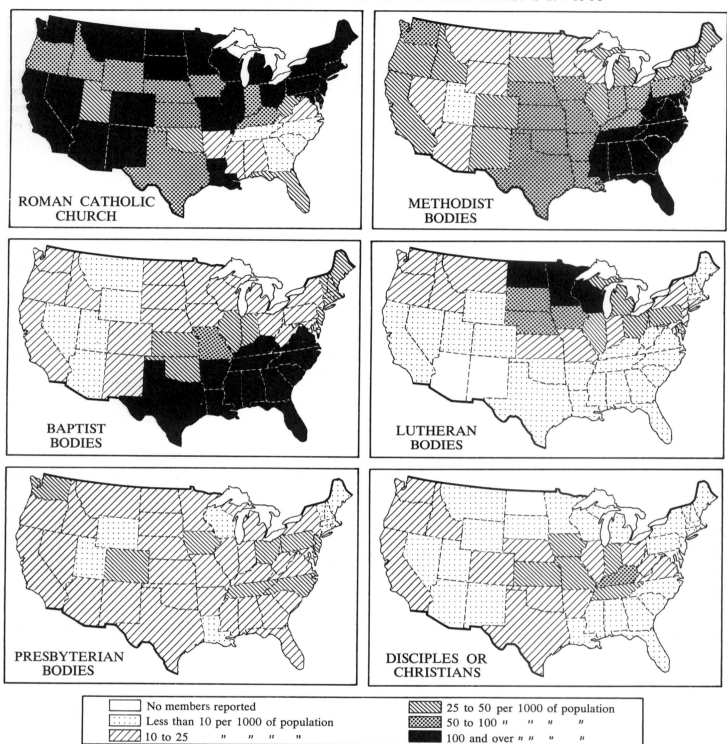

☐ No members reported	▨	25 to 50 per 1000 of population
⬚ Less than 10 per 1000 of population	▨	50 to 100 *"* *"* *"* *"*
▨ 10 to 25 *"* *"* *"* *"*	■	100 and over *"* *"* *"* *"*

Figure 34

this period. For religion that is new is religion that evangelizes with conspicuous zeal. To be sure, many who were won were merely changing "hotels," but a large segment was invariably drawn from the unchurched. Methodism, while not entirely "new" in 1800, displayed a youthful vigor that many imitated but none equaled. Of the several groups that came into being in the course of the nineteenth century, the two that made the most rapid strides were the Disciples and the Mormons. These three thriving denominations are considered here in Part II.

A large number of other religious bodies arose in this

period, for as nearly everyone is aware (either to his glee or his horror), the United States knows no equal in religious fecundity. Part III deals with a limited number of the postcolonial developments. Many of the new groups were related to millenial expectations, while others emphasized a perfection to be realized in this world. The names of Robert Owen, John Humphrey Noyes, and "Mother" Lee suggest some of the experiments in utopianism that characterize this period. Perfectionism could also work within the established denominations, not infrequently resulting in a schism sometimes temporary, some-

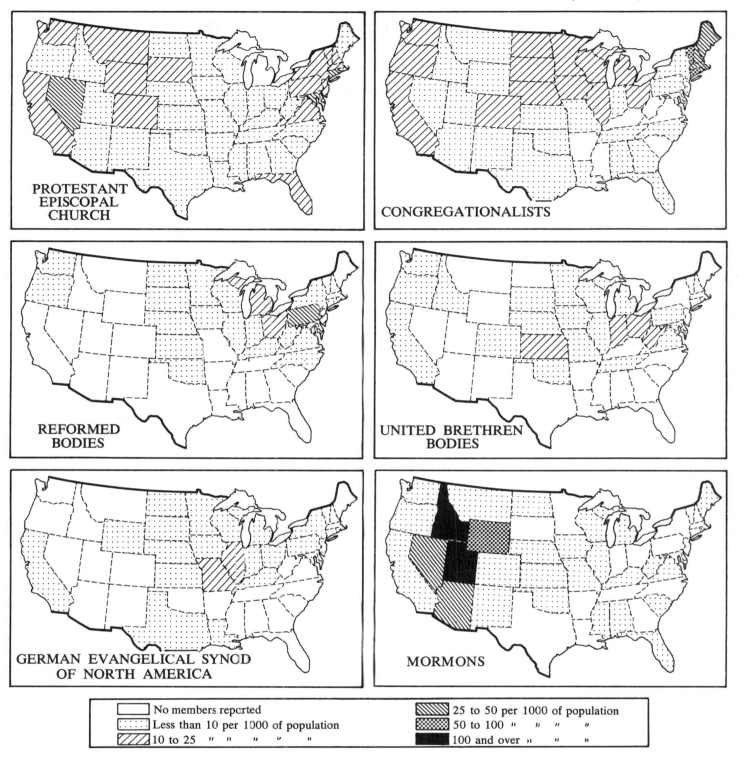

PROTESTANT EPISCOPAL CHURCH

CONGREGATIONALISTS

REFORMED BODIES

UNITED BRETHREN BODIES

GERMAN EVANGELICAL SYNOD OF NORTH AMERICA

MORMONS

☐ No members reported
⋯ Less than 10 per 1000 of population
▨ 10 to 25 " " " " "
▨ 25 to 50 per 1000 of population
▨ 50 to 100 " " " "
■ 100 and over " " "

Figure 35

times permanent. Furthermore, there were those who, like the seventeenth-century Quaker, preached under and responded to the immediate influence of the Spirit. Such persons might not affiliate with any corporate religious body, but most of them did create an institutional life. In the twentieth century, the quite rapid expansion of many of the spirit-led, "pentecostal," newer denominations is fully apparent (see Fig. 101).

(5) Finally, America's churches have multiplied and been filled by a more intangible but thereby no less powerful force: *respectability*. The faithful attendance at and support of church and synagogue has increasingly become the established pattern of American life. Advertising councils, officeholders, mottoes and movies attest to, even while they abet, this situation. To be sure, there has also been a type of "popular atheism" and almost ribald iconoclasm—Brann, Ingersoll, Mencken—but by the end of our period, it is the village atheist, not God, who has died. Anticlericalism, except for some nativist movements, has been so diffuse in America that its power has scarcely been felt.

PROPORTIONATE STRENGTH OF PRINCIPAL DENOMINATIONS
IN EACH STATE: 1906

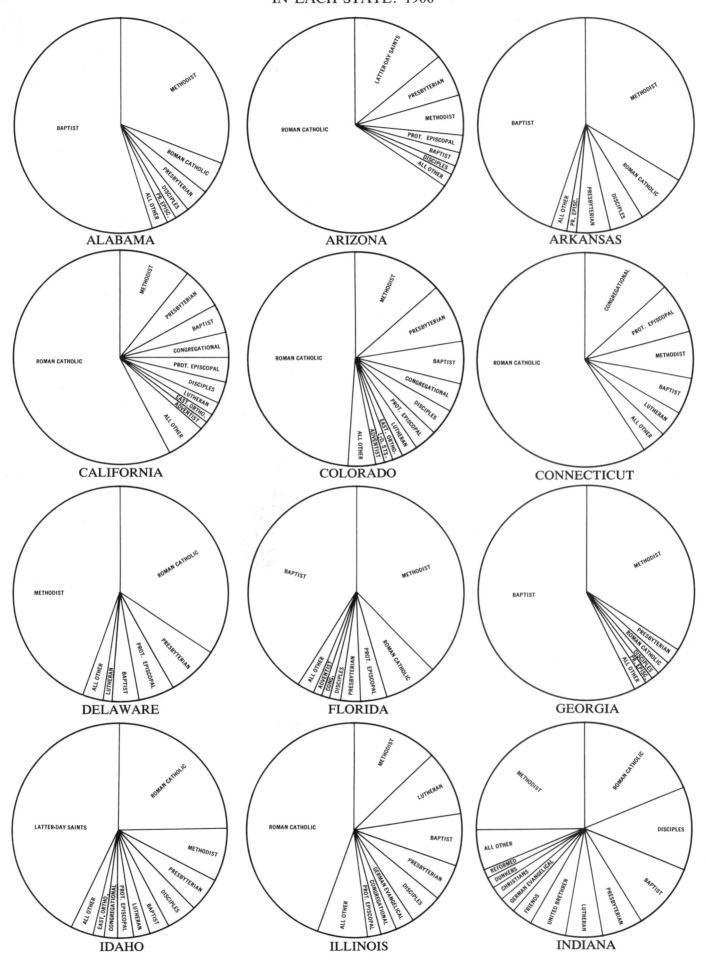

Figure 36

PROPORTIONATE STRENGTH OF PRINCIPAL DENOMINATIONS
IN EACH STATE: 1906 (continued)

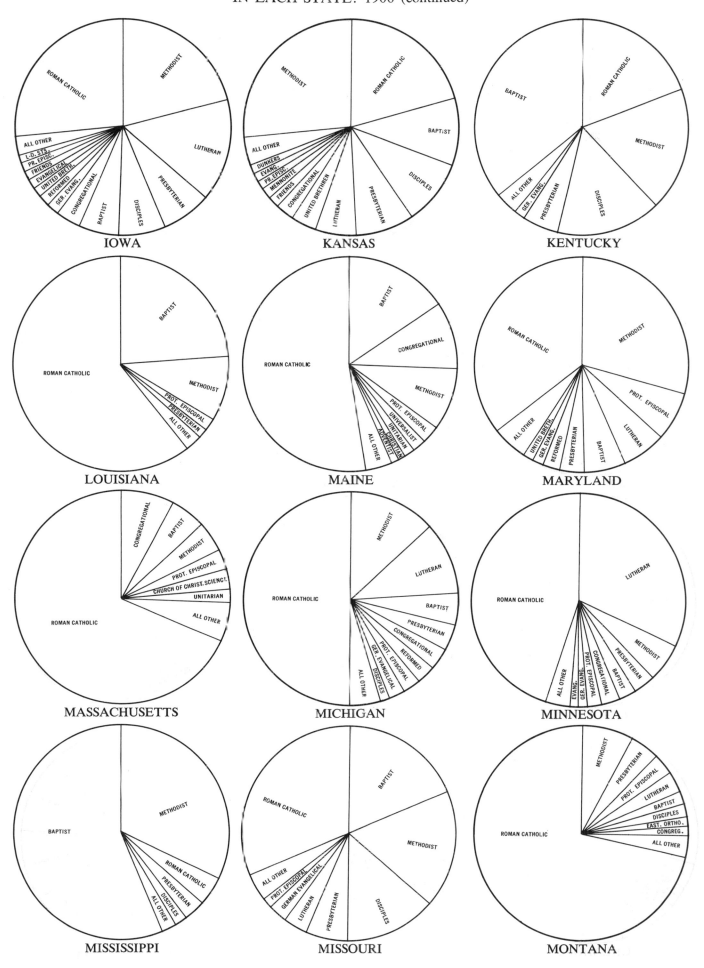

Figure 37

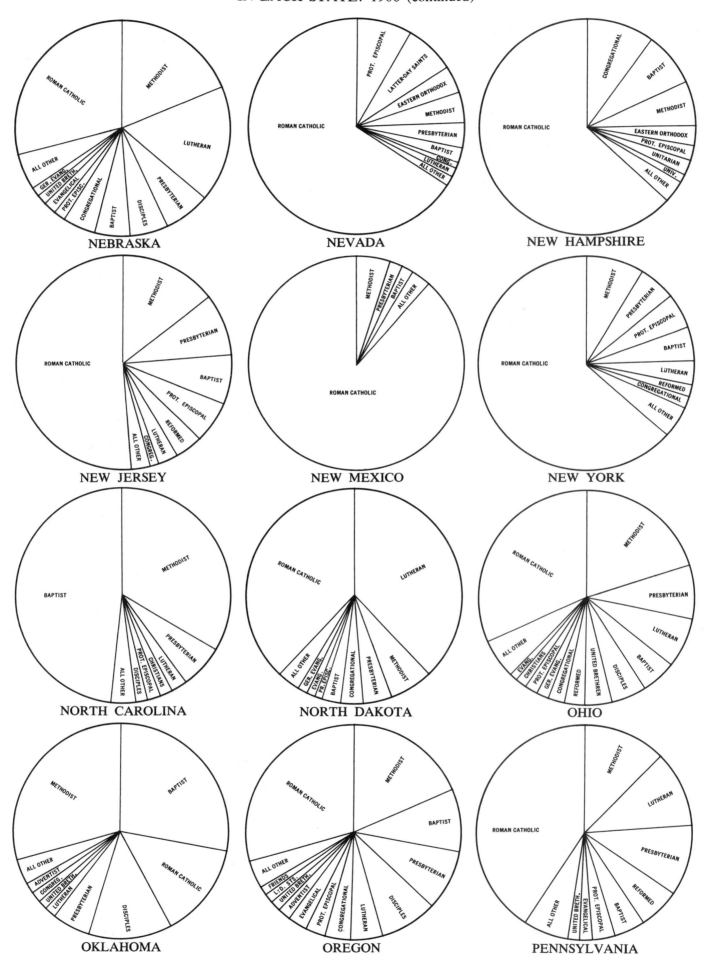

Figure 38

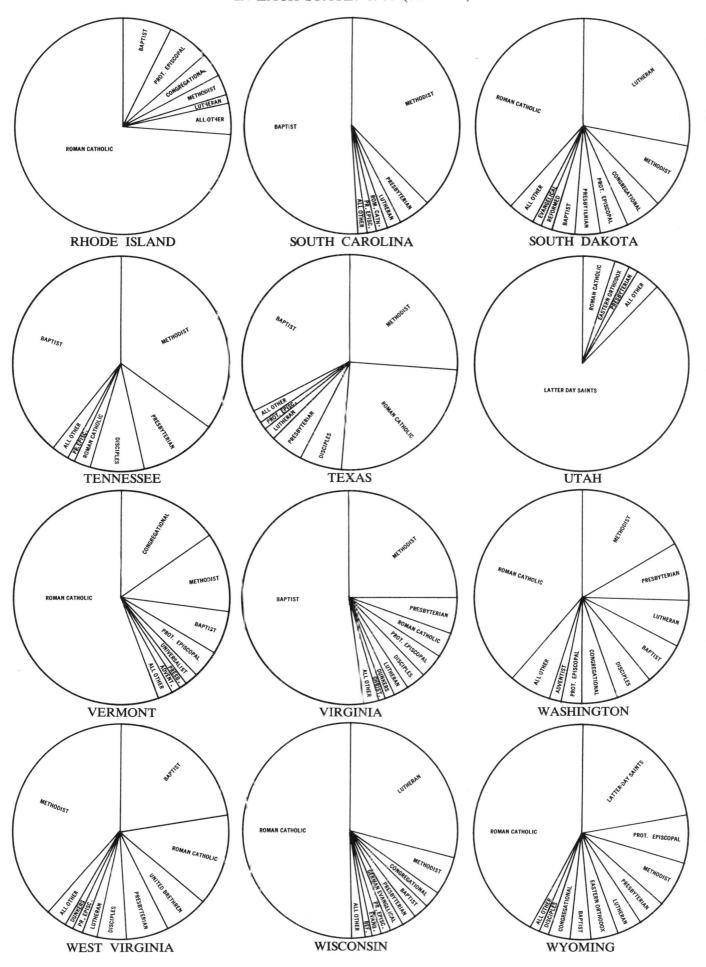

Figure 39

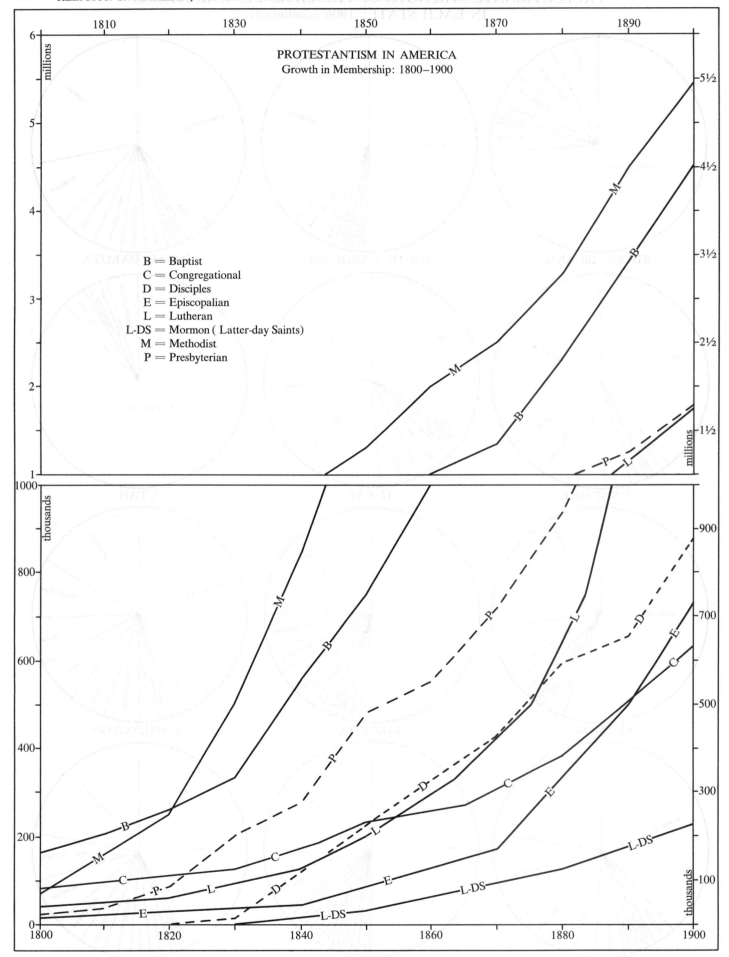

PROTESTANTISM IN AMERICA
Growth in Membership: 1800–1900

B = Baptist
C = Congregational
D = Disciples
E = Episcopalian
L = Lutheran
L-DS = Mormon (Latter-day Saints)
M = Methodist
P = Presbyterian

Figure 40

Includes only those denominations having a membership of more than 1 million by 1960.

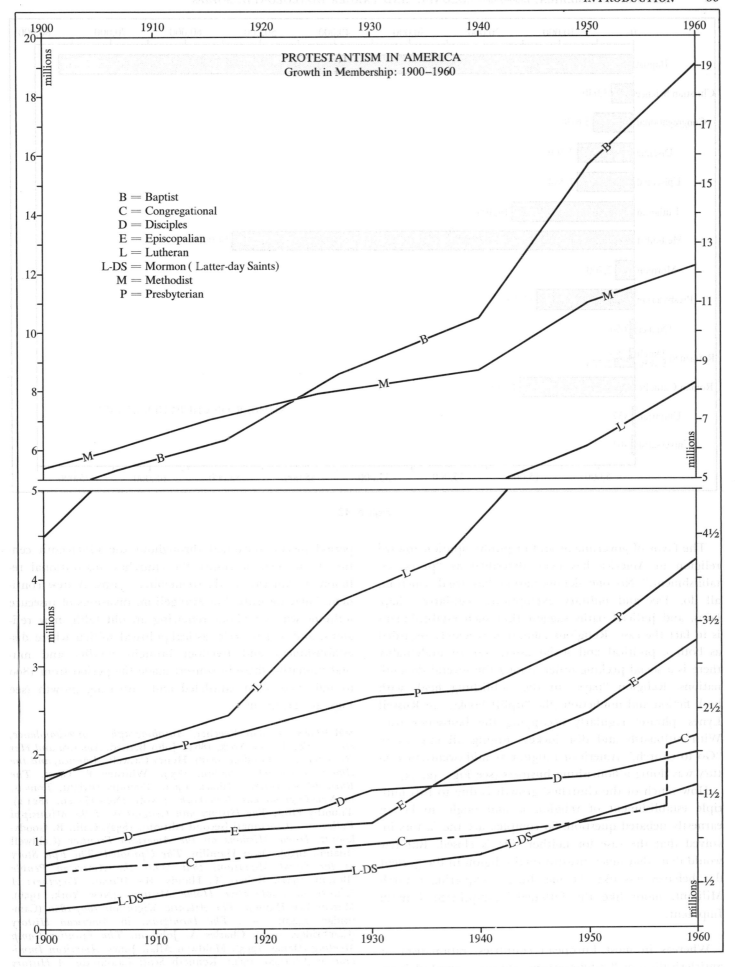

PROTESTANTISM IN AMERICA
Growth in Membership: 1900–1960

B = Baptist
C = Congregational
D = Disciples
E = Episcopalian
L = Lutheran
L-DS = Mormon (Latter-day Saints)
M = Methodist
P = Presbyterian

Figure 41

Includes only those denominations having a membership of more than 1 million by 1960.

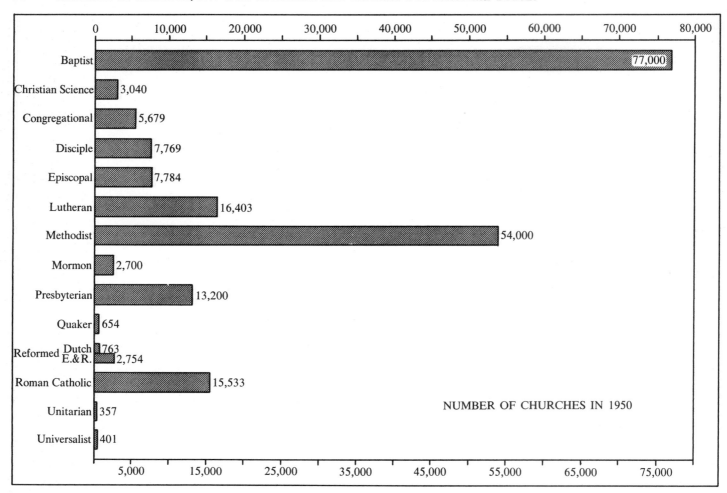

Figure 42

The favor of government and of public opinion toward religion in America has been described as "plural establishment." No one denomination has legal sanction; all do. Tax and military exemptions, legislative chaplains, and judicial oaths suggest that such establishment is in fact the case. Religious affiliation is widely regarded as both a political and social asset, though undeniably there is a social pecking order among the several denominations. Religion "pays" in the publishing field, with both fiction and nonfiction (the "uplift books," in Russell Lynes' phrase) regularly occupying the best-seller lists. With billboards and disc jockeys urging all citizens to "Go to church," American religion at mid-twentieth century was doing a flourishing business (see Figs. 42, 43).

How much of the churches' growth is due to this multiple establishment of religion is and ought to be an earnestly debated question. So complex are the factors involved that the case for neither side is closed. But few would deny that much institutional religion in the present day behaves less like the marching, conquering Church Militant, more like the fattened, tranquilized Church Impotent.

Whereas in most European countries, rationalism or anticlericalism or "indifferentism" (to use a word of Pope Pius IX, whose *Syllabus of Errors* [1864] is a revealing period piece) continued throughout the nineteenth century to weaken or empty the churches, institutional religion in America made tremendous gains. A new continent, "new measures" of evangelism, invasions of insecure millions who set about renewing an old faith, new religions, and a new ecclesiastical-political milieu where disestablishment and freedom brought vitality and mutual strength—these in concert made the period from 1800 to 1960 one of unparalleled and unceasing growth (see Figs. 40, 41, 95, 96).

SOURCES. Lyman Beecher, *Autobiography, correspondence, etc.* . . . Vol. I (New York, 1864). John Bristed, *America and Her Resources* . . . (London, 1818). Henry Caswell, *America, and the American Church* (London, 1839). Whitney R. Cross, *The Burned-Over District* (Ithaca, 1950). Timothy Dwight, *Travels; in New-England and New-York*, 4 vols. (New-Haven, 1821-2). Timothy Flint, *The History and Geography of the Mississippi Valley* . . . (Cincinnati [second edition], 1832). Colin B. Goodykoontz, *Home Missions on the American Frontier* (Caldwell [Idaho], 1939). Oscar Handlin, *The Uprooted: The Epic Story of the Great Migrations that Made the American People* (Boston, 1951). Robert T. Handy, *We Witness Together: A History of Cooperative Home Missions* (New York, 1956). Marcus Lee Hansen, *The Atlantic Migration 1607-1860* (Cambridge, 1940); ———, *The Immigrant in American History* (Cambridge, 1940). Charles A. Johnson, *The Frontier Camp Meeting* (Dallas, 1955). Maldwyn Allan Jones, *American Immigration* (Chicago, 1960). Kenneth Scott Latourette, *A History of the Expansion of Christianity*, Vol. IV (New York, 1941). William G. McGlothlin, Jr., *Modern Revivalism: From Charles*

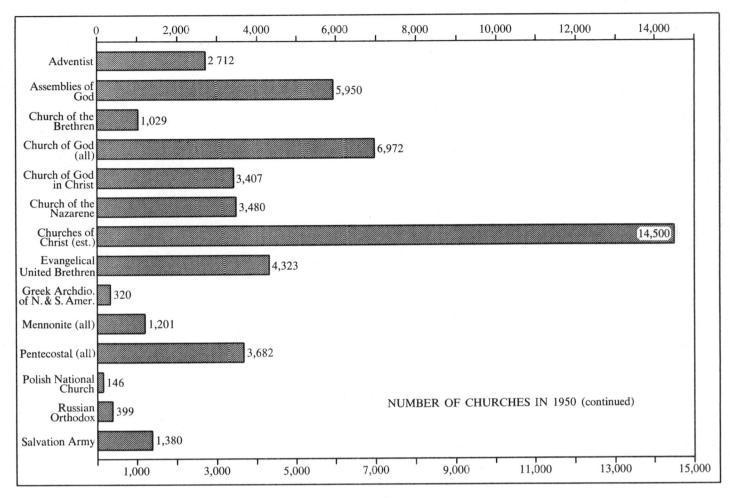

NUMBER OF CHURCHES IN 1950 (continued)

Adventist	2,712
Assemblies of God	5,950
Church of the Brethren	1,029
Church of God (all)	6,972
Church of God in Christ	3,407
Church of the Nazarene	3,480
Churches of Christ (est.)	14,500
Evangelical United Brethren	4,323
Greek Archdio. of N. & S. Amer.	320
Mennonite (all)	1,201
Pentecostal (all)	3,682
Polish National Church	146
Russian Orthodox	399
Salvation Army	1,380

Figure 43

Grandison Finney to Billy Graham (New York, 1959). Martin E. Marty, *The New Shape of American Religion* (New York, 1959). William Mulder, *Homeward to Zion: The Mormon migration from Scandinavia* (Minneapolis, 1957). Richard Niebuhr, *The Kingdom of God in America* (New York [reprint], 1959); ———, *The Social Sources of Denominationalism* (New York [reprint], 1957). Charles O. Paullin, *Atlas of the Historical Geography of the United States* [esp. Plates 67B-88] (New York and Washington, 1932). Frederick L. Paxson, *History of the American Frontier 1763-1893* (Boston and New York, 1924). Stow Persons, *American Minds* (New York, 1958). W. S. Rossiter, *A Century of Population Growth . . .* (Washington, 1909). John F. Schermerhorn and Samuel J. Mills, *A Correct View of that part of the United States which lies west of the Allegany Mountains, with regard to religion and morals* (Hartford, 1814). Timothy Smith, *Revivalism and Social Reform in Mid-Nineteenth Century America* (New York, 1957). Warren S. Thompson and P. K. Whelpton, *Population Trends in the United States* (New York and London, 1933). Reuben Gold Thwaites, *Early Western Travels 1748-1846*, 32 vols. (Cleveland, 1904-1907). Frederick Jackson Turner, *The Frontier in American History* (New York, 1920).

2. BAPTISTS

The Baptists experienced greater growth in this period than did any other religious body with the exception of the Roman Catholics. From slightly over 100,000 in 1800, they bid fair to exceed 20 million in total membership in the early 1960's (see Fig. 48). Their progress, as previously noted, was rapid, not only on the frontier, but also in the area of the original colonies (see Figs. 45 and 46). Maine, Massachusetts, Rhode Island, New York, Pennsylvania, Virginia, and the Carolinas all had sizable Baptist representation at the beginning of this period. By 1820 the South was beginning to move ahead of the states to the north, a trend which accelerated through the remainder of the century.

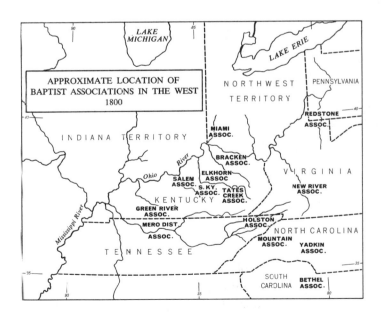

Figure 44

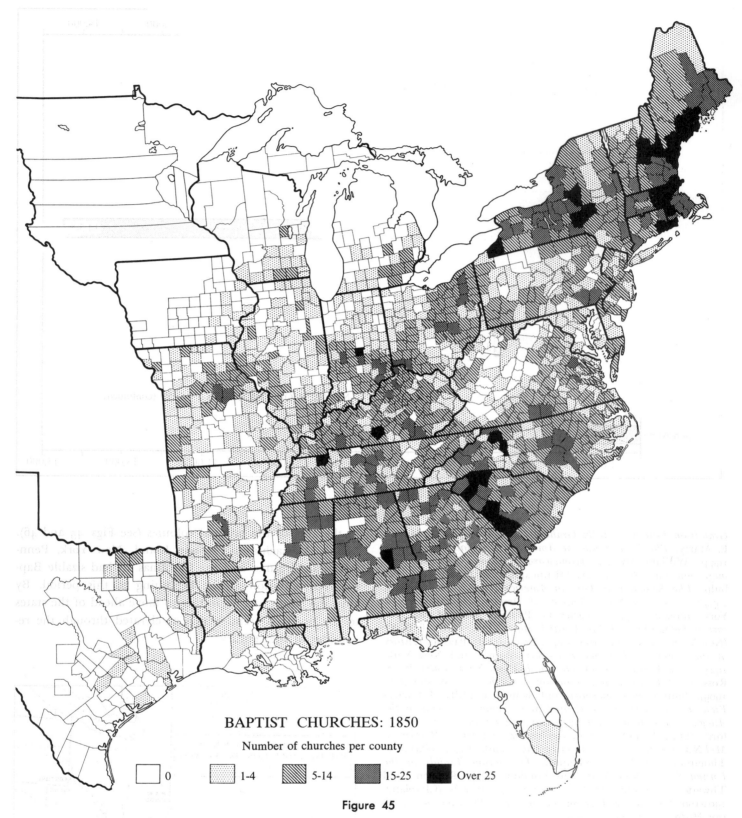

BAPTIST CHURCHES: 1850

Number of churches per county

| | 0 | | 1-4 | | 5-14 | | 15-25 | | Over 25 |

Figure 45

One church also in Sacramento County, California, and Clackamas County, Oregon

The largest group of the Baptists in 1800 was generally designated by the name "Regular Baptist." Basically Calvinist in orientation, this branch of Baptists was by far the most significant in the rapid expansion to the south and the west. The colonial Six-Principle group (see above, p. 11) grew quite slowly, from 1,600 members in 1790 to 1,800 in 1830; then the body declined, having less than

1,000 members in 1900 and only 58 in 1960. Similarly, the Seventh-Day Baptists, though also favored with an early start, made little headway. With a membership of about 2,000 in 1830, they approached 10,000 in number in the latter part of the century but had dropped to 7,000 by mid-twentieth century. More successful, numerically, were the "Free Will" Baptists, who originated in

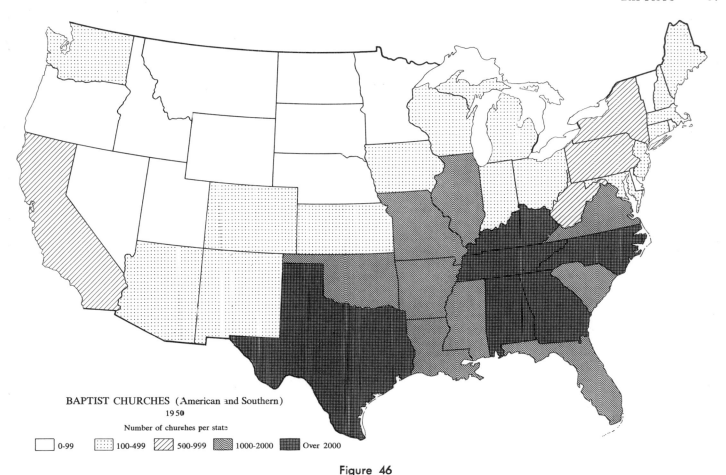

BAPTIST CHURCHES (American and Southern)
1950

Number of churches per state

☐ 0-99   ⬚ 100-499   ▨ 500-999   ▨ 1000-2000   ■ Over 2000

Figure 46

The distribution study on which this map is based did not include the Negro denominations.

Maine in the final decades of the eighteenth century. Representing, as their name implies, a reaction against the prevailing Calvinism, Free Will Baptists had, by 1830, equaled the Regular Baptists in New Hampshire, and by the middle of the century they accounted for approximately one-third of all the Baptists in Maine. In 1830 there were an estimated 400 Free Will churches in the country, with a total membership of 16,000. About 50,000 strong by mid-century, the movement had by the end of the nineteenth century reached almost 90,000 members. That was the peak. As Calvinism had become so diluted among Regular Baptists as to be unrecognizable, the Free Will Baptists' *raison d'être* evaporated. With the decline of rural population in New England, their strength was in this way also vitiated, and in 1911 the group formally merged with the American (Northern) Baptist Convention. The gradual dissolution, meanwhile, of Calvinist theology led to separations by hyper-Calvinist, "no effort" groups, the largest of which—the Primitive (Hard Shell, Anti-Mission) Baptists—had over 100,000 members at the turn of the century but only about three-fourths that number in 1950.

The principal growth, then, among white Baptists was within the ranks of the "Regulars," who increased from about 60,000 in 1790 to over 300,000 in 1830, to 754,652 at mid-century. After the emancipation of the Negro,

however, this progress was to be virtually matched by the tremendous rise of Negro Baptists (see Fig. 47). By the first decade of the twentieth century, 40% of all Baptists were Negro—a percentage that was to remain fairly constant for the next fifty years.

The period of the Civil War and the issues which gave rise to it provoked geographical and racial separations among the Baptists. As early as 1845, the dispute over slavery, centering at that moment on the question of appointment of a slaveholding missionary, resulted in the formal withdrawal of the southern states from the Triennial Convention. At Augusta, Georgia, in May of 1845, the Southern Baptist Convention came into being; soon after were added missionary and educational agencies comparable to those which had been national in scope. As is apparent in Figures 47 and 49, the southern group rather soon after the war overtook and then outdistanced the older body, now "northern" in complexion.

Prior to emancipation, the American Negroes—the vast majority of whom are Baptist (see Fig. 123)—were normally members of the white churches. There were, to be sure, some large and thriving African Baptist churches before 1860, chiefly in major metropolitan centers in the North. The real growth of Negro religious organizations, however, is a phenomenon of the late nineteenth and the twentieth centuries. Why that growth was so predom-

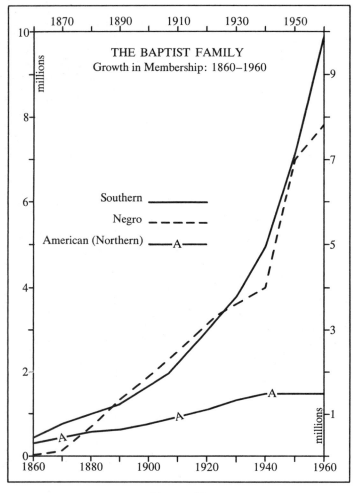

Figure 47

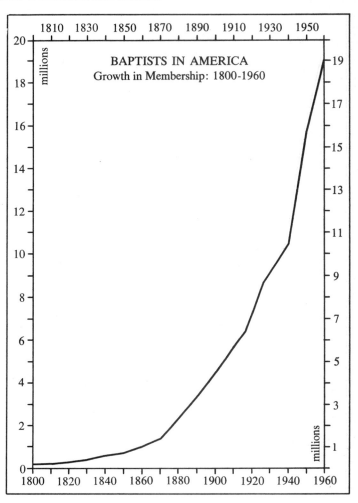

Figure 48

inantly Baptist is a question deserving a more exhaustive examination than it has yet received. The following factors, at least, were operative: (1) the extensive labors of the Baptist mission societies among the Negroes, both North and South, both post- and ante-bellum; (2) the democratic, egalitarian polity which assured to the Negro a great deal of latitude in worship and in creed, while it also assured the absence of any white bishops, superintendents, or elders; (3) the appeal of baptism by immersion, for which there was some background in African tribal custom; (4) the presence, in those states which had the greatest number of slaves, of a preponderance of white Methodists and Baptists. In 1850, for example, the leading slaveholding states were Virginia, South Carolina, Georgia, Alabama, and Mississippi, in that order. Methodists and Baptists together accounted for 90% of all the churches in Georgia, and for over 80% in all the other states. That the Negro turned more to the Baptists than to the Methodists may be owing to the Baptists' historic emphasis on, and current practice of, freedom. It was, of course, a freedom that could become anarchy, but it was also a freedom that had irresistible appeal to the newly emancipated. Gradually, and proceeding somewhat by trial and error, Negro Baptists organized themselves into state and regional conventions, and in 1880 into the National Baptist Convention of the United States of

This graph includes the following: American Baptist Convention, National Baptist Convention, National Baptist Convention Incorporated, and Southern Baptist Convention.

America. In 1915 this body was incorporated under the laws of the District of Columbia. Shortly after this legal step was taken, a large group left the parent body, assuming the all-too-similar name of the National Baptist Convention of America. For purposes of distinction, the older group is popularly referred to as the Incorporated body; the newer—and the smaller by half—as the Unincorporated. The overwhelming majority of all Negro Baptists are in these two groups.

After the withdrawal of the southern states in 1845, the Regular Baptists who remained in the Triennial Convention continued to work within their already established foreign mission, home mission, and publication societies. The need for greater centralization of these and additional agencies led to the formation in 1907 of the Northern Baptist Convention. In 1950 the name was changed to the American Baptist Convention. While there have been many discussions and speculations regarding the reunion of the two major conventions of white Baptists, the stage of serious negotiation has not yet been reached (see Fig. 47). There are areas and agencies of cooperation, however, most notably the Bap-

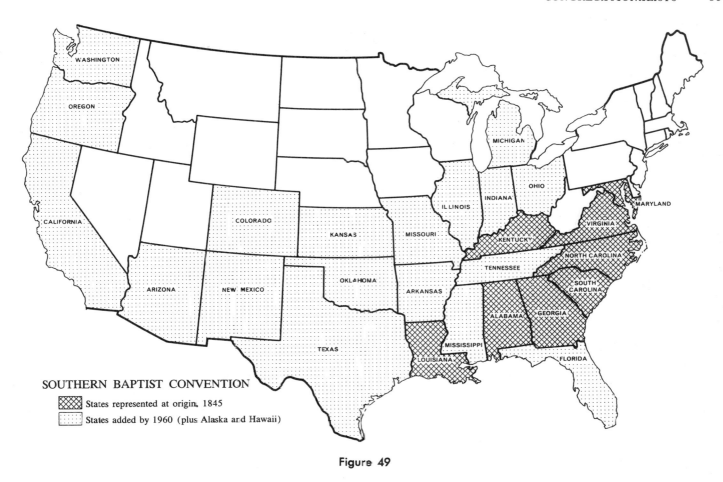

SOUTHERN BAPTIST CONVENTION

[XXX] States represented at origin, 1845

[...] States added by 1960 (plus Alaska and Hawaii)

Figure 49

tist World Alliance, organized in 1905 and directed from headquarters now located in Washington, D. C. Whereas frontier freedom and simplified theology proved eminently suitable to the headlong dash across the continent, there was evidence that Baptists in mid-twentieth century were giving renewed attention in depth to theological and ecclesiastical discussions, searching for new frontiers to cross and to conquer.

SOURCES. I. M. Allen, *The Triennial Baptist Register*, Vol. II (Philadelphia, 1836). *American Baptist Yearbook* (Philadelphia, 1868 f.). John Asplund, *The Annual Register of the Baptist Denomination . . .* (n. p. 1791). *Baptist Memorial and Monthly Chronicle* [especially useful for accounts of westward expansion] (New York, 1842 f.). W. W. Barnes, *History of the Southern Baptist Convention, 1845-1953* (Nashville, 1954). Norman Allen Baxter, *History of the Freewill Baptists* (Rochester, 1957). F. A. Cox and J. Hoby, *The Baptists in America . . .* (New York, 1836). *The Freewill Baptist Register and Saint's Annual Visitor* (Portland, 1825 f.). Winthrop S. Hudson (ed.), *Baptist Concepts of the Church* (Philadelphia, 1959). Richard Knight, *History of the General or Six Principle Baptists in Europe and America* (Providence, 1327). *The Latter Day Luminary* (Philadelphia, 1818). Lemuel Moss, *The Baptists and the National Centenary: A Record of Christian Work, 1776-1876* (Philadelphia, 1876). A. H. Newman, *A History of the Baptist Churches in the United States* (New York, 1904). Walter Brownlow Posey, *The Baptist Church in the Lower Mississippi Valley, 1776-1845* (Louisville, 1957). William Warren Sweet, *Religion on the American Frontier: The Baptists*, Vol. I (New York, 1931). Robert G. Torbet, *History of the Baptists* (Philadelphia, 1950).

3. CONGREGATIONALISTS

Ezra Stiles, in his *Discourse on Christian Union*, predicted that on the basis of Congregational strength in America in 1760 there should be, a century later, some 7 million Congregationalists. He overestimated by about 6¾ million. Admittedly he was speaking of Congregational "population" rather than church membership strictly, but even this does not greatly help his case. Granted his assumption that the population would double itself every twenty-five years (which was an excellent guess), his prophecy does not seem hopelessly farfetched. What happened?

Ethnic and geographic unity, which in the colonial period had been so great an advantage, now weighed heavily against the denomination. As for an aggressive winning of the West or an earnest enlisting of the immigrant, the Congregationalist seemed to have difficulty in getting started. As late as 1830, nine-tenths of the Congregational churches were still in New England. There simply were no Congregationalists of the Middle and Southern Colonies to move into newly opened territories. In 1850, for example, there were 224 Presbyterian churches in Kentucky, but not a single Congregational church; in Tennessee the number of Presbyterian churches was 363, with Congregationalists still totally unrepresented. The westward movement of the latter focused in New York,

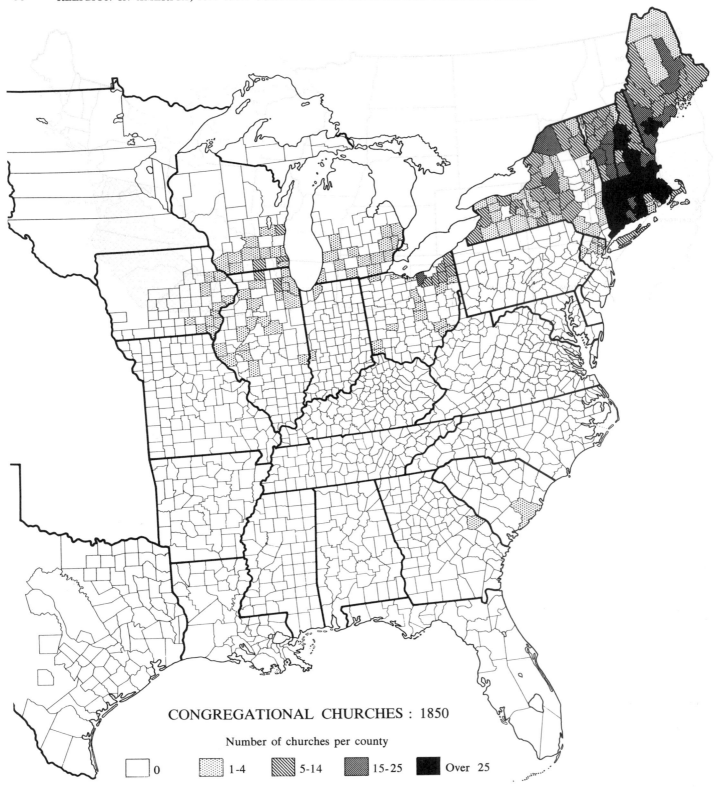

CONGREGATIONAL CHURCHES : 1850

Number of churches per county

☐ 0   1-4   5-14   15-25   Over 25

Figure 50

One church also in Clackamas County, Oregon

Ohio, Illinois, Michigan, Wisconsin, and Iowa—revealing the logical course of migration of a people located almost exclusively in the northeastern section of the country (see Fig. 50). Even by 1906, one-third of all Congregationalists were in New England with almost another one-third in the 5 midwestern states noted above. The southern states were, and remained, relatively untouched by Congregational churchmen (see Fig. 51). Nevertheless, efforts to go beyond ethnic homogeneity were consciously made as the denomination revealed an earnest willingness —particularly with the Negro and later with the German—to be something more than "New English."

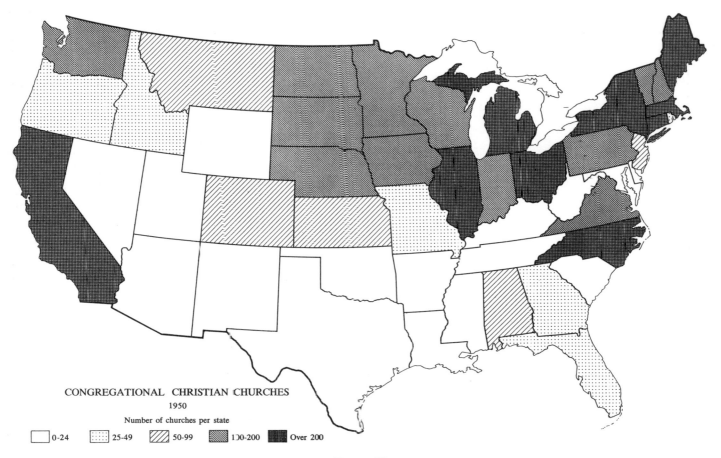

CONGREGATIONAL CHRISTIAN CHURCHES
1950
Number of churches per state

☐ 0-24   ⠿ 25-49   ▨ 50-99   ▦ 1⊃0-200   ■ Over 200

Figure 51

Political liabilities were more keenly felt as Jacksonian democracy was more fully realized. The preponderant Federalist bias of the Congregational clergy restricted their scope and sometimes their interest to areas where Federalism was a livelier option. This limitation was, of course, temporary but in the early decades of the nineteenth century it gave the freewheeling democratic itinerants of the interior a measurable advantage.

Congregationalism, moreover, had had its blood let too many times. And while medical theory of that day held that bloodletting was a healthful thing, it soon proved inapplicable to social experience. New England's Great Awakening had resulted in New Light schisms and dissensions, many of which redounded to the benefit of other denominations. Rationalism, which made its deepest penetration into New England, drained off members of the establishment to Anglicanism in Connecticut, to Unitarianism in Massachusetts, and to Tom Paine or Ethan Allen here and there in the region. While the Presbyterians were torn by similar forces, they managed—in one synod or another—to keep themselves largely under one denominational banner. By the time New England Congregationalists decided to be eclectic and irenic, much of their blood was already coursing in others' veins.

Some liabilities Congregationalism shared with other groups. Its looseness of polity was more apparent than real in New England, but it could constitute a problem

on the frontier, *if* support and personnel had to be drawn from and remain dependent upon eastern leadership. For the Baptists and the Disciples, similar polity often proved an asset rather than a liability precisely because leadership was indigenous and worship (if not creed) was spontaneous. This problem of ministerial direction was bound up with the question of ministerial training. In common with most of the colonial groups, Congregationalists were not willing to compromise on the educational standards for the clergy. And since the New England colleges could not meet the demand, the shortage of a learned ministry was acute. Untrained or semi-trained clergymen, of other loyalties, filled the vacuum. The cultured representatives of Congregationalism who crossed the Hudson and traversed the mountains reported in some dismay that frontier preachers were "generally illiterate; few are possessed of good common English learning, and there are also some who can neither read the Scriptures, nor write their names" (Schermerhorn and Mills, 38 f.). The Presbyterians, beset by the same anxious struggle, likewise lost to separations and schisms; but these, remaining "Presbyterian" in name and in sympathy, for the most part found their way back into the larger fold.

Organizationally, Congregationalism seemed better prepared than most. Through the cooperative effort of the Plan of Union (1801) and the American Board of Home

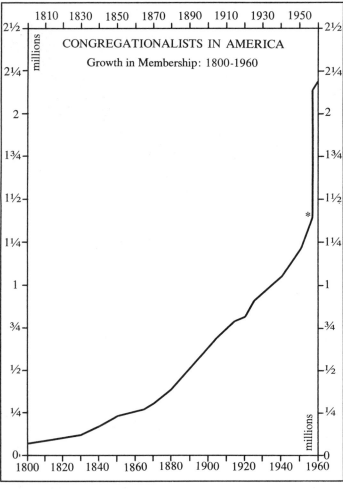

Figure 52

* Merged with the Evangelical and Reformed Church, 1957. This graph also includes the General Convention of the Christian Church, which merged with the Congregational Church in 1931.

nominational "watchcare" and control. In Ohio, the western state where Congregationalism was strongest, that denomination could claim only 100 churches in 1850, while the Presbyterians had over 6 times that number.

In education, missions, abolition of slavery, extension of the "social gospel," and exploration of paths to Christian unity, Congregationalism has had an influence, however, which often belied its failure to attain Ezra Stiles' confident prediction. The list of colleges founded by Congregationalists alone is most impressive. Three of the 7 colonial colleges were Congregational, and by 1850 the denomination had added the following (omitting those founded jointly with the Presbyterians, as well as those that were short-lived): Williams, Bowdoin, Middlebury, Amherst, Marietta, Oberlin, Mt. Holyoke, and Olivet. By the side of these one must place the many Negro schools in the South, brought into existence by Congregational mission agencies. Howard, Fisk, Atlanta, and others continue to testify to the effectiveness of this effort. In the field of missions, the Congregational-inspired American Board of Commissioners for Foreign Missions (1810) had the virtue of being the first of its kind in this country, and also of maintaining an impressive record of Christian witness. Concern for the safety and welfare of the southern Negro before, during, and after the Civil War was keenly felt in New England Congregationalism, with stalwarts such as Theodore Weld, Lewis Tappen, and Harriet Beecher Stowe exercising prodigious influence. Washington Henry Gladden, Graham Taylor, George A. Gordon, and a host of other Congregationalists led the way in the enunciation and promulgation of the "social gospel."

Finally, this "provincial" body, through its personal involvement, has pointed the way in the realm of ecumenicity. In 1931, the Congregationalists, numbering slightly less than 1 million, merged with the General Convention of the Christian Church. This latter body, having approximately 100,000 members, developed early in the nineteenth century, drawing chiefly from the ranks of Baptists, Methodists, and Presbyterians. It shared with the larger Disciples of Christ denomination a non-creedal position, acclaiming true Christian character to be the only proper test of church membership. The combined bodies took the name of the Congregational Christian Churches.

Then, a generation later, a further merger was consummated, this time with the Evangelical and Reformed Church. As in the former case, the non-Congregational group had already known something about Christian unity amid diversity. As an organizational entity, the Evangelical and Reformed Church had come into existence only in 1934, combining the resources of the (German) Reformed Church in the United States [q.v.] and the Evangelical Synod of North America, a midwestern assembly of German-speaking persons—both Lutheran and Reformed. After many years of negotiation and legal diffi-

Missions, which was organized in 1826 to execute this Plan, Congregationalists worked with Presbyterians in planting churches in the West, in forwarding mission efforts among the Indians, and in establishing centers of higher learning. "Presbygational" churches sprang up in the Western Reserve, for example, in quick succession; where there was only 1 church in 1800, there were 19 by 1810, 65 by 1820 and 149 by 1835 (Kennedy, 129 f.). "Presbygational" colleges included Western Reserve (founded in 1826), Illinois College (1829), Knox (1837), Beloit (1846), Grinnell (1846), Rockford (1849), and Milwaukee-Downer (1851). The cooperative harmony between the two denominations lasted long enough to carry them to the Pacific Coast, where they participated in the formation of a college out of which grew the University of California in 1868. By this time the Plan of Union was no more, having been rejected by a large division of Presbyterianism in 1837 and by the Congregationalists in 1852. When churches were obliged to align either with the Presbyterians or the Congregationalists, the former were more often chosen, partly because of their general numerical superiority, partly because of their greater de-

culty, the union was concluded in 1957. The resulting United Church of Christ, whose full effectiveness rests upon ratification of the merger by the local churches, enjoyed a combined membership of about 2¼ million (see Fig. 52).

SOURCES. Gaius Atkins and F. L. Fagley, *History of American Congregationalism* (Boston, 1942). Leonard Bacon, *The Story of the Churches: The Congregationalists* (New York, 1904). *The Congregational Quarterly* (Boston, 1859 f.). David Dunn *et al.*, *A History of the Evangelical and Reformed Church* (Philadelphia, 1961). William S. Kennedy, *The Plan of Union: Or, A History of the Presbyterian and Congregational Churches of the Western Reserve* (Hudson [Ohio], 1856). Lois K. Mathews, *Expansion of New England* (Boston, 1909). *The Quarterly Register and Journal of the American Education Society* (Andover, 1829 f.). John F. Schermerhorn and Samuel J. Mills, *A Correct View of that part of the United States . . .* (Hartford, 1814). Ezra Stiles, *A Discourse on the Christian Union . . . 1760* (Brookfield [Mass.], 1799). William Warren Sweet, *Religion on the American Frontier, 1783-1850: The Congregationalists*, Vol. III (Chicago, 1939). Williston Walker, *A History of the Congregational Churches in the United States* (New York, 1904).

4. DISCIPLES OF CHRIST

In the Introduction to Part II, reference was made to the vacuum of ecclesiastical authority which often obtained on the advancing frontier. Tossed by every wind of doctrine and each word of exhortation, the frontier Christian took refuge in the authority of the Bible, notably the New Testament. The Scriptures became the guide, the rule, the prophet, the court of ultimate appeal. And in no denomination was this more true than in the Disciples of Christ, a new sapling in what was to become a wilderness of fresh growth. But this sapling, in a century's span, had become American Protestantism's sixth largest family tree. That tree had grown large enough even to see one of its branches put down roots —banyan-tree style—and achieve great stature on its own.

A most sanguine promise seemed to lie in the pledge of allegiance to the New Testament: namely, that all ecclesiastical superstructure and denominational division could be abrogated, leaving nothing but the one Church of Christ. "Christian" was the only name by which those who follow Jesus should be known; all other labels should be forsaken. Like the deists, the pietists of the eighteenth and nineteenth centuries wore their ecclesiastical nomenclature lightly. And while this was true in Basel, Halle, London or Boston, it was conspicuously—even flagrantly—true in the open, turbulent, traditionless West. Why could there not be a great American Church, free in its polity, New Testament in its doctrine, and led only by the Spirit in its worship? One visitor to Illinois in 1820 was pleased "to see the people on a Sunday quietly moving to the places of worship belonging to their several persuasions, without the least symptom of disrespect

or rancorous spirit towards each other" (Thwaites, *Early Western Travels*, XII, 306). There were, of course, those who saw a different picture or at least looked through different eyes: for example, William Faux, who in 1818 wrote that intolerance was greater in America than in England: "Methodists predominate, and are brimful of bigotry; and the Catholics are very fiery and violent in all spiritual matters . . . All sects hate my reverend friend [John Wright] because he is an Unitarian . . ." (Thwaites, XI, 115). But there was enough of an irenic temper to succor those seeking a cure for Christian division.

There were times, indeed, when irenicism might go so far as to become indifferentism, when harmony might come not because churchmen loved so much, but because they cared so little. Alexander Campbell in 1827 found that "The Baptist and the Paido-Baptist, the New Light and the Old Light in the same latitudes vegetate alike." In his four-month tour of Ohio, Kentucky, Indiana, and Tennessee, he observed "pretty much the same varieties" among all the churches. "They wear different regimentals, rally round different standards, and fight under different captains; but neither the flag nor the cockade makes a difference in the soldiers. One is heroic and daring; another dastardly and timid under any insignia . . ." (IV, 9). If only Campbell could gather the heroes, Methodist or Baptist, Presbyterian or Quaker! Then he could build a real church—a truly Christian church which would win the West.

Alexander and his father, Thomas Campbell, set out to create such a church. Rejecting the creedalism and restrictive practice of communion among the Seceder Presbyterians of western Pennsylvania, the father formed the "Christian Association of Washington County, Pa." The principles upon which the independent group was founded were set forth in 1809 in a "Declaration and Address" which has remained normative among the Disciples. Denouncing the divisions in Christendom as "a horrid evil," the Christian Association averred that all congregations ought to enjoy local fellowship with all others. No creeds, of course, would be required, for not only are they divisive, they are quite unnecessary. The New Testament can guide and govern its church as perfectly as the Old Testament guided its institutions. And, in a later popular phrase, "We speak where the Scriptures speak; where they are silent, we are silent." For a time the Campbells associated with the Regular (Calvinist) Baptists, but disagreements brought that fellowship to a quick end. After the death of his father, Alexander exercised effective leadership, notably in western Pennsylvania, Ohio, and West Virginia. Until his death in 1866, Alexander Campbell wielded a mighty pen in his *Christian Baptist* (1823 to 1830), and in his *Millennial Harbinger* (1830 to the end of his life). In 1835 the first edition of his and his movement's major theological treatise was issued: *A Connected View of the Principles and Rules by Which the Living Oracles May be Intelligibly and Certainly Interpreted:*

Of the Foundation on Which All Christians May Form One Communion: And of the Capital Positions Sustained in the Attempt to Restore the Original Gospel and Order of Things; Containing the Principal Extras of the Millenial Harbinger, Revised and Corrected. It has been observed that the Disciples do not have bishops but editors; this is as evident in later days with the founding of *The Christian Century* as it was in the earlier period.

In Kentucky, a "New Side" Presbyterian, Barton Stone, had been similarly persuaded that pious men of all denominations should live and work together in love. Not separated by creeds and confessions but united by a sanctifying baptism of grace, Methodists, Baptists, and Presbyterians could form simply "the Christian Church." So it seemed, at least, in the protracted ecstasies of the great Cane Ridge, Kentucky, revival which centered in Stone's parish at the beginning of the century. By 1804 Barton Stone and others had drawn up a statement expressing views quite similar to the "Declaration and Address" which five years later was to be issued by Thomas Campbell.

By 1833 most of the followers of Stone and of Campbell had merged into one movement, and the first national convention of Disciples met in Cincinnati just before the middle of the century. Ohio and Kentucky were the early strongholds. From Ohio the Church "was carried eastward into New York and Pennsylvania; and westward into Michigan, northern Ohio and Indiana, and Wisconsin. From Kentucky it was carried eastward and southward into Virginia, Maryland, the Carolinas, Tennessee and Alabama; and westward into Indiana, Illinois and Missouri" (Gates, *The Disciples*, 212 f.). By 1850 Illinois, Ohio and West Virginia each had a Disciples college. Though the numbers are somewhat exaggerated, the relative strength of the movement from area to area is reflected in the following estimate of membership made by Alexander Campbell in 1852 (Burrows, 494):

New York, Pennsylvania, Virginia, Maryland	25,000
Ohio, Kentucky, Tennessee, Missouri	110,000
Indiana and Illinois	60,000
Iowa, Wisconsin, Michigan	15,000
Georgia, Alabama, the Carolinas	5,000
Texas	5,000
All other states	5,000

Although one might quarrel with this total of 225,000, it is clear that the Disciples were not slow to win members in large numbers. The 500,000 mark was passed in less than one half-century of corporate existence, and not even the Civil War could split an organization so young and so conscious of its vigor. While it is true that the movement had its greatest successes in the burgeoning West that had spawned it, the Disciples knew victory also in the East, particularly in Virginia and North Carolina. Their appeal was certainly not limited alone to the Baptist or Presbyterian who sought a freer, wider fellowship, but it reached the new settler who had not yet found a church, and the new settlement in which no church was yet to be found. A traveler heading for the Rockies in 1845 gave the following report of the camp located where the Oregon Trail crossed the North Platte River (Deuel County, Nebraska):

An unoccupied spectator, who could have beheld our camp today, would think it a singular spectacle. The hunters returned with the spoil [buffalo meat]; some erecting scaffolds, and others drying the meat. Of the women, some were washing, some ironing, some baking. At two of the tents the fiddle was employed in uttering its unaccustomed voice among the solitudes of the Platte; at one tent I heard singing; at others the occupants were engaged in reading, some the Bible, others poring over novels. While all this was going on, that nothing be wanting to complete the harmony of the scene, a Campbellite preacher, named Foster, was reading a hymn, preparatory to religious worship. The fiddles were silenced, and those who had been occupied with that amusement, betook themselves to cards. Such is but a miniature of the great world we had left behind us, when we crossed the line that separates civilized man from the wilderness (Thwaites, *Early Western Travels*, XXX, 53 f.).

Into that gentile wilderness, the modern Disciples were sent out to all men, preaching, teaching and baptizing (by immersion) in the name of the Father, the Son, and the Holy Spirit.

A movement so loosely organized as the Disciples of Christ might seem, in its very flexibility and local autonomy, to be secure from schism. But where two or three are gathered together, there contention may be also. A gradual separation of the "progressives" (Disciples) and the "conservatives" (Churches of Christ) took place, the division receiving a quasi-official status in 1906 by the Bureau of the Census of the federal government. In the classification of religious bodies for that year, a distinction was clearly drawn between the two wings, although no formal organization of the Churches of Christ existed. The latter group at that time reported 2,649 churches and almost 160,000 members, approximately one-half of whom were in Tennessee and Texas. The Disciples reported over 8,000 churches in 1906, and slightly less than 1 million members; Indiana, Illinois, Missouri, and Kentucky accounted for roughly one-half of their total membership (see Fig. 53).

The issues of the schism were not unlike those which have troubled earnest souls in many periods of Christian history, from first-century Corinthian chaos to twentieth-century American experimentation. Who rules the local church? When is the voice of the people known to be the voice of God? Why establish national missionary societies, with membership on a "money basis," when the New Testament speaks of no such organization? Finally, and this is the hardest question of all, how is the New Testament to be interpreted, applied, selectively quoted, or enforced in connection with an institution not of the first but of the twentieth century? In general, the Churches of Christ adopted a more sectarian, come-ye-out-from-among-them type of approach, while the Disciples moved

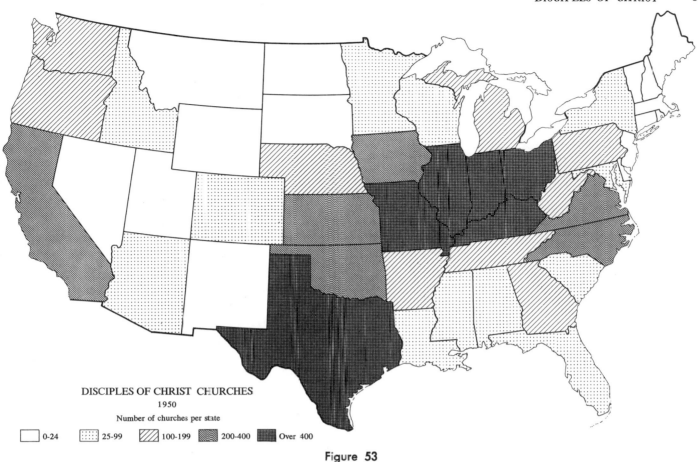

DISCIPLES OF CHRIST CHURCHES
1950
Number of churches per state

☐ 0-24   ⬚ 25-99   ⧄ 100-199   ▨ 200-400   ■ Over 400

Figure 53

There is no map for 1850 because the federal census of that year failed to distinguish adequately between Disciples and other "Christian" bodies.

in the direction of "denominationalism" with formal organization and some degree of intramural authority. The protest of the former against "human inventions," "ruling pastors," "a moneyed aristocracy," and "pride and worldliness" was distinctive in American religion only in that it was made with its greatest strength in the twentieth rather than in an earlier century.

The growth of both the Disciples and the Churches of Christ has been phenomenal (see Figs. 43 and 54), though the progress of the latter can only be approximated. For so consistent and diligent is the dedication to local autonomy that the Churches of Christ, even at the present time, have no national organization to report their strength. It seems probable, however, that since 1900 their numbers have increased at least 8 to 10 times. Colleges have been established in Nashville (Tennessee), Searcy (Arkansas), Abilene (Texas) and Los Angeles (California), from which centers the movement continues to gather vigor and personnel.

While the Churches of Christ have not stressed the ecumenicity of Alexander Campbell, eschewing any sort of "unionist" or conciliar movement, the Disciples have in the present century taken an active part in councils of churches and in merger discussions. Proposals of merger with the Congregationalists and later with the American Baptists, the three groups being of about equal size, were considered at length in recent years Apart from some

cooperatively published periodicals, however, little progress was made. Nonetheless, the Disciples of Christ (also often called Christian Churches) have contributed significantly in their own right to mutual discussions and common tasks confronting the Christian community in America. Universities such as Butler (Indiana), Drake (Iowa), Texas Christian, and Phillips (Oklahoma) help the denomination to cope with the common problem of "frontier religion"—an unlearned, untrained ministry. And colleges such as Hiram (Ohio) and Lynchburg (Virginia) reveal that learning is far from despised. Although the Disciples of Christ, "made in America," did not succeed in gathering all the wandering western sheep into one fold, they nurtured and fed many who otherwise would have discovered no fold at all. And if they did not wholly recreate the New Testament church, they extended and enlarged that church with apostolic vigilance.

SOURCES.   J. Lansing Burrows, *American Baptist Register for 1852* (Philadelphia, 1853). Alexander Campbell, *The Christian Baptist* Vol. IV (Bethany [Va.], 1827). W. E. Garrison, *Religion Follows the Frontier* (New York, 1931); —— and A. T. De Groot, *The Disciples of Christ: A History* (St. Louis, 1948). A. T. De Groot, *The Grounds of Divisions Among the Disciples of Christ* (Chicago [privately printed], 1940). Errett Gates, *The Disciples of Christ* (New York, 1905). F. E. Mayer, *The Religious Bodies of America* (St. Louis, 1954). H. K. Shaw, *Buckeye Disciples: A History of the Disciples of Christ in Ohio* [map, p. 158] (St. Louis, 1952). R. G. Thwaites, *Early Western Travels*

1748-1846, 32 vols. (Cleveland, 1904-1907). B. B. Tyler, *History of the Disciples of Christ* (American Church History Series, XII) (New York, 1893). And see the valuable bibliography by Roscoe M. Pierson in *Religion in Life* XXVI: 2.

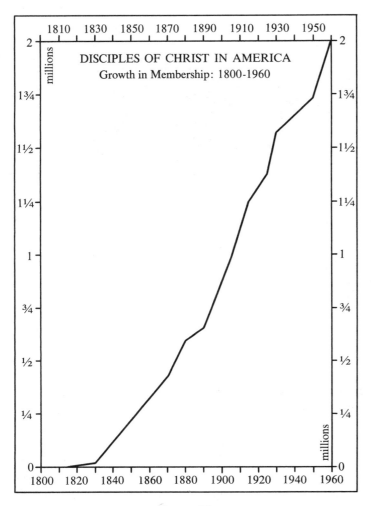

Figure 54

This graph does not include the Churches of Christ separation early in the twentieth century.

5. EPISCOPALIANS

The colonial Church of England could no longer remain the Church of England once the American upstarts had won their independence from the mother country. In 1789, therefore, a newly organized "Protestant Episcopal Church" endeavored to pick up the pieces left over from the War of Independence. (In this *Atlas*, therefore, "Anglican" refers to the colonial period and "Episcopalian" to the modern.) Amid great difficulties and no little internal dissension, the disestablished and suspect Church somehow managed to get a constitution written, a prayer book adopted, and a bishop consecrated. The last achievement was the most difficult: Samuel Seabury of Connecticut had sailed for England to receive consecration at the hand of the English bishops. But Seabury, an American, could not now take an oath of allegiance to the British Crown, while the Church in England could

not now seek an amendment to the law that would make such a consecration possible. In desperation, Seabury sought and obtained his elevation to the episcopate in Scotland in 1784; three years later, legal adjustments had been made in England which permitted William White of Pennsylvania and Samuel Provoost of New York to be consecrated in the English Church.

The early years of this suddenly orphaned Church were difficult to the point of grave anxiety. While other groups seemed to prosper and grow, the prejudices against and the tensions within this denomination seemed to enlarge rather than to diminish. Part of the problem was simply the minuteness of its new beginning. The shrinkage in the war period was so great that the Anglicans, who had in 1780 nearly shared second place numerically with the Baptists and Presbyterians behind the Congregationalists (see Fig. 6), by 1820 had dropped distinctly behind not only the Congregationalists, but also the Baptists, Methodists, Presbyterians, and Lutherans (see Fig. 31). In 1817 the Convention of the Church reported concerning the Maryland diocese:

> Of the fifty parishes which the diocese contains, the greater part are vacant. The forty clergymen, who, about fifteen years ago, laboured in the ministry, are reduced to twenty-seven. Five whole Counties . . . are without a clergyman. . . . We claim more than eighty places of worship; but of these, some do not exhibit one stone, or one brick, lying upon another . . . several [are opened] only once in two or three weeks; and many for years past, except when accidentally visited by travelling preachers, have been occupied by the fowls of the air and the beasts of the field (Hawks, *Contributions,* II, 428).

But the bottom had about been reached. Within the next two years in Maryland, there was a clergyman for every place of worship, and each parish had been visited by the bishop, who carefully noted its needs. By 1820 New York had over 4,000 communicants and 118 organized congregations; New Jersey had 800 communicants and there were twice that number in Pennsylvania. Membership was increasing in New England as well as in the South. North Carolina reported 350 on the rolls, whereas "a few years ago, the number of communicants in all our churches did not exceed fifty" (*Journal . . . of the Protestant Episcopal Church . . . 1820,* 37). Virginia, after being able to muster only 7 clergymen for the election of a bishop in 1814, was soon boasting of its numerous ordinations and vigorous building program. In 1816 "no less than ten new churches were reported as being in the process of erection, or about to be built; while eight of the old ones were undergoing repairs." And in two more years there were fully 30 clergymen in the diocese (Hawks, *Contributions,* I, 257). Discipline was tightened, prayer books and tracts were distributed, an education society was formed, a seminary was established; and by 1835 the number of churches in Virginia had passed 100.

The story was repeated elsewhere in the country. In

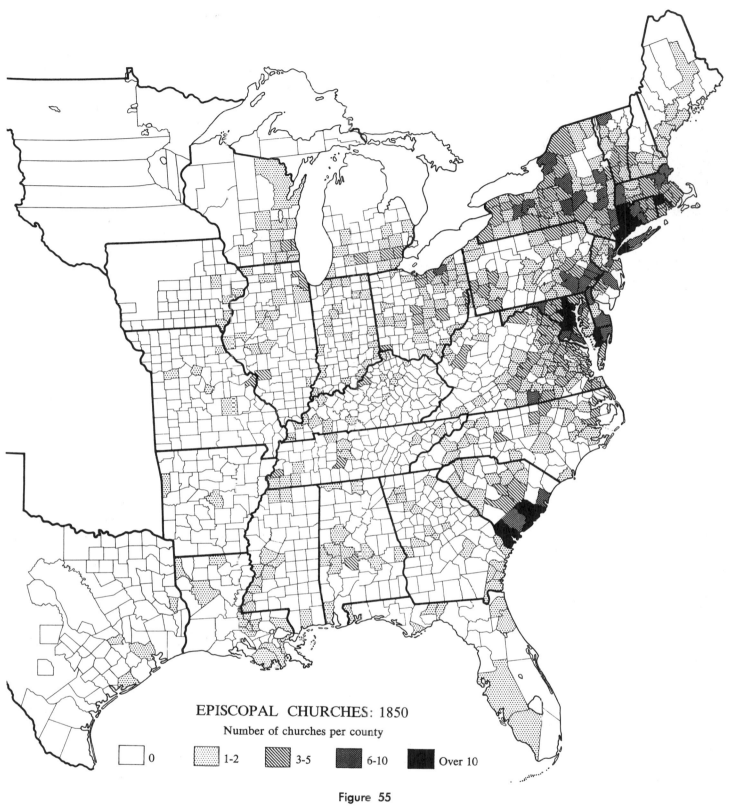

EPISCOPAL CHURCHES: 1850

Number of churches per county

0   1-2   3-5   6-10   Over 10

Figure 55

One church also in Sacramento, California

one score of years, from 1833 to 1853, the number of communicants more than tripled. Men such as John Henry Hobart and Alexander Viets Griswold led in reviving the denomination in the Northeast. General Theological Seminary was founded in 1817 and in 1821 was moved from New Haven back to New York City where it exercised an invigorating influence. Domestic and foreign missionary societies were brought into being; schools and colleges were erected; self-confidence was slowly regained. By 1830 the Church could not yet claim any numerical prominence: it numbered only about 30,000 (compared with 6 times that many Presbyterians, 10 times that many Baptists, and 18 times that many Methodists). But there was sufficient strength and vision for the Episcopalians

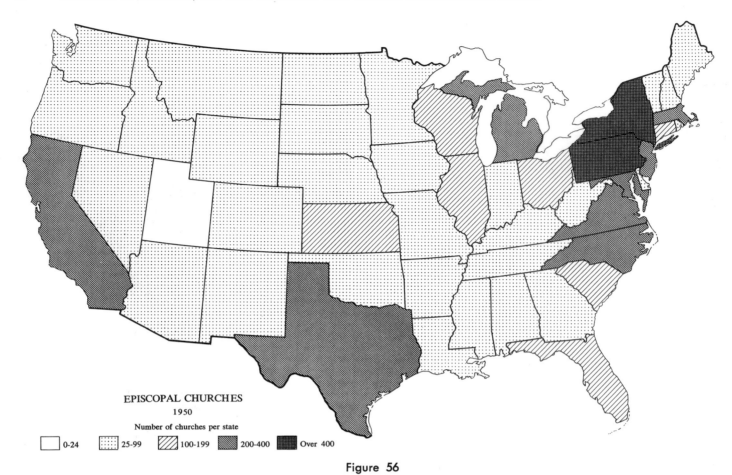

EPISCOPAL CHURCHES
1950
Number of churches per state

☐ 0-24	▦ 25-99	▨ 100-199	▧ 200-400	▤ Over 400

Figure 56

already to be engaged in that all-American enterprise: the winning of the West (see Fig. 55).

Ohio was the first western state to be penetrated by the Protestant Episcopal Church. The mission work began there in 1817, and the state was organized into a diocese the following year. There were 7 clergymen within its limits in 1820 and over 30 by 1835. Kenyon College, established in 1824, was not only an urgently needed seat of learning, it was also a center of revivals which wrought "much real benefit" (Caswell, 324). Parishes continued to out-number clergymen, however, so the use of layreaders proved "eminently successful in keeping the feeble flock together" (p. 53). Having arrived somewhat late, the Episcopalians necessarily were behind the Baptists, Methodists, and Presbyterians to whom "the great part are more or less attached." Some of those in the nonepiscopal fellowships, discovering that the authority of "the brethren and sisters" in the free churches was more galling than that of the bishops, turned to the Episcopal Church; but others "destitute of scriptural instruction of any kind . . . are indifferent, if not absolutely hostile, to religion" (pp. 319, 33).

By 1830 missionaries of the Church had also entered Kentucky, Tennessee, Alabama, and Michigan; and by 1840 Illinois, Indiana, Missouri, Wisconsin, Louisiana, and Iowa had been invaded. At this date, "the Episcopal Church had 152 ministers in the states and territories west of the Alleghenies. This was just two more ministers than the Baptist Church had in the state of Missouri alone"

(Manross, 68). But the conversion of the Church of England to the "Church of America" had been accomplished. A Kentucky traveler reports the new look as early as 1819:

The episcopalian clergy in this country, have an enjoyment seldom known in England, that is, being chosen by the people, and supported according to their respective merits; and it is my duty to add that episcopalians, as well as the ministers of most other sects, are in general "labourers worthy of their hire," virtuous in their conduct, exemplary in their deportment, exhibiting christianity in their every day conduct and intercourse with mankind, and enjoying the esteem of their congregations. There are none of those divines in the busy hive of America, which you know by the name of *dignified clergy*, partaking of the largest revenues, and doing the least possible service . . . (Thwaites, *Early Western Travels*, X, 92 f.).

These lines could have been written about any of the churches struggling to tame the savage West. That they were written of the new Anglican Church proved that the church of George III was dead; in its stead was the Protestant Episcopal Church in the United States of America.

The Civil War period did not prove as disruptive to this body as it did, for example, to the Baptists, Methodists, and Presbyterians. Although a separate ecclesiastical organization was formed by the Confederate States in 1861, the distinction was temporary. The General Convention of 1865, meeting in Philadelphia, saw Texas, Tennessee, and North Carolina already responding to the roll call—which roll call had included the southern

THE EPISCOPAL CHURCH

Province boundary · · · · · Diocese boundary   o See cities
1 Province numbers

0 | | | | | 300 MILES

Figure 57

dioceses even in the midst of war. United with an alacrity not to be found in the groups mentioned above, the Protestant Episcopal Church found itself after this war in a position of some strength and promise. The number of communicants virtually doubled within the stormy decade 1860–1870, and within a generation the number had quadrupled. Divinity schools in Philadelphia, Cambridge, Chicago, and Sewanee were soon added to the one in New York City.

If this body successfully avoided major disruption over the issues of slavery and states' rights it was not so successful in the matter of ecclesiology and church rites. Before as well as after the Civil War, the issues raised by England's Oxford Movement shook the American communion. How "Protestant" was the Church of England (and, by extension, the related Episcopal body in America)? How "Catholic"? How much fixed liturgy? How much free evangelicalism? What, really, is the nature of the Church and of her ministry? Around these earnest queries the debates revolved. Before the Civil War about 30 clergymen left the Episcopal for the Roman Catholic Church; after the war, a group of evangelicals under the leadership of the Coadjutor Bishop of Kentucky seceded to organize the Reformed Episcopal Church. The polarity of the tensions was thereby exposed. Not always in the context of schism but often in the mood of contention, discussions continued on the question of ritual, the nature

of the presence of Christ in the mass or communion, the efficacy of baptism, and a host of other questions regarding words, forms, and articles of faith. The tensions by no means disappeared in subsequent years; however, they came to be regarded by many as a potential source of strength rather than of weakness. Thus many Episcopalians currently look upon their Church as the *via media,* standing in a sense between Protestantism and Roman Catholicism, interceding for and ministering to those attracted from either wing. "High," "low," and "broad" then became—ideally at least—the tags not of mutually hostile factions but of complementary partners.

Despite the presence of its evangelical wing, the Protestant Episcopal Church never won converts in the West at the rate of some of its sister churches. And the late nineteenth-century immigrations added little to its strength, while other similarly institutional groups (e.g., Lutherans and Roman Catholics) were substantially aided by that influx. Yet the Protestant Episcopal Church has steadily grown behind the noisy frontier and later in the mushrooming suburbs (see Fig. 56). While winning new adherents among the unchurched, this body has also made significant strides through accretion from other denominations, both "high" and "low." Its ordered decency, its social freedoms, its status in the colonial and modern periods alike have made it attractive to many of the laity and clergy of other confessions. With a vigorous National

Council (organized in 1919), a thoroughly revised Prayer Book (1928), and an effective church press (established in 1952), the recent pace of 500,000 new members per decade shows no sign of slowing down (see Fig. 58).

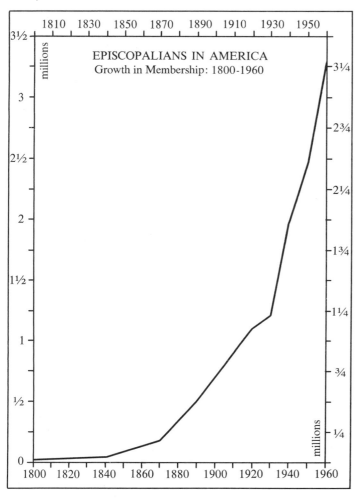

Figure 58

In 1919, the denomination expanded the term "member" to include not only communicants but all baptized members.

SOURCES. J. T. Addison, *The Episcopal Church in the United States, 1789-1931*, (New York, 1951). Henry Caswell, *America, and the American Church* (London, 1839); ———, *An Epitome of the History of the American Episcopal Church* (Lexington, 1836). E. C. Chorley, *Men and Movements in the American Episcopal Church* [valuable bibliography] (New York, 1946). Francis L. Hawks, *Contributions to the Ecclesiastical History of the United States of America*, 2 vols. (New York, 1836-39). *Journals of the General Conventions of the Protestant Episcopal Church, in the United States of America from the Year 1784, to the Year 1814, inclusive* (Philadelphia, 1817). *Journal of the Proceedings . . . of the Protestant Episcopal Church in the United States of America, in a General Convention . . . A.D. 1820* (Philadelphia, 1820). Clara O. Loveland, *Critical Years: The Reconstitution of the Anglican Church in the United States of America, 1780-1789* (Greenwich [Conn.], 1956). W. W. Manross, *The Episcopal Church in the United States 1800-1840* (New York, 1938); and, *A History of the American Episcopal Church* (New York [second ed.], 1950). Reuben Gold Thwaites, *Early Western Travels 1748-1846*, 32 vols. (Cleveland, 1904-1907). And see the bibliography in *Religion in Life* XXV:3.

6. LUTHERANS

Throughout the nineteenth century the growth of the several Lutheran synods and conferences was steady but not phenomenal. From a membership of about 35,000 the Lutheran communion rose to approximately 1½ million baptized members in 1900. By far the greater part of that growth was the result of immigration—German and Scandinavian (see Fig. 59). In the twentieth century, however, when adherents from the old countries were arriving by the dozens instead of by the thousands, Lutheranism burst forth in an amazing display of prowess and speed (see Fig. 60). At the very time when the Lutheran groups might be expected to content themselves with a holding action, they succeeded in enlarging from 1½ million in 1900 to over 8 million by 1960 (see Fig. 63).

Many factors enter into this progress, of course, some of them having already been considered in the Introduction to Part II. But a major factor, peculiar to Lutheranism, was that the besetting, enervating problem of internal dissension was being conquered. Evidence of the conquest is plentiful, but the most palpable sign was the determination to gather together elements of the scattered Lutheran flock and to begin to repair, by bits, the seamless robe of Christ. In 1850, for example, a maze of ministeriums and synods was already to be found, but these reflected differences that were primarily geographical, though sometimes doctrinal. Very soon, however, titles of Lutheran organizations began pointing primarily to differences that were ethnic: Norwegian Church (established 1853), Danish Church (1872), Finnish Church (1872), Icelandic Synod (1885). This was only the beginning, for the ethnic groups would splinter or multiply, bringing more organizational complexity into the Lutheran family.

A synodical conference formed in 1872 had, by the end of the century, gathered loosely together the Norwegian Church and the synods of Michigan (1840), Missouri (1847), Wisconsin (1851), and Minnesota (1860). Yet the hope of a closer unity and even of building a great seminary in common was shattered in the 1880's when doctrinal controversies broke out within this fellowship. The conference survived, though hardly as a nineteenth-century example of organic unity.

By the advent of the twentieth century, there were 24 separate Lutheran organizations, only 1 of which numbered more than 500,000 members. Six others had over 100,000 members, with the remaining 14 ranging in membership from 47,000 down to 482. The 7 largest groups, in the order of their size, were as follows: Evangelical Lutheran Synodical Conference of America, General Council of the Evangelical Lutheran Church in North America, General Synod of the Evangelical Lutheran Church in the United States of America, United Norwegian Lutheran Church in America, Evangelical Lutheran Joint Synod of Ohio and Other States, Evangelical Lutheran Synod of Iowa and Other States, and the Synod for the Norwegian Evan-

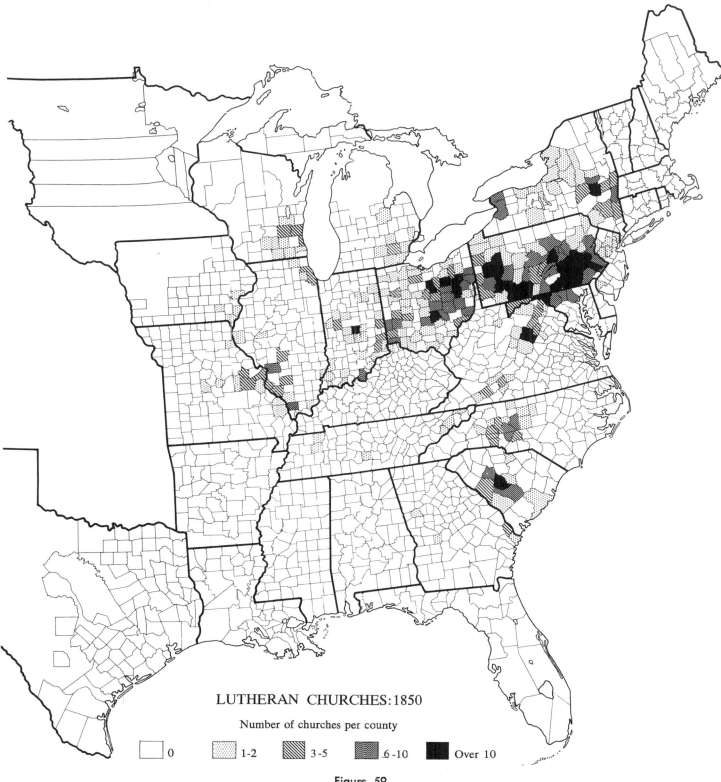

LUTHERAN CHURCHES: 1850

Number of churches per county

☐ 0   ⬚ 1-2   ▨ 3-5   ▧ 6-10   ■ Over 10

Figure 59

gelical Lutheran Church in America. That not a single one of these formal titles survived in 1960 serves as an excellent indication of the rapid shuffling which occurred in the Lutheran family.

For the twentieth century has been the era of Lutheran unity. In 1917 three synods of predominantly one ethnic background culminated several years of careful labor with the formation of the Norwegian Lutheran Church of America, which in 1946 changed its name to the Evangel-

ical Luthern Church (ELC). The next year saw the formation of the United Lutheran Church in America (ULCA), a reincarnation of an earlier comprehensive General Synod (1820) whose unity had been split on the hard rock of doctrine and the harder one of the Civil War. The surviving elements of the General Synod joined with the more conservative General Council (established in 1866) and the United Synod of the South (1862) to bring this ULCA into being. And in 1930 the American Lutheran

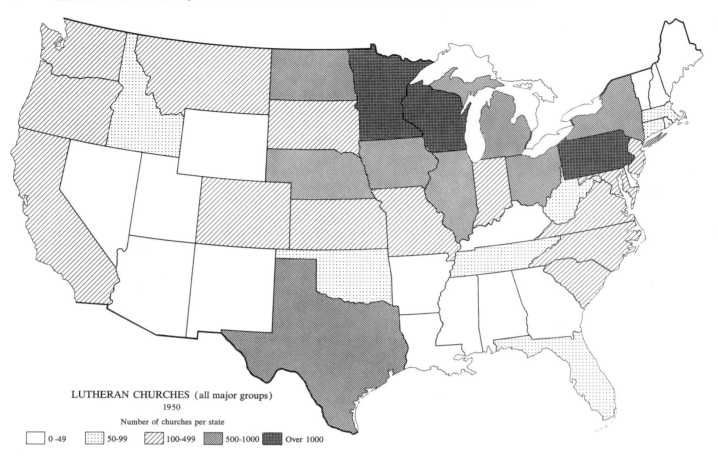

LUTHERAN CHURCHES (all major groups)
1950

Number of churches per state

☐ 0-49 ▦ 50-99 ▨ 100-499 ▨ 500-1000 ▨ Over 1000

Figure 60

Church (ALC) arose from the separate synods of Ohio, Buffalo, Iowa, and Texas. German by background and rural by location, the ALC, strengthened in its own new-found unity, assumed the role of mediator in seeking additional ways toward Lutheran reunion. Finally, in 1960, the ALC joined the ELC and a smaller group to become The American Lutheran Church, now one of Lutheranism's "big three." The other two (see Fig. 61) are the ULCA, considered above, and the Missouri Synod.

The Lutheran Church–Missouri Synod reached its present proportions not through dramatic mergers but through even more dramatic expansion. Organized in Chicago in 1847, the Synod of 12 congregations broke the bonds of language (German) and of provincialism to become in little more than a century a Synod of over 5,000 congregations. Through its rapid development of educational facilities, its energetic devotion to effective evangelism, and its unswerving loyalty to doctrinal purity, this Synod has established churches in every state in the Union, has extended itself well into Canada (where it has about 250,000 members) and has spilled over into Central America.

The drive for unity is not yet over. The Lutheran Free Church (over 80,000 members), whose leadership had envisioned being a part of the 1960 merger of the ELC and ALC, may still find it possible to enter into this union. Additional congregational referendums in these "Free" churches will be taken to determine the degree of grass-roots support by those congregations which guard their freedom with great care.

In 1960, three of the remaining ten Lutheran bodies voted to merge with the United Lutheran Church. One of

THE LUTHERAN FAMILY: 1957

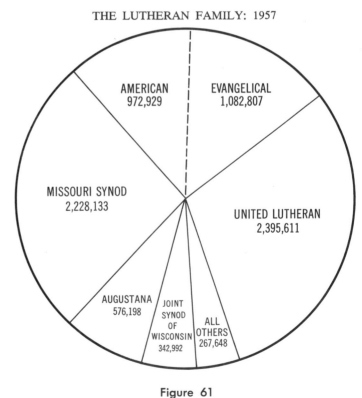

AMERICAN 972,929

EVANGELICAL 1,082,807

MISSOURI SYNOD 2,228,133

UNITED LUTHERAN 2,395,611

AUGUSTANA 576,198

JOINT SYNOD OF WISCONSIN 342,992

ALL OTHERS 267,648

Figure 61

The American and Evangelical branches merged in 1960.

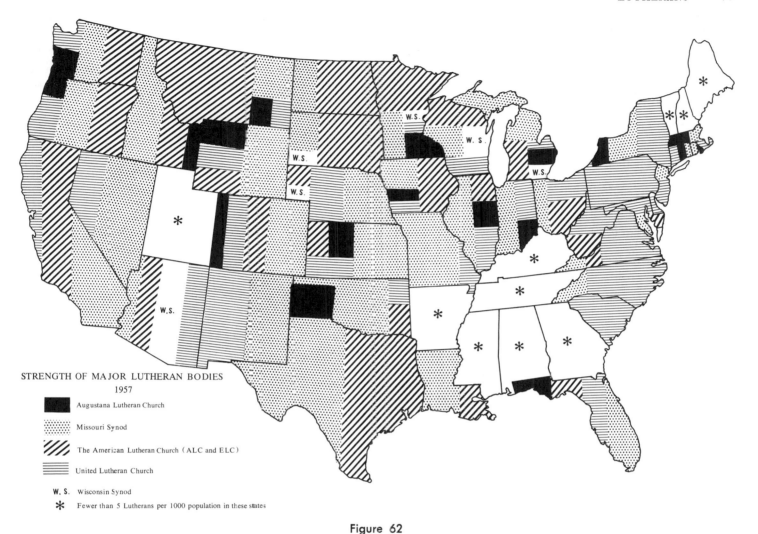

STRENGTH OF MAJOR LUTHERAN BODIES
1957

▪ Augustana Lutheran Church

⠿ Missouri Synod

▨ The American Lutheran Church (ALC and ELC)

≡ United Lutheran Church

W. S. Wisconsin Synod

✳ Fewer than 5 Lutherans per 1000 population in these states

Figure 62

The shadings indicate approximate strength of each Lutheran branch within a state; they do not indicate geographical location.

these, the Augustana Lutheran Church, is a sizable group, consisting of well over 500,000 persons of Swedish descent. While the beginnings of Swedish Lutheranism in America go back to the Delaware settlements of 1638 (see Part I, 5), the continuous history of this ethnic fellowship is traced from Andover, Illinois, where in 1850 the first Swedish Lutheran congregation was organized. Steady emigration from Sweden in the latter half of the nineteenth century led to formation of the Augustana (Latinized form for Augsburg) Church a decade later. Home mission and educational programs were systematically launched, making it possible for Augustana to reach and to hold a majority of the Swedish immigrants who were to arrive within the next fifty years. The 36 congregations existing in 1860 had within a century been multiplied virtually 40 times over (see Fig. 62).

The other two Lutheran bodies which have cast their lots with the ULCA are the Finnish Evangelical (Suomi Synod) and the American Evangelical Church. The former, enjoying a membership of approximately 40,000, was founded in 1890 after the pattern of the Church of Finland. Six years later in Hancock, Michigan, Suomi College and Seminary, in which more than 90% of the synod's

ministry is trained, was created. The growth there begun has continued until Suomi has become the largest Finnish Lutheran group in America. The American Evangelical Church, "the happy Danes," dates from 1871 when four Wisconsin pastors organized the Church Missionary Society. Retaining their native language longer than most immigrant groups, the Danish Lutherans established community halls and folk schools around which their social life—in Danish—largely revolved. Only in the present generation did "Danish" drop from the Church's title and a ministerial candidate not of Danish descent receive ordination. Having 70 churches and over 12,000 members in 1906, this group had by 1960 grown only slightly in its number of churches but had approximately doubled in its membership. When these Danes, together with the Finns and Swedes considered above, complete their projected merger (the constituting convention is set for June, 1962), the ULCA—assuming the title of the Lutheran Church in America—will have a membership of well over 3 million. The new American Lutheran Church, it may be recalled, has more than 2 million members. And the Lutheran Church–Missouri Synod alone accounts for the other great block, having in excess of 2½ million members.

The Missouri Synod, however, may not stay by itself. Indeed, since the late nineteenth century, Missouri has participated in the Synodical Conference, which while only an advisory body has made possible cooperative undertakings with the Joint Synod of Wisconsin (about 400,000 members), the Slovak Church (over 20,000) and the Evangelical Lutheran Church (of Norwegian heritage, about 14,000). A particularly effective cooperative en-

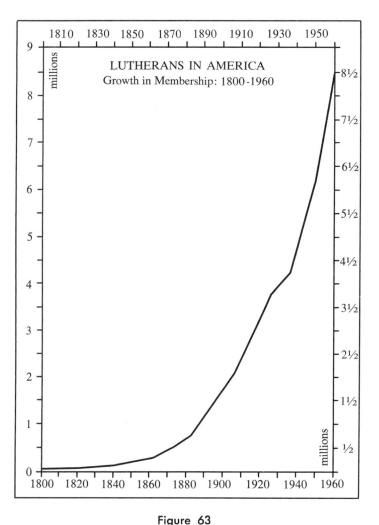

Figure 63

Includes all recognized Lutheran synods or churches.

deavor of this Conference has been its work among the Negroes in the southern states, where a native Negro ministry was trained to complement the work of the home mission appointees. Because the four groups within the Synodical Conference have a common concern for strict confessional Lutheranism, a closer tie may be forthcoming. On the other hand, anxiety for precise orthodoxy can prove to be a divisive force as well. And, in general, these four groups have been reluctant to consider any "unionism" at all, or even to work directly with the National Lutheran Council (1918), with which all other major Lutheran bodies do cooperate.

In any event, it is demonstrable that the diversifying and duplicating of the Lutheran churches has reversed

direction. From twenty-four separate organizations in 1906, there seems good reason to believe that, by 1970, Lutheranism may be reduced to three major divisions: the American Lutheran Church, the Lutheran Church in America, and the Synodical Conference. Also it appears likely that by then the last of the ethnic titles will have been replaced by one that is at a single stroke narrower in number of letters and broader in Christian love.

SOURCES.   Omar Bonderud and Charles Lutz (editors), *America's Lutherans* [reprinted from *One* magazine] (Columbus, 1955). H. E. Jacobs, *A History of the Evangelical Lutheran Church in the United States* (American Church History Series, IV) (New York, 1893). F. E. Mayer, *The Religious Bodies of America* (St. Louis, 1954). Clifford Nelson and Eugene Fevold, *The Lutheran Church Among Norwegian Americans* (Minneapolis, 1960). O. N. Nelson (ed.), *A Century of Life and Growth* (Rock Island, [Ill.], 1948). *A Statistical Handbook for the Lutheran Churches in North America* (New York, 1950). Abdel Ross Wentz, *A Basic History of Lutheranism in America* [see bibliography therein] (Gettysburg, 1955). And see the detailed bibliography by Herbert H. Schmidt in *Religion in Life* XXVII:4.

7. METHODISTS

"O America! America! it will certainly be the glory of the world for religion." These words, written by Francis Asbury in 1784, bespeak the confidence and enthusiasm with which the earliest Methodists approached the task of winning the new American nation. And whether or not that nation would prove to be the glory of the world for religion, it certainly became the glory of the world for Methodism.

For sheer pertinacity and phenomenal success, the Methodist story of expansion is hard to match. On both sides of the Alleghenies, circuit riders, colporteurs and unordained laymen began with a toehold and ended with a meetinghouse. And from this newly secured position, more riders, preachers, and propagandists would begin the next wave of invasion. The intrepid geographer, Jedidiah Morse, admittedly baffled by the tempo of Methodist expansion, wrote in 1792: "Their numbers are so various in different places, at different times, that it would be a matter of no small difficulty to find out the exact amount" (p. 269). Such wondering incredulity would not diminish as the nineteenth century unfolded.

How did all this bustle begin? Methodism was, of course, English rather than American in origin. But its nativity, coming a century after that of the Baptists, Congregationalists, Presbyterians, and Quakers, virtually coincided with the nativity of the United States of America. The two youngsters got along remarkably well. John Wesley, who had organized and directed "societies" within the Church of England, was hampered in his work across the Atlantic by a shortage of Anglican clerics favorable to his cause. On both sides of the Atlantic, however, the strength of Methodism was found not so much within the clergy as within the laity. The *ecclesiolæ in ecclesia,* the earnest, disciplined, methodical minority of men and women working and worshiping within the Anglican establishment—this was the nucleus whose energy was soon to be released.

A layman, Robert Strawbridge, introduced Methodism into Maryland in 1766, while another layman, Philip Embury, began preaching in New York City. With the help of the colorful Captain John Webb and the prayerful Barbara Heck, Embury was by 1768 able to speak from the first building in the world to be named Wesley Chapel. By this time the fiery Strawbridge had already begun sending out other preachers from his Maryland base. Captain Webb, meanwhile, having retired from the British Army, itinerated with purposive vigor, establishing a Bible class for Methodists in Philadelphia in 1768, welcoming Wesley's missionaries to New York in 1769, and in the same year assisting in the purchase of St. George's Church in Philadelphia, the oldest existing Methodist edifice in America.

Wesley, urged by Webb and others, dispatched several lay evangelists to America between 1769 and 1773. Of the many who came in that period, Francis Asbury emerged as the most effective leader. Arriving in 1771, the 26-year-old Asbury set about organizing the scattered evangels of Methodism. The next year, when there were fewer than 1,000 Methodists in all America, Asbury received from Wesley the title of "Superintendent of the American Colonies." In 1773 he made his headquarters in Baltimore and assisted in the erection of two churches (Strawberry Alley and Lovely Lane) in that and the following year. Asbury, whose 200-mile circuit sowed Methodist seed in unbelievably good soil, was aided by other successful husbandmen (Williams, Boardman, Pilmoor, King, Wright, Rankin, Shadford) in the pre-Revolutionary days.

On the occasion of the first American Methodist Conference, meeting in Philadelphia in July, 1773, the membership of the society was reckoned as follows: New York, 180; New Jersey, 200; Philadelphia, 180; Maryland, 500; and Virginia, 100. One year later this membership of 1,160 had grown to 2,073, divided among the colonies as follows: New York, 222; New Jersey, 257; Philadelphia, 204; Maryland, 1,063; and Virginia, 291 (Goss, 41 f.). It may be noted that Maryland accounted for more than one-half of the entire membership. If Methodism had not been able to adapt itself readily to the conditions of the settled East, it would never have survived to share so boldly in the conquest of the beckoning West. There were 17 itinerating Methodist preachers in the colonies in 1774, 19 in 1775, and 24 in 1776.

With the separation of the colonies from England, Methodism—even more than Anglicanism—seemed to be isolated, stranded, endangered. If the status of the Church of England was suspect in the new nation, what of a quasi-official organization, suspect even within that Church? Contrary to what might have been anticipated, however, the group with so little status soon outdistanced its more

prestigious parent. This reversal of fortune was due in the first instance to the readiness of Methodism to be a truly indigenous Church with freely chosen native leaders. It was due in the second place to the prodigious, courageous labors of those leaders.

The War of Independence did not, therefore, suddenly arrest the growth of Methodism as it did that of Anglicanism (see above, pp. 9-10). By 1781 there were more than

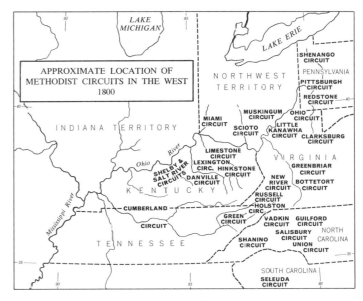

Figure 64

10,000 Methodists in America, nine-tenths of whom were below the southern boundary of Pennsylvania. Three years later there were 84 evangelists ministering to nearly 15,000 members. Such growth was possible only through the work of patriot preachers who effectively filled the void created by the withdrawal of Wesley's Loyalist missionaries. Indeed, out of the 8 preachers sent by Wesley, only Asbury remained, determined to nourish the tender Methodist plant in soil so dearly watered. And while Wesley's own outspoken rejection of the American cause could hardly be ignored, the Methodists of the United States of America showed no disposition to be ruled from abroad. In 1787, for example, when John Wesley sent written instructions that Richard Whatcoat be ordained as joint superintendent with Asbury, the ministers answered simply that they were not "ready now to obey his command" (Sweet, *Religion on the American Frontier,* IV, 40). Not until thirteen years later were they ready.

On December 24, 1784, itinerants from throughout the colonies gathered in Baltimore to establish the Methodist Episcopal Church. The Thirty-Nine Articles of the Church of England, as abridged by Wesley into twenty-four, became the doctrinal statement of the new Church; the Book of Common Prayer, as altered in Wesley's "Sunday Service," became the connecting bond between American and British Methodists. Modifications were made in matters of discipline, and an annual salary of $64 was fixed for the unmarried Methodist itinerant. But the most significant step concerned the order of the ministry.

During the growth of Methodism in America, the leaders in the colonies, as well as Wesley himself, had been gravely concerned over the unordained status of the preachers. "Members" were for the most part not "communicants" for there was no ministry authorized to administer the sacraments. Converts were received without baptism, and children were growing into adulthood without communion. The earlier dependence upon the Anglican clergy for the sacraments, never an entirely satisfactory arrangement, broke down completely during the period of the Revolution. Wesley, after much wrestling with his conscience, made his decision. On September 1, 1784, Wesley, himself a presbyter, ordained Richard Whatcoat and Thomas Vasey as deacons, and the next day ordained them as presbyters or elders. At the same time he ordained Thomas Coke as bishop or superintendent of the Methodist Societies in America. Coke, arriving in New York in November of that year, proceeded to the "Christmas Conference" in Baltimore where he read a letter from Wesley to "our Brethren in North America." The epistle stated, in part:

Lord King's Account of the Primitive Church convinced me, many years ago, that bishops and presbyters are the same order, and consequently have the same right to ordain. For many years I have been importuned from time to time to exercise this right, by ordaining part of our traveling preachers. But I have still refused, not only for peace' sake, but because I was determined, as little as possible, to violate the established order of the national Church, to which I belonged. But the case is widely different between England and North America. Here there are bishops who have a legal jurisdiction. In America there are none, and but a few parish ministers; so that for some hundred miles together there is none either to baptize or to administer the Lord's supper. Here, therefore, my scruples are at an end; and I conceive myself at full liberty, as I violate no order and invade no man's right, by appointing and sending laborers into the harvest. I have accordingly appointed Dr. Coke and Mr. Francis Asbury to be joint superintendents over our brethren in North America. As also Richard Whatcoat and Thomas Vasey to act as elders among them, by baptizing and ministering the Lord's supper. If any one will point out a more rational and Scriptural way of feeding and guiding those poor sheep in the wilderness, I will gladly embrace it (Stevens, 185 f.).

On Christmas Day, Asbury—still a layman—was ordained a deacon by Coke; the next day, Sunday, an elder; and on Monday, he was consecrated bishop or superintendent. Before the conference ended, twelve others in the assembly were ordained first as deacons, then as elders. The poor sheep now had shepherds, shepherds who set about transforming the wilderness into a fold.

The budding denomination burst forth geographically as well as numerically. As early as 1781, western Pennsylvania and the Ohio Valley were invaded by Robert Wooster, and seven years later Pittsburgh began its official membership reports to the Conference. Francis Asbury and Jesse Lee carried Methodism all the way to Charleston, South Carolina, in 1785; four years later Lee was at the other end of colonial civilization, introducing his views into Connecticut and Massachusetts. And before the century had ended, New Hampshire, Maine, Ohio, and Mississippi Territory had received the Wesleyan wayfarers (see Fig. 64). In 1780 there were 8,504 Methodists in America; in 1790, there were 57,631—a sevenfold increase in a single decade.

In 1792, at the occasion of the first General Conference, a brief setback was suffered. James O'Kelly, a prominent Virginia elder, defended the proposition that anyone dissatisfied with the appointment given him by the bishop "shall have liberty to appeal to the Conference and state his objections; and if the Conference approve his objections, the bishop shall appoint him to another circuit." For nearly a week the debate raged in Baltimore, but O'Kelly's motion was defeated "by a large majority." As a result, O'Kelly and some others withdrew from the Conference to form the Republican Methodist Church, the title revealing the pressures and passions of the day for free, nonauthoritarian religion. With special strength in the land of Madison and Jefferson, O'Kelly succeeded in drawing a sizable number away from the General Conference (membership figures dropped from 65,980 in 1792 to 56,664 in 1796), but he did not succeed in maintaining a permanent competing organization.

Early in the nineteenth century, the Negro Methodists displayed interest in having ecclesiastical organizations of their own. As early as 1787 the General Conference had exhorted preachers to proclaim the gospel to the slaves; and, in that same year, some Negroes had withdrawn to form a church in Philadelphia which, after litigation, became completely independent of the jurisdiction of whites in the Philadelphia Conference. In 1816 this church, the Bethel Society, called a general convention of Negro Methodists, inviting all to unite under the name of the African Methodist Episcopal (AME) Church. While AME growth was at first confined to the Middle Colonies, the Emancipation Proclamation opened the way for effective work in the South. By 1865 the AME Church had 2,613 clergymen and a membership of 53,670. Other organizations of Negro Methodists came into being, notably the African Methodist Episcopal Zion (AMEZ) Church in New York City in 1821. At organization time, AMEZ had 6 churches, 19 preachers and 1,426 members. In 1865 the membership figure had jumped to 30,600 and the number of clergymen to 661.

Meanwhile, the thrust into the western area was unremitting. Robert Wooster, who had carried the message into western Pennsylvania, moved on to Bracken County, Kentucky, then to Indiana. By 1787 the Redstone area centering around Uniontown, Pennsylvania, was a major propaganda station. At least seven clergymen were sent out in all directions, with circuits established for Clarksburg (Ohio) and Pittsburgh, in addition to the Redstone area. Tennessee and the western counties of North Carolina soon heard the hardy itinerant's call to meeting.

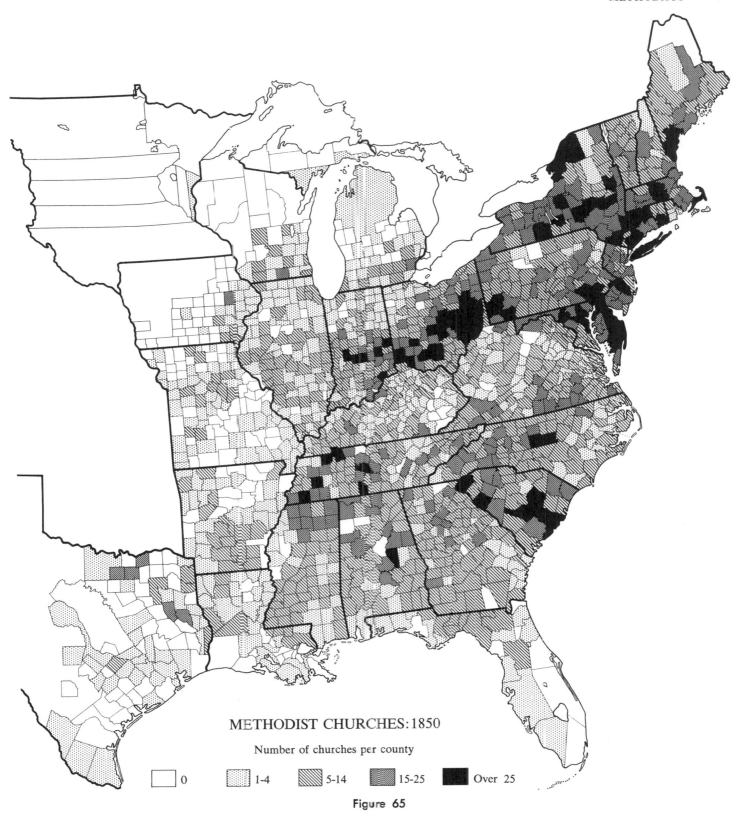

METHODIST CHURCHES: 1850

Number of churches per county

| | 0 | | 1-4 | | 5-14 | | 15-25 | | Over 25 |

Figure 65

Churches also in these California counties: Eldorado (1), Sacramento (3), and San Joaquin (1); and one church in Clackamas County, Oregon

While the circuit riders took every opportunity to deepen and broaden their work by calling forth local preachers, the burden of evangelization of these lands fell on the fervent few who could sleep on the cold ground, survive all the aches and ill humors of the wilderness, thrive on wild turkey and bear meat, evade or pacify the Indians, and still have breath and strength to preach to debtors,

adulterers, criminals, atheists, as well as to nobler sorts.

On the trail cut by Daniel Boone, Methodist preachers entered Kentucky as early as 1784, and in two or three years Kentucky was part of a regular circuit. One of the itinerants, James Haw, wrote Asbury in 1789 concerning the "Good news from Zion; the work of God is going on rapidly in this new world; a glorious victory the Son of

God has gained, and he is still going on conquering . . ." (Stevens, 228).

Asbury tried to maintain his contacts with the growing edge of Methodism, not only through written communication, but also by means of personal visitation. Tremendously boosting the spirits of lonely preacher and lonely settler alike, Asbury pushed himself to exhaustion, as did his successor, William McKendree. McKendree, whose administrative acumen greatly strengthened the sprawling,

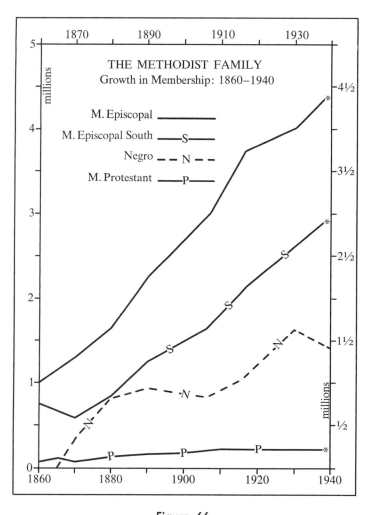

THE METHODIST FAMILY
Growth in Membership: 1860–1940

Figure 66

* These three branches merged in 1939.

expanding denomination, was, as his Church's first American-born bishop, committed to the West. His effective early labor in Virginia and later in Kentucky led to his election as bishop in Baltimore in 1808. But the West was still his home. Making his headquarters in Tennessee, McKendree moved out from this advance post to supervise the settlement of Methodists all the way to the Mississippi River.

Peter Cartwright was the Davy Crockett of Methodism. While he may not have "grinned a bear," he kept order in the camp meeting against all rowdies, bullies, and even Baptists. Powerful in body, mind, and voice, he countenanced no obstacles of man or nature which threatened to impede the progress of the gospel. From Kentucky and its

great camp meetings, the first area of Cartwright's powerful labors, he moved on to Indiana, and then to Illinois where he was twice elected to the state legislature. Impressed by his vote-getting ability, his party in 1846 nominated him for the Congress of the United States; he was defeated, however, by his Republican opponent, an Illinois lawyer named Abraham Lincoln.

Prior to the Civil War, Methodism had proved beyond doubt its mobility, its energy, its popularity (see Fig. 65). In 1800 Methodist preachers entered Mississippi at Natchez; in 1805, only two years after the happy Purchase was made, the circuit rider found Louisiana; in 1808 Michigan met the Methodists; in 1818 the steamboat and Methodism simultaneously arrived in St. Louis; Kansas was reached in 1830; the Indians of Oregon, 1834; Texas, 1841; Minnesota, 1844; California, 1849; Colorado, 1859; and Dakota Territory, 1860. Some of the Methodist "firsts" were also "firsts" for Protestantism, particularly in the Far West.

But in this forced march to the Pacific, was Methodism spreading itself too thin? Hardly. At the beginning of the nineteenth century there were 64,894 Methodists. The number was more than doubled in ten years: 174,560; almost doubled again in the next decade: 273,858. In 1830 there were 511,153, and by mid-century more than 1¼ million. At this time, 1850, there were more Methodist than any other churches in the following states: New York (1,231 churches); New Jersey (312); Pennsylvania (889); Delaware (106); Maryland (479); Virginia (1,025); North Carolina (784); South Carolina (484); Florida (87); Mississippi (454); Louisiana (125); Texas (176); Arkansas (168); Tennessee (861); Illinois (405); Indiana (778); Ohio (1,529); Michigan (119); Wisconsin (110); and Iowa (71) —20 states in all. No other religious body could approach that record. The Baptists led in only 7 states (Maine, New Hampshire, Rhode Island, Georgia, Alabama, Kentucky, Missouri); the Congregationalists in only 3 (Massachusetts, Connecticut, and Vermont); and the Roman Catholics only in California and in the Oregon and New Mexico territories. When the new homesteader drove his stakes into the ground, the echo was heard somewhere by a Methodist preacher.

But schism was never far away. The O'Kelly crisis and the Negro separations have been considered above. Next in point of time was the formation of the Methodist Protestant Church in 1830. The issue was not unlike that raised by James O'Kelly: the dissidents called for more democratic procedures and representation within the official body of the Church. Unlike the earlier groups, however, the Methodist Protestant Church maintained a structural unity, showing slow but steady growth from 105,120 members in 1830 to a little less than 200,000 a century later. This Church participated in the reunion of the Methodist bodies in 1939 (see Fig. 66).

On the critical issue of slavery, the Church was torn on both sides. Active abolitionists who failed to get the support

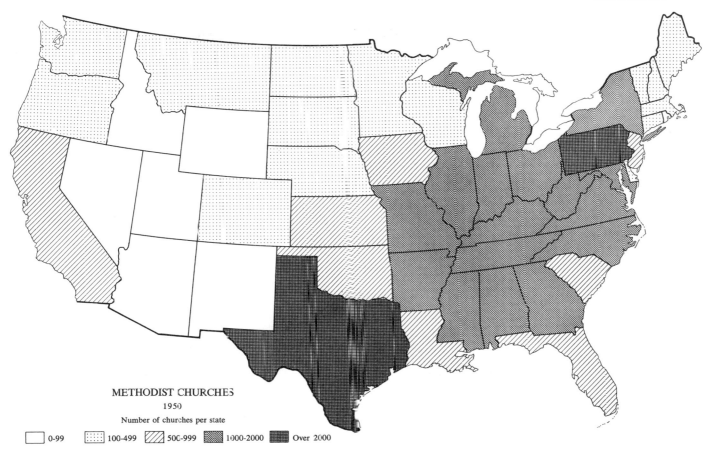

METHODIST CHURCHES
1950
Number of churches per state

| | 0-99 | | 100-499 | | 500-999 | | 1000-2000 | | Over 2000 |

Figure 67

of the General Conference in 1840 withdrew three years later to form the Wesleyan Methodist Church. At the time of the Civil War, its membership was about 25,000—a number which remained fairly constant for the rest of the century, and by 1960 was little more than 40,000. The far more serious split from the point of view of numbers was, of course, the formation in 1844 of the Methodist Episcopal Church, South.

The position of Wesley and of early Methodism on the question of slavery was hardly equivocal. Slavery was an "abomination," "the sum of all villainies," and an evil promptly to be extirpated. Methodists were to be admonished concerning the keeping of slaves and given one year in which to dispose of them; failing in this, excommunication was the only alternative. In the last years of the eighteenth century, the Methodist was as outspoken as the Quaker concerning this 'peculiar institution." But then came the cotton gin and with it an economic structure in the southern states which seemed to require great supplies of slave labor. The General Conference hedged; the state legislatures forbade emancipation; a way of life crystallized. In 1807 an Ohio Methodist gave thanks that his children were "saved from the harmful practice of trading on their fellow creatures in the manner . . . some of our old Friends have done . . . Lord have Mercy on the Methodists cause . . . when the Legislature of Virginia has determined against liberty & our preachers & people will be purchasing Slaves without a prospect of

liberating them . . ." (Sweet, *Religion on the Frontier*, IV, 171). As the distress of northern Methodists grew, the willingness of southern Methodists to concede the evils of slavery diminished. In 1844 the break came.

The separation was at first brotherly and calm, but by 1848 it had become unfriendly and tense, partly because of a northern refusal to divide properties until required to do so by a decision of the U.S. Supreme Court. In the years from 1845 to 1860, the Methodist Episcopal Church, South, grew from less than 500,000 to 750,000. In the course of the Civil War, however, the Church dropped back to near 500,000, this drop being due almost exclusively to the separation of the Negroes. Out of 207,706 Negroes in the Church in 1860, only 48,742 remained at the end of the war. "The others had joined the two African churches, which up to this time had operated mainly in the North, or had gone to the Methodist Episcopal Church [Northern], whose representatives were everywhere to be found throughout the South" (Alexander, 86). Despite this severe setback and the enormous hardship of reconstruction, the southern Church grew to well over 1 million by the end of the nineteenth century. At the time of reunion in 1939, it was nearly two-thirds the size of the northern Church. The Negro members who had remained in the southern group were invited to form their own ecclesiastical body: the Colored Methodist Episcopal Church, which grew from about 100,000 members in 1870 to virtually 4 times

Figure 68

The heavy lines indicate the five geographical jurisdictions of the Methodist Church:
Northeastern, Southeastern, North Central, South Central, and Western.

that number in 1960. In 1956 it took the name of Christian Methodist Episcopal Church.

The branch in the North, which (unlike the Baptists) remained the largest of all the Methodist groups, carried on a vigorous program of education and evangelism. Suffering also some retardation of growth during the period of civil strife, the Methodist Episcopal Church made steady gains from 1870 on. Indeed, the year 1866, taken as the occasion for a centennial celebration of the introduction of Methodism to America, was a time for extra effort in fund raising, church building and convert making. It was also a time when the Methodists began with even greater earnestness to look after their needs in formal education.

Methodism had barely come into existence as a separate entity when the first college, Cokesbury, was established in Abingdon, Maryland, in 1785. Heavy financial burdens, aggravated by fires in 1795 and 1796, resulted in the extinction of this school. Asbury College, founded in Baltimore in 1816, was also short-lived. A college established in Augusta, Kentucky, in 1822 lasted until 1841, when it merged with Transylvania University. The first Methodist college to survive was Wesleyan University, founded in Connecticut in 1831. In 1833 and 1834, the Church took over 2 colleges already existing: Allegheny

(Meadville, Pennsylvania) and Dickinson (Carlisle, Pennsylvania). Before the Civil War, altogether some 30 Methodist colleges were founded, including the following: McKendree, (1834), Emory (1836), Indiana Asbury [De Pauw] (1837), Trinity [Duke] (1838), Boston (1839), Ohio Wesleyan (1842), and Northwestern (1851). After the war, the educational activity was intensified with respect both to colleges and theological seminaries. Syracuse was opened in 1870, Vanderbilt in 1875. In 1880 the Methodists established the University of Southern California, and in 1893 the American University in Washington, D. C. Southern Methodist of Texas was opened in 1911 and Scarritt of Tennessee in 1924. At least 75 colleges currently maintain an organic relationship with The Methodist Church. While frontier preachers were largely unlettered and untrained, while suspicions against an educated ministry were as widespread among the Methodists as among the Baptists, the denomination, perhaps in defiance of a "foolish consistency," became a powerful educating force through its schools and its agencies of publication, most notably the Methodist Book Concern (1789).

In the area of social concern and applied Christianity, few of America's religious bodies could point to a comparable record. Methodism, as its own historians note, "was born in a prayer meeting, but it learned to walk on a battlefield" (Luccock and Hutchinson, 463). Of this development, at least, John Wesley would have whole-heartedly approved. For that indomitable spirit had personally (and sometimes singly) waged war against the English smuggler, the conscienceless liquor merchant, the inhuman administrators of prisons, the indifferent trader in slaves, and all who lived in or for cruelty, frivolity, and sin. His spiritual children forsook not the way

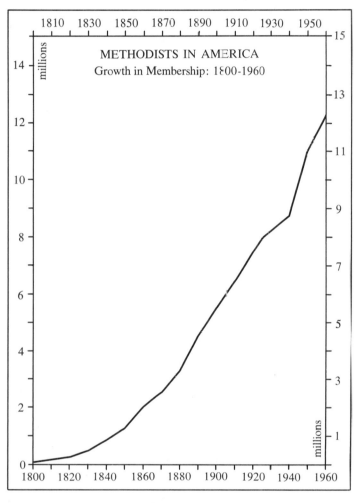

METHODISTS IN AMERICA
Growth in Membership: 1800-1960

Figure 69

This graph includes the three constituent bodies of The Methodist Church as well as three Negro denominations (African Methodist Episcopal Church; African Methodist Episcopal Zion Church; Christian [Colored] Methodist Episcopal Church).

of their father. While the protest over slavery suffered a regional limitation, the protest over alcohol could be heard all over the land. Particularly from the Civil War to the passage of the Eighteenth Amendment in 1920, Methodists were responsible for, or were actively engaged in, the antiliquor movements. The Prohibition Party, the Anti-Saloon League, and the Woman's Christian Temperance Union were among the many organizations in which Methodists were conspicuous by their presence. And Frances E. Willard won international notice by the diligence and incessancy of her warfare, a warfare not unrelated to the broader question of woman suffrage. In

1908 the denomination's General Conference, considering the relevance of New Testament love to America's social structure, adopted "The Social Creed of the Methodist Episcopal Church." In the same year, the Federal Council of Churches, representing the largest cooperative association of America's proliferating Protestantism, was formed; its influential "Social Creed of the Churches" closely followed the pattern set by the Methodists. For the next half-century, Methodism's mission included the responsibility to consider the claims of Christian conscience in matters of labor and management, war and peace, exploitation and justice.

Wholly engaged in the affairs of world-wide Protestantism, Methodists made their greatest contribution to ecumenicity by solving their own difficulties of dissension. Alone among the larger denominations which split before or during the Civil War, Methodism healed its breach before World War II. But the difficulty and delicacy of reunion negotiations can be appreciated when one recognizes that 1874 marked the beginning of a rapprochement which was not consummated until 1939. Irritations, uncertainties, and great procrastinations notwithstanding, the Methodist Episcopal Church, the Methodist Episcopal Church, South, and the Methodist Protestant Church became one: The Methodist Church (Fig. 66). Of course, success was not complete, for there were many Methodists still outside the pale, particularly the Negro Methodists. In 1960 approximately 2 million Methodists were members of the two leading Negro denominations, the African Methodist Episcopal and the African Methodist Episcopal Zion. Within the reunited Methodist Church itself, the controverted Central Jurisdiction, the only jurisdiction set up on a racial basis, accounted for approximately 370,000 Negroes, and the membership of the Colored [now Christian] Methodist Episcopal Church approached 500,000. Less than 1% of the white Methodists remained outside of the 1939 union.

Having considered Methodism's strides in nineteenth-century America, in education and publishing, in social witness and ecumenicity, one need only note that the twentieth-century advance is hardly less impressive (see Fig. 68). A membership of 5½ million at the beginning of the century had doubled itself at mid-point (see Fig. 69). And early in 1960, Bishop G. Bromley Oxnam served notice that when life is discovered on another of the universe's planets, The Methodist Church will be ready with its rocket riders.

SOURCES. Gross Alexander, *History of the Methodist Episcopal Church, South* (American Church History Series, XI) (New York, 1894). George C. Baker, Jr., *An Introduction to the History of Early New England Methodism 1789-1839* [excellent bibliography] (Durham, 1941). Wade C. Barclay, *History of Methodist Missions* [this six-volume work, of which three volumes have now appeared, will constitute the most exhaustive and reliable account of the expansion of Methodism] (New York, 1949–). J. M. Buckley, *A History of Methodists in the United States* (American Church History Series, V) (New York, 1896). C. C. Goss, *Statistical History of the First Century of*

American Methodism . . . [invaluable] (New York, 1866). James Dixon, Methodism in America: with the personal narrative of the author . . . [see Part IV, pp. 251-391, for the geographical extent of the conferences] (London, 1844). Nolan B. Harmon, The Organization of the Methodist Church (New York, 1948). John Lednum, A History of the Rise of Methodism in America . . . (Philadelphia, 1862). Halford E. Luccock and Paul Hutchinson (with two final chapters by Robert W. Goodloe) The Story of Methodism (New York, 1946). Jedidiah Morse, American Geography . . . (London [second edition], 1792). Walter B. Posey, The Development of Methodism in the Old Southwest 1783-1824 (Nashville, 1933). Abel Stevens, A Compendious History of American Methodism [abridged from the author's four-volume History of the Methodist Episcopal Church] (New York, 1867). William W. Sweet, Methodism in American History (Nashville [rev. ed.], 1954); ———, Religion on the American Frontier, 1783-1840: The Methodists, Vol. IV (Chicago, 1946); and ———, Virginia Methodism (Richmond, 1955). And see the bibliographies with discriminating commentary by Edward T. Fortney in Religion in Life XXIV: 3; and Frederick A. Norwood in Church History XXVIII:4 for Part I; XXIX:1 for Part II.

8. MORMONS

When discussing the Church of Jesus Christ of Latter-day Saints, it is not difficult to keep in mind the territorial expansion of America. Indeed, it is impossible not to do so. For the growth, persecution, exile, flight, adventure, courage, march, war, politics, ideals, and colonization of the Mormons are so much a part of America's nineteenth-century epic that the evolution of this church at any other time and in any other place is inconceivable. The contrary temptation is to consider Mormonism as exclusively or provincially American; but to yield here would be to go widely astray, for the Church began its ministry abroad even before it had won any degree of security at home. The portrait of Mormonism in America can easily be drawn altogether in black and white—a black villain against a white background, or a white hero against a black background. There is enough black and enough white, in both instances, to etch out such a picture. But whatever the artistic merits of this type of endeavor, the service to history would be negligible.

In April of 1830, 24-year-old Joseph Smith, together with five friends, organized in Fayette, New York, the "Church of Christ." After the writing of the Book of Mormon (first published in 1830), young Smith had felt the necessity of a formal organization through which the revelations of the past and of the future might be channeled. He also had seen visions of a great gathering of the saints, a holy community, a new heaven on earth, made possible by the revelation of God; in these latter days, to peculiarly American saints. As these visions were shared, and as new inspiration came, the Mormon Church grew by the hundreds before even the remaining months of 1830 had passed.

And Joseph Smith grew, too. Born in Sharon, Vermont, in 1805, he had moved a decade later with his family to Wayne County, New York. In that area, Smith later wrote, there was "an unusual excitement on the subject of religion" (see, e.g., Cross). This excitement began among the Methodists,

but soon became general among all the sects in that region. Indeed, the whole district seemed affected by it, and great multitudes united themselves to the different religious parties, which created no small stir amongst the people, some crying "Lo here!" and others, "Lo there!" Some were contending for the Methodist faith, some for the Presbyterian, and some for the Baptist (Joseph Smith's Own Story, 1).

Fourteen years of age at this time, Joseph was moved by the public religious excitement but also by "great uneasiness" in his own meditation. And though favorably inclined for a time toward the Methodists, Smith decided that the strife and confusion among the denominations was too great "for a person as young as I was . . . to come to any certain conclusion who was right and who was wrong."

Engaged in a variety of boyhood pursuits, and working on his father's farm, Joseph determined "to ask of God" the way out of his spiritual darkness. In 1820 he experienced the "First Vision," the vision of the Father and the Son. Three years after having received a series of revelations from the Angel Moroni, Joseph Smith brought forth the completed Book of Mormon, for him the supreme vindication (as the Koran was for Mohammed) of the validity of his religious experience. This book may be regarded as an American Testament, complementing Biblical history which was conspicuously silent on American affairs. According to Smith's revelation, the continent of the present United States was occupied many centuries before Christ by the Nephites and Lamanites—both descendants of the House of Israel. Constant warfare between these two groups resulted in the destruction of the Nephites, but not before one of their number, Mormon, recorded the history of his tribe. This record, discovered by or revealed to Smith, constitutes the Book of Mormon.

Following the organization of the 6-member church in Fayette, the vigorous, expanding Mormon community moved—an activity in which the Mormons would soon become quite accomplished. To Kirtland (now Kirtland Hills), Ohio, Joseph Smith and his followers came in 1831. Encouraged to take this step by Sidney Rigdon, an ex-Baptist and an ex-Disciples preacher, Smith set about to establish both a community and a church. With little in hand but an iron will and an unwavering faith, Smith made plans for an entire city, foresaw the building of an impressive temple, and directed the Mormon colonizing of the Missouri frontier. It was not long before money and men were both at his disposal. One of those men, Brigham Young, was among the 2,000 and more converts who had come into Kirtland by 1832 "in rude vehicles, on horseback, on foot . . . filling on their arrival every house, shop, and barn to the utmost capacity" (West, 39). Money was a more difficult problem, but this need was met through (1) donations to the communal treasury by new converts; (2) extensive borrowing from eastern sources,

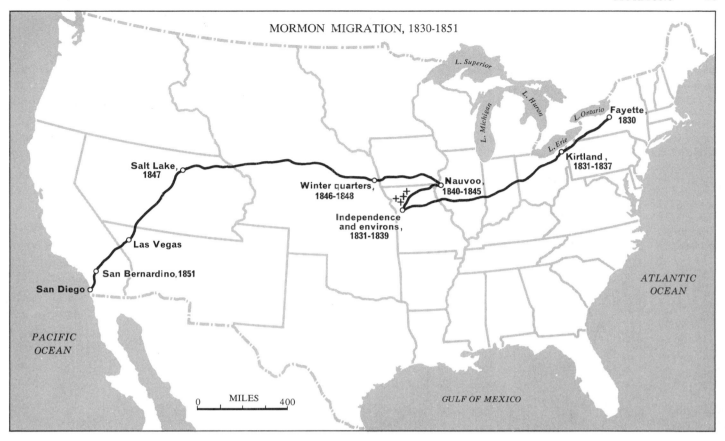

MORMON MIGRATION, 1830-1851

L. Superior

L. Michigan   *L. Huron*

L. Ontario Fayette,
1830

L. Erie

Kirtland,
1831-1837

Salt Lake,
1847

Winter quarters,
1846-1848

Nauvoo,
1840-1845

Independence
and environs,
1831-1839

Las Vegas

San Bernardino, 1851

San Diego

*PACIFIC
OCEAN*

*ATLANTIC
OCEAN*

MILES
0   400

GULF OF MEXICO

Figure 70

professional and personal; and in 1836, (3) the establishment by Smith of his own bank. When the Ohio legislature failed to grant a charter to the Mormon bank, the saints were undaunted: *Bank* notes simply became *anti-banking* notes, and business continued as usual. Early in 1837, however, as a harbinger of the panic that was soon to spread across the nation, Smith's bank, or anti-bank, failed; creditors sued; the faithful faltered; and a troubled follower acknowledged that there "were not twenty persons on earth that would declare that Joseph Smith was a prophet of God" (Brodie, 203).

In the Missouri settlements, conditions were, if anything, worse. From 1831 on, the Mormons of this frontier area had known little peace. Persuaded, however, that the wide-open spaces on or across the Missouri River held promise as a great homeland for Zion, the battered, dispirited community hung on. Driven from Jackson County by neighbors suspicious of the Saints' dealings in land, of their friendship with Indians, of their acceptance of free Negroes and of their presumptive intimacy with God, the Mormons went into Clay County. For three years they met with general acceptance by their neighbors. But old issues and old animosities made another move necessary, this time into an unpopulated section of Ray County, which they later, in 1836, organized into Caldwell County. In their newly formed county seat of Far West, it seemed that the Kingdom might, after all, be at hand. Prosperity and growth, however, while giving assurance to the Saints, were alarming to the Gentiles. As migrants from Ohio

swelled the Mormon community in the counties of Daviess, Carroll, and Ray, animosity, suspicion, and insecurity grew. When, on August 6, 1838, the Gentiles sought to prevent the Saints from voting, the first "Mormon War" began. Several months of bitter raiding, looting, and murdering, with excesses on both sides, led in April of 1839 to another Mormon move, this time to Illinois. A peculiar people began to learn the price of peculiarity.

While some questioned whether the price was too high or the procedure too irregular, Joseph Smith possessed of undiminished hope, purchased more land in Iowa and Illinois. One parcel of land, located on a sharp bend of the Mississippi, near the point at which the Iowa–Missouri border met the river, became the new home of the scattered flock: Smith named it Nauvoo. In 1840 the city of Nauvoo was formally, if somewhat irregularly, chartered, and once again the elaborate plans for efficient communal living were put into execution. The town was laid out in carefully prescribed order, another and more ambitious temple was envisioned, city government was organized and an all-Mormon militia of 2,000 men was raised.

At this time—the early 1840's—the preponderance of Mormons was in Illinois. A contemporary, writing in 1844, estimated the total number of Mormons to be 18,000 "distributed nearly as follows:—Nauvoo and vicinity, eight thousand five hundred. Other parts of the United States and Canada, three thousand. Great Britain, six thousand

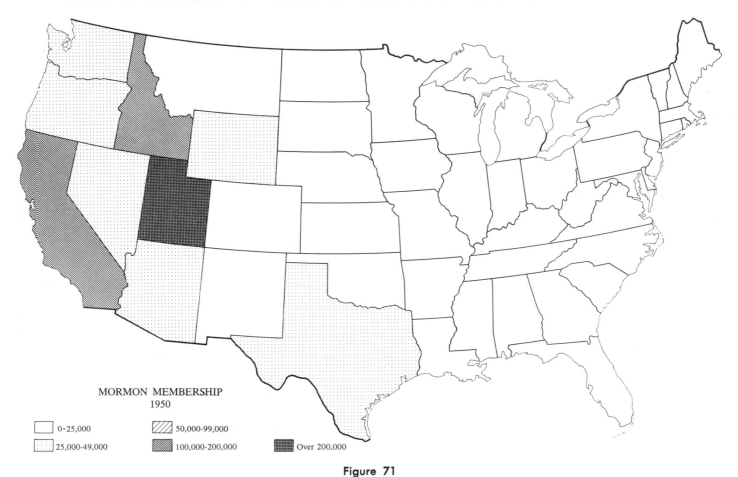

MORMON MEMBERSHIP
1950

☐ 0-25,000   ▨ 50,000-99,000

▤ 25,000-49,000   ▧ 100,000-200,000   ▦ Over 200,000

Figure 71

Statistics for the number of churches per state were not available.

five hundred" (Kidder, 7). However, another contemporary suggests that there were 18,000 Mormons in Nauvoo alone (Hunt, v) in the year 1844. Finally, a Mormon publication reported a census in 1845 which showed a "population of 11,057 in the city and one-third more outside the city limits" (O'Dea, 51), suggesting a happy mean of about 15,000 Mormons in and around Nauvoo during these days of deceptive calm.

For Mormon troubles were not over. In 1840 malarial attacks reduced the Nauvoo community in strength and in number. An already impoverished, exiled people discovered that they were not too poor to be robbed, as a fraudulent land agent sold land, on both sides of the river, that was not his. In 1843 Joseph Smith made known his special revelation concerning the legitimacy of polygamy, and what was privately whispered soon became publicly decried; opposition to the doctrine, moreover, was by no means restricted to the Gentiles. But to the Gentiles of Illinois the marital novelties of the Mormons, added to all the familiar charges against the sect, made further hospitality impossible. Newspapers published sharply critical accounts of the community's finances, of the Church's doctrine, of Smith's integrity. In June, 1844, an angry Mormon mob destroyed the newspaper press of two Nauvoo apostates; two weeks later Joseph Smith was arrested and jailed; and on June 27 an angry Gentile mob, storming the jail where the 38-year-old Smith was quartered, killed him.

With the death of its leader, the Mormon Church again hung between life and death. The dark days of Ohio, of Missouri, of early Nauvoo returned to make even darker the blackness of the murder of Joseph Smith and the bleakness of the Church's future. Sidney Rigdon wanted to lead the community back to the East, to redress and retrench. Lyman Wight took a group to Texas; J. J. Strang, a group to Wisconsin; Cutler, Cowles, Emmet, and others led small groups away, generally to oblivion. The bullets which ended Joseph Smith's life seemed also about to end his bold dream for Zion. And well they might, had it not been for Brigham Young.

A self-made, self-taught, self-reliant man, Brigham Young prepared at the age of 43 to assume the fallen hero's mantle. Twelve years earlier, in 1832, he had been immersed in baptism at Mendon, New York. Since that hour he had shown himself to be a strong right arm as he organized congregations in New York and Canada, built houses and a temple in Ohio, collected money in Pennsylvania and New England, led a march to Missouri and another one 1,000 miles back to Kirtland, defended Joseph Smith against attacks within and without the Church, and directed the pathetic flight of 20,000 bedraggled men, women and children out of a hostile Missouri into a momentarily hospitable Illinois. From Nauvoo, Brigham Young had been dispatched to England in 1839, where already some 1,500 Mormon converts lived. When he left England the next year, there were 5,000 Saints enrolled.

Back in Illinois, Young gradually rose to leadership within the town council and within the second highest governing body of the Church, the Council of Twelve. His apprenticeship had been hard; but, like any good apprenticeship, it prepared him for even harder tasks ahead.

When Brigham Young addressed the thousands of disillusioned, bone-weary Saints assembled on the meadow overlooking the Mississippi River, he made that August afternoon of 1844 seem brighter. A new leader had been given to Israel; as surely as God raised up Brother Joseph, He had raised up Brother Brigham; deliverance would come. How costly, how arduous, how daring that deliverance would be, no one—not even Brother Brigham—could know.

The first step toward unity and the restoration of morale was work. For a tired, dispirited, grieving community—work. Missionary efforts were intensified, construction of the temple was accelerated, authority of the Twelve was imposed. For the next two years, as the Nauvoo community worked and prospered, negotiations were held with state officials for the right of a peaceable departure from Illinois. Anti-Mormon activity, having moderated briefly following the mob murder of Smith, waxed hot once again. Young, hoping to forestall the shedding of more blood, made known in 1845 the plan of the Saints for "a general exodus in the spring"—an exodus from the newly completed temple, from Illinois, from civilization. Even this promise, however, did not cool the tempers of the Gentiles, who in February of 1846 renewed their persecution. What had been planned as an orderly evacuation became, of necessity, a disorderly, hurried, sometimes frenzied flight. By May, almost all of the Mormons who could travel had left. The ill and aged remained, fending off attacks and raids as long as possible. When finally forced to surrender, they were given 24 hours in which to leave Illinois. Many who left got only as far as the other side of the Mississippi River where, in Iowa soil, they were buried.

The main body, which had begun leaving Nauvoo in the sub-freezing February of 1846, made its way as far as "Winter Quarters," the present site of Omaha, Nebraska. There more than 11,000 Mormons were quartered by the fall of 1846; between Nauvoo and Omaha, another 5,000 were making their slow, painful way west (West, 171). On April 16 of the next year, Brigham Young led a pioneer company of 148 persons and 72 wagons toward the savage, uncharted, but by-faith-redeemable West. Somewhere between the Platte River and the Pacific Ocean a Promised Land awaited.

Stories of this and the later Mormon migrations to Salt Lake City have been often told (see Fig. 70). History here needs no embellishment. While this move forms part of the great saga of western migration, the Mormon drama is heightened by the additional hazards of persecution, of poverty, of challenge to authority, of finding a Jerusalem that would not be destroyed by enemies of righteousness, of building a Kingdom worthy of the hope that lay within

them (see, for example, the excellent chapters, "Pillar of Cloud" and "Whether It Be Fat or Lean: Canaan," in Bernard DeVoto's *The Year of Decision*). On July 24, 1847, an ill Brigham Young raised himself up from the rumbling wagon, viewed the Salt Lake Valley spread out below him and said, "This is the place."

To that place came Mormons from all over the continent and beyond, first by the hundreds and soon by the thousands. "Give us ten years in this place," said President Young, "and we'll ask no odds of Uncle Sam or the devil." Then in September, on his way back to the Missouri River, he wrote the faithful who stayed in the valley to water the wastelands into life:

We have now fulfilled the mission, one which we were set, by selecting and pointing out to you a beautiful site for a city, which is destined to be a place of refuge for the oppressed, and one that is calculated to please the eye, to cheer the heart, and fill the hungry soul with food . . . (West, 192).

There were 1,671 persons at Salt Lake in the winter of 1847-48. To create a prosperous "State of Deseret," these Mormons needed both labor and luck. To the first they were no stranger, and to the second they were at last about to be introduced. The miracles of gulls in '48 and of gold in '49 saved the isolated community from serious, if not fatal, reverses. A plague of giant crickets—now "Mormon crickets"—threatened to destroy the entire harvest of the first year's crops, a calamity of incalculable proportion. After exhausting themselves and every conceivable method in a futile effort to halt the relentless advance, the Mormons seemed lost; suddenly the sky was black, not with crickets, but with sea gulls who devoured the insects and saved a portion of the harvest. In the rush to California for gold in 1849, Salt Lake City immediately became a strategic trading post where wagons were built or repaired, outfitted or traded, where goods and services were bartered for or bought, and where, in consequence, Zion mightily prospered.

Migration and immigration into the valley had just begun. Over 11,000 persons were settled in Utah by 1850, and by 1870 more than 86,000; of these probably 95% were Mormons (Anderson, 279). The immigrant element in this expansion deserves special mention, for the Latter-day Saints succeeded in organizing a remarkable and unique program in Church-sponsored, Church-financed, Church-directed immigration of foreign converts. While the Saints were still in Nauvoo, Brigham Young and others had established councils in the major cities of England, Scotland, and Wales. Working with such groups, Young arranged transportation for those who wished to emigrate to Illinois, hiring ships to carry only Mormon passengers, and arranging for their proper reception at an eastern port. A mission to the Scandinavian countries was begun in 1849 and to Germany in 1851; here the same careful procedures were employed. And in view of the great spread of land in Utah, the promises held out to the converts could be as expansive as the desert itself. The far-sighted Young, envisioning San Diego as the best potential port of entry for Mormon immigrants, "established settlements from Provo to Las Vegas to . . . make a highway along what he conceived to be a Mormon corridor to the sea" (O'Dea, 85). Through the Mormon agency at Liverpool alone, 4,750 emigrants sailed between 1840 and 1846. And by the end of the century close to 90,000 had left a tried and familiar homeland for an unknown, unproven storyland.

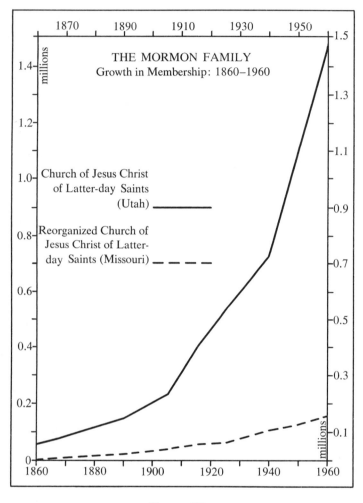

THE MORMON FAMILY
Growth in Membership: 1860–1960

Church of Jesus Christ of Latter-day Saints (Utah) —————

Reorganized Church of Jesus Christ of Latter-day Saints (Missouri) — — —

Figure 72

The appeal which could bring so many so far on so little has perhaps been nowhere better understood or expressed than by a bitter opponent of the exiled church. The Honorable John Thompson delivered a speech in the United States House of Representatives on January 27, 1858, the principal thesis of which was to persuade Congress to increase the size of the U. S. Army in order to put "Governor Young" in his place. Disturbed at the same time that he was enthralled by the move of thousands across the waters, Congressman Thompson spoke with eloquence:

What wonder that the down-trodden, famishing masses from Wales, Scotland, Sweden, Germany, France and all parts of the other world, without education, without moral instruction, are caught by the picture, and start in Troops for this earthly Paradise? What marvel that eager crowds begrimed with the soot of the dark mine, or pale from the faintness of the heated factory—what marvel that victims of an ecclesiastical system, that is known only by its oppressions; and taxes and tithes, while it fails to bless or enlighten—what marvel that they crowd round the earnest man in the thronged marts of the continents, or on the corners of the rural hamlets of England, and drink in his words, blazing with his own enthusiasm as he paints the earthly glories of the God-defended Eden of the West, which sparkles to the eye of faith in the distance, the embodiment of all excellence that the imagination ever painted? And then comes in the aid of 'organized emigration'; in vast communities, with the order and precision of an army, they set their faces resolutely for their new home; and along every avenue, from the Atlantic and Pacific alike, in winter and summer, toil on with a dogged energy, that is itself morally sublime. Sixty thousand souls at least own the sway of this occidental hierarchy (p. 5).

It was a reluctant but glowing tribute to a people who made the desert bloom.

In 1850 there were 16 Mormon churches in America; in 1860, 24; and in 1870, 189. Of this latter number, 160 were in Utah, indicating the position of strength of the Salt Lake community. A major group which separated from this Church and managed to survive the difficulties of the nineteenth century took the name of the Reorganized Church of Jesus Christ of the Latter-day Saints. Maintaining that the only true successor to Joseph Smith must be within his own family, Joseph, Jr., in 1860 gathered together most of the Saints who had not gone on to Winter Quarters with Young or to Wisconsin with Strang or to Pennsylvania with Rigdon. In 1884 Joseph Smith III claimed for this branch of the church 18,000 members "scattered from Maine to New Mexico, Oregon and Florida; some in England, Wales, Denmark, and Australia, and Society Islands" (Kennedy, 256). Early in the twentieth century the Reorganized Church reported almost as many churches (501) as Brigham Young's branch, but its membership (40,851) was less than one-fifth that of the larger body. Fifty years later the gap between the two had become even greater, the proportion being approximately 10 to 1.

Two other factors relating to the growth of Mormonism require particular mention. One is the practice of sending a great number of young men on a mission, foreign or domestic, on behalf of the Church. In pairs, the young men take the world as their parish—teaching, preaching, sowing the seed which (often in the form of the *Book of Mormon*) is left behind to germinate. Priding itself on its nonclerical, nonprofessional ministries, the Utah Church takes with great seriousness the priesthood of every believer. And even should the young evangelist in his two- or three-year missionary endeavor fail to win a single convert, he himself returns to his daily work a confirmed, convinced, earnest disciple of the Palmyra prophet.

The other factor concerns the teaching of the Salt Lake Church regarding the Negro. In the early days of Mormon history there was little to suggest any rejection of or discrimination against the Negro. Indeed, one of the problems troubling the Saints in Missouri was their open acceptance of the free Negro into their fellowship; further, they were suspected of being abolitionists, though this was likely intended only as an inflammatory charge. Later in Utah, when Horace Greeley pressed Brigham Young on the issue of slavery and Utah's stand thereon, Young replied that Utah, if admitted, would be a free state, for he, personally, regarded slavery as "generally a curse to the masters." It remains true, however, that the Mormon

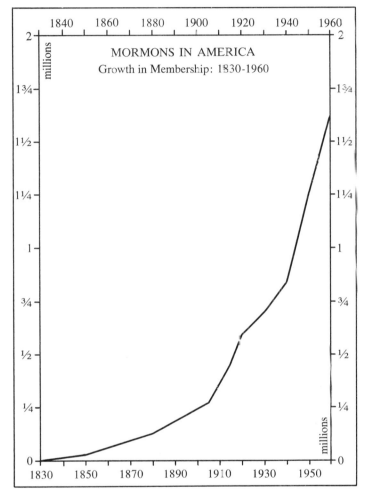

MORMONS IN AMERICA
Growth in Membership: 1830-1960

Figure 73

Membership totals include both groups cited in Figure 72.

Church does, on theological grounds, discriminate against the Negro. While he may become a member he cannot hold the priesthood, which prohibition automatically excludes him from all the temple rites, including baptism for the dead, and celestial marriage. Few Negroes are members. According to President Joseph Fielding Smith, grand-nephew of Joseph Smith, "It was well understood by the early elders of the Church that the mark which was placed on Cain and which his posterity inherited was the black skin" (p. 107). This current limitation in Mormon catho-licity seems fated for repeal or reinterpretation. Polygamy, which had much stronger doctrinal and even liturgical support, fell away; the exclusion of the Negro from the full privileges of a Church which has itself known so

much of prejudice and abuse is an anomaly which its most liberal and loving spirits must soon sweep away.

A socio-economic community as well as an ecclesiastical institution, the Mormon Church holds much fascination for the student of America's civilization. For it shared with the nation which gave it birth the ideals of human freedom and of a kingdom of God that was just around the corner. Recognizing this common heritage, one does not now find himself writing in the spirit of a pamphlet of 1841, entitled *The Mormons, or Knavery Exposed. Giving an Account of the Discovery of the Golden Plates . . . Documents printed by order of the Senate of the United States. The Whole Being designed as a Caution to the Ignorant and Unsuspecting Against One of the Most Barefaced and Blasphemous Devices which has ever been witnessed. Affording a Lamentable Exhibition of the Credulity and Weakness of Human Nature, in so Readily Allowing Itself to be Made the Dupe of Artful and Designing Knaves* (Philadelphia, 1841). While Mormon historiography has not been noted for its dispassionate character, Americans more recently give evidence of their desire to understand and to appreciate the new Israelites—these Saints of a latter day who dwell in their midst (see Figs. 71 and 73).

SOURCES. Nels Anderson, *Desert Saints: The Mormon Fron-tier in Utah* (Chicago, 1942). Fawn M. Brodie, *No Man Knows My History: The Life of Joseph Smith* (New York, 1945). W. R. Cross, *The Burned-Over District: The Social and Intellectual History of Enthusiastic Religion in Western New York, 1800-1850* (Ithaca, 1950). Bernard DeVoto, *The Year of Decision 1846* [chaps. 3 and 16] (Boston, 1942). Norman F. Furniss, *The Mormon Conflict 1850-1859* (New Haven, 1960). L. R. and A. W. Hafen (eds.), *Journals of Forty-Niners Salt Lake to Los Angeles* [exact route shown on map following p. 324] (Glendale [Calif.], 1954). James H. Hunt, *Mormonism: embracing the Origin, Rise and Progress of the Sect . . .* (St. Louis, 1844). Milton R. Hunter, *Brigham Young the Colonizer* [maps showing western settle-ments, p. 363, p. 365, p. 367] (Salt Lake City, 1940); ———, *The Mormons and the American Frontier* (Salt Lake City, 1940). J. H. Kennedy, *Early Days of Mormonism: Palmyra, Kirtland and Nauvoo* (New York, 1888). Daniel P. Kidder, *Mormonism and the Mormons: A Historical View of the Rise and Progress of the sect self-styled Latter-Day Saints* (New York, 1844). Thomas F. O'Dea, *The Mormons* (Chicago, 1957). *Joseph Smith Tells His Own Story* [brochure] (Independence, [n.d.]). Joseph Fielding Smith, *The Way To Perfection* (Independence [eighth edition], 1949). John Thompson, *Mormonism—Increase of the Army* (Washington, 1858). Ray B. West, Jr., *Kingdom of the Saints* [see map on end papers] (New York, 1957). And see the discern-ing article on "The Historiography of Mormonism" by Marvin S. Hill in *Church History* XXVIII:4.

9. PRESBYTERIANS

As noted in Part I, the Presbyterians presented a heart-ening unity as they faced the nineteenth century, for the first General Assembly gathering in 1789 bound together in the new Republic over 20,000 Presbyterians. Except for the small movements related to the Scottish Secession Church, America's Presbyterians were of one fellowship—and of one mind: to evangelize America. In the pursuit of that common goal, however, differences of principle and of procedure erupted into major separations.

The first break, coming quite early in the century, occurred in the Cumberland Presbytery of eastern Kentucky and Tennessee. Beginning in 1802, this presbytery, enjoying conspicuous success in its revival measures and seeking immediate leadership for its young churches, relaxed some of the educational requirements for the ministry. The overseeing Synod of Kentucky, already suspicious of the outbursts and irregularities of the revivals, first censured the Cumberland Presbytery, then in 1806 dissolved it. When the actions of the synod were supported by the General Assembly, leaders in the "Cumberland country" resolved

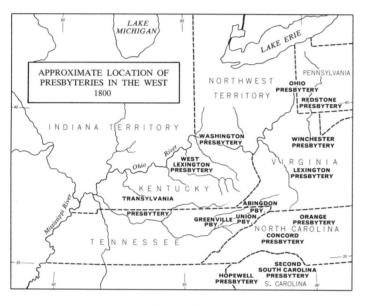

Figure 74

in 1810 to form their own independent presbytery. The ministers McAdow, Ewing, and King, "having waited in vain more than four years . . . for a redress of grievances, and a restoration of our violated rights, have, and do hereby agree, and determine, to constitute into a presbytery, known by the name of the Cumberland presbytery" (Armstrong *et al.* eds., 117). In this break, even the Westminster Confession sustained a crack; for the ministerial candidates, fresh from evangelistic successes, were not required to accept "the idea of fatality, that seems to be taught under the mysterious doctrine of predestination."

While there was originally some hope of reunion with the Synod of Kentucky, it was soon apparent that the independent presbytery had become an independent Church. In 1813 a general synod was constituted and 3 presbyteries formed. Fifteen years later there were 4 synods, 18 presbyteries and about 8,000 members. In 1840 there were 500 churches; in 1853, 1,250 churches; by 1875, over 2,000 churches; and in 1906, nearly 3,000 churches and almost 200,000 members. In that year a major portion of the Cumberland Presbyterian Church elected to merge with the Presbyterian Church in the United States of America—thus accounting for the drop in membership

evident in Figure 77. (This merger greatly assisted the "northern church" in becoming more nearly a "national church.") Of 195,770 Cumberland Presbyterians in 1906, less than one-half (72,052) remained in their original Church a decade later. In the fifty years following the 1906 merger, the residual denomination made little gain in membership and lost in the number of its churches. The only Presbyterian denomination specifically for Negroes grew out of the Cumberland Church in 1869 when, by mutual agreement, the Negroes separated to form the Colored Cumberland Presbyterian Church. Never a thriving group, this body's strength lies almost exclusively in 4 states: Kentucky, Tennessee, Alabama, and Texas.

The main body of "regular Presbyterians" was rent in 1838 by issues that were both old and new. While several disputants looked back to the 1801 Plan of Union agreement with the Congregationalists (see above, p. 62), and even further back to the revival excesses of the Great Awakening, others looked forward to the problems of slaveholding and abolition (Armstrong *et al.* eds., ch. 6). There was, in any case, provocation sufficient for bitter quarrel and for a sad but sharp cleavage between Old Side and New Side Presbyterians (see above, p. 20). For approximately a generation (1838-1869), there were in the United States two distinct General Assemblies, each claiming to speak for the Presbyterians of the nation. The division was fairly even, with some edge going to Old Side Presbyterianism which in 1840 had 126,583 members; its membership had doubled by 1869, reaching a total of 258,903. New Side Presbyterianism began (in 1840) with 102,060 members, which number had risen to 172,560 in 1869 (*Presbyterian Reunion*, 494, 503). Overwhelmed by the greater issues plaguing a divided nation and overtaken by yet another schism, Old Side and New Side reunited in 1869. In Pittsburgh, forgiving each other's errors and abuses, they joined hands at the same time their nation, by means of a transcontinental railroad, joined shores. [Note: The chart "Presbyterian Family" (Fig. 77) anticipates this reunion by nine years, presenting the combined membership of Old Side and New Side under the name of the Presbyterian Church, U.S.A.].

A major portion of the joy over this reunion was lost, however, in the recognition of even more serious fractures besetting the denominational body. The familiar issue of slavery, over which so many of America's churches had agonized, also taunted and tormented the Presbyterians. While New Side Presbyterians were more outspoken in their abolitionism, both Old and New Side had forces within them which threatened years before the Civil War to destroy any remaining semblance of Presbyterian unity. Only by the most cautious and sometimes compromising maneuvers was schism postponed until the actual outbreak of hostilities.

As in the case of the Methodists, the Presbyterians were, in the Revolutionary period, convinced of the evil of slavery. The Synod of New York and Philadelphia indi-

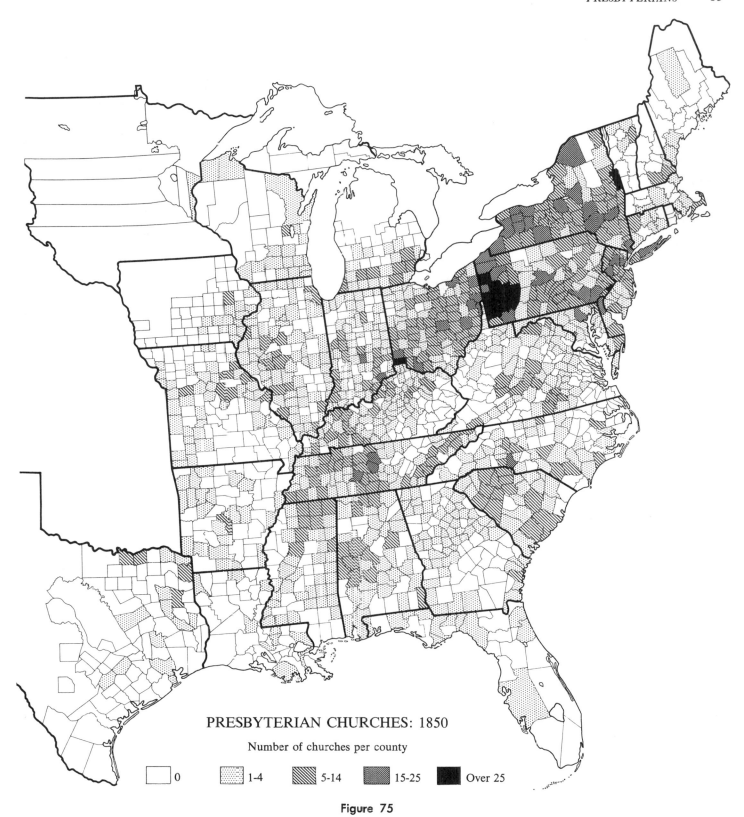

PRESBYTERIAN CHURCHES: 1850

Number of churches per county

☐ 0 ▦ 1-4 ▨ 5-14 ▨ 15-25 ■ Over 25

Figure 75

One church also in each of these counties: Sacramento, San Joaquin, and Solano, California; and Clatsop, Oregon.

cated in 1787 its readiness "to procure eventually the final abolition of slavery," while the Covenanters decreed by 1800 "that no slaveholder should be allowed the communion of the Church." In the early decades of the nineteenth century, however, official statements began to betray a regional character. While the Synod of Michigan decried the buying, selling, and owning of slaves "to be

A Sin Before God and man," the Charleston Union Presbytery observed in the same year, 1835, that "the holding of slaves, so far from being a sin in the sight of God, is nowhere condemned in his Holy Word" (Armstrong *et al.* eds., 199). The testimony of a New Side missionary, Timothy Hill, indicates that by 1845 the "Yankee" had difficulty gaining full acceptance even in a border state.

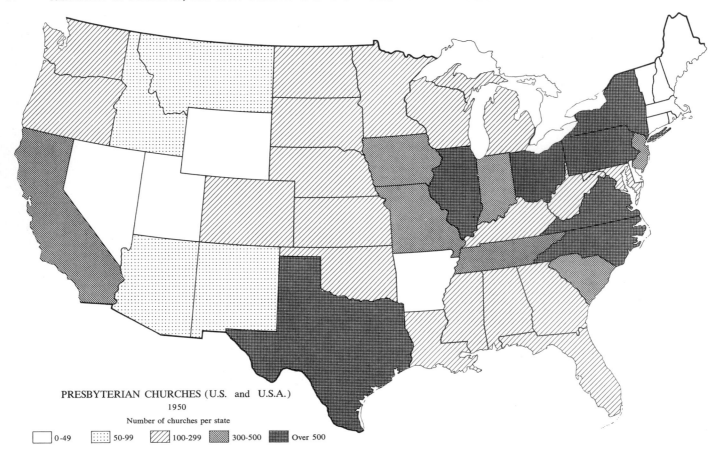

PRESBYTERIAN CHURCHES (U.S. and U.S.A.)
1950
Number of churches per state

☐ 0-49   ▦ 50-99   ▨ 100-299   ▧ 300-500   ▮ Over 500

Figure 76

In that section of Missouri to which he had ministered, Hill was not aware of any religious instruction at all being given to the slaves. Furthermore, "I could not say a syllable in private to the slaves themselves without setting in motion a train of opposition which would soon drive me from the State . . . I have come to the conclusion to wait quietly and discharge every duty in my power until the close of the year, and then as quietly *leave this State,* and seek a field of labor in a State where the curse of Slavery is not found . . ." (Armstrong *et al.* eds., 182). With so strong a division of opinion, with so unmistakable a shaking of the dust from one's feet, the wonder is not that the Church split, but that it did not do so until 1861. In that year of secession, the Old Side General Assembly, declaring its obligation "to strengthen, uphold, and encourage the Federal Government," made inevitable the separation of the southern presbyteries. On December 4, 1861, 47 presbyteries banded together to form the General Assembly of the Confederate States of America. Earlier in 1857, 21 presbyteries had withdrawn from the New Side General Assembly to form the United Synod of the Presbyterian Church. Then, in 1864, these two newly created southern groups joined to bring into existence the Presbyterian Church in the United States (Presbyterian, U.S.).

Although showing a steady progress, the southern Presbyterians remained roughly one-fourth the size of the reunited northern group: the Presbyterian Church, U.S.A.

While the U.S. Church grew from 82,014 members in 1870 to 678,206 in 1950, the U.S.A. Church expanded, in the same period, from 446,561 to 2,318,615 (see Fig. 77). The strength of the Presbyterian Church, U.S. has remained largely in those states in which it began (see Fig. 79), unlike that of the Southern Baptist Convention, which moved with vigor both to the west and to the north (cf. Fig. 49). Discussions of merger between the U.S. and the U.S.A. churches were carried on for eighty years, with high hopes of fulfillment being raised in the 1950's. On the presbytery level, however, the southern branch defeated the proposal for merger. Though the vote was almost equally divided (42 presbyteries for merger; 43 against), approval by a minimum of three-fourths of the presbyteries was required before any plan of union could be adopted.

The group which did successfully merge with the Presbyterian Church, U.S.A. was a Scottish communion: the United Presbyterian Church of North America. This latter body had come into existence in 1858, gathering the larger sections of two groups related to the Scottish Secession and Covenanter movements. Although the immediate result of this 1858 union was more rather than fewer Presbyterian bodies, the strength of most of the continuing smaller bodies was permanently sapped. In 1865 there were nearly 68,000 United Presbyterians; by the turn of the century, about 100,000; and in 1950 the membership figure was 213,810. After exactly a full century of corporate existence, the United Church added its nearly 250,000 members to the 3 million members of the Presbyterian Church, U.S.A. to form in 1958 the new fellowship: The United Presbyterian Church in the U.S.A. (see Fig. 80).

Since 1869 the main branch of the Presbyterian family tree has been the Presbyterian Church, U.S.A. First through the College of New Jersey (established in 1746 and renamed Princeton University in 1896) and later through

realms of theology and social action, charges of heresy, modernism, reaction, and obscurantism crackled in the electrified air. As in other denominations, the right of the Church and its leaders to make judgments about unions and working conditions, housing and public health, equity and race relations was bitterly contested; but by 1936 a Department of Social Education and Action had won its place in the ecclesiastical structure. In the area of theology, heresy trials, receiving a full press, plunged the

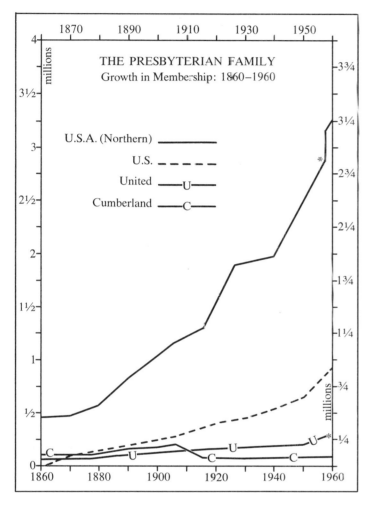

Figure 77

*The U.S.A. and United branches merged in 1958.

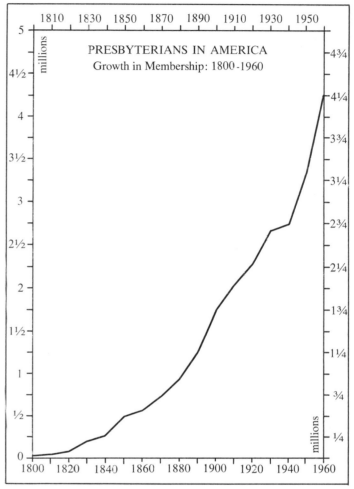

Figure 78

Membership totals include all groups cited in Figure 77.

Princeton Seminary (established 1912) as well, this Church sent out scores of graduates who became leaders, not only in religious circles, but in the educational and political affairs of the young republic. In New York, Pennsylvania, Delaware, Kentucky, and California, schools operated today by the states had their beginning under Presbyterian auspices. And while many of the schools founded prior to the Civil War have either moved away from official affiliation with the Presbyterian Church, U.S.A., or else have ceased to exist, there are currently some 40 institutions of higher learning connected with the denomination.

In the closing years of the nineteenth century and continuing into the twentieth, the Church was beset with struggles more ideological than organizational. In the

denomination into turmoil. While the specter of a great conservative–liberal split haunted the Church for decades, the separation which did come in 1937 proved to be neither so large nor so serious. The Orthodox Presbyterian Church and the Bible Presbyterian Church, both plucked from the right wing, together amounted in 1960 to less than 1% of the membership of the parent body.

The newly formed United Presbyterian Church in the U.S.A. gave every indication of carrying on in an even more effective way the consistent witness of its two constituent bodies. And together with the southern Church, America's Presbyterians maintain an institution which is "a rock immovable in her principles amid surrounding change, a river pouring a widening and deepening tide

THE PRESBYTERIAN CHURCH, U.S.

⎯⎯⎯⎯ Synod boundaries   ⎯⎯⎯ Presbytery boundaries   ⎯ ⎯ ⎯ State lines not Presbytery boundaries

0 ⎯⎯⎯⎯⎯ 200 MILES

Figure 79

of saving influences for the healing of our own and other lands" (Baird, viii; see Fig. 78).

SOURCES. Maurice W. Armstrong, *et al.* (eds.), *The Presbyterian Enterprise: Sources of American Presbyterian History* (Philadelphia, 1956). Samuel J. Baird, *A Collection of the Acts, Deliverances, and Testimonies of the Supreme Indicatory of the Presbyterian Church* (Philadelphia, 1856). Charles A. Briggs, *American Presbyterianism. Its Origin and Early History* (New York, 1885). C. M. Drury, *Presbyterian Panorama* [story of home missions] (Philadelphia, 1952). Robert V. Foster, *A Sketch of the History of the Cumberland Presbyterian Church* (American Church History Series, XI) (New York, 1894). Thomas C. Johnson, *History of the Southern Presbyterian Church* (American Church History Series, XI) (New York, 1894). Walter Bronlow Posey, *The Presbyterian Church in the Old Southwest 1778-1838* (Richmond, 1952). *Presbyterian Reunion: A Memorial Volume 1837-1871* (New York, 1870). James Brown Scouller, *History of the United Presbyterian Church of North America* (American Church History Series, XI) (New York, 1894). Robert E. Thompson, *A History of the Presbyterian Churches in the United States* (American Church History Series, VI) (New York, 1905). William Warren Sweet, *Religion on the American Frontier: The Presbyterians 1783-1840*, Vol. II (New York, 1936). Herman C. Weber, *Presbyterian Statistics Through One Hundred Years 1826-1926* [invaluable] (n. p., 1927). And see the bibliography by Thomas H. Spence, Jr., in *Religion in Life* XXV:4.

10. QUAKERS

Creedal ambiguity, as was noted in the discussion of the Disciples (Part II, 4), is no guarantee against ecclesiastical separation. Indeed, there appears to be no guarantee; for of all the colonial religious bodies, that buffeted band of Quakers, busy quarreling with all the world, seemed least likely to have time to quarrel with one another. Yet the early eruption of the Keithian schism (see above, p. 25) served as a woeful harbinger of darker days ahead. Howard Brinton's "third period" of Quaker history, 1800-1900, is, he observes sadly, a period of "conflict and decline" (p. 175).

Revivalism and all the furniture of a vigorous evangelistic religion had, in one denomination after another, raised points of sore contention. New Light/Old Light, New Side/Old Side, enthusiasm/formalism, uncouth/unconverted—by these and other names, men censured or withdrew fellowship from their denominational colleagues. Among the Friends the context of argument differed while the themes echoed a familiar ring. How "evangelical" was Quakerism to become? how dependent upon human contrivance and "studied preaching"? how dependent upon God and His Grace? To these questions, which were not new, the nineteenth-century Quaker added others: What is my authority—Scripture, "the unity of the meeting," the convincement of the Inner Light? Whence is my salvation—the incarnation, the crucifixion, the indwelling Christ? What is my duty—sobriety, exhortation, passivity?

To these queries, Elias Hicks (1748-1830) had over a

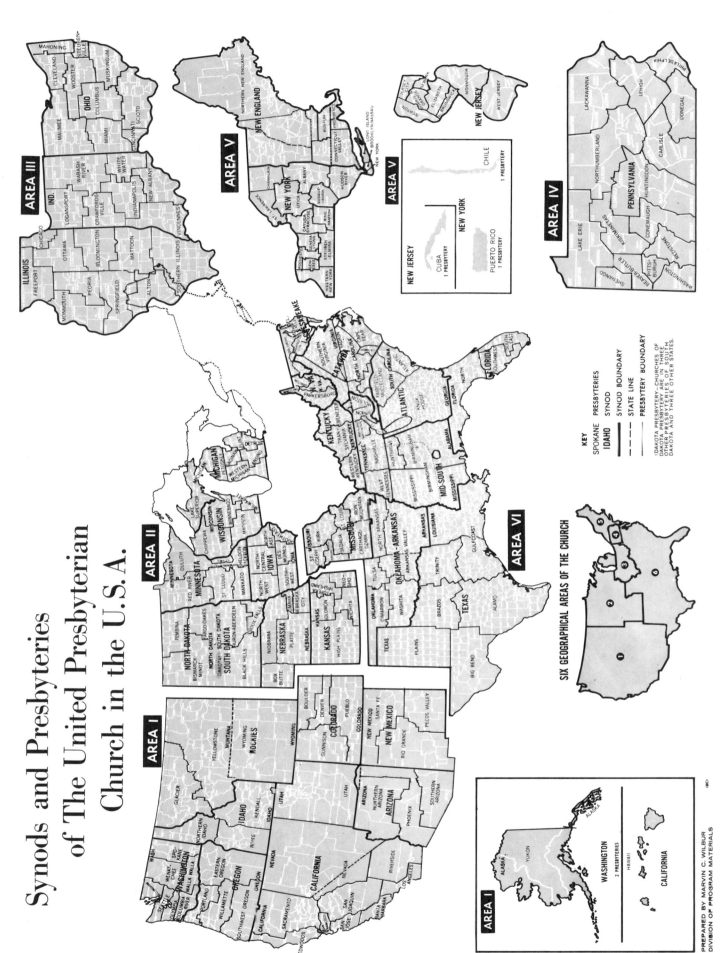

Synods and Presbyteries
of The United Presbyterian
Church in the U.S.A.

SIX GEOGRAPHICAL AREAS OF THE CHURCH

KEY

SPOKANE — PRESBYTERIES
IDAHO — SYNOD
— SYNOD BOUNDARY
— STATE LINE
— PRESBYTERY BOUNDARY

¹DAKOTA PRESBYTERY—CHURCHES OF
DAKOTA PRESBYTERY ARE IN THREE
OTHER PRESBYTERIES OF SOUTH
DAKOTA AND THREE OTHER STATES.

PREPARED BY MARVIN C. WILBUR
DIVISION OF PROGRAM MATERIALS

Figure 80

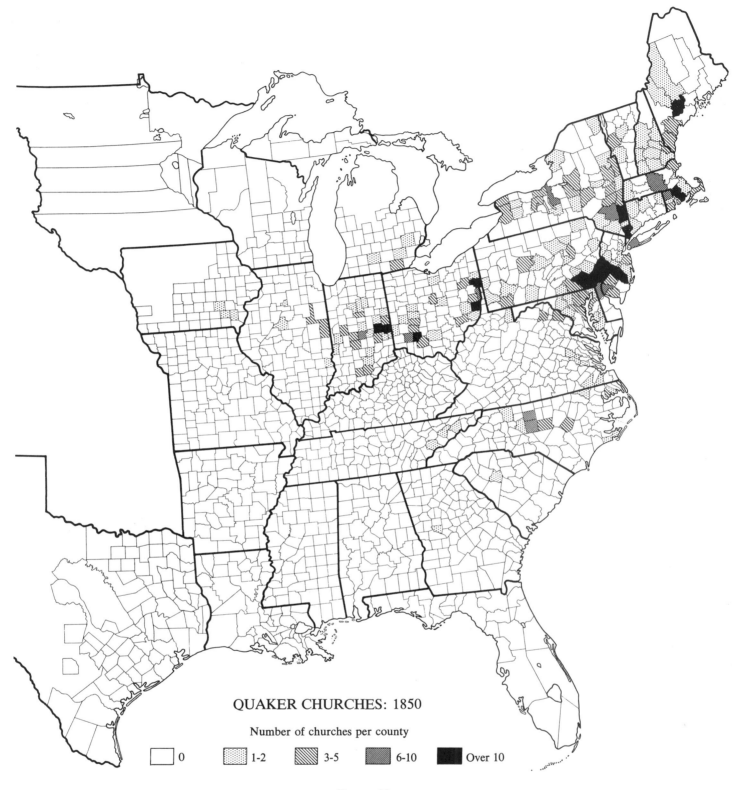

QUAKER CHURCHES: 1850

Number of churches per county

☐ 0   ▦ 1-2   ▨ 3-5   ▧ 6-10   ■ Over 10

Figure 81

period of many years been offering his answers. Born on Long Island, New York, Hicks had grown up in a Quaker family, had accepted with "dread and fear" the "heavenly call" to a public ministry, and had been heard with appreciation and respect by large numbers of America's Quakers. While making no sharp, self-conscious departure from traditional doctrine, Hicks gradually assumed a distinct position. History, revelation, education, and tradition grew dim in the shadow of the all-sufficient Inner

Light. Once a man possesses and is possessed by

this gift of Grace, this Light, there is no necessity for us to be careful about what we believe and what we won't believe; because nothing can give us true belief but this Light . . . You need not trouble yourselves to recommend to your friends what they must believe, that they must believe this or that—it is all nonsense; because a man . . . cannot believe anything but what the divine Light gives him an evidence of, and this he must believe, and he cannot resist it (Jones, I, 447).

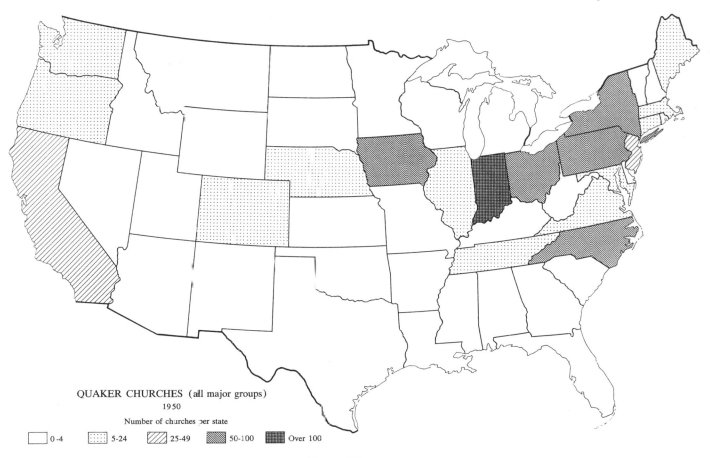

QUAKER CHURCHES (all major groups)
1950

Number of churches per state

☐ 0-4   ⣿ 5-24   ▨ 25-49   ▨ 50-100   ▦ Over 100

Figure 82

Unmerited, divine, irresistible grace; antimission, anti-effort, antievangelical Church.

While criticism was expressed and discomfort felt as early as 1808, the Quaker community at large took no step until in 1822 ten elders of Philadelphia gave Hicks formal notification of disagreement: "We feel it a duty to declare that we cannot have religious unity with thy conduct nor with the doctrines thou art charged with promulgating" (Jones, I, 462). Since Hicks did not stand alone, however, there was no question of private admonition or even of public trial. The question, rather, was which party, "Hicksite" or "Orthodox," spoke for Quakerism in America. For the next five years leaders wrangled and positions hardened. Then at the Philadelphia Yearly Meeting in 1827, the inevitable occurred: those sympathetic to the position of Elias Hicks resolved to make "a quiet retreat from this scene of confusion," professing that they had no new system of discipline to impose nor any "new gospel to preach; nor any other foundation to lay than that already laid . . . 'Christ within, the hope of glory.'" The die was cast and, as Rufus Jones observes, "once the schism-habit got launched it was extremely difficult to stop it or to limit it." Other Yearly Meetings, where the issue of loyalty to doctrine versus obedience to the Inner Light was clearly drawn, divided in turn so that by the end of the next year the Quaker community was widely and permanently rent.

The division between the two parties varied markedly from one Meeting to another. In the Baltimore Yearly Meeting, about four-fifths of the membership became Hicksite, while in the newly formed (1821) Indiana Yearly Meeting, the preponderance of Friends remained Orthodox. In the Yearly Meetings of New England, North Carolina, and Virginia, no major separation occurred. New York was heavily Hicksite, one report showing 12,532 members for the latter as opposed to less than half that number (5,913) for the Orthodox. In Ohio the split was approximately even. In the Philadelphia Meeting, where the schism began, the numerical advantage lay with the Hicksites, even though a majority of ministers and elders chose the Orthodox party. Totals may only be guessed at: there were perhaps 20,000 to 25,000 Hicksites by 1830 with at least twice that number in the opposing group. The greater growth has belonged to the Orthodox, though the progress of neither group has been phenomenal. At the end of the nineteenth century there were 21,992 Hicksites; a decline in the first half of the twentieth century appeared to have been arrested by 1950.

While the strength of the Hicksites remained largely in the East (particularly New York, New Jersey, Pennsylvania, and Maryland), the Orthodox had by 1850 moved in surprising strength across the Alleghenies into the West (particularly Ohio and Indiana; see Fig. 81). In addition to the usual causes provoking a westward move, Quakers were motivated by the desire to escape the compromises and calumnies involved where slavery was condoned. Often entire Meetings would agree that the Spirit of God was leading them to the West. By 1843 more than half of the Orthodox strength was across the mountains. The following estimate has been made of Yearly Meeting membership of the Orthodox for that year: Philadelphia, 8,686; New York, 11,000; New England, 10,000; Baltimore, 800; Virginia, 500; North Carolina, 4,500; Ohio, 18,000; and Indiana, 30,000 (Jones, I, 434). In 1857 the Western Yearly

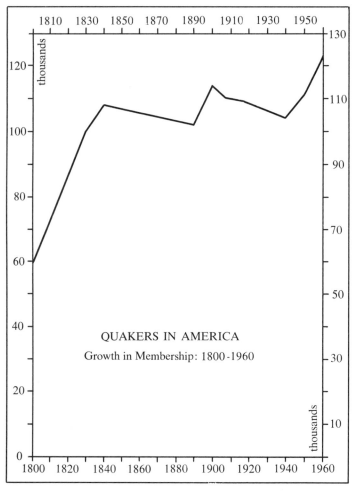

Figure 83

The principal meetings of the Quaker family are included.

Meeting, comprising parts of Indiana and eastern Illinois, was formed; Iowa had its Yearly Meeting by 1863; Kansas, by 1872. By the end of the century, there were similar Meetings both in Oregon (1893) and California (1895).

Before the middle of the nineteenth century, the Orthodox branch of the Quaker family was once again torn asunder, this time as a result of disputes between John Wilbur (1774-1856) and Joseph John Gurney (1788-1847). The issues were not dissimilar to those which had already brought about the earlier separation, but now, of course, they were debated only by the Orthodox. The question, in brief, was this: How orthodox are the Orthodox? Is their doctrine really pure? their reliance upon Scripture genuinely complete? their acceptance of Christ as Savior wholly uncompromised? Gurney (of Norwich, England)

pushed orthodoxy even further in the direction of biblical authority and doctrinal purity, rejecting mysticism and carefully limiting the scope of the Inner Light. With equal sincerity, Wilbur (of Hopkinton, Rhode Island) defended the Inner Light as the essence of the Quaker position, arguing that Gurney's attachment to the letter left insufficient room for the Spirit. "The most full and literally sound acknowledgment of faith in the blood and sacrifice of Jesus Christ, our blessed Redeemer, may be still in the oldness of the letter without the quickening of the inward living Power" (Jones, I, 512). When Gurney came to America in 1837, his popularity and success were phenomenal. Wilbur was heard but not heeded, and in 1845 the New England Yearly Meeting, long since persuaded by Gurney's eloquence and wit, forced Wilbur and his followers into separation. Out of a Meeting of around 7,000 members, approximately 500 joined in Wilbur's withdrawal. But, as in the case of the Hicksite disturbance, the shock waves reached other Meetings, particularly those in Philadelphia and Ohio. The latter divided in 1854, with the larger number following Wilbur. By the desperate expedient of cutting off their official correspondence with (and thereby recognition of) other Yearly Meetings, the Philadelphia group avoided a major schism. For by this means it was possible to avoid taking sides in the far-flung battles. Separations farther west occurred in 1877, and by 1890 the followers of John Wilbur had 52 churches and over 4,000 members. But the movement was too small to keep afloat in the main stream of cultural change, and by mid-twentieth century, it had shrunk to less than one-half of its 1890 size.

Growth for all of Quakerism was in the nineteenth century a thorny and painful problem. The schisms, of course, weakened and discouraged. Discipline and enforced separation from the world not only proved too heavy a yoke for many to bear, but also isolated the Church from its larger community. There was, moreover, still enough of the element of quietism to prevent the sect's wholehearted embrace of evangelical methods for expansion and advance. In 1850 there were 726 Quaker churches in America, but only 692 twenty years later. Some recovery had been made by the end of the century, however, as the total number of churches (Orthodox, Hicksite, and Wilburite) exceeded 1,000. In the first six decades of the twentieth century, there was generally some decline in the number of churches for all major Quaker groups, while the total membership showed slight gain (see Figs. 82 and 83).

The impressive quality of twentieth-century Quakerism lies not in its statistical profile, but in its dogged and often heroic social witness. The American Friend's Service Committee has, for its ministry during two world wars, won the gratitude and admiration of the world, of which the Nobel Peace Prize, awarded in 1947, was a fitting token. Thousands of non-Quakers, attracted by a humanitarianism that countenanced no artificial restriction, have in sympathy joined the Wider Quaker Fellowship or have joined in the enterprising, sensitive labors of Quaker love. The Inner Light, wrote Rufus Jones, "is an experience of God revealed in the soul of man." The modern Friend is a bearer of and a witness to that Light.

SOURCES.   Howard Brinton, *Friends for 300 Years* (New York, 1952). W. W. Comfort, *Quakers in the Modern World* (New York, 1949). Bliss Forbush, *Elias Hicks: Quaker Liberal* (New York, 1956). Rufus Jones, *The Later Periods of Quakerism*, 2 vols. (London, 1921). Francis B. Lee, *New Jersey as a Colony and as a State*, Vol. III (New York, 1902). Ezra Michener, *A Retrospect of Early Quakerism; Being extracts from the records of Philadelphia Yearly Meeting* [shows relative location of all Quarterly Meetings] (Philadelphia, 1860). Allen C. and Richard H. Thomas, *History of the Society of Friends in America* (American Church History Series, XII) (New York, 1894). Frederick B. Tolles, *Quakers and the Atlantic Community* (New York, 1960). Stephen B. Weeks, *Southern Quakers and Slavery* [includes map of Quaker communities in Maryland, Virginia, the Carolinas, Georgia and Tennessee] (Baltimore, 1896).

11. REFORMED

Dutch Reformed. While favored with an early, endowed beginning in the colonial period, the Dutch Reformed, as was noted in Part I, did not take great numerical strides before 1800. Slow growth continued to be the rule in succeeding years. Unable to break the bonds of either ethnic or geographic provincialism, the Church suffered the further hazard of schism. Although English began to be used in New York City in 1763, contention within the churches regarding the general displacement of the Dutch by the English language continued well into the nineteenth century. And though there were nearly 300 Dutch Reformed churches in America in 1850, nine-tenths of them were in only 2 states: New York and New Jersey (see Fig. 84).

The nineteenth century held many promises of church unions or cooperative associations. Sharing the basic theological orientation of others in the "Reformed tradition," the Dutch explored, as early as 1743, the possibility of union with the Presbyterians and the German Reformed. These efforts, renewed shortly after the Revolution, met with no success. Around 1820, the Dutch Reformed and the Associate Reformed were in the final stages of merger negotiations before their efforts collapsed. In 1822 and more strenuously in the 1870's, leaders in the several Reformed bodies sought union, as they were to do once more in 1886. Apart from a degree of cooperation in missions, however, there was little to show for decades of conscientious effort. On the contrary, while the hope of union was being pursued, the reality of schism was catching up.

On October 22, 1822, five ministers withdrew on doctrinal grounds from the Dutch Reformed communion. For the next generation, this disaffected group (the "True Dutch Reformed Church") increased very slowly; it might possibly have expired, had it not been for a separation in Holland in 1835 of a group protesting against certain practices and beliefs of the State Church. Immigrants from this separated group set up the Christian Reformed Church in 1857, which within a generation provided refuge for the descendants of the 1822 American schism. When, early in the 1880's, the Dutch Reformed refused to deny the Church's fellowship to members of any secret fraternal society, another separation occurred, adding once more to the strength of the Christian Reformed. Beginning in 1857 with only 3 churches in Michigan, the new group quickly spread throughout the state and westward into Wisconsin and the Dakotas. By 1890 there were over 100 churches and 12,470 members, of whom more than one-half were in Michigan. Employing an extensive system of Christian elementary schools, the Christian Reformed Church ably propagated its doctrine and steadily added to its fellowship. Indeed, by 1960 it had overtaken the older body, having attained a membership of over 250,000 (see Fig. 88).

Despite all the debilitating difficulties, the Dutch Reformed managed to do more than settle for the status quo. With 137 churches at the beginning of the nineteenth century, this denomination reorganized itself into 2 Particular Synods: New York (having the Classes of New York, Bergen, New Brunswick, Poughkeepsie, and Paramus) and Albany (having the Classes of Ulster, Albany, Rensselaer, and Montgomery). By 1830 there were 194 churches, much of this increase being attributed to the greater "support given to the College and Theological Seminary at New Brunswick" (*Quarterly Register,* III, 225). A mission society, organized in 1822, sent out as many of the seminary's graduates as could be recruited to minister to the pastorless churches (of which there were 33 in 1830) or to open up new territory. In the 1830's the operations of this society were gradually assumed by a Board of Missions which directed both the domestic and foreign program of the Church. A church was formed in Fairview, Illinois, in 1837 and within five years the number of congregations in the West was sufficient to organize the Classes of Illinois and of Michigan. Due in part to political pressures on the state Church, immigration from Holland accelerated after 1845, making possible more rapid expansion of the Dutch Reformed in America. From 1850 to 1870, the churches increased from fewer than 300 to nearly 500, many of the new congregations being established in the midwest. Even as late as 1950, however, less than one-half of the states had a Dutch Reformed church within their borders (see Fig. 85).

In addition to Rutgers (see above, p. 28), the denomination in 1866 obtained a charter for Hope College in Holland, Michigan; three years later a seminary was added there. About the same time (1864), Rutgers became independent of the control of its founding church, though it maintained an affiliation until 1920. In 1945 this colonial school officially became the State University of New Jersey.

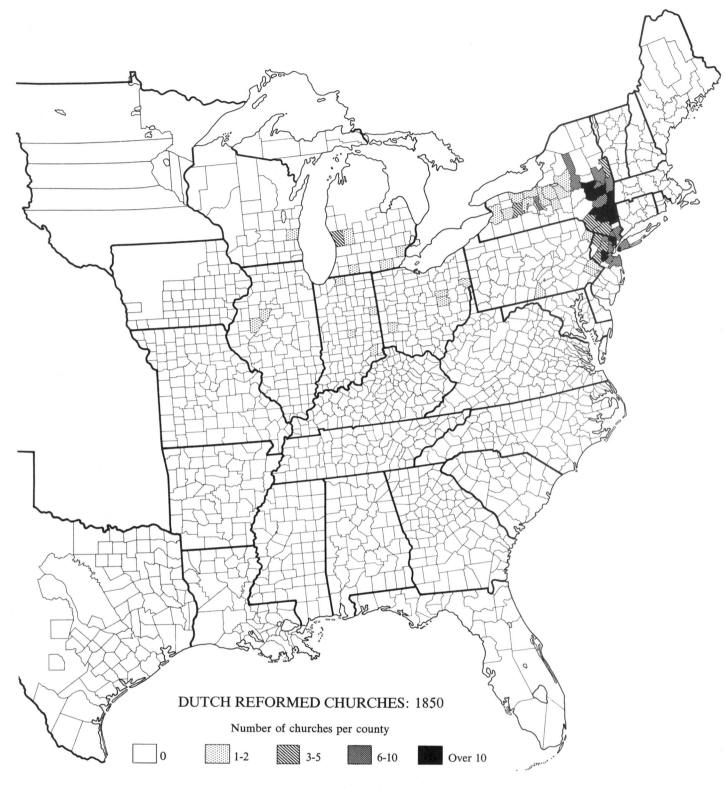

DUTCH REFORMED CHURCHES: 1850

Number of churches per county

☐ 0   ▦ 1-2   ▨ 3-5   ▨ 6-10   ■ Over 10

Figure 84

A seminary founded in 1784 in New York, which later related itself to Rutgers, remained in the control of the Church. Together with the Presbyterians and Congregationalists, the Dutch participated in the organization of Union College in Schenectady in 1795. And in 1916 the Baptists sold Central College in Pella, Iowa, to this Reformed body. The ecumenicity in these latter instances reflects the proper character of the Reformed Church in America (the name adopted in 1867) which, while it found

many doors closed in its search for a way out of its ethnic limitations, has not ceased to open those that would yield. A charter member of the Federal Council of Churches (1908) and of its successor, the National Council (1950), the Reformed Church in America has discharged soberly and honorably its ministry to America.

German Reformed. At the time of the first synod of the German Reformed Church, held at Lancaster (Pennsyl-

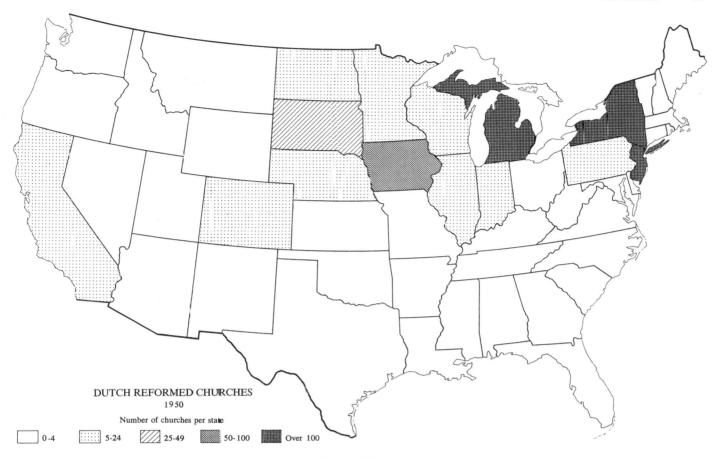

DUTCH REFORMED CHURCHES
1950

Number of churches per state

0-4   5-24   25-49   50-100   Over 100

Figure 85

vania) in April, 1793, there were about 15,000 members and 178 churches in that communion. Pennsylvania was the center of strength, of course, but churches were to be found northward to New York and southward to Virginia. A generation later, the line extended from Nova Scotia to South Carolina. From the point of view of ministerial supply, the line extended too far. Beset by a critical shortage of preachers, the problem of expansion for the German Reformed, as for the Dutch, was aggravated by the difficulties of language. The language situation kept the New York congregations from aligning with the Dutch, who could provide ministerial services but not in German; on the other hand, lack of German-speaking clergy gradually forced the Lutheran-Reformed settlement at Waldoborough, Maine, into the hands of the Congregationalists, who could and did provide services in English to the younger generation. And, as noted above (p. 28f.), the barrier of language prevented any widespread proselyting, propagandizing activities.

The growth, therefore, of the German Reformed continued in the nineteenth century, as it had been in the eighteenth, to be chiefly the function of natural increase and immigration. While churches were established in Kentucky, Tennessee, and Ohio, seldom were these western congregations able to maintain, nor were they interested in maintaining, a close connection with the "Eastern" Synod. The frontier communities particularly lacked the ministerial leadership that might have made coordinated

mission activities possible. The Reformed Church, moreover, was frequently a union church, as the newly settled German immigrants, Lutheran or Reformed, would jointly build and dedicate a house of worship. Settlement tended to be by national origin rather than by religious doctrine: in Maryland, for example, the counties which in 1850 had German Reformed churches were exactly the same ones that had Lutheran churches (Allegany), Baltimore, Carroll, Frederick, and Washington; compare Figs. 84 and 86). Appropriately, there were in the first quarter of the nineteenth century serious negotiations aimed at union of the Lutherans and German Reformed in America, particularly after these two groups were by law united in Prussia in 1817. After several years of exploratory conversations, however, this effort was dropped.

The ministerial problem was acute, not only because of a shortage of numbers, but also because of a deficiency in quality. Education, in the first quarter of the nineteenth century, was admittedly inadequate. A plan for a seminary, proposed to the Synod of 1820, was after much difficulty put into operation in 1825 with the opening of the Theological Seminary of the Reformed Church in Carlisle, Pennsylvania. Removed to York in 1829, then to Mercersburg in 1837, this first seminary, particularly under the influence of John Williamson Nevin and Philip Schaff, went far toward solving the problem of inadequate preparation, even while it intensified problems of theological diversity. In 1871 the seminary once more moved, this

GERMAN REFORMED CHURCHES: 1850

Number of churches per county

0   1-2   3-5   6-10   Over 10

Figure 86

time to Lancaster, Pennsylvania.

The Reformed Church in the United States (the "German" having been dropped from the title in 1869) found new strength after the Civil War as its eastern and western synods joined for reunited effort. In 1824 the Classis of Ohio had resolved itself into the "Evangelical Reformed Synod of Ohio" in protest against the restrictive ordination policy of the Pennsylvania group. Competing for the droves of Germans moving into the interior, this "Western Synod" struggled for stability along the sect-infested, revival-burdened frontier. By mid-century, a seminary and a college (Heidelberg) had been successfully launched in Ohio. Relations between the two sections of the Reformed Church were maintained all through these years, but only the formation of a General Synod in 1863 brought organizational integrity back to the German Reformed. Thus revived, the Church by 1880 exceeded 150,000 in membership.

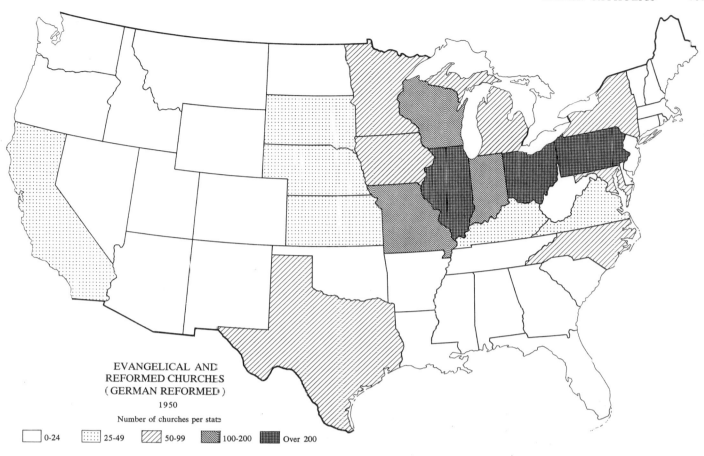

EVANGELICAL AND
REFORMED CHURCHES
(GERMAN REFORMED)
1950
Number of churches per state

| | 0-24 | | 25-49 | | 50-99 | | 100-200 | | Over 200 |

Figure 87

In the twentieth century this Church not only continued its quiet growth but also proved itself remarkably tolerant in the matter of union with other bodies. In 1924, remnants of the old Hungarian Reformed Church were taken in, and a decade later the German Reformed concluded a merger with the Evangelical Synod of North America. The latter body, with a membership of over 250,000 at the time of union, was the American counterpart of the Prussian-pressured combination of Lutheran and Reformed churches. While the theological heritage of the Evangelical Synod was drawn largely from Luther, and that of the German Reformed chiefly from Calvin or Zwingli, yet the two bodies, sharing a common ethnic heritage, found it possible to unite in mutual trust. The new organization, the Evangelical and Reformed Church, had in concert over 600,000 members and nearly 3,000 churches (see Figs. 87 and 89).

As early as 1942, only in the eighth year of its denominational life, the Evangelical and Reformed Church began exploring merger possibilities with the Congregational Christian Churches (see above, Part II, 3). A 1947 decision to complete the union, frustrated for a time by legal battles, was executed in June, 1957. The resulting ecclesiastical body took as its name the United Church of Christ; and, if the explicit intent of this comprehensive title finds fulfillment, then the German Reformed fellowship, which began with the Palatinate refugees in 1708, has not yet finished its ecumenical mission in America.

SOURCES. Henry Beets, *The Christian Reformed Church* (Grand Rapids, 1946). E. T. Corwin, *History of the Reformed Church, Dutch* (American Church History Series, VIII) (New York, 1895); ———, *A Manual of the Reformed Church in America* (New York [4th ed.], 1902). David D. Demarest, *History and Characteristics of the Reformed Protestant Dutch Church* (New York, 1856). Joseph H. Dubbs, *History of the Reformed Church, German* (American Church History Series, VIII) (New York, 1895). David Dunn, "The Evangelical and Reformed Church," in Vergilius Ferm (ed.), *The American Church of the Protestant Heritage* (New York, 1953); David Dunn *et al.*, *A History of the Evangelical & Reformed Church* (Philadelphia, 1961). Hugh Hastings (ed.), *Ecclesiastical Records. State of New York*, 7 vols. (Albany, 1901-1916). Milton J. Hoffman, "The Reformed Church in America," in Vergilius Ferm (ed.), *The American Church of the Protestant Heritage* (New York, 1953). *The Quarterly Register and Journal of the American Education Society* (Andover, 1829 ff.; title and place of publication vary).

12. ROMAN CATHOLICS

For most of America's religious bodies, the nineteenth century was a time for cutting new trails across a virgin land, for erecting a chapel, mission or church where none had been before. Although Roman Catholicism was likewise engaged in this onward march of Christian soldiers, the West was for this Church neither so new nor so empty. The Mississippi Valley constituted a great basin of French Catholicism, while Spanish Catholicism had long since

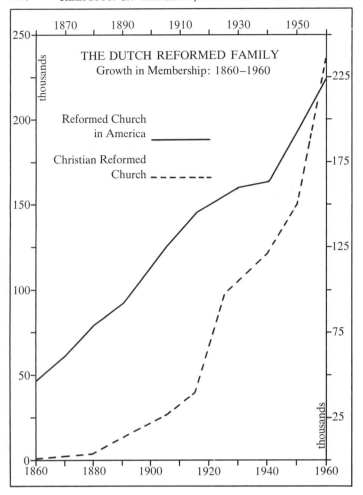

Figure 88

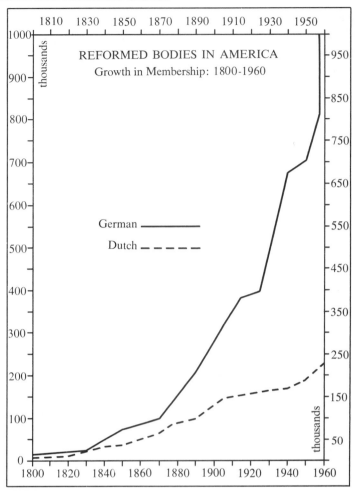

Figure 89

Dutch Reformed membership in this graph does **not** include the Christian Reformed Church (see Fig. 88); German Reformed membership **does** include the 1934 merger with the Evangelical Synod of North America and the 1957 merger with the Congregational Christian Church.

secured several positions in the Southwest and the far West (see above, p. 29 and Fig. 116). Roman Catholics, therefore, were in a sense just filling in the gaps between the Atlantic and Pacific shores.

It would be a mistake, however, to regard the status of Catholicism in the interior as being very advanced or very stable in 1800. Missionaries from the eastern seaboard were as likely to be disheartened as they were to be encouraged by the kind of religious practices they found among the Indians, the traders, the soldiers, and scattered settlers. And many a bishop of "all outdoors" found himself confronted with an impossible, thankless task, often lacking the comfort even of knowing that Rome was sensitive to the enormity of his difficulties. The first "Bishop of Louisiana and the Two Floridas," Cuban-born Luís Peñalver wrote in 1795 that those in his charge "do not listen to, or if they do, they disregard, all exhortations to maintain in its orthodoxy the Catholic faith, and to preserve the innocence of life." Of the "eleven thousand souls composing this parish, hardly three to four hundred comply with the precept of partaking at least once a year of the Lord's supper" (Ellis, *Documents*, 182). Protestant missionaries twenty years later found the area scarcely improved: Bishop DuBourg, they noted, "laments the degraded state of [the] church in Louisiana, and mourns over the depravity and wickedness of the place in which he re-

sides . . ." (Schermerhorn and Mills, 34 f.). And, around the beginning of the nineteenth century, Father John Dilhet wrote from Michigan Territory:

I had to exhort and instruct these people, make them tractable and docile to the voice of the priest, destroy the spirit of faction, reform their morals, root out scandals such as drunkenness, the selling of strong drink to the Indians, restrain their love for amusement, carousing and dancing which was carried on to a great excess . . . (Nuesse, 125).

Under circumstances such as these, it is moot whether Roman Catholicism had a real "head start" in the settlement of the West. Yet, however stunted its growth might in some particular place appear to be, the spiritual roots went deep, and the day of flowering was not a great way off. The progress of Catholicism during the nineteenth century was phenomenal; nonetheless, it was not a progress unaccompanied by pain.

Three broad areas of difficulty were encountered by the Roman Catholic Church in the rising American republic. The first area, already hinted at above, involved the enormous internal diversity—cultural, national, and linguistic—which created potential, if not actual, faction or separation within the Church. Like the Lutherans and the Reformed, but to a far greater degree, the Catholics were obliged first to settle sharp differences and soothe impassioned jealousies within their own communion. In 1818 Archbishop Maréchal of Baltimore, noting that there were fifty-two priests in his diocese, indicated their diverse origins: 14 were French; 12 were American; of the Irish, there were 11; Belgians, 7; English, 4; Germans, 3; Italians, 1. And this was years before the intensive immigration had really begun! The complexity would only increase.

Even in this comparatively early time, however, tension was already keen between the French and the Irish. The Baltimore prelate, a Frenchman, could freely praise the priests of all other origins, but the Irish drew his censure. Difficulties in church order and discipline in various parts of his diocese the archbishop attributed to "those priests from Ireland who were given over to drunkenness or ambition, together with their accomplices, whom they win over to their side by means of innumerable artifices." These Irish had even gone so far as to try to persuade their countrymen "that the Bishops of Boston, Bardstown, and myself intended secretly to establish a French hierarchy in these provinces and to expel the Irish priests" (Ellis, *Documents*, 217). And when an Irish congregation was obliged to receive as its pastor a French priest, low boiling points were passed. The problem mushroomed as the number of Irish laymen increased without a proportionate increase in Irish clergy; French priests and bishops, fleeing from the excesses of their country's revolution, were in great abundance. Of the 10 bishops in the United States in 1830, "six were either French or French sympathizers, while two were Irish-born, and two were of American birth, but Irish ancestry" (Ellis, *American Catholicism*, 47). On issues where the hierarchy had to make decisions or offer counsel to Rome, there tended to be a French faction versus an Irish faction in the American Church.

A few years later, as the French influence declined and the Hibernian influence expanded, the Irish and the Germans in the East and Middle West were contesting for recognition and authority. Protests lodged in Rome in 1886 indicated a German resentment over alleged inadequacies or discrimination in their treatment by the American hierarchy. In the same decade, Italian immigrants by the thousands began arriving, taxing the facilities of the Church beyond its capacity and raising again the problems of ethnic and linguistic diversity. In a single generation, 1880 to 1910, the increase of Italians in America was almost fiftyfold. One-third million Hungarians had also arrived by 1910; Canadians, Poles, Czechs, and Latin Americans were to be added to a pot kept so full that little melting could occur. Apart from jealousies and frictions brought on in this overwhelming invasion, the law of supply and demand—in its simplest terms—created hazards and shortages aplenty. And when there was no competition, there certainly was waste; in a single community French Catholic, Italian Catholic, Irish Catholic each built his own church, honored his own national saint, and bowed only before his own altar.

A second broad area of difficulty into which and through which the Roman Catholic Church moved was related to the peculiar nature of the American environment. The United States, a freedom-fascinated country without an established church, presented a circumstance so new that adjustment, whether in Rome or in America, came hard.

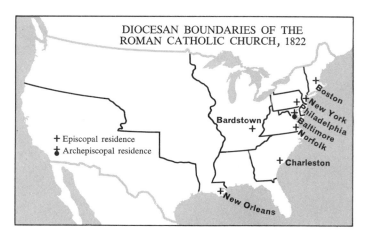

Figure 90

Archbishop Maréchal, with excellent understanding of the situation, wrote in 1818:

. . . the American people pursue with a most ardent love the civil liberty which they enjoy. For the principle of civil liberty is paramount with them, so that absolutely all the magistrates, from the highest to the lowest, are elected by popular vote . . . Likewise all the Protestant sects, who constitute the greater part of the people, are governed by these same principles, and as a result they elect and dismiss their pastors at will. Catholics in turn, living in their midst, are evidently exposed to the danger of admitting the same principles of ecclesiastical government (Ellis, *Documents*, 219).

Not only did some Catholic congregations aspire, like their neighbors, to choose or reject a pastor, but they also proposed to hold the title to the property on which the place of worship had been built. This issue of "lay trusteeism," as it was called, arose shortly after the Revolution when in 1786 the trustees of St. Peter's Church, New York City, made the choice of a pastor their own affair. On this occasion, Bishop John Carroll (then "Superior of the Missions" in America), in a letter of remonstrance to the trustees, noted that were their principle of self-determination to be accepted

the unity and catholicity of our Church would be at an end; and it would be formed into distinct and independent societies, nearly in the same manner as the congregational Presbyterians of our neighboring New England States (Ellis, *Documents*, 156).

The very next year, 1787, a group of German Catholics in Philadelphia, with even greater initiative, organized

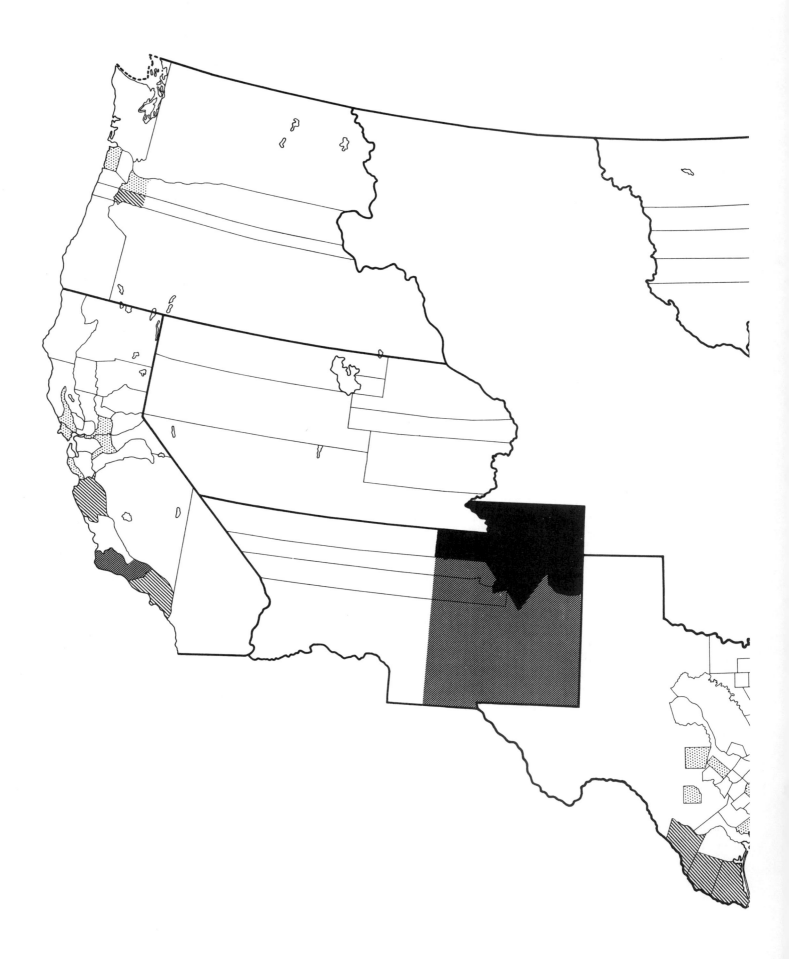

Figure 91

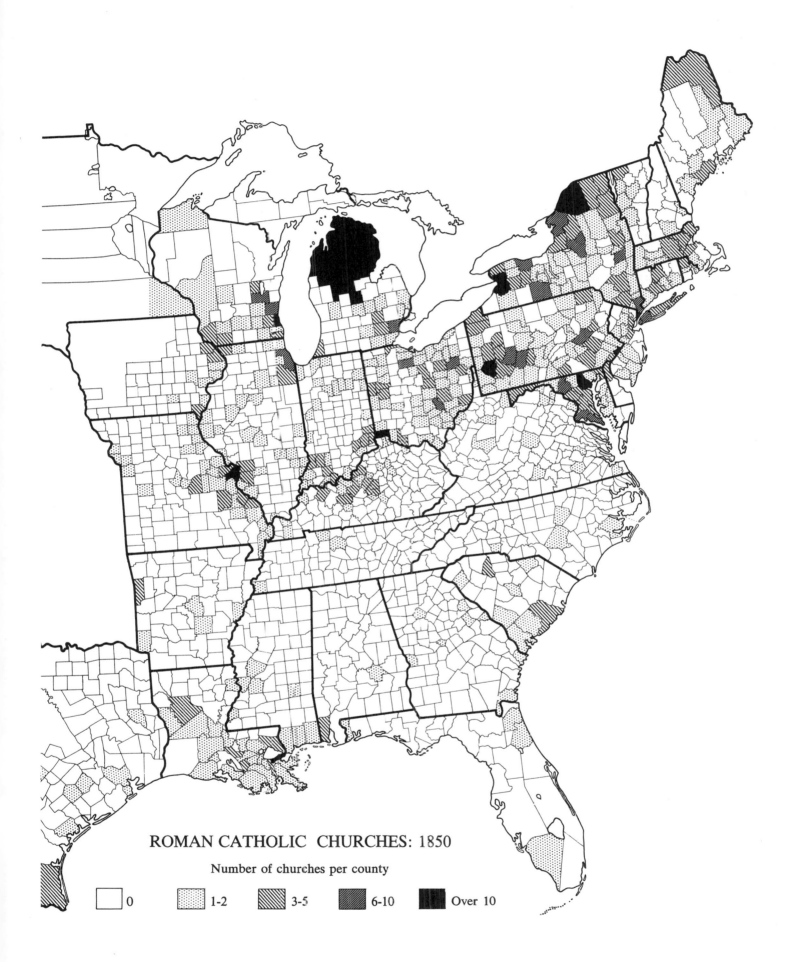

ROMAN CATHOLIC CHURCHES: 1850

Number of churches per county

0   1-2   3-5   6-10   Over 10

Figure 91

a parish, obtained legal incorporation, built a church (Holy Trinity) and in 1789 called their own pastor in defiance of the expressed wish of John Carroll, now America's first bishop. Troubles grew so acute in this instance that Holy Trinity Church was actually schismatic from 1796 to 1802.

The ramifications of the laity's claims were, as Carroll had stated, of great consequence. Was there to be a new ecclesiology for the Roman Catholic Church in America? Was there, indeed, to be a new institution: the American Catholic Church? Many of the hierarchy feared so, and many of the laity acted so. In 1819 the "Board of the Roman Catholic Church and Congregation of Norfolk" declared, with remarkable lack of equivocation, that their archbishop, not being a Virginian (nor, for that matter, an Irishman either), "has no right at all to interfere with these congregations or any of their religious matters, whatever." Further, "the impertinence of the demand of the Right Reverend Archbishop of the Catholic Church of Baltimore" was "a most glaring violation of their civil rights and religious liberties and in direct opposition to the state laws of Virginia . . ." (Ellis, *Documents,* 226 f.). In view of such intemperate language, it is not surprising that schism occurred here, too, as well as in Charleston, New Orleans, and Buffalo. While creating genuine crises in authority, trusteeism probably did its greatest damage by keeping alive ethnic jealousies and by creating suspicions in Rome of the entire American effort.

Trusteeism was, however, symptomatic of the urgent problem of adapting old ecclesiastical forms to a new national environment. To the solution of this problem some of the ablest members of the hierarchy gave their critical attention. The First Provincial Council of Baltimore drafted in 1829 a pastoral letter (probably written by Bishop John England of Charleston) to the laity which set the issue in focus:

As our congregations have in a great measure been hitherto an emigrant population, so has our ministry been to a considerable extent composed of adopted citizens. But the children of the former, and the successors of the latter have for some time past assumed more of our native character, and must necessarily become chiefly, if not altogether national, henceforth (Guilday, *National Pastorals,* 22).

But what was "our native character," and in what sense could the Church or its members become "national"? De Tocqueville noted, in 1835, that Roman Catholicism was by no means insulated from the democratizing tendencies of America, "the most democratic country in the world" (II, 30). Of the flood of Irish Catholic immigrants, this astute Frenchman observed:

These Catholics are faithful to the·observances of their religion; they are fervent and zealous in the belief of their doctrines. Yet they constitute the most republican and the most democratic class in the United States (I, 311).

While Catholicism may predispose the faithful to obedience, he added, it "certainly does not prepare them for inequality."

Could Catholicism prepare the faithful for American democracy, for religious liberty, for a pluralistic society? Men such as the vigorous Bishop John England certainly thought so. In an address before the United States Congress on January 8, 1826, he declared that "no special form of human government for civil concerns has been generally established by divine authority." Which form of government is to be adopted by any society is a question appropriately settled by the people themselves and not by the Church. Regarding the separation of church and state, England stated this understanding of the Constitution:

You [Congress] have no power to interfere with my religious rights; the tribunal of the church has no power to interfere with my civil rights. It is a duty which every good man ought to discharge for his own and for the public benefit, to resist any encroachment upon either (Nuesse, 186 f.).

After England, other leaders in the American Church sought to prepare the faithful for and in their new home: notably, John Joseph Keane (1839-1918), first rector of the Catholic University of America and later Archbishop of Dubuque; John Ireland (1838-1918), Archbishop of St. Paul; and James Cardinal Gibbons (1834-1921), Archbishop of Baltimore and a man of far-reaching influence. To be sure, there were those in the Roman Church who opposed the efforts of England and others, with the result that nineteenth-century Catholicism in America revealed "two fairly discernible schools of thought."

The one, to which men like Gibbons, Ireland, and Keane generally adhered, was inclined to interpret the Church's attitude [in certain social or civil matters] in a broad and somewhat tolerant manner, in the dual hope that this approach would better serve the end of assimilating the thousands of foreign-born Catholics to the spirit and institutions of their American home, and at the same time deprive enemies of the argument frequently used that the Church was un-American. The other group, numbering bishops like Corrigan [of New York], Katzer [of Milwaukee], and McQuaid [of Rochester], took a more strictly legalistic view, were fearful of the germ of philosophical liberalism which they thought they detected in the ranks of the opposition, and were less inclined to show a spirit of accommodation to American ways (Ellis, *James Cardinal Gibbons,* II, 1).

Adherents of both schools of thought were quoted and misquoted abroad. European Catholics, particularly in France, tended to "take sides," and, in so doing, often assumed positions more extreme than their American counterparts. When a French visitor to the United States returned to Europe in 1895 to write that "The Church is tolerant, she is democratic, she is, in fine, American," he may have pleased the republicans in France but to the royalists he could have brought only distress. Fractious partisanship in Europe more than honest exploration in America led in 1899 to the condemnation of "Americanism" by Pope Leo XIII. So far as the American hierarchy was concerned, Leo's apostolic letter, *Testem benevolentiae,* condemned a heresy that no one was quite sure existed. Cardinal Gibbons forthrightly responded to the pontiff that the so-called "Americanism" has "nothing in

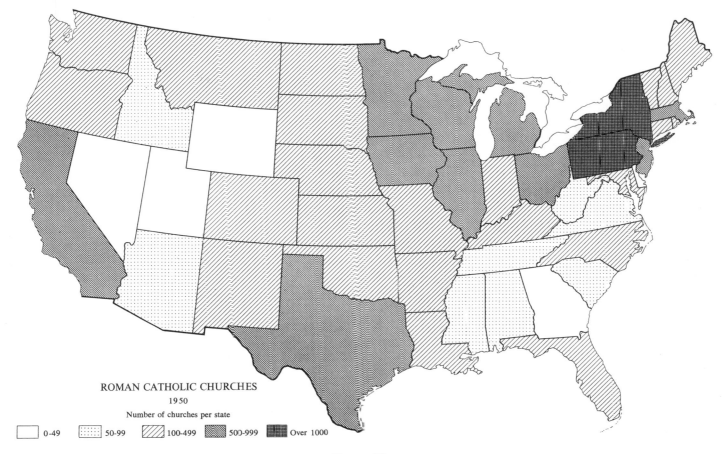

ROMAN CATHOLIC CHURCHES
1950
Number of churches per state

| | 0-49 | | 50-99 | | 100-499 | | 500-999 | | Over 1000 |

Figure 92

common with the views, aspirations, doctrine and conduct of Americans" (Ellis, *Documents*, 553-62).

To a large group of American citizens, it would have come as a great surprise (or more likely, as a clever, sinister plot) that Roman Catholics were charged with being too American. To members of this group, Catholics did not deserve to be considered Americans at all. Here we enter the third broad area of difficulty encountered by Roman Catholicism in nineteenth-century United States: bigotry. Religious persecution, suspicion, hostility, and fear were, of course, part of the daily diet in colonial America (see Part I). Jealousies and animosities, however, were so widely scattered and so mutual that their total effect was partially annulled. As the nineteenth century progressed, sectarian striving among Protestant denominations survived largely in the form of small jokes and blunted barbs, with the more bitter battles being reserved for intra-family feuds. The great clamor about tithes and establishment, heresies and anarchy was heard no more, as the Congregational lion lay down beside the Baptist lamb (or was it the other way round?).

In all of this new charity and American liberty, Roman Catholicism in its numerical infancy seemed likely to share. But as the tremendous flood of Catholic immigrants after 1820 inundated the eastern seaboard, cries of "no popery" more shrill than before rang out from Boston to Savannah. The immigrants were poor, they were "foreign," and there were so many of them. Nativism, latent in any society, found much to deplore and even

more to fear as the immigration grew to fantastic proportions. In 1830 *The Protestant,* an anti-Catholic weekly, was founded with its "sole objects" being "to inculcate Gospel doctrines against Romish corruptions—to maintain the purity and sufficiency of the Holy Scriptures against Monkish Traditions" and to defend all Protestantism "against the creed of Pope Pius IV . . . no article will be admitted into the *Protestant* which does not contribute to these desirable results." Thus was "the Protestant Crusade" born (Billington, 53 *et passim*).

Most Americans are vaguely familiar with the excesses and extravagances of the American Protestant Association (1842), the Know-Nothing party (1854), the Ku Klux Klan (1865; 1915), the American Protective Association (1887) and countless local, ephemeral organizations. It is not a pretty record. While the motives and means of anti-Catholic organizations could and certainly did vary, the effect was to imply at best a second-class citizenship for America's Roman Catholics. An Ursuline convent in Charlestown, Massachusetts, burned to the ground the night of August 11, 1834, while the mob who had fired it stood around admiring their handiwork. Ten years later rioting gangs in Philadelphia burned St. Michael's Church and an adjoining seminary, then moved on that same night to put the torch to St. Augustine's Church. In the supercharged atmosphere of these and other cities on such occasions, plots and counterplots, real or imagined, were rumored or announced; books, tracts, handbills were circulated; passions were unleashed and blood was spilled.

The longevity and complexity of America's anti-Catholicism arises from a maze of related issues: xenophobia in general or of a particularly irritating, agitating, displacing minority; economic grievances concerning labor that was abundant and cheap, or families that were destitute and dependent on charity; education and the establishment of an inclusive public school system; freedom and the authoritarianism of a powerful, historically vulnerable Church; democracy and diplomatic representation to and from the Vatican; the right to political office and the fear of ecclesiastical pressure. Some of the issues were raised in sincerity and good faith; others were not. Some were the manifestation of intelligent concern; others of uncritical reaction or contempt. Together they made the Church's adjustment to the American scene—already a problem of herculean proportion—turbulent and troubled. The suspicion that anti-Catholicism had by the twentieth century been outgrown was noisily, raucously set aside in the 1928 Presidential campaign of Alfred E. Smith. In the campaign of 1960, on the other hand, scurrilous anti-Catholicism was less in evidence. And however the complexities of voting patterns and religious blocs were judged, the victory of John F. Kennedy made one conclusion inescapable: 40 million Americans had not, on the day of their baptism, surrendered their birthright to the highest office in the land.

Despite these areas of difficulty, the nineteenth century was for Catholicism a time of remarkable growth. That growth, of course, was directly responsible for those very difficulties. With a membership of about 50,000 in 1800, the Church by the end of the century could boast of a membership of more than 12 million. In 1800 Roman Catholicism had fewer adherents than did the Baptists, Congregationalists, Methodists, or Quakers. By 1850 it had exceeded them all (compare Figs. 42 and 94). From that time to the present, it has been the largest religious body in America.

As has already been noted, the major impetus in this swelling of membership came from nineteenth-century immigration. In 1790 the population of the United States was 3,172,444. Of this number, about 61,000 were Irish; 17,000, French; and 176,000, German. In 1850 when the nation's population was over 23 million, the number of foreign-born citizens was about 2¼ million. Of this group, almost 1 million were Irish. The next largest national body was German, with over 500,000. In this same year, 1850, there were only 3,679 native-born Italians. By 1900, however, there were 484,207 persons of Italian birth living in America. There were not enough Poles in the country in 1850 to warrant a separate listing in the census; by 1900 there were 390,000. Emigrants from Austria-Hungary, who numbered less than 1,000 in 1850, were by 1900 more than 500,000. Finally, there were 147,711 persons of Canadian birth in America in 1850 but more than 1 million in 1900. While the countries mentioned here are obviously those whose population was heavily Roman Catholic, the selection has not been arbitrary: these were the countries providing a majority of all immigrants, the only principal competitors being the United Kingdom and the Scandinavian countries. In the order of their contribution of inhabitants to America, the leading nations in 1900 were as follows: Germany, Ireland, Canada, England, Austria-Hungary, Sweden, Russia, and Italy (Rossiter, 226). Of the total number of approximately 17 million immigrants into America from 1850 to 1900, it has been estimated that nearly 5 million were Catholics (Shaughnessy, 145 f.). Since the actual increase in Catholic membership in this period was approximately 10 million, the remaining 5 million members came from natural propagation and new adherents.

In 1795 a geographer wrote: "The whole number of Roman Catholics in the United States is estimated at about fifty thousand, one-half of which are in the state of Maryland" (Winterbotham, I, 383). The nineteenth century saw the complete overthrow of such geographic concentration. By 1850 there were Roman Catholic churches in every state and territory (except Utah) in the nation (Fig. 91): the state of Maryland had fallen far behind New York, Pennsylvania, and Ohio; Wisconsin and Massachusetts had caught up with it, and New Mexico had passed it.

As early as 1785, Catholic families began emigrating from Maryland to Kentucky, largely for economic reasons. By 1791, there were 6 colonies of Catholics in Kentucky's northern counties; two years later, Father Stephen Badin "estimated that there were about three hundred families in the region" (Nuesse, 122). In 1808, Bardstown, Kentucky, was made the episcopal residence of the first diocese to be laid out west of the Allegheny Mountains (Fig. 90). The bishop appointed to this sparsely settled area, however, was so poor (and Archbishop Carroll who consecrated him was no richer) that his departure was delayed for many months. After horseback, flatboat, carriage, and ambulation, the prelate arrived in 1811 to say his first Mass on an altar for which no cathedral had yet been built (Ellis, Documents, 202 f). A generation later, there were bishoprics in Nashville, Cincinnati, Dubuque, Vincennes, Chicago, and Milwaukee. Colonization societies organized for the Catholic immigrant, more successful among the Germans than the Irish, urged a westward move in order to relieve the congestion and misery in the overcrowded cities of the East. Between 1876 and 1881 Bishop John Ireland of St. Paul was the most conspicuously successful organizer and colonizer as he negotiated with the railroad companies, served as land agent, provided religious succor to rootless migrants, and in general made of Minnesota "the center of Catholic culture for the entire Northwest" (Shannon, 267; map, p. 7).

Those that migrated beyond the Alleghenies, if not impoverished when their journey began, were certainly

ROMAN CATHOLIC CHURCH ARCHDIOCESES
AND DIOCESES OF THE UNITED STATES

——— Province boundary ——— Diocese boundary – – – State lines not Diocese boundaries

● Archdiocese   ○ Diocese

0   MILES   200

Figure 93

so when it ended. Though there were 80,000 Catholics in Illinois by mid-century, the entire diocese was destitute. A priest ministering to 8 churches had to carry chalice, missal, and altar stone from church to church for none could afford them. But the mission moved on, leaving new parishes and earnest priests behind. It was not long before the "gaps" between the Spanish Catholicism of Santa Barbara, the French Catholicism of St. Louis, the English Catholicism of Baltimore, met and mingled in a Catholicism which was American.

In the twentieth century there was no abatement in the Church's rapid advance. From 1900 to 1950, membership multiplied 2½ times; in these fifty years, the increase was more than 16 million (see Fig. 92). In the 1950's an extra burst of speed was manifest, with a growth of more than 12 million in only a single decade (see Fig. 94). In 1908, when there were approximately 15 million Catholics in America, the Vatican reached an understandable conclusion: the Church in the United States was no longer a mission field. Removed from the protective shelter of the Congregation for the Propagation of the Faith, the Church was free to make its own way in America.

A separation of Polish Catholics in 1907, creating the Polish National Catholic Church, represents the only major enduring schism in America's Roman Catholicism.

In 1960 this independent Church numbered more than 250,000 in membership.

Restrictive immigration laws in 1921 and the years following cut off a major source of the Roman Catholic membership supply. By 1921, however, the Church, 20 million strong and growing both in wealth and in influence, was secure; a century earlier, it was not so. Indeed, at mid-twentieth century, the Church in America occupied a commanding position in the Roman Catholic community abroad, as befitted its victories at home. For, by this time, there were American missions, American orders, American cardinals, and before long there was even to be an American saint.

SOURCES. Ray A. Billington, *The Protestant Crusade 1800-1860: A Study of the Origins of American Nativism* [includes informative maps] (New York, 1938; reissued, 1952). *Catholic Historical Review* [Vol. II contains an important article by J. F. R. Canevin; Vol. VI contains *The Laity's Directory* for the year 1822] (Washington, 1915-   ). John Tracy Ellis, *American Catholicism* (Chicago, 1955); ———, *The Life of James Cardinal Gibbons, Archbishop of Baltimore 1834–1921*, 2 vols. (Milwaukee, 1952); and, as editor, *Documents of American Catholic History* (Milwaukee, 1955). Peter Guilday, *A History of the Councils of Baltimore (1791-1884)* (New York, 1932); ———, *The National Pastorals of the American Hierarchy (1792-1919)* (Washington, 1923). Oscar Handlin, *The Uprooted: The Epic Story of the Great Migration that Made the American People* (Boston, 1951). Theodore Maynard, *The Story of American Catholicism* (New York, 1943). C. J. Nuesse, *The Social Thought of American*

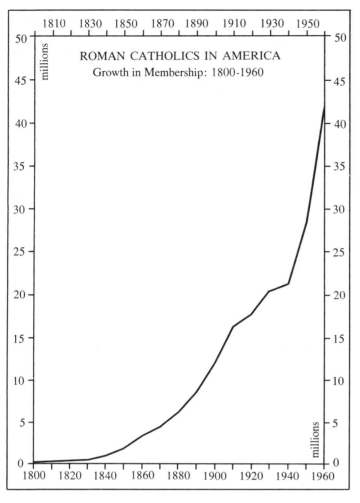

Figure 94

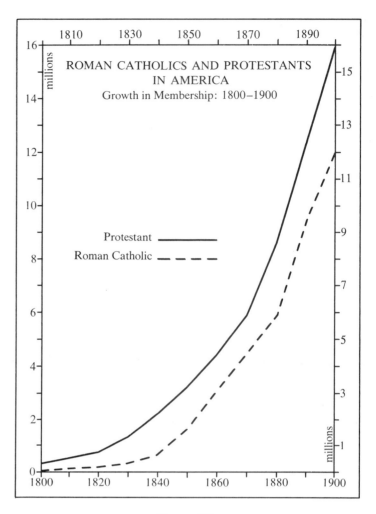

Figure 95

In Figures 95 and 96, the term "Protestant" is limited to the denominations covered in Part II, omitting the Mormons.

Catholics 1634-1829 (Westminster [Md.], 1945). Thomas O'Gorman, *A History of the Roman Catholic Church in the United States* (American Church History Series, IX) (New York, 1895). W. S. Rossiter, *A Century of Population Growth* (Washington, 1909). John F. Schermerhorn and Samuel J. Mills, *A Correct View of that part of the United States which lies west of the Allegheny Mountains* . . . (Hartford, 1814). James P. Shannon, *Catholic Colonization on the Western Frontier* (New Haven, 1957). Gerald Shaughnessy, *Has the Immigrant Kept the Faith? A Study of Immigration and Catholic Growth in the United States 1790-1920* [indispensable] (New York, 1925). John Gilmary Shea, *History of the Catholic Church in the United States*, 4 vols. (New York, 1886-92). Alexis de Tocqueville, *Democracy in America*, 2 vols. (New York, [reprint] 1954). William Winterbotham, *An Historical, Geographical, Commercial, and Philosophical View of the American United States* . . . 4 vols. (London, 1795). And see the eminently useful compilation by John Tracy Ellis, *A Guide to American Catholic History* (Milwaukee, 1959).

13. PROTESTANTS AND ROMAN CATHOLICS

Valid comparisons between Protestant and Catholic growth are difficult to make. There is a well-worn story of the army sergeant preparing to indicate religious affiliation on the new recruit's identification tag. The recruit, however, was not quite sure of his classification. Whereupon the sergeant inquired, "Are you a Catholic?" "No,"

was the decisive reply. "Are you a Jew?" "No," once more. "Well, then," said the sergeant, having deftly solved another of life's great puzzles, "you are a Protestant!" —and bang went the "P" on the tag. On the other hand, when does the baptized Catholic cease to be a Catholic? When he forsakes the Mass and defies his priest? When he ignores the days of fast and has only a civil marriage? When he, by deed and by word, contradicts all that is right and worthy in his Church? Such problems of classification and exclusion are so intricate that any proffered solution must seem arbitrary.

In Figures 95 and 96, "Protestant" has been deliberately —and arbitrarily—limited. Instead of reckoning every non-Jewish, non-Catholic ecclesiastical institution as "Protestant," the latter term has been limited to the larger, historic bodies considered here in Part II. Mormons have been excluded on the grounds that they do not consider themselves Protestants. Many large and rapidly growing bodies within American Christendom are, therefore, not shown in these two Figures; most of those discussed in Part III could fairly be added to the Protestant column.

The term "Catholic" has also been restricted, its application here extending only to those in communion with Rome. In the twentieth century, notably, there has been a considerable advance in the size of Eastern or National Catholic Churches (see Part III, 3). In 1950 the Polish National Church, the Russian Orthodox Church, and the Greek Archdiocese of North America together accounted for a membership of over 1½ million (see Figs. 41 and 100). Clearly, then, Figures 95 and 96 are *not* to be read as though all Christians in America were represented on one line or the other.

In the religious history of America there are two walls: one is Jefferson's explicit "wall" of separation between church and state; the other is the people's implicit wall of separation between Protestant and Catholic—"a scandal and an offense against Christian charity," in the words of Reinhold Niebuhr. In recent years there have been serious attempts to breach or at least to peek around this second wall. For example, John A. Hardon of the Society of Jesus wrote for Catholics a book entitled *The Protestant Churches of America* (Westminster [Md.], 1957). In its preface, he noted:

Catholics deal with Protestants on every level of human relationship, from the intimacy of family life to the less personal but very important associations in the professional and business world. Yet they often have only the vaguest notion of what Protestants believe, how they worship, and what their religion means to them (xv).

On the other side of the wall, Jaroslav Pelikan, a Protestant, wrote *The Riddle of Roman Catholicism* (New York, 1959) for those many Americans who

know more about the batting averages of the Yankees or the marriages and divorces of Hollywood than they do about the life and workings of the most formidable religious institution in the history of America and of the world (12).

Nor do these volumes stand alone. Considering only the most recent decade, others by Roman Catholics include J. J. Kane, *Catholic-Protestant Conflicts in America* (Chicago, 1955), G. H. Tavard, *The Catholic Approach to Protestantism* (New York, 1955) and Gustave Weigel, *Faith and Understanding in America* (New York, 1959). Protestant offerings in the same time span include Stanley Stuber, *Primer on Roman Catholicism for Protestants* (New York, 1953), Winthrop Hudson, *Understanding Roman Catholicism* (Philadelphia, 1959), and E. K. Skydsgaard, *One in Christ* (Philadelphia, 1957). Conversations within the covers of a single volume occur in Robert McAfee Brown and Gustave Weigel, *An American Dia-*

logue (New York, 1960), and in a work edited by Thomas T. McAvoy entitled *Roman Catholicism and the American Way of Life* (Notre Dame [Indiana], 1960).

Suspicions are, nonetheless, far from extinct, and trust is far from complete. Not even the storehouse of dirty weapons is altogether emptied. Yet if the dialogue can be

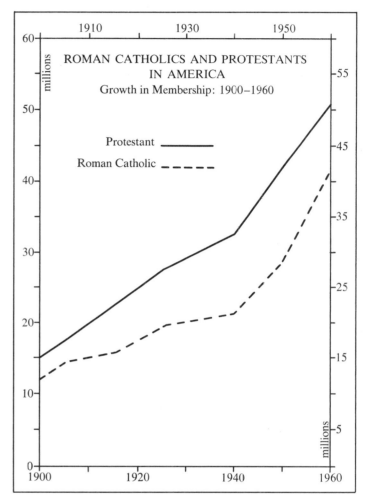

Figure 96

The Protestant total for 1900 is lower than in Figure 95 because in the twentieth century the Churches of Christ are no longer counted as part of the Disciples of Christ denomination.

carried on at the level and in the spirit of the works just cited, there is solid ground for hope. In the words of Mark de Wolfe Howe, "From the beginning of time men have found it difficult to live with each other. Reasonable men, however, have found it less difficult than have the impassioned" (*Religion and the Free Society* [New York, 1958], 62).

PART III

Religion in America, *1800–1960:*
Additional Noncolonial Bodies

1. INTRODUCTION

Ideally, Part III would encompass the remaining religious bodies of America. Practically, to follow such a principle of inclusiveness would be to reduce the treatment of the remaining organizations (more than 200) to a mere cataloging of name, place and number. To avoid this, Part III treats only a modest segment of these organizations, the choice being made on the grounds of numerical strength or historical continuity. The following are considered: Seventh-day Adventist, Jehovah's Witnesses, Eastern Orthodoxy, Assemblies of God, Church of God, Church of the Nazarene, Unitarian, Universalist, Christian Science, Evangelical United Brethren, and Mennonite.

One of the results of America's separation of church and state was the virtually unlimited freedom granted for religious expression. When to this one adds the national spirit of experimentation, the freshness of a land where tradition was absent and novelty omnipresent, the heterogeneity of a population whose differences were only partially melted, and the geographical and cultural mobility of a society, then the extraordinary diversity in American religion begins to be believable. And what is often the despair of the theologian may be the delight of the sociologist who, in the United States, has a laboratory of social grouping, shuffling and status-seeking that could hardly have been dreamed of and certainly not duplicated.

There have been many studies of the "cults" and "sects" in America, singly and en masse, sympathetically and critically. A major problem is that of classification. In the free-form ecclesiology of America, when is a religious body a "cult," a "sect," a "denomination," a "church"? Is there a line of theological progression or deterioration here? Is there a pecking order of social respectability or repugnance implied? Is there even the slightest suggestion of political privilege or penalty involved? The difficulty, of course, lies in the continuing search for some convenient, uncontroverted, objective standard by which to make such distinctions. Where there is a state-supported church, the difficulty disappears: all disestablished groups are sects, while the officially sanctioned one is The Church. Where theological or liturgical conformity is required, the solution is equally easy: all nonconformists are dissenters, schismatics or heretics, perhaps not to be tolerated

by, but certainly not to be confused with members of The Church.

Life for the American classifier is not so simple. Not only are the lines or boundaries vague, but they are also frequently crossed. Ernst Troeltsch, the great German sociologist of religion, distinguished between "church" and "sect" largely in terms of the social participation of each: the church embraces society, while the sect flees from society. The church seeks to redeem the whole; the sect separates itself from the whole. Between these two concepts, as the American church historian Sidney E. Mead has pointed out, lies "denominationalism," a position in which the religious body assumes only a limited liability for the welfare of its members, leaving great areas of life to society and the state. In America, the seventeenth-century sect may be the nineteenth-century denomination; on the other hand, a newly arrived church (e.g., one of the Eastern Churches) may seem more like a sect, withdrawn and introverted. The groups treated in Part III are divided according to a relatively simple but nonetheless vulnerable classification: (1) adventist, (2) Eastern, (3) holiness or pentecostal, (4) liberal, and (5) others.

SOURCES. Sidney E. Mead, "Denominationalism: The Shape of Protestantism in America," *Church History,* XXIII:4. H. Richard Niebuhr, *The Social Sources of Denominationalism* (New York, 1929; 1957). Ernst Troeltsch, *The Social Teachings of the Christian Church,* 2 vols. (London, 1931; latest reprinting, New York, 1960). On sects and cults, see the extensive bibliography in Nelson R. Burr's *Critical Bibliography of Religion in America* (Princeton, 1961), 308-346.

2. ADVENTIST BODIES

The hope for and expectation of a visible return of Christ to the earth has a long and uneven history in the Christian Church. One wave of "premillenialism" (i.e., the view that Christ would come before the millenium—the 1,000 years of peace prophesied in Revelation 20:4) swept over the United States in the first half of the nineteenth century. The "last days," the "end of the age," the "fullness of time"—all were at hand according to pronouncements made in most of the Protestant denominations during the 1830's.

In upstate New York, William Miller (1782-1849), a

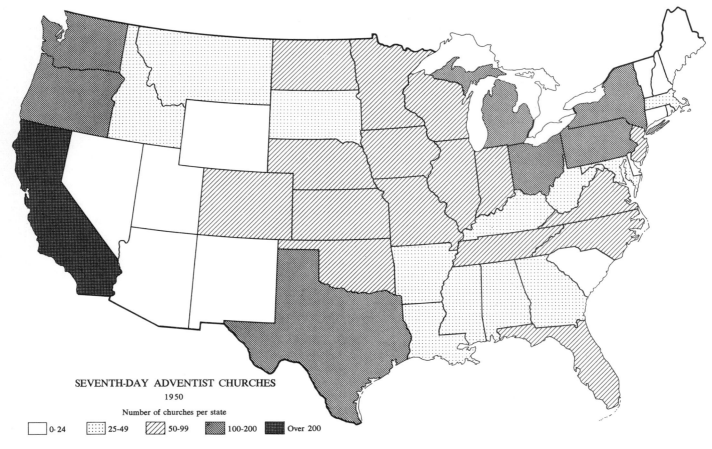

SEVENTH-DAY ADVENTIST CHURCHES
1950
Number of churches per state

☐ 0-24   ▦ 25-49   ▨ 50-99   ▩ 100-200   ■ Over 200

Figure 97

sheriff, soldier, farmer, deist, Baptist preacher (in that order, attracted great attention and a sizable following through his dramatic lectures concerning the approaching end of the world. Having devoted eight earnest years to the study of the Bible, reconciling apparent contradictions and wrestling with obscure prophecies, Miller announced that Christ would appear sometime between March 21, 1843, and March 21, 1844. (Miller based this prophecy on Daniel 8:13 f. and 9:24 f., where the promise was made that after 2,300 "years" the sanctuary would be cleansed —this "cleansing" involving, in Miller's view, the return of Christ to the earth. Since the prophecy was judged to have been made in 457 B.C., 2,300 years from that date pointed inescapably to 1843.) When Miller's prophecies were not fulfilled by March 22 of 1844, a recalculation put the date in October, to correspond with the Jewish Day of Atonement. And when these expectations failed to be realized many of the thousands who had been attracted to Miller sought succor elsewhere. Some returned to their earlier denominational affiliation; some forsook Christianity and its apparently misleading book; some continued to look for Christ's imminent return.

Many of this last group met the next year (1845) at Albany to gather, if possible, all those who had shared in the Great Disappointment, but efforts to effect a union were not successful. Out of the many ridiculed and uncertain knots of believers surviving the year, one group achieved stature:

Seventh-day Adventists. In Washington, New Hampshire, certain Adventists, under the influence of Seventh-Day Baptists (see above, p. 11), adopted the position that the Old Testament commandment regarding the Sabbath was in no way abrogated by the events described in the New Testament. The Christian was still obliged to keep the Sabbath day—Saturday—holy, even as the Orthodox Jews had been doing for many, many centuries. By the end of 1844, the first Seventh-day Adventist congregation had been formed. Meanwhile, other "Millerites," examining the Scriptures once more, concluded that 1843 had been the year when the *heavenly* sanctuary was cleansed —a step preparatory to Christ's return to cleanse the *earthly* tabernacle. The prophecy of William Miller was correct in every point, save one: Christ must first enter Heaven's Holy of Holies and there wash away all sin. Then he would be ready to make his visible, bodily, and still-impending return.

This new interpretation of the advent and this new day of worship were themselves not enough out of which to build a great church. To these elements, however, Mrs. Ellen G. White (1827-1915) added her steadying hand as theologian, comforter, reprover, and inspired guide. Her visions restored a confidence that had been badly shaken and her leadership provided a purposiveness that was sorely needed. By 1849 the first newspaper (*Present Truth*) appeared in Middletown, Connecticut; and by 1852 Mrs. White's husband was operating Adventism's first printing office. Again the message of Christ's coming was circulated, by press and from pulpit. In 1854 the group, aided by a $200 loan from John Preston Kellogg, purchased its first meeting tent, and the next year the Whites and others agreed to move their headquarters to a small village in Michigan: Battle Creek. There in 1860 the name "Seventh-day Adventist" was officially adopted, and in May of 1863 the General Conference was organized with 125 churches and 3,500 members.

While religion since its primitive days has had something to say about food, it has rarely said it so wholeheartedly as in Battle Creek. Although there were evidences in the East of a general circumspection in caring properly for the body—the temple of the Spirit—in Michigan this concern received distinctive emphasis. In 1866 the Western Health Reform Institute (later Battle Creek Sanitarium) was established and the publication of *Health Reformer* begun. Not only was diet a consideration; preventives and therapies which emphasized the "natural" as opposed to the artificial were advocated. In the days when current medical practice involved repeated bleedings and massive doses of calomel, Mrs. White's prescription had much to commend it: "Pure air, sunlight, abstemiousness, rest, exercise, proper diet, the use of water, trust in divine power—these are the true remedies."

In 1876 Dr. John Harvey Kellogg became medical superintendent of the Battle Creek Sanitarium. Publishing frequently on subjects ranging from hydrotherapy to digestion, Dr. Kellogg also led in the search for healthful foods to substitute for meat. For the Adventist Church had not only condemned the use of alcohol, tea, coffee, and tobacco, it had also concluded that Adam's God-given diet was the natural and healthy diet for man. And while the Adventist was not forbidden to eat meat, he was urged not to do so, and particularly not to eat any of the "unclean" meats described in chapter 11 of Leviticus. In the pursuit of his wide interests, John Henry Kellogg built a modest empire to health in Battle Creek. His brother, W. K. Kellogg, also built an empire, not so modest, on the cereal foods which had first been developed to vary and enrich the diet of the vegetarian Adventist.

Financial successes in this and in other areas have had some part in the great growth of Seventh-day Adventism. The unquestioned liberality of the rank and file member, however, has been an even more significant factor, as the per capita giving of the Adventists far outstrips that of the larger denominations. By the end of the century, there were over 50,000 Seventh-day Adventists, and with the removal of their headquarters from Battle Creek to Washington, D. C. in 1903, any uncertainty about the Church's survival was a thing of the past.

World-wide missionary efforts were undertaken as the twentieth century began, and before that century was half over, the Church had demonstrated convincingly the vigor and earnestness of its zeal (see Fig. 97). Publishing houses, hospitals, colleges, food factories, and churches are currently in operation all over the world. The proportions of this missionary activity are evidenced by the fact that in 1960 approximately two-thirds of all Seventh-day Adventists were outside of America.

To many who have looked for the world's imminent end, social reforms and long-term investments seemed pointless. Of the Adventists, however, this is emphatically not true. In the span of a single century, the denomination has not only formed 12,000 churches (3,000 in America) but has done a remarkable work in medical missions (107 hos-

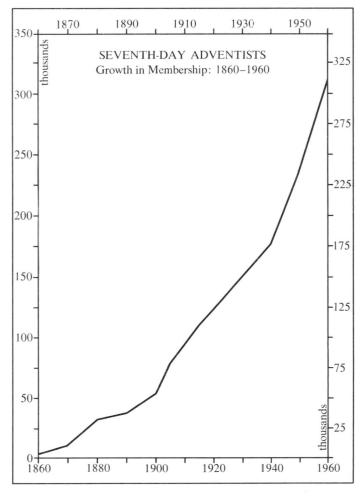

Figure 98

pitals and sanitariums), has at great sacrifice built and maintained over 300 colleges and academies, and, more recently, has turned its attention to homes for the aged and the orphaned. The vast educational program includes a wide network of elementary schools as well as 3 graduate schools: a theological seminary in Washington, D. C., and medical and dental schools in southern California. After World War II, the Adventists (who urge a noncombatant status for their servicemen) made mighty contributions toward the relief of the hungry and ill-clad. While expecting a kingdom of God from the heavens, they work diligently for one on the earth.

Jehovah's Witnesses. Not related so directly to the Millerite expectations of the 1840's, a younger adventist group arose in the 1870's. Founded in 1872 by Charles Taze Russell in Allegheny, Pennsylvania, the Jehovah's Witnesses were at first simply a group of "Christian persons met together . . . to consider the Scriptures relative to the coming of Christ and His Kingdom" (Stroup, 4). Affirming that the cosmic contest between Satan and Jehovah would end with a personal return of Christ to the earth and a fierce battle in which Satan and all his host would be destroyed, Russell's coterie attracted additional followers. By 1884 the group was large enough to justify incorporation as "The Zion's Watch Tower Tract Society."

Five years earlier (1879), the first issue of *Zion's Watch Tower* had come off the press; this publication has continued without interruption to the present-day—something of a record for religious periodicals. Colporteurs, enlisted by the thousands, sold this early literature where they could and gave it away where they could not. The *Watch Tower,* in its second year of publication, called for 1,000 preachers who would

go forth into large or small cities, according to your ability as Colporteurs or Evangelists, [and] seek to find in every place the earnest Christians, many of whom you will find possessed of a zeal for God, but not according to Knowledge; to these seek to make known the riches of Our Father's grace, and the beauties of His word, giving them tracts; and as a work of kindness and love to them, endeavor to sell them the "Day Dawn" [book written by J. H. Paton], or take their subscription for the "Watch Tower" (or if interested, but too poor to purchase, presenting the same as a gift from God) . . . (*Jehovah's Witnesses in the Divine Purpose,* 28).

Book agents and others responding to Russell's plea discovered that he did not want order takers or deliverymen; he wanted preachers, laborers "who will work for heavenly wages, rather than for the price of a paper or book, be that ever so needful. No, we want those only who can explain the paper and book and plan, who as they go will *preach* . . ." At this point, Russell's call was heard by about 300 colporteurs or "pioneers," to use current Witness terminology. But the 1,000 called for would not be long in coming; indeed, they soon would come in tens of thousands.

In 1893 the first national assembly of Witnesses was held at Chicago with about 360 persons in attendance. With permission to use the baptismal facilities of the Calvary Baptist Church of that city, 70 converts "symbolized their baptism into Christ's death by immersion in water." By 1900, following a trip abroad by Russell, the first branch office outside of the United States was opened in London, England. Nine years later, the main office in America was moved to Brooklyn, New York, where the former parsonage of Henry Ward Beecher was converted into a staff home for Jehovah's Witnesses, and a former mission of Beecher's Plymouth Congregational Church was dedicated as the new headquarters on January 31, 1909. Since the Pennsylvania charter did not legalize property holdings in New York, a new corporation was formed: The People's Pulpit Association.

The Witnesses, having survived occasional internal struggles for power (some of which were occasioned by President Russell's divorce in 1906), had built up a sizable organization by the time of World War I. Membership was around 15,000 and *Watch Tower* circulation over 50,000. (This body tends to measure progress more in terms of literature distribution than of membership accretion.) Russell, a popular lecturer, used special trains in his ceaseless sweep of the country, still finding time to publish a weekly sermon and to travel annually abroad. In 1911 and 1912, Russell and a committee of seven toured the world, "spreading seeds of truth that, in time, brought into fruitful action more groups of anointed Christians in far-flung areas of the globe." Russell also availed himself of the new developments in phonograph records and motion pictures, devising a "Photo-Drama of Creation" at a cost of $300,000. Much of this activity was in prospect of a promised cataclysm or advent to occur in 1914, when "the lease of power to the Gentiles" will end, when "the final end of the kingdoms of this world and the full establishment of the Kingdom of God will be accomplished" (*Jehovah's Witnesses in the Divine Purpose,* 55). While the outbreak of World War I gave some plausibility to this prophecy of long standing, yet 1914 did not include a "full establishment" of God's kingdom on earth. Like the Seventh-day Adventists considered above, the Witnesses, after further examination of the Scriptures, concluded that it was the heavenly kingdom which Christ established, the heavenly Temple which He cleansed. Christ did return in 1914, in spirit; He does rule, in heaven. All this was understood as a prelude to the visible, personal return, the Battle of Armageddon, the consequent restoration of righteousness to the earth and of perfection to man. This lies yet in the future, but not very far: "Millions now living may never die."

Those words were made famous by (Judge) Joseph Franklin Rutherford (1869-1942) who was serving as the Society's chief legal counsel when Charles Taze Russell died on October 31, 1916—appropriately, on a lecture-tour train. For two months following Russell's death, the Society was managed by a temporary executive committee of three. Then in January of the next year, J. F. Rutherford was unanimously selected as the successor. (At this time, a contribution of $10 entitled the donor to 1 vote in the corporation; Russell had often cast 25,000 votes because he had contributed over the years about $250,000. This voting procedure was altered in 1944.)

Born in Missouri in 1869 of Baptist parents, Rutherford went to law school, was at age 22 admitted to the Missouri bar, and later served briefly as substitute judge in that state's Fourteenth Judicial District. Becoming a member of the Society in 1906, he soon occupied a prominent position. While some objected to having a mere layman as successor to the sainted Russell, Rutherford's legal training was to prove at least as valuable as any theological training could have been.

As noncombatants in any war except Jehovah's War (and therefore theologically not pacifists), the Witnesses had a difficult time after the entry of the United States into World War I. Embroiled in growing internal disputes about Rutherford's leadership, and weakened by a major disruption in the board of directors (probably 4,000 left the Society in 1917-1919), the Witnesses also met resistance from the United States government. The charge was sedition. On June 20, 1918, Rutherford and seven other leaders of the movement heard their sentences pronounced in the U. S. District Court, Eastern District of New York: twenty years in the Federal penitentiary of Atlanta. While their followers sang "Blest Be the Tie that Binds," the eight men were remanded to the Brooklyn jail to await their departure for Atlanta on the Fourth of July.

Despite the formidable sound of Judge Rutherford's twenty-year sentence (twenty years on four separate counts, the terms to run concurrently), the end of World War I raised hopes for his early release. In March of 1919, he and those imprisoned with him were granted bail and returned to Brooklyn; in May of the next year the government announced that it would not reopen the prosecution. Revived and united, the Society strengthened its Brooklyn base, then held a national convention in Cedar Point, Ohio, attended by 7,500 of the heartened faithful. The dark days seemed over, the bright days ahead.

The Golden Age made its appearance on October 1, 1919, and by 1920 this magazine had a printing of 4 million copies. New presses purchased, the Society decided to meet its own insatiable demands for more literature. In the 1920's the Jehovah's Witnesses outgrew one building after another, adding each time to their corporate responsibilities and physical facilities. In addition to periodicals, books were printed on Witness presses, with translations into other languages being assumed as a sacred obligation. In 1922 books were bound at the rate of 2,000 per day; in 1928, at a rate of over 10,000 per day. In 1924, with the licensing of Station WBBR, the power of the air waves was added to that of the press. Then sound car and transcription machines (1933), house-to-house phonograph playing (1937), and modest training schools (1942) intensified the incessant drive. In 1950, the Society issued its own official translation of the Bible: the *New World Translation of the Christian Greek Scriptures.*

Not until 1931 did the name "Jehovah's Witnesses" receive official sanction. Many nicknames had been and continued to be used: Dawnites, Russellites, Watch Tower Bible people, Bible Students, Rutherfordites and others. In their own publications, terms such as "the Lord's anointed," "the brethren," "footstep followers of Jesus," frequently appeared. At the convention in Columbus, Ohio (July, 1931), a resolution was adopted which declared that "we joyfully embrace and take the name which the mouth of the Lord God has named, and we desire

to be known as and called by the name, to wit, 'Jehovah's witnesses'—Is. 43:10-12; 62:2; Rev. 12:17" (*Jehovah's Witnesses in the Divine Purpose,* 126). And while it is singular in religious history, the Witnesses are popularly called by the very name which they themselves chose and prefer.

In 1942 J. F. Rutherford died, but his demise was not the signal for any bitter palace intrigue as Russell's had been in 1916. Only five days after Rutherford's death, the previously elected vice-president, H. N. Knorr (1905——),

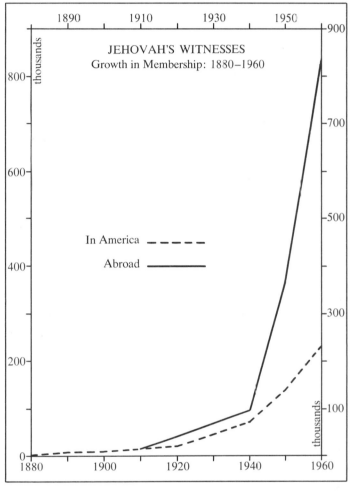

Figure 99

was quietly and unanimously elected president of the Pennsylvania and New York corporations. The new president, unlike his two predecessors, does not issue quantities of books and articles in his own name, nor does he direct lecture trains across the country. There can be no question, however, of the effectiveness of an administration which has overseen a growth in "ministers" from less than 100,000 in 1940 to nearly 1 million (worldwide) in 1960. In the United States alone, there were about 250,000 ministers and over 4,000 congregations (Fig. 99). The Society maintains branches or offices in 84 countries, with particularly strong work in Great Britain, Canada, Brazil, Mexico, West Germany, and the Philippines. In these countries, as well as in the United States, "pioneers" (full-time workers) and "publishers" (part-time workers) carry their message, often leaving behind them one of the more than 86 million [!] copies of the *Watch Tower* currently printed each year.

One of the most engrossing chapters in America's recent religious history concerns the Jehovah's Witnesses and the law. In 1933 the Society began keeping a count of arrests of its members—the servant with "a record," of course, being honored rather than despised. In that year there were 269 arrests; in 1936 there were 1,149; and in the early 1940's more than 3,000 arrests per year took place. The charges were many, some of nuisance value only, others of more consequence. "Pioneers" and "publishers" were charged with disturbing the peace (that omnium gatherum), with selling without a license, peddling without a permit, violating Sunday "blue laws," failing to pay a license tax, trespassing, libeling and, again, sedition. Soon the Society found it necessary to establish its own legal department in Brooklyn and to issue a brochure to all members telling them what legal rights to claim, what legal procedures to follow. And while there is no record of any separate department being established in government (local, state, or federal), it is a safe guess that Witness litigations kept many departments of government occupied for years. Every adverse decision handed down against the Society was appealed, that appeal often going to the U. S. Supreme Court. Time and again the decisions of magistrates, police courts, and other lower courts were reversed and their judgments set aside.

One of the most widely publicized cases dealt with the refusal to salute the flag of the United States; the Witnesses regarded such an action as "unchristian image worship." The Gobitis Case, involving the failure of the two Gobitis children (ages 10 and 12) to salute the flag, and their subsequent expulsion from a Pennsylvania grammar school, reached the Supreme Court in June, 1940. This time, the Court (with Justice Harlan Stone dissenting) rendered a decision against the Witnesses, declaring that a public school is within its rights in requiring the pupils to salute the national flag. With this support and with the pending peril of war, many citizens assumed a personal, extralegal responsibility for making "good Americans" out of the Witnesses. Property was damaged; persons were abused; taunts and insults were hurled. The American Civil Liberties Union observed: "Not since the persecution of the Mormons years ago has any religious minority been so bitterly and generally attacked as the members of Jehovah's Witness—particularly in the spring and summer of 1940." If this was true of a country boasting of its freedom in religion, one can hardly be surprised to learn that Witnesses have been persecuted by the Nazis, sentenced to penal camps by the Russians, and violently attacked in the Dominican Republic. In the non-Communist countries, they have regularly been charged with being Communists or Communist sympathizers, while in Communist countries they have been arrested as secret agents of capitalistic imperialism. The Washington *Post*

(March 21, 1959), commenting editorially on the "extended denunciation" of the Witnesses in *Pravda*, wrote of "the courage and obduracy of the Witness prisoners and [of] their ability to withstand intimidation and even torture." The same newspaper also pointed out that people who proclaim that all existing forms of government are satanic (they even urge their fellow Americans not to vote) have an undeniable appeal to those "who live under the more totalitarian and tyrannous forms of government."

Since Witness doctrine held that the number of the Lord's anointed, the Remnant, in the heavenly kingdom would be only 144,000 (Revelation 7:4), there could understandably be a tendency or temptation to keep the fellowship small. In the 1930's, however, attention turned to the "other sheep" who, while not of the inner fold, were still to participate in the kingdom's inheritance. No ceiling, moreover, was placed on the number of "other sheep" to be gathered in. Public selling of literature and "follow-up" visitation of those showing interest were also revived in the late '30's, having fallen into disuse after World War I. As a result, then, of (1) a theological reorientation concerning the number to be redeemed, (2) an intensified and improved program of disseminating the message, and (3) persecution, the Jehovah's Witnesses made sudden progress after 1940, all but eclipsing the development of the first sixty years. As is true of many of the younger religious groups, the period of the Witnesses' greatest growth appears to be the present (see Fig. 99).

The Seventh-day Adventists and the Jehovah's Witnesses, differing in a great many respects, do jointly demonstrate the vigor of a religion which demands much of its laity and expects much of its God. And while the Witnesses have not so dramatically looked after the bodily welfare of those in need, they have organized ambitious relief programs, particularly following World War II. Together, these two bodies scuttle the generalization that millenial expectations thrive only on crude emotionalism and unrestrained passions. A soberer, more serious service of worship than those offered by these two groups would be difficult to find. Whatever may be true of adventism generally, as represented by these groups it is scholastic rather than ecstatic.

SOURCES. Marley Cole, *Jehovah's Witnesses: The New World Society* (New York, 1955). W. R. Cross, *The Burned-over District: The Social and Intellectual History of Enthusiastic Religion in Western New York, 1800-1850* [Adventist map, p. 289] (Ithaca, 1950). Booton Herndon, *The 7th Day* (New York, 1960). "Information File, Seventh-day Adventists" (issued by the Bureau of Public Relations, Washington, D. C., [no date]). *Jehovah's Witnesses in the Divine Purpose* [valuable source data] (Brooklyn, 1959). F. E. Mayer, *Jehovah's Witnesses* (St. Louis, 1942). Francis D. Nichol, *The Midnight Cry* (Washington, 1944). Royston Pike, *Jehovah's Witnesses* (New York, 1954). Horace B. Powell, *The Original Has This Signature—W. K. Kellogg* (Englewood Cliffs [N.J.], 1956). *The Story of Our Church* [Published for the Department of Education, General Conference of Seventh-day Adventists] (Mountain View [Calif.], 1956). Herbert H. Stroup, *The Jehovah's Witnesses* (New York, 1945).

3. EASTERN ORTHODOXY

In Christendom's ancient separation of East from West, of Greek from Latin, of Byzantine from Roman, another rich and brightly colored vein of America's ecclesiastical mine is to be found. The Eastern Church, eschewing the papal polity of the West, failed to maintain an organizational unity, dividing along lines primarily national but occasionally theological or liturgical. As, therefore, immigrants from the several Eastern countries began arriving in the United States, the numerous administrative entities came to have their counterparts on American soil. And, as if to prove their Americanism, there were new separations, indigenous innovations.

On the American scene, the Eastern Churches have become statistically significant only within the last half-century. At the beginning of the twentieth century, their collective membership was only about 100,000. By 1960, however, the combined membership approached three million. With the exceptions of the Church of Armenia and the Jacobites, both modest in number, the Eastern Churches come within the compass of Eastern Orthodoxy. It is to this ancient Orthodoxy, then, that we turn for a view of that Catholicism not in communion with Rome.

Two groups merit major attention: the Russians and the Greeks. Of the Eastern Churches, the Russian Orthodox Church has clear title to temporal priority in the North American continent. As early as 1743, Alaskan natives were baptized by a Cossack who gave his name as well as his blessing to the Andreanof Islands. The first preacher to the Aleutians arrived in 1759, and before the end of the century eight monks were laying a firm foundation for Russian Orthodoxy in North America (see Part IV, 5 below). Late in the next century, 1872, the diocesan headquarters for the Russian Church in the West was moved from Sitka, Alaska, to San Francisco, California. There Russians, Serbs, and Greeks all received the ministries of the Russian Orthodox Church. In the final decade of the nineteenth century, vigorous episcopal direction—under Nicholas—resulted in the establishment of churches as far east as New York. (The Russian Orthodox Church has the distinction of being the only major religious group in America to expand from West to East.) Nicholas, like his predecessor Vladimir, was also glad to receive several Uniate congregations into the fellowship of his Church. The Uniates, who had much earlier been under the aegis of the Russian Church, often found their current affiliation with Roman Catholicism restrictive and irritating. Led by a Ruthenian congregation in Minneapolis, Uniate groups across the country returned to the Russian fold.

Around the turn of the century, Russian emigration to the United States increased, producing thereby rapid increase in the membership and status of Russian Orthodoxy. In 1901 the Church of St. Nicholas was erected in New York City, and in 1905, with the transfer of the episcopal see from San Francisco to New York, this became the cathedral church. Shortly thereafter, both a seminary and a monastery were established in America, the whole American enterprise now being of sufficient stature to warrant the elevation of Bishop Tikhon to the rank of archbishop. In 1906 there were nearly 20,000 members and 60 churches in America (excluding Alaska); a decade later, membership had risen to approximately 100,000, distributed among 169 churches.

The Russian revolution of October, 1917, and the resultant rise of the Communist party created confusion and embarrassment within the Russian Church abroad as it created harassment and suffering within that Church at home. Out of the shattered organization in the United States, some order was wrought in 1919 when an "All-American" convention, meeting in Pittsburgh, declared the Russian Church in America to be "temporarily autonomous." In 1922 Archbishop Platon was elected head of this Church, an election confirmed by the American churches two years later. This bold move was made in open defiance of a Soviet appointee, Reverend John Savitz Kedrovsky, who sought to take over direction of the American archbishopric in the name of the Moscow Patriarchate. Rejected by virtually all resident leadership, Kedrovsky nevertheless won a court decision granting him legal title to the Cathedral of St. Nicholas. The ejected Platon, now taking the title of Metropolitan, accepted the gracious offer of the Episcopalians to use the chapel of Trinity Parish in New York until such time as another cathedral could be built. In 1934 the Most Reverend Theophilus succeeded Platon upon the latter's death that year, and in 1950, the Most Reverend Leonty became Ruling Bishop of what is now known as The Russian Orthodox Greek Catholic Church of America.

This communion is much the largest representative of Russian Orthodoxy in the United States, enjoying a membership of over 750,000 in 1960. "The Russian Orthodox Church Outside Russia," organized abroad in 1920, moved its headquarters to the United States (Lake Mahopac, New York) in 1950, at which time it reported an American membership of 45,000. The body which maintains an official tie with the Soviet Union bears the title "Russian Orthodox Catholic Church, Archdiocese of the Aleutian Islands and North America." Providing no statistics concerning its present size or rate of growth, this group—consisting of perhaps 5 churches—represents no significant strength in the total power of Russian Orthodoxy in America. Rather, the church guided by the steady hands of Vladimir (1888-1891), Nicholas (1891-1898), Tikhon (1898-1907), Platon (1907-1934), Theophilus (1934-1950) and Leonty (1950-   ) is the one whose history is intermixed with that of the American people. And virtually alone among the Eastern Churches, this one succeeded in demonstrating a real missionary concern and in manifesting a genuine catholicity.

The second major group within Eastern Orthodoxy arose as a result of Greek immigration to the United States, beginning in the final years of the nineteenth century. Before 1900, Greek Catholic churches were organized in New York and Chicago, and by World War I the number of Greek Catholics in America exceeded 100,000. In 1918 the Archbishop of Athens, under whose jurisdiction

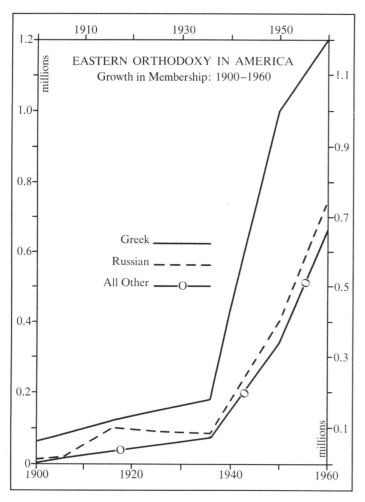

Figure 100

the American Greeks had been placed a decade earlier, came to the United States with the intention of forming a Hellenic diocese. Such were the disorders and frictions, however, that this attempt yielded only frustration. Not until 1930 was a real unity established among the Greeks, permitting the formal creation of an Archdiocese of North and South America to become truly meaningful. In 1936 there were nearly 200,000 members of this Archdiocese in the United States and 241 churches, with the greatest concentration being in New York, Massachusetts, Pennsylvania, Illinois, and Ohio.

After World War II, Greek Catholic membership exceeded 1 million. And while the geographical sweep of this Archdiocese extends to all of the western hemisphere, the

bulk of the membership is in the United States. In 1960 a membership of 1,200,000 was reported, making this church the largest representative of Eastern Orthodoxy in the Western world. Together with the Russians, the Greeks constitute the overwhelming majority of all those in America whose worship follows the Eastern liturgies (see Fig. 100).

The remaining ethnic groups—Albanian, Bulgarian, Rumanian, Serbian, Syrian, and Ukrainian—are, in American ecclesiology, children of the twentieth century. The Albanian Orthodox Diocese in America, the smallest of these churches, had less than 1,000 members at the time of World War I; in 1960, there were 15 churches, claiming a total membership of 14,000. The Bulgarian Eastern Orthodox Church, consisting of only 4 churches in 1916, did not receive a bishop until 1938, and in general showed little growth before World War II. By 1960 there were 21 churches, located chiefly in the Midwest. The Rumanian Orthodox Episcopate of America, which received its first priest in 1902, had less than 2,000 members in 1916 but had risen to a membership of approximately 50,000 by 1960. The Serbian Eastern Orthodox Church—after the Greeks and Russians the next largest ethnic group within Eastern Orthodoxy—began the century with over 10,000 members. Migrating from Syria, Egypt, Palestine, and Iraq, Syrians built their first cathedral in Brooklyn in 1902, although their first bishop was not appointed until 1927. Now divided into two groups (both of which, however, regard Antioch as their spiritual base), the Orthodox Syrians had in 1960 over 100 churches and more than 150,000 members. Among the latest to arrive in the United States, the Ukrainians had by 1960 succeeded in splitting themselves among three separate ecclesiastical organizations. With fewer than 40 churches prior to World War II, the Ukrainians together had 145 churches in 1960.

Like Lutheranism, Eastern Orthodoxy found itself beset and bewildered by the cultural and administrative diversity which, within the confines of the United States, became so readily apparent and so admittedly artificial. Several efforts have been launched, either as broad movements or as new churches, to rise above the political or ethnic character of the divided Eastern Churches. Often those efforts take the form of an open embrace of or a definite adjustment to the American environment. The use of English in the services has been a first and obvious step, as has the replacement of the Julian calendar—authoritative in the East—with the Gregorian calendar—normative in the West. Other reforms, such as the use of mixed choirs, the introduction of instrumental music, and the provision of seating for the congregation, parallel the kind of adaptation for which Reform Judaism also labored (see Part IV, 3, below). Such groups as the Holy Eastern Catholic and Apostolic Church (1922), the Holy Orthodox Church in America (1927), the American Holy Orthodox Catholic Apostolic Eastern Church (1932), and the Orthodox Catholic Patriarchate of America (1951) are representative of these attempts to form a church that is either more American or more catholic. Of these efforts, one can only say that, by 1960, the statistical results were meager indeed. Out of Eastern Orthodoxy's membership of approximately 3 million, less than 1% seem to have found their way into those churches which minimized or set aside the heritage of the Old World.

SOURCES. Michael Constantinides, *The Orthodox Church* (London, 1931). C. W. Emhardt, *The Eastern Church in the Western World* (New York, 1928). Rene Janin, *The Separated Eastern Churches* (St. Louis, 1933). Kenneth Scott Latourette, *A History of the Expansion of Christianity*, IV (New York, 1941). Eugene Smirnoff, *A Short Account of the Historical Development and Present Position of Russian Orthodox Missions* (London, 1903). Matthew Spinka, "The Eastern Orthodox Churches in America," *Encyclopedia Britannica*, XVI (Chicago, 1956). *St. Vladimir's Seminary Quarterly*, V:1-2 (1961), is devoted entirely to a discussion of the Orthodox Church in America. And see the remarkably complete bibliography of Eastern Churches in Nelson R. Burr's *Critical Bibliography of Religion in America* (Princeton, 1961), 493-506.

4. HOLINESS AND PENTECOSTAL BODIES

"For God has not called us unto uncleanness, but unto holiness." "Be ye therefore perfect, even as your Father in heaven is perfect." "Since, therefore, we are now justified by his blood, much more shall we be saved [sanctified] by him. . . ." With the implications of these sentences, written in the first century of the Christian era, many disciples were yet wrestling in the nineteenth century of that era. Spiritual struggles with the issues raised in the latter century could be found in several church groups, but it was largely within or on the edges of Methodism that those issues were most mightily contested. For Wesley himself had earnestly emphasized the doctrine of sanctification and the hope of perfection; and as late as 1884, on the occasion of the Centennial Conference of American Methodism, the delegates thereto affirmed:

We remind you, brethren, that the mission of Methodism is to promote holiness . . . In all the borders of Methodism this doctrine is preached, and the experience of sanctification is urged. We beseech you, brethren, stand by your standards on this subject (Redford, 38).

To the eye of many, however, Methodism failed to measure up to its own standard. Disagreements between the "holiness" and "anti-holiness" factions within Methodism were among the first indications that new denominations might soon be born. Even as Methodism itself had begun as a wing within a larger church, so many Holiness churches began simply as groups of like-minded Methodists working within the broader frame. The National Association for the Promotion of Holiness, organized in New Jersey in 1867, was neither a new church nor the competitor of any existing ecclesiastical body. That it might foster both was soon obvious.

By way of Baptists such as John Q. Adams and A. B.

Earle, Lutherans such as S. S. Schmucker, Presbyterians like William E. Boardman, and Congregationalists like Thomas C. Upham, the concern for holiness spread generally throughout American Protestantism between 1840 and 1870. Combining such diverse elements as revivalism and transcendentalism, mysticism and asceticism, pietism and pragmatism, the drive for the "Higher Christian Life"

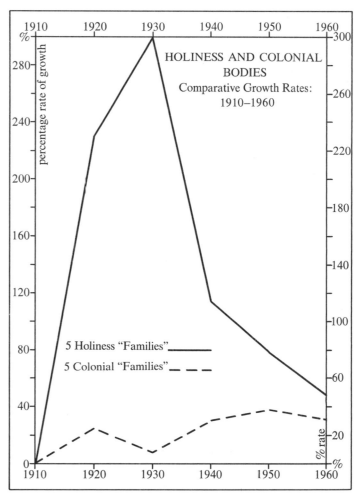

Figure 101

The colonial "families" included are Anglican, Baptist, Congregational, Lutheran, and Presbyterian. The holiness "families" included are Assemblies of God, Churches of God, Church of God in Christ, Church of the Nazarene, and the major Pentecostal bodies.

gathered great momentum. Men of lofty official position within the denominations and men of no official position joined in and inspired the march.

Timothy L. Smith (see his *Revivalism and Social Reform*) has distinguished carefully between the Oberlin and Wesleyan types of perfectionism, both of which had a large and sometimes overlapping following. In the former, perfection was attainable through a growing in grace; the process was gradual. In the latter, sanctification was wholly a gift of grace; the change wrought in this "second blessing" was, like that of the first, instantaneous. In both cases, one attained to Christian purity, to perfect love. The first allowed more room for Bushnell's "Christian Nurture," the other granted greater prominence to the work of the Holy Spirit. As the movement attracted other groups, it became necessary to draw a further distinction between those for whom the Spirit's gift of "entire sanctification" was (as it was for Wesley) marked by a life of disciplined devotion to God; and those for whom this gift had its immediate manifestation in the form of ecstatic trances, glossolalia and extreme emotionalism. Sometimes the word "holiness" is reserved for the former, the term "pentecostal" for the latter. (The Church of the Nazarene, for example, was the "Pentecostal Church of the Nazarene" until in 1919 the "Pentecostal" was dropped in order that the Church might more readily distinguish itself from this second type.) Examples of both types are considered in this section.

Before briefly examining certain of the larger holiness or pentecostal denominations, some notice should be given to the phenomenal rate of growth manifest in the group as a whole. The "Third Force in Christendom" (see *Life Magazine,* June 9, 1958), filled with youthful vigor and holy vitality, has in the present century spurted ahead, burying last year's statistics under a mass of new adherents, new churches, new territories. In Figure 101 the rate of progress for 5 "young" holiness family groups is compared with the rate for 5 "old" church families, to the obvious advantage of the former. It is no less obvious, however, that as these young denominations mature, they too slow down, making it possible for still other "reborn" believers to react against their formalism, deadness or worldliness.

Though sociological generalizations are risky, it is probably fair to say that the greater appeal of the groups considered here has been to the lower economic stratum, to those who, finding worldly goods denied them, have denied the world. At the same time they have affirmed a nobility of life which not only clearly distinguishes them from the world, but promises somehow to redeem elements of that world. For there is a "social gospel" here too, though it is one which places most hope in the power of the pure in heart, not only to see God, but also to call down His power. Ernst Troeltsch once wrote:

The really creative, church-forming, religious movements are the work of the lower strata. Here only can one find that union of unimpaired imagination, simplicity in emotional life, unreflective character of thought, spontaneity of energy and vehement force of need, out of which an unconditional faith in a divine revelation, the naivete of complete surrender and the intransigence of certitude can rise (H. R. Niebuhr, 29).

Whether or not these features are invariably wedded to a particular level of society, their continuing presence is manifest in several representatives of the holiness and pentecostal fellowships.

Some groups noted in this section are still engaged in intraparty struggles, and may indeed dissipate their strength through protracted strife and schism. A lack of historical continuity makes the statistical or geographical treatment of such "families" most tenuous (e.g., Fig. 103).

On the other hand, there are those who, having laid a firm foundation, proceeded faithfully and steadily to build thereon (e.g., Fig. 104). The following groups are considered: Assemblies of God, Churches of God, and the Church of the Nazarene.

Assemblies of God. The largest of the Pentecostal bodies, with a 1960 membership of more than 500,000, is less than half a century old. A Pentecostal editor, E. N. Bell, near the end of 1913, issued in his newspaper, *Word and Witness,* a call for "A General Convention of Pentecostal Saints and Churches of God in Christ" to meet the following April in Hot Springs, Arkansas. Editor Bell warned that this meeting was

only for saints who believe in the baptism with the Holy Ghost. Neither is this meeting for any captious, contrary, divisive or contentious person. But we leave for the body itself to take up any subjects it desires . . . (Winehouse, 29).

What the body itself desired to take up was the urgent question of unifying the diverse, scattered, ofttimes competing efforts of a multitude of Pentecostal groups that had come into existence during the previous two decades. There were groups tracing their origin to Charles F. Parham's Bethel Bible College in Topeka, Kansas, or to William J. Seymour's Azusa Mission in Los Angeles, or to G. B. Cashwell's rented warehouse in Dunn, North Carolina, or to a number of other modest and obscure beginnings; together they sent more than 300 delegates to Hot Springs that April of 1914. In the manner of the organizers of nearly every new church, these delegates pledged themselves "not to organize or charter a church, denomination or sect." Rather, they agreed to "have an ANNUAL COUNCIL, made up from all Pentecostal Assemblies, Churches and individuals to meet once a year to advise scriptural methods of unity and to attend to business for God" (Winehouse, 34). Thus the Assemblies of God denomination was born.

A General Council was incorporated in order to give the necessary recognition and legal status to the missionaries who were already carrying around the world the Pentecostal message of a baptism by the Spirit. A small school as well as a small printing press were set up in Findley, Ohio, and procedures for issuing or withholding ministerial credentials were determined. To all of this sudden structure there was, of course, a measure of resistance; complaints were heard against those who dared to "place restrictions on the moving of the Holy Spirit," but opposition to organization per se was soon overcome.

More serious was the baptismal formula controversy which in 1915-16 threatened to wreck a program scarcely begun. A significant segment of the infant denomination, believing that baptism should be "in the name of Jesus" only, rebaptized those who had received the rite with the usual Trinitarian words. Of the more than 500 ministers recognized by the first General Council, 150 dropped away

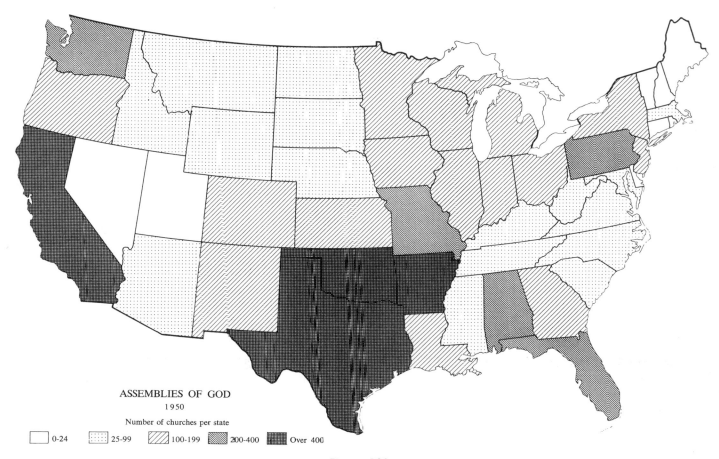

ASSEMBLIES OF GOD
1950

Number of churches per state

☐ 0-24   ▦ 25-99   ▧ 100-199   ▨ 200-400   ▓ Over 400

Figure 102

during these days of contention. But the Assemblies of God held to Nicene orthodoxy, and by 1917, the storm weathered, the number of clergymen was up once more to 573.

In 1918 the General Council met for the first time in Springfield, Missouri, which city was to become the world headquarters of the movement. There were at this time approximately 10,000 members and 200 churches. By 1925 membership had reached 50,000, with the number of churches approaching 1,000. A decade later membership had trebled, the largest representation of the Church being in Texas, Oklahoma, Arkansas, and Missouri. In 1950 (see Fig. 102), there were more than 6,000 churches, to be found chiefly in Texas (930), California (721), Oklahoma (479), and Arkansas (455). In September of 1955 the denomination's first liberal arts college, Evangel College in Springfield, Missouri, opened its doors.

A vigorous "Mission U. S. A." serves a large number of special groups in the continental United States. Indians and Jews have a separate ministry, as do the deaf and the imprisoned. Foreign language "branch" churches are to be found among Italian, Ukrainian, German, Polish, and especially among Central and South American immigrants. In 1958 there were 26 Assembly of God churches in Alaska and 20 in the Hawaiian Islands. In these and the numerous preaching stations from the Fiji Islands to the Congo, the salvation available to all men is boldly proclaimed. And they who have received the grace of God

may, by means of the direct witness of the Spirit, know of their new estate. The initial witness is the "physical sign of speaking with other tongues as the Spirit of God gives them utterance. Acts 2:4." But of even greater significance is the outward evidence of salvation: a life of righteousness and holiness. In the "Constitutional Declaration" adopted in 1927, the Assemblies of God voiced their earnest conviction that "entire sanctification is the will of God for all believers, and should be earnestly pursued by walking in obedience to God's Word. Heb. 12:14; 1 Peter 1:15,16; 1 Thess. 5:23,24; 1 John 2:6" (Winehouse, 209).

Churches of God. In few instances is the problem of terminology more difficult than in the case of the several "Church of God" groups currently in the United States. The unlimited, unmodified inclusiveness of the title is deliberate, for these bodies, like so many others in American history, desired not to create a new sect or denomination but only to recreate the New Testament church. Not only are there at least seven groups claiming the title "Church of God," there are "Churches of God" which are not to be confused with the singular form—even though historically these two titles were not carefully distinguished.

The first American use of the title "Church of God" was by John Winebrenner early in the nineteenth century. Winebrenner, a German Reformed minister of Harrisburg, Pennsylvania, was greatly influenced by the techniques and fruits of revivalism. Resisted in his own communion as

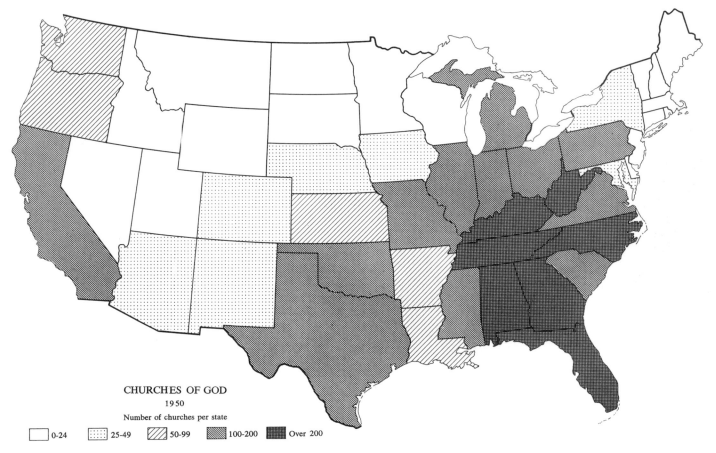

CHURCHES OF GOD
1950
Number of churches per state

☐ 0-24   ▦ 25-49   ▨ 50-99   ▩ 100-200   ▦ Over 200

Figure 103

his attachment to a more pietistic, emotional religious expression grew, Winebrenner and six friends in 1830 organized the General Eldership of the Church of God. Near the end of the century, the "Church" of the title was changed to "Churches of God," by which they are now known (with the phrase "General Eldership" usually added for clarity). Though having a significant chronological lead over similarly named denominations, the Winebrennerians did not make comparable progress, having 479 churches in 1890, but only 378 in 1957. At the beginning of the twentieth century, the membership of approximately 25,000 was heavily concentrated in 4 states: Pennsylvania, Ohio, Indiana, and Illinois. With the addition of Maryland, this area of concentration remained the same through 1950. In that year there were over 30,000 members, roughly half of them residing in Pennsylvania.

The Church of God (Anderson, Indiana), next in point of time to adopt the name, was founded by Daniel S. Warner in October, 1881, at Beaver Dam, Indiana. Warner, for whom the Church's publications division is now named, became a follower of John Winebrenner in 1872. Five years later, influenced by the National Association for the Promotion of Holiness, he accepted the doctrine of perfectionism and spoke of his own experience of entire sanctification. The General Eldership, rejecting this theology, in 1878 withheld Warner's license to preach, and for three years Warner moved about Indiana as an independent holiness evangelist. Then, as noted, in 1881 he

founded a church—or did he? The doubt arises as one recognizes Warner's great determination not to establish a church, but rather to create an open fellowship for all Christians unimpeded by distinctions of name or doctrine. At the beginning Warner sternly opposed all human organization, but then he saw a difference between *organizing a Church* (the Body of Christ) and *organizing the work of the Church* (missions, publications, education, worship, etc.). The latter, Warner concluded, was permissible; thus, once again in American religion, anarchy bowed before necessity. Technically known as the Church of God Reformation Movement, this body is usually distinguished by the designation of its headquarters: Anderson, Indiana. Here, in addition to the main offices, may be found the group's press, its principal college and its only seminary. While beginning in the Midwest, the denomination now has a large portion of its strength in the South and the Far West. At the end of the first quarter of the twentieth century, the Church of God (Anderson) had almost 40,000 members; by mid-century, it had a membership of over 100,000 (see Fig. 103).

In 1886 a movement in Tennessee led first by R. G. Spurling and later by A. J. Tomlinson resulted in the establishment of not one but many "Church of God" organizations. Among the bewildering multiplicity of offshoots, the largest is generally designated by its headquarters location: Cleveland, Tennessee. The problem is not fully solved thereby, however, since there are several

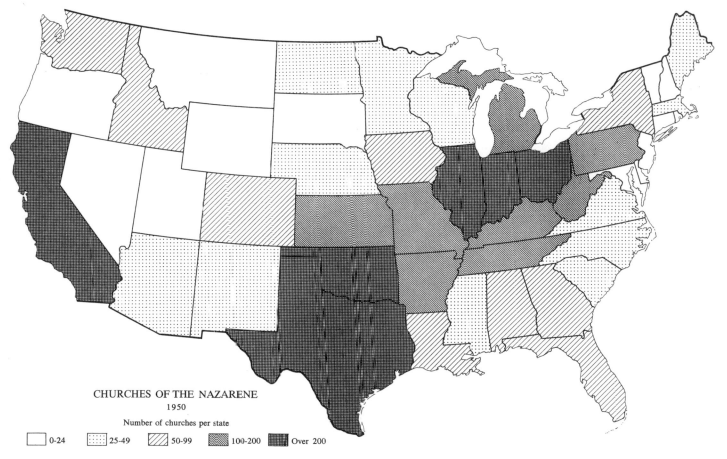

CHURCHES OF THE NAZARENE
1950
Number of churches per state

☐ 0-24   ▦ 25-49   ▨ 50-99   ▩ 100-200   ■ Over 200

Figure 104

groups which have their headquarters in Cleveland. The large group of which James A. Cross is currently General Overseer is the one referred to in Fig. 103. With emphasis upon speaking in tongues, the imminent return of Christ, and the three rites instituted by Jesus (baptism, Lord's Supper, washing of feet), the several institutional survivors of the efforts of Spurling and Tomlinson show a penchant both for growth and for separation. The name, "Church of God," was not taken until 1907 when an organizational meeting of 150 members and 5 churches gathered at Union Grove, Bradley County, Tennessee. Two decades later there were 932 churches, and by 1936 over 1,000. In 1950 there were 3,368 churches and approximately 175,000 members, with the group's strongest representation in the following states: Georgia, Florida, Alabama, North Carolina, and Tennessee.

Church of the Nazarene. Like the Christian and Missionary Alliance (founded by a Presbyterian, Dr. A. B. Simpson, in 1887) and the Free Methodist Church (established in 1860 by the Rev. B. T. Roberts), the Church of the Nazarene belongs to the conservative wing of the holiness movement. Each of these three bodies regards itself as preserving the Methodist tradition in purity, in sobriety, and in honor, obeying the command of John Wesley to "preach full sanctification, preach it definitely, preach it explicitly, preach it strongly, preach it wherever you have an opportunity."

The Church of the Nazarene was founded in Los Angeles in 1895 by Dr. P. F. Bresee, a pastor and presiding elder of the Methodist Episcopal Church. Many who had been caught up in the joy and hope of the holiness movement, feeling unmoved by or even unwelcome in their own denominations, believed that new organizations were necessary. The Nazarene Church, as one such organization, had the special gift of forming intimate alliances with similar developments and associations across the country. In 1907 the Church merged with an Eastern holiness body: the Association of Pentecostal Churches of America, founded in New York in 1895. They were of approximately equal size: the California group brought to the merger 52 churches and a membership of 3,827; the New York group, 47 churches and 2,371 members. In the next year, 1908, this "Pentecostal Church of the Nazarene" united with a holiness movement in the South, giving a truly national scope to the body. This southern addition, the Holiness Church of Christ, had a membership of 2,307 in 92 congregations. Fifteen years after its beginning in Los Angeles, the Church of the Nazarene (no longer "Pentecostal") had over 10,000 members. Twenty years later (1930), it had passed the 100,000 mark, and by mid-century there were already 225,000 members. From 135 charter members to 225,000 in a period of fifty-five years represents a respectable rate of growth indeed (see Fig. 104).

The mergers—east, west and south—also made possible an early dispersement of institutional centers of strength.

In the first decade of the twentieth century there were three bases for the Church's educational training: Deets Pacific Bible College (Los Angeles; later moved to Pasadena, becoming Pasadena College in 1915); Pentecostal Collegiate Institute (North Scituate, R. I.; later moved near Boston, becoming Eastern Nazarene College in 1918); Nazarene Bible School and Academy (Pilot Point, Texas; later absorbed with many other institutions, ultimately becoming Bethany Nazarene College, Bethany, Oklahoma). As the area between these three widely scattered points was evangelized by the Church and as other mergers were consummated, more schools were established: Trevecca Nazarene College (Nashville); Olivet Nazarene College (Olivet, then Kankakee, Illinois); Northwest Nazarene College (Nampa, Idaho). In 1945 the denomination's first graduate school of theology, the Nazarene Theological Seminary, was opened in Kansas City, Missouri.

SOURCES. C. E. Brown, *When the Trumpet Sounded: History of the Church of God* (Anderson [Ind.], 1951). H. K. Carroll, *The Religious Forces of the United States* (American Church History Series, I) (New York, 1893). Vergilius Ferm (ed.), *The American Church of the Protestant Heritage* (New York, 1953). M. E. Gaddis, "Christian Perfectionism in America" (Unpublished doctoral dissertation, University of Chicago, 1929; revised, 1939). F. E. Mayer, *The Religious Bodies of America* (St. Louis, 1954). Frank S. Mead, *Handbook of Denominations in the United States* (New York, 1951). H. Richard Niebuhr, *The Social Sources of Denominationalism* (New York, [reprint] 1957). M. E. Redford, *The Rise of the Church of the Nazarene* (Kansas City, no date). Timothy L. Smith, *Revivalism and Social Reform* (New York, 1957). Irwin Winehouse, *The Assemblies of God* (New York, 1959). A history of the National Association for the Promotion of Holiness (now National Holiness Association) is a major desideratum.

5. LIBERAL BODIES

From a mid-twentieth century point of vantage, several ecclesiastical or semi-ecclesiastical groups might well be considered among the "liberal bodies." This term, however, is here restricted to two denominations which not only have a history of significant duration but have officially accepted the label "liberal" in their cooperative organization, the Council of Liberal Churches. These two bodies, the Unitarians and the Universalists, moreover, voted in 1960 to become a single fellowship: the Unitarian Universalist Association.

Unitarians. While objections to or qualifications of Trinitarian orthodoxy go back at least as far as the Arianism of the third and fourth centuries, American Unitarianism as an organized entity dates from the early nineteenth century. As an anti-Calvinistic mood and movement, its roots lie in eighteenth-century New England where *The Beginnings of Unitarianism in America* have been perceptively described by Conrad Wright (Boston, 1955).

The institutional origin of American Unitarianism took the form of schism from the established Congregational churches of New England. (Joseph Priestly transplanted British Unitarianism into Pennsylvania, establishing a church in Northumberland in 1794 and one in Philadelphia in 1796, but the indigenous American movement did not rise from these efforts.) In 1810 there were 361 Congregational churches in Massachusetts; in the theological strife and legal struggle of the next few years, "ninety-six of these same churches passed over to Unitarianism, besides thirty parishes, where the same views predominated . . . and consequently the withdrawal of the churches from their meetinghouses. So that one hundred and twenty-six places of worship, with their appurtenances, and parish and church funds, were lost to the cause of evangelical religion and gained to its opposite" (Clark, 270).

The rift in Connecticut was not nearly so serious because, as a contemporary wrote, "that class of population, somewhat elevated by taste and education, which in Massachusetts became Unitarians, have in our commonwealth chosen to be Episcopalians, so that the material has here been wanting for proselytes to their faith" (*Contributions to the Ecclesiastical History of Connecticut* [the words are those of Abel McEwen], 274). By 1850 there were only 3 Unitarian churches in Connecticut (1 each in Fairfield, Hartford, and Windham counties), and none of those represented an actual split in a Congregational parish.

At the time of William Ellery Channing's famous ordination sermon in Baltimore, May 4, 1819 (often taken as the unofficial beginning of the denomination), Unitarianism was virtually limited to eastern Massachusetts. "A radius of thirty-five miles from Boston as a center would sweep almost the whole field of its history and influence" (Allen, *Historical Sketch of the Unitarian Movement*, 195). In Boston itself, every Congregational Church except one, rejecting the Calvinist doctrine of God and even more emphatically the Calvinist doctrine of man, had become Unitarian. But from this "hub of the universe" the organization did not move far in its earliest days.

In May of 1825 the American Unitarian Association was formed, providing some denominational direction to the progress of the churches. There was a Unitarian fellowship in Washington in 1820, in Cincinnati and Louisville in 1830, in Buffalo one year later, and in New Orleans (1833), St. Louis (1834), and Chicago (1836) before the decade had passed. As evident from the testimony of an English gentleman and scholar, Richard Flower, who migrated to Illinois in 1818, there was even some Unitarianism on the frontier. In Albion, Illinois, where any "hireling" ministry was severely frowned upon, Flower himself assisted in the leading of public worship, reading from either "the Reformed or Unitarian Liturgy, the Scriptures, and Sermons from our best English authors." And whereas dire predictions had been made regarding this "wicked infidel settlement," Flower proudly reported that in the three years which had "passed since the solemn

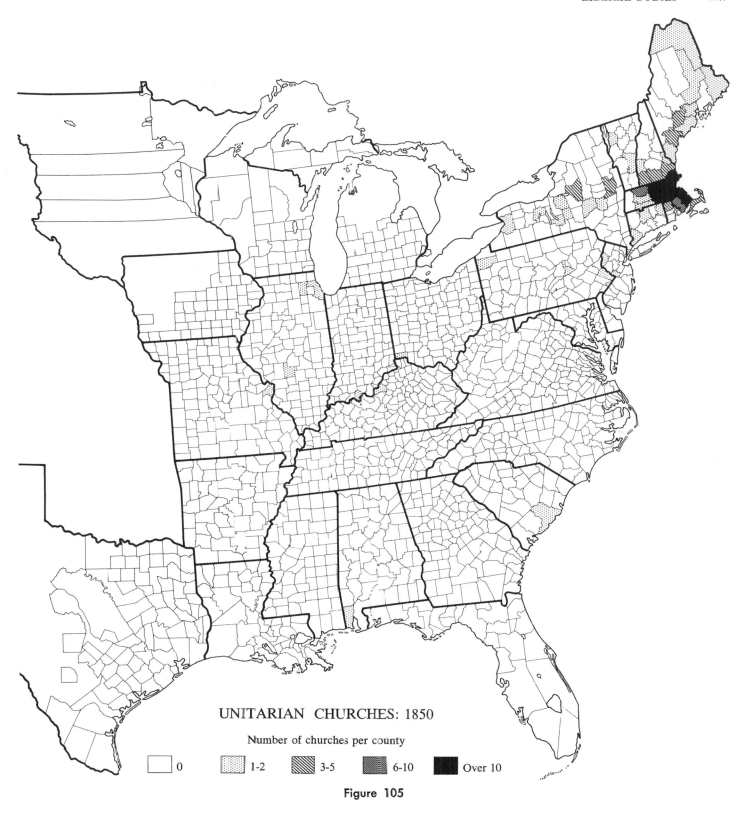

UNITARIAN CHURCHES: 1850

Number of churches per county

| | 0 | | 1-2 | | 3-5 | | 6-10 | | Over 10 |

Figure 105

warning was given," not only had a church "on the moderate candid Unitarian plan" been formed but also an "Episcopal Church of England" and one "for the use of the Calvinistic baptists" (Thwaites, X, 107 f.; 144 f.; 160 f.). But "moderate" plans of any sort were not suited to the competitiveness of the frontier, and in 1850 over 90% of all Unitarian churches were still to be found in New York and New England (see Fig. 105).

Unitarians not only had difficulty achieving geographical breadth, they also had a problem in building numerical strength. Part of that problem is now familiar to the reader: the originators of a new denomination had no desire to originate a new denomination. The very name "Unitarian" was rejected by many as sectarian, narrow, and divisive when all that was really intended was "a larger intellectual and religious life, free of the restraints imposed by a doctrinal system." And in that larger life, there was room for much controversy and dissension among the Unitarians themselves; a generation of struggle over miracles and the meaning of "Unitarian Christianity" pre-

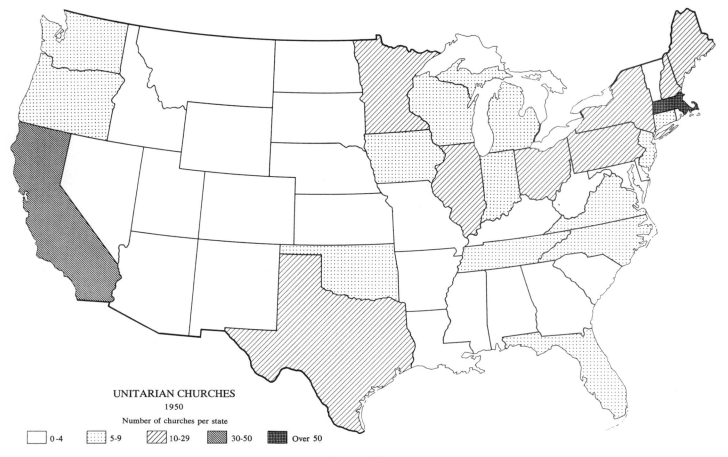

UNITARIAN CHURCHES
1950
Number of churches per state

☐ 0-4   ▦ 5-9   ▨ 10-29   ▧ 30-50   ■ Over 50

Figure 106

cluded any forceful expansion as each move toward tighter administrative control or direction found ready and powerful opposition. Furthermore, concerning the whole question of evangelizing or proselyting there was enough uncertainty or antipathy or divided opinion to obstruct an effective mission program. A present-day spokesman for the body responded to the question "Do Unitarians try to make converts?" with an unequivocal "No" (Rosten, 148).

The result has been a severely limited numerical progress by the American Unitarian Association. The vacillating from 246 churches (1850) to 455 (1900) and back to 357 (1950) suggests retrogression rather than progression (see Fig. 109). In membership, however, there has been some growth. In 1900 there were about 70,000 Unitarians; the denomination in 1950 reported a membership of 75,389 —a gain of 5,000 in fifty years. But by 1958 there had been a surprising jump to over 100,000. Nonetheless, the first half of the twentieth century for both the Universalists and the Unitarians was from a statistical point of view a time of relative stagnation or decline.

The strength of Unitarianism, however, has more often been measured in terms of influence than of numbers; particularly in the nineteenth century, Unitarianism, by this measuring, loomed large. Transcendentalism, rationalism, biblical criticism, and other currents which ran deep into American life first trickled out of and through New England Unitarianism—so much so that Unitarianism may be appropriately treated as a full and exciting chapter in America's intellectual history. In 1805 Congregationalists regarded Harvard as having been captured by the enemy. And to mention the names of John Adams, John Quincy Adams, Ralph Waldo Emerson, Nathaniel Hawthorne, Oliver Wendell Holmes, and Horace Mann is to suggest the weight of the impact which this group made in nineteenth-century America. In 1950 (see Fig. 106) the major centers of Unitarian strength were Massachusetts (145 churches), California (33), New York (27), Illinois (22) and New Hampshire (18); while every state in the union except Wyoming and Montana had at least 1 Unitarian church, 25 states had less than 5 within their respective borders.

Universalists. Like the anti-Trinitarian position of the Unitarians, the anti–eternal-damnation position of the Universalists has an ancient history. This denominational label points beyond the belief that Christ died for all men rather than only for a preordained and limited elect to the view that not only *can* all men be saved but all men *will*, in fact, be saved. An early "profession of belief," adopted in Winchester, New Hampshire, in 1803 declares that God "will finally restore the whole family of mankind to holiness and happiness."

Also, like Unitarianism, the institutional history of this other liberal body began in New England. In 1785 the first distinct organization was formed in Oxford, Massachusetts: an "Independent Christian Society, commonly called Universalists." This was the work of John Murray,

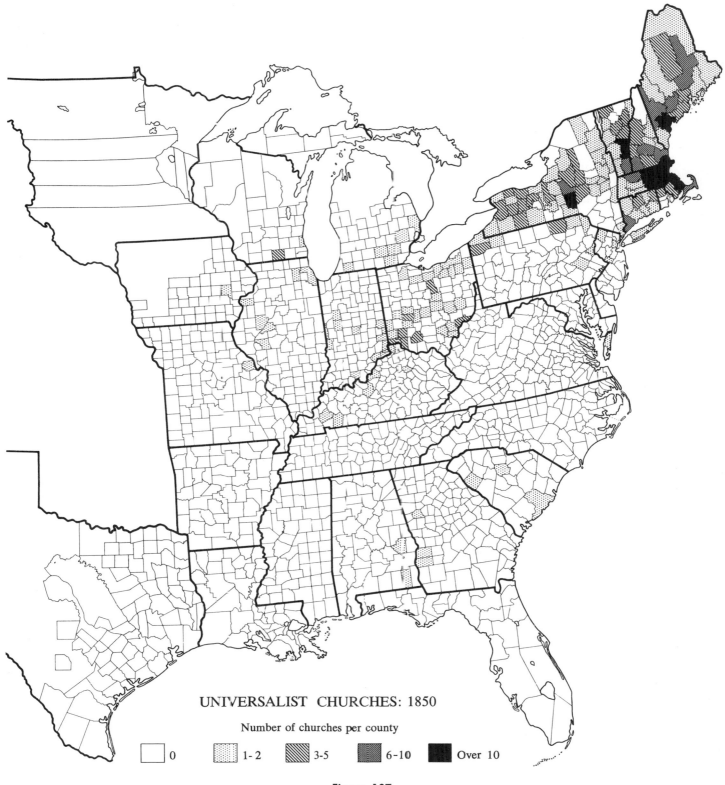

UNIVERSALIST CHURCHES: 1850

Number of churches per county

☐ 0　▦ 1-2　▨ 3-5　▨ 6-10　■ Over 10

Figure 107

an ex-Methodist, who in 1770 emigrated from England and set about preaching the views of Universalism from Philadelphia to Gloucester. Having at first no design to create a new church, he sought, as had others before him (e.g., Charles Chauncy, Jonathan Mayhew, George De Benneville and Richard Clarke), merely to persuade practicing Christians that the doctrine of hell and eternal retribution was inconsistent with their belief in a just and loving God.

Elhanan Winchester, a Baptist preacher converted to

Universalism in 1781, organized that year a "Society of Universal Baptists" in Philadelphia. Following this example, a number of Baptist ministers and laymen in Pennsylvania "fell in with Elhanan Winchester's notion of universal restoration. The rage for this doctrine prevailed for a time to a considerable extent" (Eddy, 411). One contemporary Baptist historian ruefully noted that "Nicholas Cox, a preacher in Kingwood, now grown wiser than his fathers, mounted the fractious steed of 'general provision'

UNIVERSALIST CHURCHES
1950
Number of churches per state

☐ 0-4   ⬚ 5-9   ⧄ 10-29   ▨ 30-50   ■ Over 50

Figure 108

and rode furiously on to the barren, hopeless, desolate plains of Universalism" (Eddy, 412). At a convention held in May, 1790, the delegates (who counted among their number Dr. Benjamin Rush, the well-known surgeon and signer of the Declaration of Independence), drawn largely from former Baptist churches, professed their faith in Christ Jesus

who, by giving himself a ransom for all, hath redeemed them to God by his blood; and who, by the merit of his death and the efficacy of his Spirit, will finally restore the whole human race to happiness (Eddy, 414).

While this was a far cry from the theory of atonement to be espoused in the next century by Hosea Ballou, it does reveal the gradual drift of this assembly toward the camp of John Murray. The organization of "Universal Baptists" dissolved soon after this convention, joining with Murray's "Independent Christian Society." By 1800, societies had been established not only in Pennsylvania and Massachusetts, but also in Maine, Vermont, New Hampshire, New York, and New Jersey.

In the nineteenth century, Universalism shifted deliberately in the direction of Unitarianism. Hosea Ballou, "the most eminent and influential of all the preachers of Universalism," led in this move. His *Treatise on Atonement* (1805) abandoned the ransom theory (noted above) holding in its stead that Christ's death was a mighty moral demonstration of God's love for all men. God sought no

vengeance, demanded no payment, wrought no retribution. The atonement was to change the heart of man, not the mind of God. Regarding the work of Christ, then, more in its natural than in its supernatural aspects, Universalists came gradually to speak of the "spiritual leadership of Jesus" rather than in terms appropriate to Nicene orthodoxy. In this way, a rapprochement with Unitarianism was made possible. A Unitarian historian stated in 1854, perhaps with some exaggeration, that Universalists "without exception, now hold Unitarian opinions" (Winebrenner, 206).

Although the Universalists, like the Unitarians, were at this time heavily concentrated in New England (in 1850, 285 out of 529 churches were in that region), yet the former body had achieved a greater geographical spread than the latter (compare Figs. 105 and 107). State conventions were organized in Virginia (1835), North Carolina (1824), South Carolina (1830), and Georgia (1838), but growth in these areas was never great. More successful was the work in the West, particularly Ohio, where Timothy Bigelow first preached the message of final reconciliation for all men in 1814. Universalism also enjoyed a measure of success in Indiana, which had a state convention by 1837. Illinois was organized into a convention in 1837; Michigan, Iowa, and Kentucky, in 1843; and Wisconsin, in 1848.

The hundred years from 1850 to 1950 were not years of steady progress for Universalism in America (see Fig. 110).

The peak of its growth in churches was at the end of the nineteenth century, when the number of separate societies reached almost 1,000. In terms of membership, there were about 50,000 Universalists in 1890. The federal census for 1906 reported 64,158 members, and in 1950 the denomination's report was 64,655 members—a precise preservation of the status quo. While Universalism had earlier enjoyed a numerical advantage over Unitarianism, this lead dropped away completely in the twentieth century. And

phony Hall, the vote was cast in favor of such a move (725 for the merger to 143 against, on the Unitarian side; 365 for the merger to 65 against, on the Universalist side). The new body, the Unitarian Universalist Association, has within its ranks a membership of over 170,000, divided among approximately 700 churches.

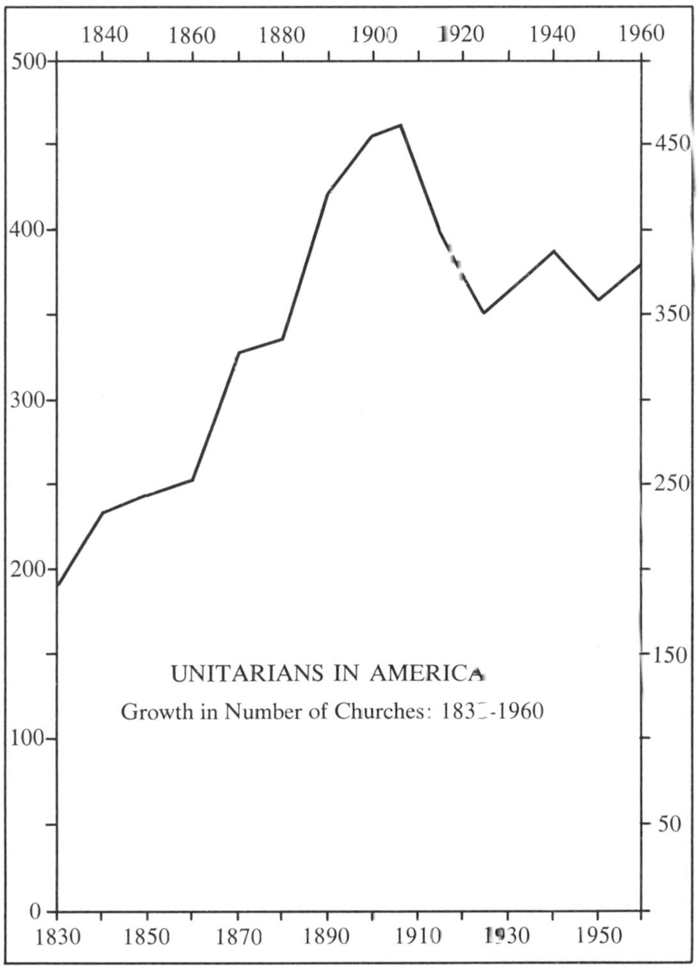

SOURCES. Joseph Henry Allen, *Historical Sketch of the Unitarian Movement Since the Reformation* (American Church History Series, X) (New York, 1894); ———, *Our Liberal Move-*

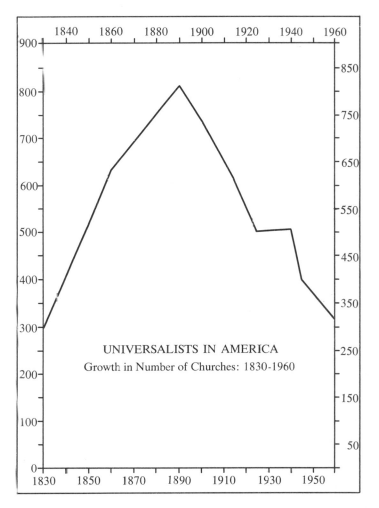

Figure 109

Figure 110

while Universalism showed early promise of breaking away from geographical parochialism, by 1950 it was, even more than Unitarianism, a phenomenon of the northeast. Of over 300 churches reported, about 200 were in the 5 states of New England, and another 40 were in New York (see Fig. 108).

Having grown closer together in their advocacy of liberal religion, and perhaps having felt the need of a strength that might be found in unity, Unitarians and Universalists moved in the direction of organic union. As early as 1937, the two denominations issued a common hymnbook. In October of 1959, as a result of four years of careful study by a joint commission, the machinery for actual merger was set into motion. On May 23, 1960, in Boston's Sym-

ment in Theology . . . (Boston, 1882). Hosea Ballou, *A Treatise on Atonement* . . . *and its glorious consequences in the Final Reconciliation of All Men To Holiness and Happiness* (Boston [6th. ed.], 1848). Joseph S. Clark, *A Historical Sketch of the Congregational Churches in Massachusetts from 1620 to 1858* (Boston, 1858). *Contributions to the Ecclesiastical History of Connecticut* . . . (New Haven, 1861). Richard Eddy, *History of Universalism* (American Church History Series, X) (New York, 1894). E. H. Gillett, "History and Literature of the Unitarian Controversy," [includes bibliography] *Historical Magazine*, XIX (1871). William Hutchinson, *The Transcendentalist Ministers* (New Haven, 1959). Leo Rosten (ed.), *A Guide to the Religions of America* (New York, 1955). Reuben Gold Thwaites, *Early Western Travels 1748-1846*, 32 vols. (Cleveland, 1904-1907). Earl Morse Wilbur, *A History of Unitarianism in Transylvania, England and America* (Cambridge, 1952); ———, *Our Unitarian Heritage* (Boston, 1925). John Winebrenner, *History of Religious Denominations in England and Scotland* . . . (Harrisburg, 1854). Conrad Wright, *The Beginnings of Unitarianism in America* (Boston, 1955).

6. OTHERS

Three groups are treated in this section: Christian Science, Evangelical United Brethren, and the Mennonite family.

Christian Science. A relative newcomer to the American denominational scene, Christian Science was founded in Boston in 1879 by Mary Baker Eddy (1821-1910). Having

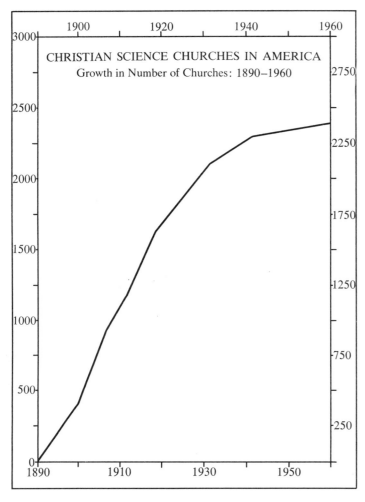

CHRISTIAN SCIENCE CHURCHES IN AMERICA
Growth in Number of Churches: 1890–1960

Figure 111

experienced the healing effect of right thinking in 1866, Mrs. Eddy spent some years informally telling others of her discovery. In 1875 she published *Science and Health with Key to the Scriptures,* a volume which later was to occupy a place of special authority in her Church. Of her book, Mrs. Eddy wrote: "I was only a scribe echoing the harmonies of heaven in divine metaphysics . . ." (Mayer, 528). These echoes are, for the contemporary Scientist, the means whereby the complete and perfect truth of the Bible can be known; without such means, the Bible remains shrouded in mystery.

Although some of the comments in *Science and Health* suggest a hesitation about or possibly even an opposition to formal church organization, Mrs. Eddy, like so many before her, concluded that such organization was neces-

sary. Twenty-six members secured a charter in 1879 from the state of Massachusetts for "The Church of Christ (Scientist)." Without a building of its own, this early group met in rented halls or members' homes. In 1881 Mrs. Eddy received another charter for a Massachusetts Metaphysical College, where for eight years (first in Lynn, then in Boston) she trained followers in the art of divine healing. Neither the Church nor the college was a permanent institution, the latter closing down in 1889 and the former being dissolved to make way in 1892 for the First Church of Christ, Scientist—the Mother Church. By this time the message of Mrs. Eddy had already reached Chicago and even California. When Mrs. Eddy appeared in Chicago's Central Music Hall in 1889, over 4,000 persons were on hand to greet her.

Though many Methodists, Baptists, Lutherans, and others might have some difficulty in naming immediately their denomination's first American church, no such difficulty will be experienced by the Christian Scientist. For the Mother Church, through its Board of Directors, from the beginning exercised a powerful and ever-present influence over each new society and, to a degree, over each new member. By this Church, lecturers are sent out, practitioners are recognized, new societies are approved. No literature is authorized, no instruction is permitted except as directed by the Mother Church. Scientists, moreover, may have a dual membership, being enrolled in their local church and in the Mother Church as well. This feature makes membership statistics an unreliable index to the growth of Christian Science.

By 1890 there were over 200 churches in the United States. Early in the twentieth century the Christian Science churches were to be found chiefly in the following states: Illinois (54), New York (51), California (35), Iowa (34), Ohio (34), Michigan (33), and Massachusetts (33). By 1910 there were more than 1,000 churches and, by 1930, over 2,000. This growth, however, was not unaccompanied by conflict.

When Mary Baker Eddy, Discoverer and Founder, died on December 3, 1910, so careful had been her organization that no major disruption was suffered by the young Church. The new structure of the Mother Church had been dedicated four years earlier, a tremendous First Church of Christ, Scientist had been opened in London, and Scientists in Edinburgh, at the time of her death, were preparing to build their "First Church." Also, a potential competitor, Mrs. Augusta Stetson of New York, had been ejected from the Church. For some time prior to 1910 Mrs. Eddy had withdrawn from the detailed management of her Church, leaving an approved Board of Directors to supervise and regulate the Society. Thus, one week after her passing, public notice was given that "the direction of the spiritual and business affairs of the Church [was] entirely in the hands of the Christian Science Board of Directors" and would continue so to be (Braden, 61).

Inescapable and puzzling difficulties arose, however,

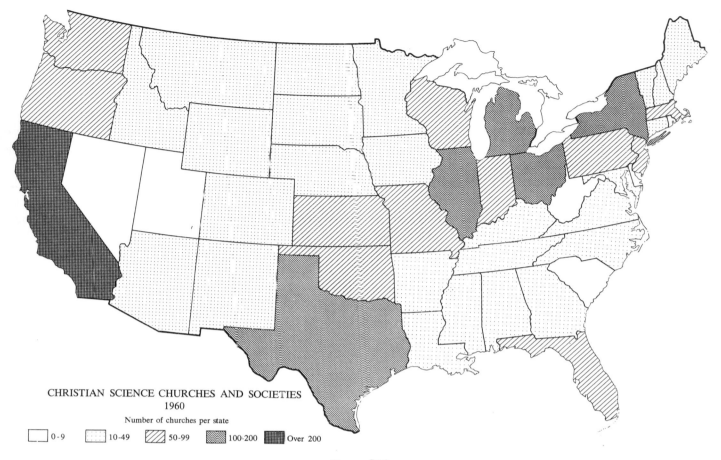

CHRISTIAN SCIENCE CHURCHES AND SOCIETIES
1960
Number of churches per state

☐ 0-9   ▢ 10-49   ▨ 50-99   ▦ 100-200   ■ Over 200

Figure 112

from the anomalous situation that prevailed in Mrs. Eddy's absence. The Church's *Manual* made most vital decisions dependent upon the approval of Mrs. Eddy herself, and it was by no means clear what, if anything, was to be substituted for that final confirmation. Some even suggested that this was the Founder's way of saying that, after her departure, the human organization of this divine metaphysics should cease to exist. The organization, however, rather than preparing itself for an early demise, grew in numbers and influence, both in the activities of the Mother Church and in the printed matter of the Publishing Society (founded in 1898). And it was a protracted conflict between the governing boards of these two organizations which in the years 1918 to 1921 produced the Great Litigation. The question before the courts of Massachusetts was whether the Church's Board of Directors was the final authority in all matters pertaining to the organization created by Mrs. Eddy, or whether the two boards of directors —that of the Mother Church and that of the Publishing Society, both established by Mrs. Eddy—were to enjoy autonomy, though working together in harmony. Clearly the latter view had support within the Publishing Society, else the legal wrangle would have been unnecessary. Ultimately, the courts recognized the Board of Directors as the supreme and final authority in the Church, though a wide measure of independence is preserved by the Society, which publishes such familiar and respected items as the *Christian Science Monitor* (1908) and the *Christian Science*

Journal (1883). Other dissatisfactions and minor schisms notwithstanding, the Church's progress, especially in the period after World War I, continued apace (see Fig. 111).

Without a public ministry, without a program of evangelism, what factors promote the twentieth-century growth of Christian Science? First, there are the numerous, strategically located, capably staffed propaganda centers: the Christian Science Reading Rooms. Attractive and accessible, they draw many shoppers, idlers, and seekers into their alcoves. Second, though there are no priests or deacons, there are lecturers (about 30) who speak not only to the congregations but, more significantly, to the public at large. For the Christian Science lecture, in any given community, is a major event, usually held in a capacious hall and invariably heralded by widespread, tasteful publicity. Third, there is literature—quantities of carefully edited, attractively printed, freely circulated literature. Airport and train terminals, hotels, and supermarkets serve as repositories for journals, newspapers, and pamphlets that, subtly or directly, turn the reader's mind toward Christian Science. With the possible exception of the Jehovah's Witnesses, no religious group in America has done so much so effectively with the printed page. Fourth, there is organization which is both skillful and tight, preventing a dissipation of energies, a dilution of doctrine. Fifth, the Wednesday evening service featuring personal testimonies of recent healings provides the most effective engine of conversion ever known: "Once I was blind, but now I see."

Though the size of this growing membership is not revealed by the Mother Church, the nature of that membership may be known in part. It is typically urban and upper middle class. Practitioners (those who pray for the sick and enjoy official recognition in this capacity) are predominantly women, by a proportion of more than 10 to 1. The absence of an aggressive social program has something to do with the relative scarcity of young people in the churches, though Christian Science's focus on problems of health also has greater impact in post-adolescent years. In 1960 about one-sixth of all Scientist churches in America were to be found in California. As Figure 112 shows, the states with the next largest number of churches were New York (173), Illinois (142), Ohio (116), Michigan (113), and Texas (112). The message of the eternal reality of Spirit, Life, Truth, Love, and Principle had even reached the outposts of America, with 5 churches or societies active in Alaska and 5 in Hawaii.

Evangelical United Brethren. This Church reached its present form in 1946 as a result of a merger of the United Brethren and the Evangelical Church. Deriving from a background among German-speaking residents of Pennsylvania, Maryland, and Virginia, both of the bodies—eager for a more intensely personal, experimental religion—were founded about the beginning of the nineteenth century. Oriented toward Methodism (this was especially true of the Evangelical Church), the movements sought to bear their share in Christianizing along the expanding frontier.

Of the two constituent bodies, the United Brethren was the first to be established. Philip William Otterbein (1726-1813), a German Reformed minister, joined with a Mennonite preacher, Martin Boehm (1725-1812), in conducting revivals among the Germans of the Middle and Southern Colonies. By 1800 a definite organization was formed under the leadership of Otterbein and Boehm. The task of developing that organization, however, fell to Christian Newcomer (1749-1830), also of Mennonite background. Bishop Newcomer organized the first classes in 1813, urged the adoption of a Confession and a Discipline, and personally led in the westward expansion of the Church. The first General Conference of the United Brethren Church was held at Mt. Pleasant, Pennsylvania, in 1815, by which time preaching stations had been established in Ohio, Indiana, and Kentucky. The creation of a conference in 1810 west of the Alleghenies (Miami Conference) demonstrated the greatest frontier center of strength: Ohio's Miami Valley. At this time there were also three eastern conferences: Pennsylvania, Maryland, and Virginia. Recognizing rather early the conflict between an aggressive evangelistic program and a continued use of the German language, the United Brethren began a gradual shift to English. Before the end of the century, less than 5% of their churches were German-speaking.

In 1870 there were 1,445 separate organizations of United Brethren in America. The states in which the denomination was at that time most strongly represented were Ohio (370), Pennsylvania (201), Iowa (188), Indiana (184), and Illinois (125). In 1890 the Church had a membership of over 200,000, with approximately one-half of that membership residing in Ohio, Pennsylvania, and Indiana. At the occasion of the merger in 1946, these were still the principal centers of strength (see Fig. 113). Membership at that time was less than 500,000.

The Evangelical Church resulted principally from the efforts of Jacob Albright (1759-1808), a Lutheran layman, who near the end of the eighteenth century came strongly under the influence of Methodism. (Indeed, a proposal to form a German branch of Methodism was later turned down by Bishop Francis Asbury.) In 1803, at the first council of the Evangelical Association (*Evangelische Gemeinschaft* was the early name of the denomination), held in Pennsylvania, 16 followers acknowledged "Jacob Albright as a true Evangelical preacher in word and deed" (Spreng, 400). Twenty-eight persons attended the first General Conference, held in 1807 in Kleinfeltersville, Pennsylvania. Albright died the next year, but the infant body was carefully nurtured by other able men, notably John Driesback (1789-1871) and John Seybert (1791-1860). The record of the latter reads like that of a Methodist circuit rider, which, among the German families, Seybert virtually was: 175,000 miles by horse from 1820 to 1860; 9,850 sermons in that time, and 46,000 pastoral visits. Not as ready to abandon the German language as the United Brethren had been, the Evangelicals continued to preach and publish in German throughout the nineteenth century; the anti-German reaction during World War I did much to diminish the use of the language.

By 1870 the Evangelicals had over 800 churches, their greatest concentration being in Pennsylvania (256), Wisconsin (179), and Ohio (157). In 1890 this Church had over 130,000 members, approximately one-half of them in these 3 states. At the 1946 merger, Ohio, Michigan, Illinois, and Wisconsin were, with Pennsylvania (far ahead of all), the areas of greatest strength (see Fig. 113). Membership at that time was approximately 250,000.

On November 16, 1946, these two ecclesiastical organizations met in Johnstown, Pennsylvania, to consummate a half century of ecumenical labors and overtures. The two groups seemed ideally suited for this appropriate climax. Since they had originated in the same area (Lancaster County, Pennsylvania), about the same time (beginning of the nineteenth century), among the same people (German-speaking—whether Lutheran, Reformed, Mennonite, or Dunkard), the wonder is that they took so long to find each other. But as has often been brought out in the earlier pages of this book, the nineteenth century was—with rare exception—the time of schism; the twentieth century—with some promise—the time of union. The combined strength of 750,000 members and over 4,000 churches, still heavily concentrated in half a dozen states,

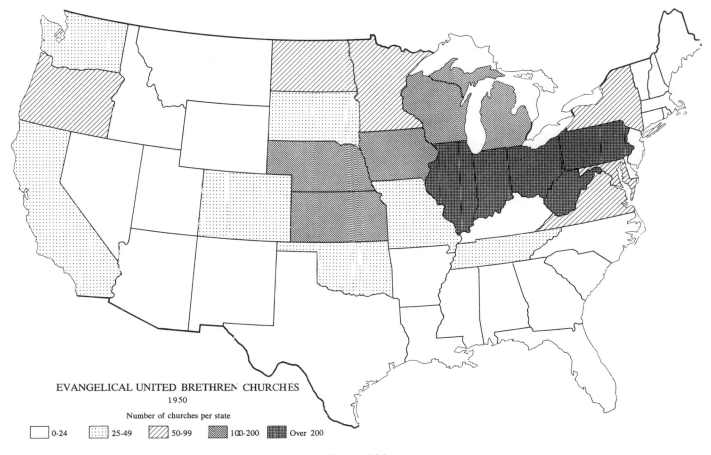

EVANGELICAL UNITED BRETHREN CHURCHES
1950
Number of churches per state
☐ 0-24   ⊞ 25-49   ⧄ 50-99   ⧄ 100-200   ⊟ Over 200

Figure 113

will help take the "German Methodist" light out from under a bushel and set it upon a stand.

Mennonite. Unlike the two groups described above, the Mennonites constitute a loosely organized or sometimes quarreling family rather than an administrative unity. With at least 16 separate organizations in 1960, this religious body has made its impact on American life in ways other than numerical. No attempt is made here to deal with each segment of Mennonite institutional life, but only with the principal branches of the family tree.

Comparatively speaking, the Mennonites had an early start in America, having established their first permanent settlement in the Philadelphia area in 1683. For a generation thereafter, however, their numbers in the New World were not significantly augmented. But after 1710 a sizable Mennonite immigration (mostly Swiss) began. Demonstrating from the first a powerful social cohesion, these new arrivals settled in the Conestoga and Pequea valleys of Lancaster County, Pennsylvania, as well as in the area of Souderton, Pennsylvania, in portions of Montgomery and Bucks counties. In the course of the eighteenth century, some of those in the East moved west, and were joined by additional brethren coming directly from Europe. Virginia, Ohio, and Indiana were penetrated early.

In the nineteenth century more Swiss Mennonites arrived, settling chiefly in Wayne County, Ohio, and Adams County, Indiana. There was also a large number of Swiss

Amish who in this time found their way into western Pennsylvania and even further west. The Amish, descended from a 1693 separation among Swiss Mennonites, took their name from Jacob Ammann, an elder who stood for greater resistance to cultural accommodation and for greater severity in disowning the excommunicated brother.

In the last quarter of the nineteenth century, and following the two World Wars of the twentieth, many Mennonites left Russia for the Western Hemisphere. The earlier immigrants settled chiefly in Minnesota, South Dakota, Nebraska, and Kansas, while the later ones for the most part went either to Canada or to South America. By 1890 there were over 40,000 Mennonites in the United States, and 550 churches. Of the latter, Pennsylvania led with 188; Ohio had 77; Kansas, 62; Indiana, 51; and Illinois, 32. At the turn of the century, there were approximately 50,000 Mennonites in America. At mid-century, membership was 130,000 and the number of churches over 1,000.

The ecclesiastical fortune of the Mennonites has been clouded by repeated schism, more often on questions of social than of theological propriety. At the beginning of the nineteenth century, only two groups were recognized in America: the Mennonites and the Amish. Around the middle of that century, a major split rent the Mennonites into (1) the Mennonite Church and (2) the General Conference of the Mennonites of North America. The second group, the "New Mennonites," were less severe in their discipline and less rigid in their isolation. Showing a de-

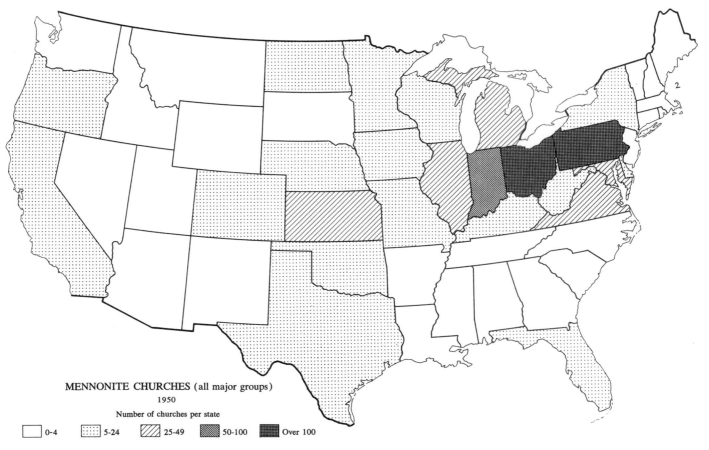

MENNONITE CHURCHES (all major groups)
1950
Number of churches per state

| 0-4 | 5-24 | 25-49 | 50-100 | Over 100 |

Figure 114

sire to participate more fully in the main stream of American life, this body practices open communion, cooperates with other denominations, treats ceremonial footwashing as optional, and permits instrumental music in the churches. Like all Mennonites, these of the General Conference embrace the doctrine of nonresistance and reject the taking of any oath.

The first group named above, the Mennonite Church or "Old Mennonites," is the largest division of this fellowship. With over 70,000 members, this Church can claim almost one-half of all America's Mennonites. Regarding itself as the original group in the United States, the Mennonite Church has steadily maintained its numerical superiority. Toward the end of the nineteenth century, Sunday Schools, mission programs and colleges were added to the denominational structure, thus provoking the schism of the Old Order Mennonites who rejected such trappings. At mid-century, the group's 500 churches (see Fig. 114) were to be found principally in Pennsylvania (195), Ohio (50), Virginia (42), and Indiana (39).

The Amish in America are represented chiefly by the Old Order Amish, "the extreme traditionalists of the Mennonite family." Not all Amish are encompassed in the "Old Order," but the great majority are. Though less than 20,000 in number, these people, because of their determined separateness, are rather well known. The peculiarities of manner and dress, the rejection of modern plumbing and lighting, the adherence to the German lan-

guage as well as to the horse and buggy—these have received wide reporting via press, pulpit, and Broadway.

These three divisions among Mennonites (the General Conference, the Mennonite Church, the Old Order Amish) account for approximately four-fifths of the entire communion. A group strongly influenced by the holiness concern for entire sanctification, the United Missionary Church, has a membership of over 15,000. The remaining groups, however, lack significant numerical strength, ranging in membership from about 5,000 to about 400. In three counties of the United States, the Mennonites in 1950 were the leading religious body [see color map]: Holmes, Ohio; Lagrange, Indiana; and Oscoda, Michigan.

SOURCES. Raymond W. Albright, "Churches Can Unite," *Christian Century*, LXIII:43 (October 23, 1946). Norman Beasley, *The Cross and the Crown* (New York and Boston, 1952). D. Berger, *History of the Church of the United Brethren in Christ* (American Church History Series, XII) (New York, 1894). C. S. Braden, *Christian Science Today: Power, Policy, Practice* (Dallas, 1958). *The Christian Science Journal*, LXXXVIII:7 (July, 1960). Paul H. Eller, *These Evangelical United Brethren* (Dayton, 1950). Vergilius Ferm (ed.), *The American Church of the Protestant Heritage* (New York, 1953). F. E. Mayer, *The Religious Bodies of America* (St. Louis, 1954). Lyman P. Powell, *Mary Baker Eddy* (Boston, 1930). E. Mary Ramsay, *Christian Science and Its Discoverer* (Boston, 1923; revised 1935). Leo Rosten (ed.), *A Guide to the Religions of America* (New York, 1955). Samuel P. Spreng, *History of the Evangelical Association* (American Church History Series, XII) (New York, 1894). John C. Wenger, *Glimpses of Mennonite History and Doctrine* (Scottdale [Pa.], 1947); ———, *Separated Unto God* (Scottdale [Pa.], 1951).

PART IV

Special Aspects of Religion in America

1. INTRODUCTION

By no means can all of America's religious development be encompassed by or fully understood through a purely denominational account. Though this limitation applies pre-eminently to any broadly conceived cultural history, it is true even of a study that is primarily statistical and geographical. Among the many topics deserving a more extended treatment, five "special aspects" of American religion are considered here. The Indians, the Jews, and the Negroes, constituting historically definable ethnic communities within the national community, have presented particular challenges to, or new expressions of, institutional religion in America. Alaska and Hawaii, latest members of the American federation, have similarly presented unusual challenges and novel expressions: Hawaii, as the most diverse racially and religiously of all the 50 states; Alaska, as the last great land mass to be developed as the nation answered its westward call to the Pacific.

Part IV is concluded by a brief backward glance at three hundred years of religion in America.

2. INDIANS

The story of the Indian in the white man's America is one of sharpest contrasts: brotherhood and hate, missionary devotion and senseless spoliation, noble sacrifice and base betrayal. On both the white and the Indian sides there was enough suspicion of motive throughout three hundred years of contact to prevent the kind of "blending" and "intermixing" into one people which Thomas Jefferson envisioned. What took place, rather, was a series of massacres and wars, treaties and migrations, interspersed with earnest efforts to understand and even to aid each other.

To the million Indians who roamed the rich lands of North America in the sixteenth century, the "white man problem" could be viewed only as an unwelcome, intolerable invasion. To the white colonists of the seventeenth century, the "Indian problem" was seen principally in terms of savage hordes to be converted, subdued, or exterminated. So antithetical were the positions, so contrary the drives, so irreconcilable the cultures that the wisdom of a Solomon could hardly have found a peaceable solution. Yet there were men who proved that the Indian could be dealt with fairly and could deal fairly in return. There also were men who proved that the command to go, baptize and preach had not been forgotten and would not be ignored.

The earliest efforts to convert the Indians to Christianity, made by the Roman Catholics, have been briefly considered in Part I. The missionary heroism and vision evident in the demanding days of the sixteenth and seventeenth centuries hardly lessened in the succeeding years, and the disappointments appeared only to increase. As the power of Spain and France disappeared from the continental United States, the promise of widespread successes among the Indians often disappeared too. Furthermore, Mexico's fight for independence from Spain early in the nineteenth century failed to give any comfort to the Franciscan Fathers in the West. In 1833 the secularization of the California missions began, with land being turned over to secular authorities or to Christian Indians, with funds in Mexico being confiscated, and with some missions even being sold at auction. By mid-nineteenth century, the old colonial order had passed away; new strategy and new organization were necessary to execute the obligation of the Church to go "unto all the nations."

Early Protestant efforts had the advantage and at the same time the liability of being largely unofficial and nonpolitical. The advantage lay in the absence of an obvious and frequently crass imperialism which had proved a constant embarrassment to the Catholic missionaries. The liability was that Protestant missions were generally on a small, if often daring, scale. In 1613 the Anglican cleric Alexander Whitaker advertised among the assets of Virginia the opportunities which it offered for compassion toward "the miserable condition of those naked slaves of the divell. . . ." In response to Whitaker's *Good Newes from Virginia* and even more to the socially successful visit of Pocahontas to England in 1616, the Church of England began parish collections for the education and conversion of Virginia's Indians. Plans proceeded apace until 1622 when a brutal Indian massacre of 300 Virginia whites brought missionary interest to a sudden stop. English population dropped from 2,960 in 1622 to 1,800 by the following year.

In New England the harvest was more rewarding. The first Indian Congregational church was established on Martha's Vineyard in 1642. This island, as well as Nantucket, had been purchased by Thomas Mayhew the previous year. Under the remarkable leadership of the Mayhew family through five generations, missionary labors there continued among the Indians, though the Indian population of the islands steadily dwindled throughout the eighteenth century. Another Congregational church for Indians was gathered in Sandwich (Massachusetts) in

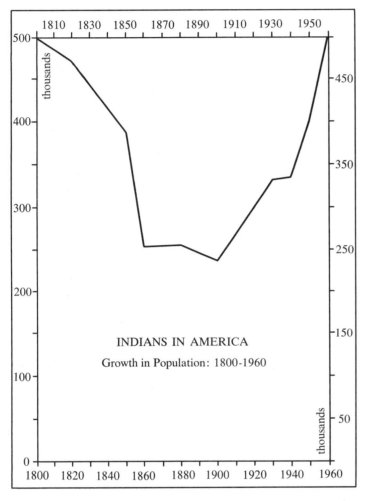

Figure 115

1658, 1 at Natick in 1660, 3 at Middleborough (for different tribes) in 1665, and 1 each at Mashpee and West Tisbury in 1670 and 1680 respectively. Cotton Mather judged that by the end of the century there had been 3,000 Indian converts on Martha's Vineyard and Nantucket alone.

The first Bible to be printed in America was in behalf of the Indians: the famous "Indian Bible" of the Congregational missionary, John Eliot. In 1661 he published in Cambridge *The New Testament of our Lord and Saviour Jesus Christ. Translated into the Indian Language, And Ordered to be Printed by the Commissioners of the United Colonies in New-England, At the Charge, and with the Consent of the Corporation in England For the Propagation of the Gospel amongst the Indians in New-England;* in 1663 the Old Testament was added. As early as 1646 Eliot had begun preaching to the Indians of Massachusetts, and by 1651 he had established a settlement at

Natick, 18 miles southwest of Boston. A decade later he founded a church, exercising great care that those admitted to full communion were well informed concerning the significance of the step. By the time of the publication of his Bible in phonetic equivalents of the Algonquin language, other Congregationalists in New England had taken up similar labor. All of this effort was very nearly lost by a devastating, organized Indian attack: King Philip's War, 1675-76. In terms of the proportionate losses to the settlers, it was America's severest war, for more than 600 English colonists were killed and more than a dozen towns razed. Between 10% and 20% of the Indian population of Massachusetts and Rhode Island were casualties of the war.

In the eighteenth century, missionary activity among the Indians was renewed as a result of the wave of revivalism which swept over the colonies. The Boston pastor, Benjamin Colman, observed in 1742 that "the Clans or Tribes of *Indians,* the Reliques of *Mokeage, Pequots* and *Niantic's . . .* who have obstinately continu'd in *Infidelity"* did during the Great Awakening apply for "Instruction to the Pastors about them, and receive it greedily, and with great Thankfulness, and Numbers of them seem savingly wrought upon" (*Proceedings of the Massachusetts Historical Society,* LIII, 213). A Mohegan convert from New London, Samson Occom, the first pupil of Eleazar Wheelock's Indian school in Lebanon, Connecticut, became New England's first ordained Indian. Delawares from New Jersey and Iroquois from New York traveled to the Charity School at Lebanon, frequently returning to their own people in the capacity of Christian missionaries.

One Connecticut youth, David Brainerd, was to have an influence among the Indians extending far beyond his brief and poignant life (1718-1747). Working chiefly with the tribes of New York and New Jersey, Brainerd preached with a single-minded saintly devotion "of the love and compassion of God in sending his Son to suffer for the sins of men." Stricken by tuberculosis, Brainerd died at the age of 29, being ministered to in his last days by his fiancée, Jonathan Edwards' daughter, who shortly after joined him in death. Edwards gave him enduring fame, however, by publishing the *Memoirs of Rev. David Brainerd,* taken chiefly from the latter's diary. This account, going through many reprints, editions, and enlargements, served as a powerful magnet, drawing others into a commitment to the Indian cause. Before the eighteenth century ended, Protestant missions had been founded not only in the New England and Middle Colonies, but as far west as Ohio and as far south as Georgia.

In the nineteenth century, Protestants and Catholics alike, though faced with a multitude of problems attending the westward thrust and the immigrant shove, continued to found new Indian missions and send out more preachers. The difficulties in winning the Indian to Christianity were many. (1) The linguistic diversity appeared to be limitless; in order to be heard by each knot of a few hundred or possibly only a few dozen, an entire language had to be mastered and perhaps written symbols had to be invented. (2) The religious diversity was such that Christianity had to be presented in widely differing terms, the strategic approach shifting from tribe to tribe. (3) The broad geographical spread, as well as the high mobility of the Indian, often made mission efforts a nightmare; the continuity and intensity so necessary to any fruitful, meaningful indoctrination seemed impossible to obtain. (4) Hostility to and suspicion of all that was the white man's was, understandably, a continuing element in the individual or tribal life of a majority of Indians. And conversely, (5) the white man's exploitation and bungling, as well as his diseases and drinks, made many missionary labors a hollow mockery.

Early in the nineteenth century, the government of the United States began dealing with the Indians on grounds other than extermination—the "ultimate solution." In 1819 Congress offered legislation to prevent "the further decline" of the Indians and to introduce among them "the habits and arts of civilization." An annual appropriation of $10,000 was voted for the education of the Indian in agriculture and the three "R's." Since, however, the federal government had no machinery for the administration of these funds, the money was granted as subsidies to the several missionary schools already serving the Indian. Indirectly, the government was therefore (as Kenneth Scott Latourette points out) "effectively subsidizing the efforts of the churches to win the Indians to the Christian faith" (*A History of the Expansion of Christianity,* IV, 301). The agencies of government indeed often had to depend on those whom the Indians trusted, from Roger Williams, who in 1636 helped Massachusetts forestall a potentially disastrous alliance between the Pequots and the Narragansetts, to Father De Smet, who in 1868 interceded between the angered Sioux and the United States to bring about peace. In the twentieth century all federal aid to mission schools ceased, though the government continued to act as a third party in contracts between the tribes and the schools.

From the $31 spent for Indian affairs in 1800 to the more than $62,000,000 spent in 1950, the United States government has sought acceptable adjustments between a relentless, land-hungry white advance and a dispirited, land-loving Indian retreat. Into the tangled web of Indian Affairs—of stewardship honored and abused, of treaties made and broken, of land given and taken away, of hospitals and schools established or postponed, of legal and physical protection proffered or denied—it is not possible to enter here. It must be noted, however, that governmental policy toward the Indians was not unrelated to the progress or failure of evangelical missions among the Indians. Sometimes the churches and the national policy were at loggerheads; at other times, official policy reflected the recommendations of the missionaries who themselves were on occasion appointed as executors of that policy.

Following the collapse of European influence in the American continent, Roman Catholicism continued its Indian work under the leadership of its American bishops. John Carroll of Baltimore joined the Bishop of Boston in maintaining the work begun in Maine two centuries earlier by the French (see Part I, 9). Bishops Benedict Flaget of Bardstown and Edward Fenwick of Cincinnati likewise sought to revive the dying embers of holy fires started by Jesuits in and around the Mississippi Valley. The first Bishop of Marquette, Frederic Bavaga, began his work in America as a missionary to the Indians, using his personal wealth and raising additional funds from Europe to further the Christian cause among the aborigines. Bishop Du Bourg of Louisiana and the Floridas (see above, p. 102) invited the reconstituted Society of Jesus to take up once more its interrupted task in his diocese. Diligent, though often frustrated, efforts made in behalf of the Osages, Kickapoo, Potawatomi, Miami, Ottawas, and Chippewas produced Indian converts over a wide area west of the Mississippi.

Many of the Jesuits involved in these labors were from Belgium, and the best known of all Belgian Jesuits in nineteenth-century America was Pierre Jean De Smet (1801-1873). On March 27, 1840, Father De Smet set out from St. Louis on his first trip to the Rockies, traveling via the Oregon Trail, "the broadest, longest, and most beautiful road in the whole world—from the United States to the Pacific Ocean," in De Smet's own words (Garraghan, II, 253). His mission, said Bishop Rosati, was "to visit and evangelize the various tribes of aborigines living beyond the Rocky Mountains, some of whom, in particular those called the Flatheads, have through deputies dispatched repeatedly to St. Louis signified a most ardent desire for the Catholic faith and have earnestly begged for a priest by whom they might be instructed. Therefore, in order to accede to the wishes of the little ones asking for bread and for a minister to break it unto them, we send this strenuous herald of the Gospel in very truth even to the ends of the earth . . ." (Garraghan, II, 253).

A permanent mission was formed among the Flatheads the next year, and in succeeding years among other tribes of the Northwest as well. De Smet, who also came to know well the Blackfeet and the Sioux, toiled ceaselessly and planned imaginatively for the Indians he loved, looking forward in confidence to that day when "the scalping-knife might . . . soon be laid aside," when instead of the war whoop which "has for centuries resounded" there might be heard "the canticles and praises of the true and only living God" (Thwaites, XXIX, 172).

The extent and number of other Catholic enterprises may be noted in Fig. 116. Missions among the Choctaw in Louisiana, the Sioux in Minnesota, the Apaches in

INDIAN MISSIONS,
1567-1861

B. = BAPTIST
C. = CATHOLIC
CO. = CONGREGATIONALIST
E. = EPISCOPALIAN
F. = FRIENDS
L. = LUTHERAN
M. = METHODIST
MO. = MORAVIAN
P. = PRESBYTERIAN
PR. = PROTESTANT

Texas, the Navahos in New Mexico, the Hopi in Arizona and the Blackfeet in Montana suggest the breadth of the parish ministered to by the Roman Catholic Church. In 1874 the Bureau of Catholic Indian Missions was formed both to aid in the over-all direction of a scattered flock and to improve co-ordination with the federal government. Later, Mother Katherine Drexel (1858-1955) poured her wealth and her energies into the American missions, founding in 1891 the Sisters of the Blessed Sacrament for Indians and Colored People. Sisters and Brothers, seculars and laymen, in the twentieth century extended the Indian work, making possible by mid-century a gathering of approximately 100,000 Indian Catholics.

As Protestantism crossed the Alleghenies, pushing the imaginary frontier line ahead of the sparse settlements,

the Indian continued to be the object of the missionary's concern. Sometimes, indeed, the missionary found himself in the anomalous position of resenting the advance of his own people and resisting the policies of his own government. Newly organized home mission societies kept in view not only the advancing white settler but also the now more accessible red hunter. While some of the Protestant efforts were of an interdenominational nature, directed by such entities as the American Board of Commissioners for Foreign Missions (1810), the Society for Propagating the Gospel among the Indians (1787), and the National Indian Association (1881), most of the work was denominational in character.

Baptist Isaac McCoy (1784-1846) led in the organization of a large number of Indian missions. Persuaded

Figure 116

that the aboriginal American would be better off separated from the avaricious, whisky-drinking white, McCoy argued for the creation of an Indian Territory in the West and for a while served under the federal government to this end. Methodist Jason Lee (1803-1845) paved the way for his denomination generally in Oregon Territory, laboring with particular effectiveness among the Indians of Willamette Valley. As "promoter, developer, business adviser, and constant advocate of the Americanization of the country," Lee led in the formation of a territorial government, protected the material and political interests of the Indians, and was instrumental in the founding of Willamette University. Presbyterian Sheldon Jackson

(1834-1909) began his missionary career in 1858 in a school for Choctaw boys at Spencer, Indian Territory. In 1859 he was transferred to Minnesota, and in 1870 he was made superintendent of the vast area which encompasses the present states of Montana, Wyoming, Utah, Colorado, New Mexico, and Arizona. For a dozen years he wrought mightily in this region, earning more than enough laurels on which to rest; but instead of resting he launched in 1877 a second career in Alaska (see Part IV, 5). Episcopalian Eleazar Williams (c. 1789-1858), himself a half-breed, under the direction of Bishop Henry Hobart translated the prayer book and hymns into the Iroquois language, led a group of converts from New York to a

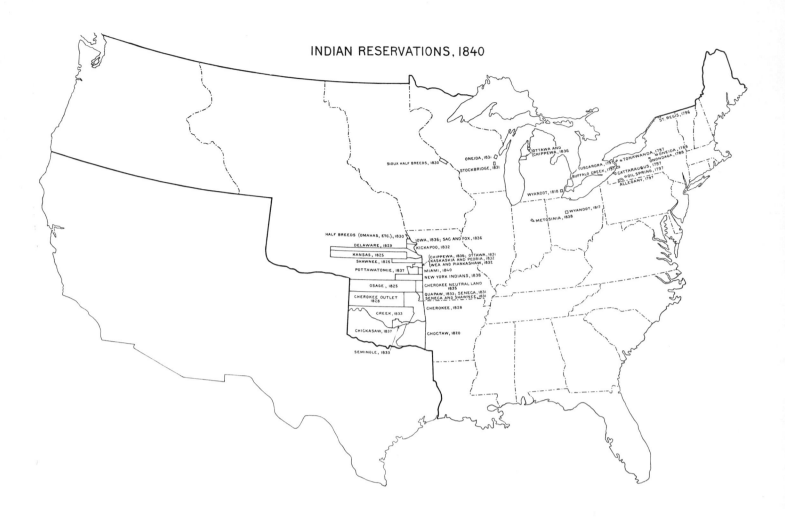

INDIAN RESERVATIONS, 1840

INDIAN RESERVATIONS, 1875

Figure 117

INDIAN RESERVATIONS, 1900

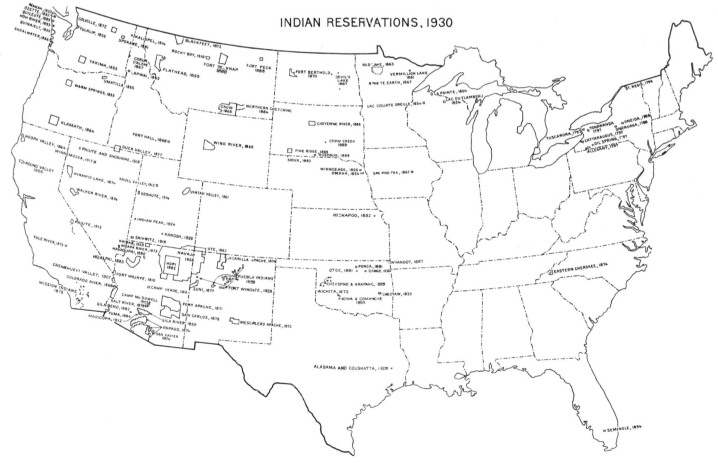

INDIAN RESERVATIONS, 1930

Figure 118

new home in Wisconsin, and started a school in Green Bay. A colorful and controversial figure, Williams was for some of his aberrations dropped by his Church in 1832, the Church reaping a more enduring harvest from the careful cultivating of Bishop William Hobart Hare (1838-1909), "Apostle to the Sioux." Congregationalist Stephen R. Riggs (1812-1883) began in 1837 his lifework among the Sioux along the upper Minnesota River. Under the auspices of the American Board of Commissioners for Foreign Missions, he soon became the recognized authority on the language of the Sioux, providing grammars and reading books for the Dakotas, as well as translating major portions of the Bible, all of *Pilgrim's Progress,* a hymnbook and other items. "Time would fail me to tell" of Moravian work in Georgia, Quaker fair dealings from New York to the far West, Lutheran labors in the Midwest, and a host of other efforts which presented to the native American the white man's better face.

What were the results of these prodigious efforts, Protestant and Catholic? Such a question evades easy answer. To measure results on a statistical scale alone is to miss much, possibly most, of the fruit. And statistics themselves cannot be confined only to conversions, for the work through hospitals, schools, orphanages and agencies of government must not be slighted. While many mission schools have closed down or have been absorbed by the federal government, others continue in operation to the present time. The role of the entire missionary movement in encouraging a greater humanitarianism on the part of the government gives the former some claim in the following figures. In 1952 the U. S. Indian Service operated 61 hospitals for Indians and arranged for the hospital care of Indians where no special facilities existed. Schools run by the Indian Service at that time included 56 in Arizona and the same number in New Mexico, 46 in South Dakota, 18 in North Dakota, 11 in Oklahoma, 9 in Montana, 7 in Mississippi, 5 in North Carolina, and one or more in 12 additional states. Alaska alone had almost 100 government schools for Indians in 1952.

In 1849 Indian Affairs were transferred from the Department of War to the newly created Department of Interior. Three-quarters of a century later (1924), United States citizenship was granted to the Indian. The passing of an Indian Reorganization Act in 1934, the renewed attention to welfare and rehabilitation, to legal claims and financial loans, suggested that the rights of this citizenship might be taken seriously. Of the approximately 500,000 Indians now in the United States (see Fig. 115), probably less than half that number can be claimed as converts—in any degree—to Christianity. But all can look to a continuing Church lobby and an expanding Christian charity intended to strengthen and to deepen the introduction of the Indian to "the habits and arts of civilization."

SOURCES. H. M. Chittenden and A. T. Richardson, *Life, Letters and Travels of Father Pierre-Jean De Smet, S. J.,* 4 vols. (New York, 1905). Harold E. Driver, *Indians of North America* (Chicago, 1961). Jonathan Edwards, *Memoirs of the Rev. David Brainerd; Missionary to the Indians on the Borders of New-York, New-Jersey, and Pennsylvania* . . . (edited by Sereno Edwards) (New Haven, 1822). Harold E. Fey and D'Arcy McNickle, *Indians and Other Americans* (New York, 1959). Gilbert J. Garraghan, *The Jesuits in the Middle United States,* 3 vols. (New York, 1938). Oliver La Farge, *A Pictorial History of the American Indian* (New York, 1956). Kenneth Scott Latourette, *A History of the Expansion of Christianity,* Vols. III and IV [see bibliographies therein] (New York, 1939; 1941). G. E. E. Lindquist, *The Red Man in the United States* (New York, 1923). D'Arcy McNickle, *They Came Here First* (Philadelphia and New York, 1949). C. O. Paullin, *Atlas of the Historical Geography of the United States* [see bibliography, p. 17] (Washington and New York, 1932). *Report with respect to the House Resolution Authorizing the Committee on Interior and Insular Affairs to Conduct an Investigation of the Bureau of Indian Affairs* [House Report #2503] (Washington, 1953). Reuben Gold Thwaites, *Early Western Travels,* 32 vols. (Cleveland, 1904-1907). And see the essay and bibliography published by the Institute of Early American History and Culture, *American Indian and White Relations to 1830* (Chapel Hill [N. C.], 1957).

3. JUDAISM

Judaism in colonial America was a modest enterprise. In 1654 a Jewish community was founded in New Amsterdam. About twenty years later, there was a second fellowship in Newport, Rhode Island, but no other for the remainder of the century. In the second quarter of the eighteenth century, synagogues were established in Savannah (1734), Charleston (1741), and Philadelphia (1745). These 3 were, with New York and Newport, the only religious communities of Jews that had been formed by the end of the colonial period. The first federal census, 1790, counted only 1,243 Jews out of a total population of 2,810,248—less than one-twentieth of 1%.

The earliest Jews coming to America were of Portuguese heritage, descendants of those who had fled the Inquisition of the fifteenth, sixteenth or seventeenth centuries. A large number of those searching for a hopeful refuge had settled in Amsterdam where they participated in the world-wide Dutch colonial enterprise, which included migrations to Brazil. When the Portuguese reasserted their power in Brazil in 1654, the Jews who had moved there fled—some returning to their earlier home in Amsterdam and others proceeding north to the New Amsterdam. The provoked Peter Stuyvesant and his Dutch Reformed minister were not happy about this development. The minister (Samuel Megapolensis) poured out to the West India Company his mournful tale:

For as we have here Papists, Mennonites and Lutherans among the Dutch; also many Puritans or Independents, and many Atheists and various other servants of Baal among the English under this Government, who conceal themselves under the name of Christians; it would create a still greater confusion, if the obstinate and immovable Jews came to settle here (Hastings, I, 335 f.).

But as had often happened before, the Company felt otherwise, this time motivated in part by the large capital investment which some of the Portuguese Jews had made in the Company itself. Thus, the director granted the Jews permission "to sail to and trade in New Netherland and to live and remain there, provided the poor among them shall not become a burden to the Company or the community. . . ." In Newport too the Jews were of the "Sephardim," that is, from Spain or Portugal, or descendants of those having departed from the Iberian Peninsula. Indeed, the Sephardic rite was followed in all 5 of the colonial synagogues.

In the eighteenth century, however, "Ashkenazim" Jews (that is, Jews from Germany or descendants of German Jews living elsewhere) also arrived in America, though at first in very small numbers. In 1802 the first synagogue of the Ashkenazic rite was established in Philadelphia, and a generation later the major migration of German Jews began. In 1820 there were only about 4,000 Jews in America, but by 1850 there were over 50,000 (see Fig. 119). According to the census of that year, there were 30 synagogues in the country, distributed as follows: New York, 9; Pennsylvania, 7; 3 in South Carolina and in Ohio, 2 in Connecticut, and 1 each in Massachusetts, Rhode Island, Virginia, Kentucky, Missouri, and Louisiana. These figures, however, are not complete, a total of 50 synagogues throughout the United States being a closer estimate (Glazer, 24). German Jews continued to emigrate during the remainder of the nineteenth century, but by 1880 they were outnumbered and almost overwhelmed by a vast migration of Jews from eastern Europe, notably Russia, Rumania, Poland, and Austria.

In 1880 there were about 250,000 Jews in America and 270 synagogues; at the end of the century, just twenty years later, there were 1 million Jews and 1,000 synagogues. Most of this fourfold increase was the direct result of the East European emigration. But while American Jewry was greatly strengthened by this tremendous influx, it was also sharply divided. Many of the German Jews, particularly those arriving after 1840, had participated in Europe in a program designed to reform traditional Judaism. These reformers, now in America, proposed that worship be modified to allow preaching in the vernacular, that Hebrew prayers be translated, that organs be installed, mixed choirs encouraged, and seating by families (instead of by sexes) permitted. They further proposed that the intellectual life be altered to make room for a rigorous historical scholarship and a sweeping reinterpretation of the place of Jewish law. To a majority of East European Jews, such a program constituted a shocking and blasphemous sacrilege. To others of the newcomers, such a program was irrelevant and silly, because Jews must forsake their devotion to religion—no matter how refashioned or reformed—in favor of a commitment to political or secular goals. On the one hand more rigid

than the German Jew, or on the other more radical, the immigrant from eastern Europe dashed all hope for a unified movement of reform.

Those who clutched their orthodoxy tightly, resisting reform and cultural accommodation, sometimes found their religion slipping away nonetheless. And even if they managed to hold on successfully, their children more often did not. Nathan Glazer explains the lapse in this way:

> Only the practices of Judaism were taught. One was brought up to observe the commandments, and, for this reason, as soon as one came in touch with a kind of thought which questioned fundamentals, one was at a loss. In other words, it may be said Jews lost their faith so easily because they had no faith to lose: that is, they had no doctrine, no collection of dogmas to which they could cling and with which they could resist argument. All they had, surrounding them like an armor, was a complete set of practices, each presumably as holy as the next. Once this armor was pierced by the simple question, Why? it fell away, and all that was left was a collection of habits (69 f.).

Thus, though there were about 1,000 synagogues in 1900 and 1 million Jews, in 1950 there were 5 times that many Jews but barely 2 times the number of synagogues.

Between the Orthodox and the Reform groups in twentieth-century American Judaism, there arose a third body: the Conservative (see Fig. 120). To understand this tripartite division, it is necessary to return to the development of the reform movement. Under the leadership, most conspicuously, of Rabbi Isaac Mayer Wise (1819-1900), German Jewry established a seminary (Hebrew Union College) in Cincinnati in 1875. In 1889 Wise organized the Central Conference of American Rabbis which, as its name implies, was designed to include, or at least to be open to, all rabbis ministering to America. For a time the reform movement showed promise of being the recognized leader of a Judaism finding its way in a strangely ghettoless society. But the problems created by mass immigration were aggravated and accentuated by the recognition that the Jewish reformers were doing more than merely tinkering with synagogue seating arrangements.

The Pittsburgh Platform, adopted in 1885, signaled the direction and degree of theological revolution in the movement that now could speak for only a segment, school, or wing of American Jewry. A program for reform now became Reform Judaism. In the words of Will Herberg, the Pittsburgh Platform

> represented a drastic revision of traditional Jewish teaching along lines of German idealism and American Protestant liberalism . . . It relegated the Talmud and Talmudic Tradition to the margin of Jewish life. It converted the messianic hope and expectation into an affirmation of the nineteenth century doctrine of progress, and eliminated Zion (Palestine) from the Jewish vision of fulfillment (176).

To this length, many who had been generally sympathetic with the liturgical or synagogal alterations were not prepared to go. Under the leadership of Sabato Morais

(1823-97), a dozen or so congregations pulled away from the Union of American Hebrew Congregations, protesting a platform which seemed to undermine the most sacred Torah and to destroy those habits of life which had distinguished Judaism for 3,000 years. Out of this reaction against a reform that seemed too encompassing or else too damaging came Conservative Judaism. The year of the Pittsburgh assembly, 1885, saw the formation of a

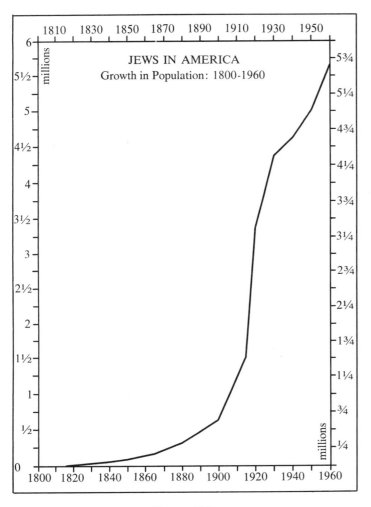

Figure 119

Conservative institution, the Jewish Theological Seminary of New York, and in 1913, with the seminary as its locus, the United Synagogue of America came into being. Although at first the Conservative movement seemed to languish and even to approach being reabsorbed by Reform Judaism, among the 20,000 Jews landing annually on American shores, Conservative Judaism found its vital role. Led by the scholarly Solomon Schechter (1847-1915) and the capable Cyrus Adler (1863-1940), the Jewish Theological Seminary was revived early in the twentieth century, and with it the whole Conservative force, ministering to "the children of East European Orthodox parents who found Orthodoxy too severe and Reform too unJewish."

With the adoption of the National Origins Act in 1924, the mass deluge of Jewish immigration ceased. Judaism

then set itself to the task of stabilizing its religious communities and retaining its own children. As noted above, second generation Jews, sensitive to the "foreignness" of their parent's Orthodoxy and eager to be accepted as American, frequently cast off all ties to the religion of their fathers. In the third generation, however, a perceptible "return" to Judaism could be traced as the synagogue in suburbia joined the urban synagogue in attaining new prominence in the life of the American Jew (see Herberg, 186-198). In this revived institutional life, the familiar American pattern of "men's clubs, sisterhoods, junior congregations, youth groups, 'young marrieds,' Sunday School classes, discussion circles, adult education projects, breakfasts, 'brunches,' dinners, and suppers" ap-

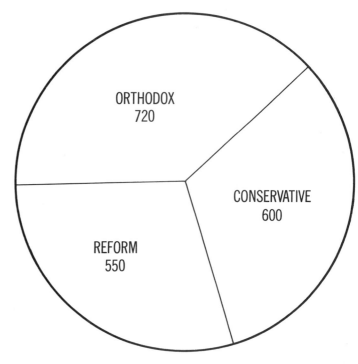

NUMBER OF CONGREGATIONS OF JUDAISM: 1957

Figure 120

peared in all three branches of Judaism, as there was deliberate adjustment to the new environment. The relative success of Orthodox, Conservative, and Reform in this process, however, is difficult to assess with precision. Special studies have been conducted across the country in an effort to discover in what direction American Jewry is going—both with respect to the three synagogue assemblies and with respect to the larger question of any active synagogue affiliation at all. It is difficult and perhaps unwise to attempt generalizations on the basis of studies that are neither comprehensive in scope nor comparable in method.

Figure 120, based on statistics given in the *American Jewish Yearbook 1958*, is only an approximate indication of relative size. As they become available, other measuring rods should be used. The weekday Jewish school en-

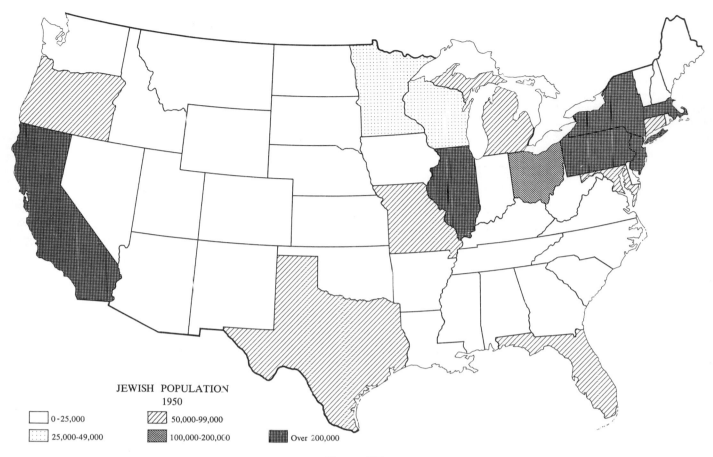

JEWISH POPULATION
1950

☐ 0-25,000   ▨ 50,000-99,000
▦ 25,000-49,000   ▧ 100,000-200,000   ▨ Over 200,000

Figure 121

rollment, for example, reveals roughly a division which places the Conservative in front (40%), followed by the Reform (31%) and the Orthodox (28%). A B'nai B'rith study of "Small Town Jewry" revealed that 50% of the Jews surveyed indicated a preference for Conservative, 27% for Reform, and 18% for Orthodox. The strength of the Orthodox lies, of course, not among the "Small Town Jewry" but in the large metropolitan centers—New York in particular—where the size and unity of the Jewish community make obedience to the halakhah (Jewish law) possible. Whether the strength of Orthodox Judaism also lies largely or solely within the ranks of the first generation American Jew is a question not yet fully resolved. Reform Judaism, while also strong in New York and New Jersey, is at the same time widely scattered across the country, with about one-fourth of its synagogues (temples) being found west of the Mississippi River. Over 80 Reform temples are in the southern states. (For further data regarding the present status of Reform Judaism, see the quite helpful "First Annual Congregational Survey," a mimeographed booklet prepared in 1958 by Stanley F. Klein, Director of Research and Evaluation for the Union of American Hebrew Congregations.) Conservative Judaism appears to have the larger number of sympathizers who, while they prefer that program, may find it easy to evade genuine involvement in it. How many of America's 5½ million Jews are personally caught up in the work and worship of the synagogues? Again

the evidence is inconclusive, but probably about one-half of that population regularly attends to the cry, "Hear, O Israel, the Lord thy God is one God . . ." (see Herberg, 195).

The hundreds of thousands of Jews who entered America in the last two decades of the nineteenth century and the first two decades of the twentieth left behind bloody pogroms and bitter anti-Semitism. As the United States came to have the largest concentration of Jews in the world, anti-Semitism made its unwelcome appearance here too. The forms which it took tended, however, to be more in the nature of subtle snobberies and "gentlemen's agreements" than in acts of violence. Yet in the present decade, as pressure for the rights of the Negro has mounted, synagogue bombings have blackened the American scene. Anti-Semitism has been explained from the aspects of theology, history, psychology, and economics. The fact is that anybody who hates mankind, for whatever reason, sooner or later hates the Jew. And anyone who hates the Jew sooner or later becomes the enemy of humanity itself. Recent bombing of American synagogues and haranguing of "half-penny Hitlers" offer a most vivid testimony to the existence of that bell which, when it tolls for one, tolls for all.

SOURCES. Charles P. Daly, *The Settlement of the Jews in North America* (New York, 1893). Philip S. Foner, *The Jews in American History 1654-1865* (New York, 1945). Nathan Glazer, *American Judaism* [see bibliography therein] (Chicago, 1957).

Abram V. Goodman, *Jewish Rights in Colonial Times* (Philadelphia, 1947). Oscar Handlin, *Adventure in Freedom: Three Hundred Years of Jewish Life in America* (New York, 1954). Hugh Hastings (ed.), *Ecclesiastical Records. State of New York,* 7 vols. (Albany, 1901-1916). Will Herberg, *Protestant-Catholic-Jew* (New York, [revised] 1960). "Jewish Statistics in the U. S. Census of Religious Bodies (1850-1936)," *Jewish Social Studies,* IX (1947). Lee J. Levinger, *A History of the Jews in the United States* [high school text] (Cincinnati, 1932). Harry S. Linfield, *The Communal Organization of the Jews in the United States*

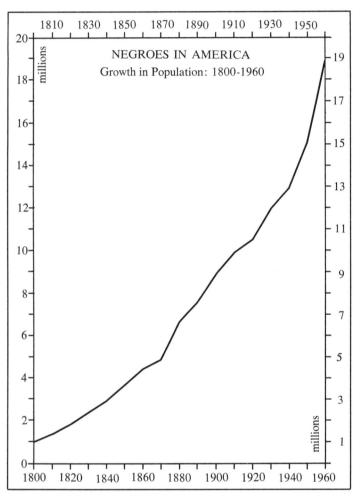

Figure 122

(New York, 1930). Jacob Radar Marcus, *Memoirs of American Jews 1775-1865,* 3 vols. (Philadelphia, 1955); ———, *American Jewry: Documents, Eighteenth Century* (Cincinnati, 1959). Moses Rischin, *An Inventory of American Jewish History* [valuable critical bibliography] (Cambridge, 1954). Marshall Sklare (ed.), *The Jews: Social Patterns of an American Group* (Glencoe [Ill.], 1958).

4. NEGROES

At the beginning of the eighteenth century there were about 50,000 Negroes in America; at the end of that century there were 1 million. Of that million (one-fifth of the nation's population in 1800), 90% (893,602) were slaves, 10% (108,435) were free men. When the slave trade was outlawed in 1808, the involuntary immigration of the Negro, while it did not completely cease for some

time, underwent a sharp decline. And though Negro population continued to grow (see Fig. 122), it did not keep pace with the mushrooming white population. By 1920, therefore, the proportion of Negroes in the total population had declined from 20% to slightly less than 10%. Even at the latter percentage, however, the Negro constituted a conspicuous and vital minority of many millions. In the religious history of America, what is the place of the Negro?

In the colonial period, the Negro—slave or free—had a limited share in the institutional religion of his master or emancipator. His own native religion, generally some form of primitive animism or, occasionally, of Islam, could maintain no strong hold as tribal organization broke down completely and as a continuing ritual or tradition proved, in so radically altered a way of life, utterly impossible. A slave could and often did attend the same church as his owner, hear the same sermon, share in the same communion. Missionaries, both domestic and foreign, responded to the challenge presented by the Negro as they had to that presented by the Indian. Yet these missionaries were often obliged to report that white masters offered little cooperation in, and sometimes overt hostility to, the religious instruction of their own slaves. David Humphreys, for example, while proclaiming in 1730 the noble efforts of the Society for the Propagation of the Gospel in Foreign Parts to instruct and convert the Negroes, bemoaned the reluctance of their owners to assist in that enterprise. And so far as Sunday worship was concerned, many slaves were granted only that one day in which "to clear Ground and plant it, to subsist themselves and Families." Whether from conviction or from convenience, some white masters, Humphreys wrote, "have been so weak as to argue, the Negroes had no Souls; others, that they grew worse by being taught and made Christians: I would not mention these if they were not popular Arguments now . . ." (p. 234 f.). Earlier, another of the Society's apostles, James Adams, reported in 1709 from Pasquotank, North Carolina, that he could instruct but not baptize the slaves, the masters "having a false notion that a Christian slave is, by law, free" (Hawks, *History of North Carolina,* II, 311). This "false notion" was indeed a type of common law tradition in the history of the Christian Church. There was enough logic to recognize that if in Christ all men are brothers, then slavery was ruled out; there was not enough courage to proceed on the basis of that logic to make all men brothers.

The Great Awakening which enveloped the colonies in the eighteenth century moved with sufficient force to reach the Negro, even as it did the Indian. Gilbert Tennent in 1742 noted the "multitude of awakenings" in the Boston area among "children, young people and Negroes." By the time of the Revolutionary War, a large number of Negroes had heard at least fragments of the gospel and had responded to that gospel with amazing alacrity.

As the number of Negroes increased to the point where they became the dominant group in a community or a church, both Negro and white groped for new solutions. The Negro gallery, the onlookers at the side door, the mixed seating in the pew—none seemed fully satisfactory. Negroes, even before 1800, grew restive under white domination and discrimination in the services of worship, and whites grew uneasy over the changing complexion and character of those services. In some cases the Negroes made the first move for an independent and separate church. Richard Allen, for example, after his own withdrawal from the St. George Methodist Episcopal Church of Philadelphia in 1787, formed the Free African Society, then proceeded to encourage other freed Negroes in Baltimore, Wilmington, Salem, and elsewhere to organize their own independent churches. Thus the African Methodist Episcopal Church was launched. On other occasions, the initiative for separation lay chiefly with the whites, as in the instance of the First African Baptist Church of Richmond, Virginia. In 1841 Richmond's First Baptist Church had 387 white members and 1,708 Negro members; the whites that year withdrew to form their own church at another location, deeding the church's original property to the Negro members. By such means, renewed church life and a Negro denominational structure came into being, the most significant developments in this direction taking place within the Methodist and Baptist fellowships (see Part II, 2 and 7).

In a situation of growing irritations and tensions, another plan suggested itself: repatriation. The Negro, who had been brought to America against his will, could be returned to Africa, thus avoiding the further festering of a worrisome social sore. The idea of Negro resettlement, which had been proposed as early as 1776 by Congregationalist Samuel Hopkins, led to the organization in 1817 of the American Colonization Society. Honorably conceived and broadly supported, the Society in 1821 sent the first shipload of free Negroes to Liberia. Though clergymen of several denominations labored heroically to save the ambitious but impractical project, within a decade its decline had begun. On the one hand, Liberia was plagued with poverty and disease; on the other, slavery was required by cotton and its new gin. Churches which in 1790 had considered excluding the slaveholder were, fifty years after, considering the exclusion of the abolitionist.

Notwithstanding the turbulence and the tragedy of the Negro's life in nineteenth-century America, the progress of Christianity among the "poor unfortunate blacks" was astounding. A non-Christian people, enslaved and oppressed by a Christian majority, turned with zest and almost with unanimity to the oppressor's religion.

Among no other body of peoples of non-European stock did nineteenth century Christianity make such large numerical gains. By 1914 Protestant churches had approximately as large a total of members among the Negroes

of the United States as they had among all the peoples of Asia and Africa. In other words, all the extensive Protestant missionary efforts of Europeans and Americans in Asia and Africa in the century between 1815 and 1914 had resulted in no greater numerical gains than had been achieved among the Negroes of the United States in the same period (Latourette, IV, 327).

This expansion was in part the result of direct mission efforts by the major religious bodies in America.

Except for Maryland and Louisiana, Roman Catholicism was not strong in those states where Negro population was greatest. This fact alone helps explain the modest gain among Negroes made by the Roman Catholic Church. Yet societies were formed and schools were established with the conversion and cultivation of the Negro directly in view. In the early years of emancipation, however, men newly freed resisted the authoritarian aspect of Catholicism, with the result that many thousand hard-won Negro Catholics abandoned this institution in the postwar years. By the end of the nineteenth century, the number of Negro Catholics in America was about 150,000.

Protestant missions of the nineteenth century were on a larger scale and their results were greater. In addition to the colonization effort considered above, much Protestant energy was expended on the causes of education and emancipation of the Negro. As early as 1789, Philadelphia Quakers organized the Society for the Free Instruction of Orderly Blacks and People of Colour. The philanthropy of a Pennsylvania clergyman, Charles Avery, led to incorporation of Avery College in Allegheny City, Pennsylvania, in 1849. Five years later, Ashmun Institute, the forerunner of Lincoln University, was chartered by Pennsylvania Presbyterians. In 1856 a university for Negroes was begun in Ohio by the Methodists; this school, Wilberforce, had had its beginnings in a seminary established by the African Methodists near Columbus in 1847. Berea College of Kentucky, though opened in 1869 as a school for both Negro and white students, gradually lost its bi-racial character, becoming a school for whites; in 1950 a bi-racial policy was once more assumed.

It was after the Civil War, however, that the marked progress in Negro education took place—and it took place in the areas where the Negro masses could obtain the maximum benefit. Freedmen's Aid Societies, the American Missionary Association, and individual denominations or philanthropists assumed responsibility for the schooling of the Negro from the primary grades through college. Theological schools for the training of the Negro ministry were also maintained. As the first fruits of these institutions were harvested, Negro leadership assumed the direction of the fortunes of these and other schools. Among the institutions of higher learning, Baptists established such schools as Shaw (Raleigh), Roger Williams (Nashville), Storer (Harpers Ferry), Morehouse and Spelman (Atlanta). Methodists, the other major religious body in the midst of the Negro's southern population, founded Walden (Nashville), Rust (Holly Springs, Mississippi), Morgan

(Baltimore), Claflin (Orangeburg), and Clark (Atlanta). In the case of both Methodists and Baptists, the initiative and resources for these schools came almost exclusively from the northern branches of the respective denominations. The American Missionary Association, which though open to all nonslaveholders "of evangelical sentiments" was backed chiefly by Congregationalists, led in the formation of Avery Institute at Charleston, Ballard Normal

NEGRO CHURCH MEMBERSHIP: 1936

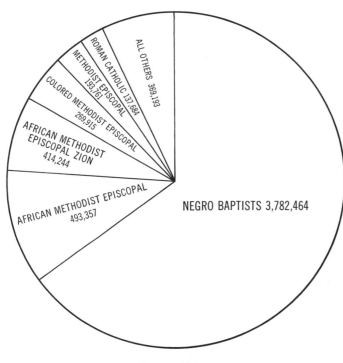

ALL OTHERS 369,193

ROMAN CATHOLIC 137,684

METHODIST EPISCOPAL 193,761

COLORED METHODIST EPISCOPAL 269,915

AFRICAN METHODIST EPISCOPAL ZION 414,244

AFRICAN METHODIST EPISCOPAL 493,357

NEGRO BAPTISTS 3,782,464

Figure 123

School at Macon, and Washburn at Beaufort, North Carolina—all in 1865. The next year 3 more schools were organized by the Association, among them the important Fisk University of Nashville. By 1870 this same group had sponsored 14 other schools, including Hampton Institute in Virginia. Howard University of Washington, D. C., though it received governmental aid, emerged in 1867 also as a result of Congregational support. Other denominations, including the rising Negro bodies themselves, likewise participated, though to a lesser degree, in education's reconstruction for the southern Negro.

A portion of Protestant denominational efforts directed toward emancipation has been considered in Part II. Quakers especially had been active in the demand for slavery's abolition, and in 1776 Congregationalist Samuel Hopkins petitioned the Continental Congress to abolish the institution. Methodists four years later declared slavery to be "contrary to the laws of God, man, and nature, and hurtful to society." Baptist bodies condemned slaveholding, and several prominent Virginia Baptists freed their slaves before the end of the eighteenth century. Presbyterian David Rice and Disciple Barton W. Stone urged their fellows in Kentucky to manumit all slaves. Surges of

Protestant piety and waves of revivalism generally led to intensified abolitionist activity (see Timothy Smith, chs. 12 and 13), though—as previously noted—this activity took on a northern cast as the nineteenth century developed.

Evangelism, in addition to education, constituted a major part of the Protestant effort on behalf of the Negro. At the beginning of the nineteenth century there were approximately 15,000 Negro Methodists and approximately 20,000 Negro Baptists. With more modest memberships in other denominations or independent churches, Negro Christians probably numbered between 40,000 and 50,000 in 1800. At the end of the nineteenth century, Negro church membership was approximately 3 million. In 1800, 4% to 5% of the Negro population was within a church; in 1900, over one-third of the population was so enlisted.

Over 95% of that church membership was Protestant and the vast majority of the Protestant membership was Baptist. Figure 123 represents the latest report by the Bureau of the Census on the denominational make-up of the Negro churchman. Unfortunately, no comparable data later than 1936 are available. At that time, there were more than 5½ million Negroes in America's churches, this total representing over 40% of the Negro population and about 10% of the country's entire church membership. Baptists accounted for two-thirds (67%) of the Negro church membership and Methodists for 25%. All other religious bodies had only the remaining 8% of Negro membership to divide among themselves. The African Methodist Episcopal Church was the leading Negro denomination in Delaware, Montana, Washington, and Wyoming, while the Baptists led in every other state except Maryland. The Methodist Episcopal Church, which held the edge in Maryland, was the only white denomination with a significant number of Negro churches in its ranks; the same was true in 1960 of the reunited Methodist Church. A study in 1933 by Benjamin E. Mays and Joseph W. Nicholson revealed that while Negroes made up one-third of the population of Atlanta, they had more than one-half of the city's churches. Of the more than 1,000 Negro churches then in Atlanta, 661 were Baptist, 209 were Methodist, 95 were Holiness; there were 17 Catholic, 16 Episcopalian, 12 Presbyterian, 11 Congregational, 6 Disciples, 6 Seventh-day Adventist, and 5 Lutheran. In 5 northern cities (Baltimore, Chicago, Cincinnati, Detroit, Philadelphia), the denominational distribution did not greatly differ. Of the thousand-plus churches, 466 were Baptist, 244 were Holiness, 160 were Methodist, and 78 were Spiritualist; the remaining churches, less than 100, were divided among 14 denominations (Mays and Nicholson, 210, 214).

The Negro's more than 50,000 churches of the present day have occupied a larger place in the Negro community than the white's churches have in his community, generally speaking (see Fig. 124). With so many avenues of social expression cut off, the church was called upon for a variety of services.

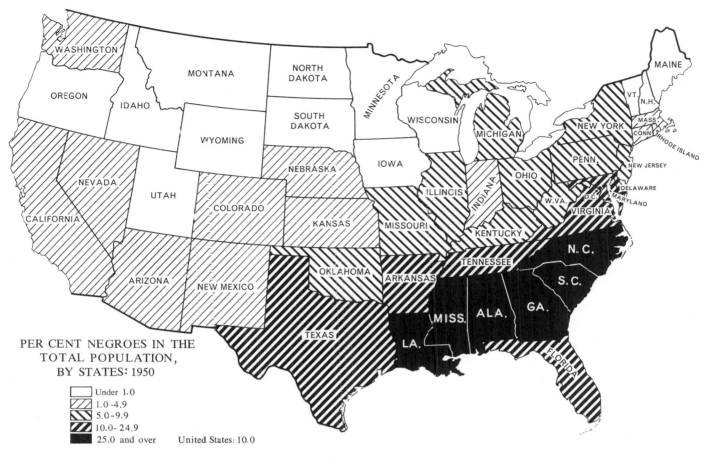

PER CENT NEGROES IN THE
TOTAL POPULATION,
BY STATES: 1950

Under 1.0
1.0 - 4.9
5.0 - 9.9
10.0 - 24.9
25.0 and over   United States: 10.0

Figure 124

. . . every public man has had to reach the Negro through his church. The lecturer . . . asks for a hearing there; the phrenologist holds his seances in this sanctuary; the spurious "foreigner" in quest of a collection seeks there the opportunity to tell a credulous people about wonders of other lands; and the race leader demands this rostrum from which he, like a watchman on the wall, sounds the alarm for an advance against the bold enemy who, if not checked, will fix upon the race disabilities and burdens until all the hopes of liberty will be lost (Woodson, 272 f.).

The ministry, for many years the only profession open to the Negro, was likewise broadened in scope to include the services of a "walking encyclopedia, the counselor of the unwise, the friend of the unfortunate, the social welfare organizer, and the interpreter of the signs of the times" (Woodson, 281). And the Negro laity in the field of music made its most original and enduring contribution to America's religious history.

Prior to the twentieth century, the Negro was content to express his newly received Christian faith largely in older denominational contexts. In this regard, concentrating upon three or four denominations, he showed himself more conservative than his white Protestant neighbor. Toward the end of the previous century, however, the holiness movement (see Part III, 3) made its way among the Negroes and, led by Elder C. H. Mason, a Negro holiness church in 1897 took the name of the Church of God in Christ. Its membership of 30,000 in 1925 had risen to 400,000 by 1960. In number of churches, this denomination in 1950 had grown as large as the Unitarian, Universalist,

Quaker, Dutch Reformed, and Salvation Army groups combined (see Figs. 42 and 43). More recently the Negro has, like the whites before him, developed many exotic and often ephemeral sects which seem to be dependent wholly upon their founder for their character and possibly for their survival. Such groups as the Father Divine Peace Movement, the "Black Jews," the "Black Muslims" or "Moorish Americans," and various spiritualist bodies may be mentioned. None of these by mid-twentieth century had attained statistical significance, though the Black Muslims in the early 1960's were, according to C. Eric Lincoln (*The Black Muslims in America*, Boston, 1961), "the fastest growing social movement in America," having a determined membership of at least 100,000. Church life as a whole, however, proved increasingly significant statistically for the Negro in the twentieth century, as it did for the white. Indeed, if the denominational reports are accurate—and some appear to be estimates rather than exact head counts—the proportion of Negroes who were church members by 1958 exceeded the 63% which marked the proportion for the country as a whole.

Since the 1954 Supreme Court decision sounding the death knell for the "separate but equal" doctrine in public education, racial crises in American life have erupted with distressing frequency. In the midst of this heightened tension, the churches, Negro and white, have been the butt of outspoken criticism. "The most segregated hour of the week" is the epithet sometimes applied to the Sunday morning worship hour, and the social conservatism of the South's white congregations has drawn frequent caustic comment. Yet, to look at the problem, if not *sub specie aeternitatis,* at least under the aspect of a century, is to see the churches as not altogether derelict in their duty. Further, even in the present decade the churches are neither silent nor impotent. Roman Catholic bishops in Louisiana and North Carolina, to cite only two conspicuous examples, have forthrightly demanded the end of segregation in their respective dioceses. Protestant ministers in Atlanta and Little Rock, again to cite only two instances, have issued manifestoes declaring the relevance of the Christian conscience to desegregation. On the Negro side, the most dramatic and quite possibly the most effective move for the Negro's civil rights has been led by a Baptist pastor in Alabama, Martin Luther King. Articles and books such as Kyle Haselden's *Racial Problem in Christian Perspective* (New York, 1959) and King's *Stride Toward Freedom* (New York, 1958) have brought the witness of the Christian churches to bear on this pressing issue.

This is not to suggest that the churches have fully lived up to the demands of their ancient charter any more than the citizens of the United States have fully lived up to theirs. Catholic parishes have been divided, Protestant seminaries have been embroiled, clergymen's voices have been lifted in reaction and rancor. On January 1, 1963, the nation celebrates the first centennial of Abraham Lincoln's Emancipation Proclamation; and it was Lincoln who had urged: "with firmness in the right, as God gives us to see the right, let us strive on to finish the work we are in. . . ." Every honest American recognizes that this work is not yet finished.

SOURCES. Herbert Aptheker (ed.), *A Documentary History of the Negro People in the United States* (New York, 1951). A. H. Fauset, *Black Gods of the Metropolis* (Philadelphia, 1944). John T. Gillard, *The Catholic Church and the American Negro* (Baltimore, 1929; 1941). Francis L. Hawks, *History of North Carolina . . .* (Fayetteville, 1858). L. L. Haynes, *The Negro Community within American Protestantism, 1619-1844* (Boston, 1953). David Humphreys, *An Historical Account of the Incorporated Society for the Propagation of the Gospel in Foreign Parts* (London, 1730). Kenneth Scott Latourette, *A History of the Expansion of Christianity,* Vols. III & IV (New York, 1939; 1941). Benjamin E. Mays and Joseph W. Nicholson, *The Negro's Church* (New York, 1933). H. Richard Niebuhr, *The Social Sources of Denominationalism* (New York, 1929; reprint 1957). Liston Pope, *Kingdom Beyond Caste* (New York, 1957). J. Saunders Redding, *The Lonesome Road* (New York, 1958). Timothy L. Smith, *Revivalism and Social Reform* (New York, 1957). W. D. Weatherford, *American Churches and the Negro* (Boston, 1957). Carter G. Woodson, *The History of the Negro Church* (Washington, [second edition] 1945).

5. ALASKA

In 1867 the United States paid Russia $7,200,000 for a piece of land variously described as "a hyperborean solitude," "Johnson's Polar Bear Garden," "Seward's Icebox," and "a barren, worthless, God-forsaken region." Before a century passed, however, most Americans agreed that, at less than 2¢ an acre, the bargain was not bad. But at the time of purchase, all of the ingenuity and energy of Secretary of State William H. Seward was required to cajole the Senate into approving the purchase treaty and the House into appropriating the money. Persuading Russia to sell had been no problem, for the vast Alaskan empire had proved economically burdensome and diplomatically troublesome. There had even been, moreover, a rumor that Brigham Young's Mormons might move into Russian America.

The first missionaries had entered Alaska more than three-quarters of a century before, under the aegis of the Russian Orthodox Church. In 1792 eight monks from western Russia arrived on Kodiak Island, where they built the first Eastern Orthodox church on the American continent. Here and on the nearby Alaska Peninsula, the missionaries enjoyed quick successes among the natives, baptizing several thousand before the eighteenth century closed. As had often been true of mission activities in the New World, the Russian Church found the strongest opposition to its program not among the heathen, but among its plundering countrymen, whose economic ravages were being threatened by the introduction cf Christian missionaries. Though some Christianization of the natives was casually and superficially undertaken, some was earnestly and heroically accomplished. In the latter category were the labors of John Veniaminoff. Kenneth Scott Latourette thus describes Veniaminoff and his work:

A native of Siberia, he had been trained in the seminary in Irkutsk. Athletic, of towering stature, forceful and impressive, in 1824, when not quite twenty-seven years old, he arrived in Unalaska, one of the Aleutian Islands. Here he set himself to raise the moral and religious tone of the debased, nominally Christian population. He became expert in the language, manners, and institutions of the Aleuts. He prepared a catechism and a Bible history in the native tongue and translated portions of the New Testament. He conducted schools to such good effect that in time in some localities most of the Aleuts were literate. Later he moved to Sitka, the capital, and still later was made bishop of a new see which embraced Kamchatka, the Kurile Islands, and the Aleutians. He was zealous in encouraging the clergy to master the local idioms and to prepare literature in them. Between 1841 and 1860, 4,700 Indians are said to have been baptized (IV, 311 f.).

The work of the Orthodox Church did not come to a sudden end with the sale of Alaska to the United States. On the contrary, during the long years of the new landlord's neglect of Alaska and its native population, Russian priests struggled to prevent the degradation and starvation of the inhabitants. By the end of the nineteenth century, the Orthodox Church was the strongest religious force in Alaska with over 10,000 members, or approximately one-sixth of the population.

When the United States took possession of the northern empire, little was known of the land, the resources, the people. Not until 1890 was an extensive effort made by the federal government to secure reliable data concerning this "hyperborean solitude." Before that time, however, churches in America had begun to respond to the opportunities for evangelism which Alaska offered. The most significant response was made by the Presbyterians, who in 1876 organized in Wrangell the first Protestant church in American Alaska. (In 1842 a Lutheran chapel had been established at Sitka for the German and Finnish employees of the Russian American Company.) Within the next dozen years, the Presbyterians started missions among the Tlingit Indians at Juneau and Sitka, took over a government school at Point Barrow on the Arctic coast, and built 4 houses of worship.

The leading spirit in the Presbyterian work in Alaska was Sheldon Jackson, who had already proved himself a prodigious evangelist in the western United States (see above, p. 141). His first visit to Alaska in 1877 convinced him that the natives were in great need and that remedies must be on a large scale. On his return to the United States, he appealed to his friends, to his home mission board, and to his government for aid. He urged the Secretary of the Interior to push forward an educational program in Alaska and he himself petitioned Congress to provide courses in the "common branches of an English education, the principles of a republican government, and such industrial pursuits as may seem best adapted to their circumstances" (Lazell, 64). In 1885 Jackson was appointed General Agent of Education in Alaska, in which capacity he fought lawlessness and immorality, corruption and cynicism, witchcraft and slavery, in an effort to raise the educational level of the Alaskan native. It was no mean challenge, for in 1890 there was 93% illiteracy among the Indians and 72% in the population as a whole. (Progress was not rapid; in the 1950's, out of an Indian population of 35,000, the average number of college graduates per year was 5; of high school graduates, 75.) Jackson's most dramatic contribution to the life of Alaska, however, lay not in the realm of its education but of its economy. In 1891 in an effort to save the Eskimos from possible starvation as a result of the white man's depletion of the whale and seal herds, Jackson introduced from Siberia Alaska's first reindeer. On July 4, 1892, the first small herd was placed on the mainland of Alaska at Port Clarence. To Jackson's great delight, the reindeer—and thus the Eskimos as well—survived. As he rightly foresaw, this alteration in the economy would "do more than preserve life. It will preserve the self-respect of the people and advance them in the scale of civilization. It will change [them] from hunters to herders. It will also utilize the hundreds of thousands of square miles of moss-covered tundra of Arctic and sub-Arctic Alaska. . . ." By 1905 there were nearly 13,000 reindeer in Alaska; a generation later the number stood at 600,000.

Other denominations, in addition to the Presbyterians, responded early to Alaska's needs. Before 1880 the Episcopalians were at work along the Yukon River, at Anvik and Nuklukayet. The Congregationalists took over a government school at Cape Prince of Wales. The Baptists assumed the development of Kodiak Island as their responsibility, establishing a children's home on Woody Island in 1886. In the same decade, Moravians traveled on foot or with dog sleds in the country north of Alaska Peninsula, at Nushagak and at Bethel on the Kuskokwim River. The first Methodist missionary arrived in 1886, beginning his work on the Shumagin Islands, off the southern tip of the Peninsula. A little farther to the east, in the Aleutian chain, Methodists opened in 1890 the Jesse Lee Home on Unalaska, moving it later to Seward Peninsula. Roman Catholics first established a church at Wrangell near the site of the Presbyterian mission, but later abandoned this location for Juneau, where by 1890 the Church of the Nativity had 325 white members. Catholic missions were also established along the Yukon River at Nulato, Kozerevsky, and Tununuk.

In 1890 the leading religious group was still the Russian Orthodox Church with its 27 churches or chapels and more than 10,000 communicants. Next were the Presbyterians who had 5 churches and approximately 500 members. The Roman Catholics had roughly the same number of members distributed among 4 churches. The Episcopalians, the Moravians and the Swedish Free Mission each had 2 churches, which with 1 nondenominational church at Metlakatla made a total of 12 Protestant churches in Alaska in 1890. In that year, there were 16 United States public schools and 19 private schools. Of the latter, 6 were Russian, 4 were Presbyterian and 2 were Roman Catholic.

For two generations after these noble beginnings, religious progress in Alaska was not rapid: it was, in fact, hardly discernible. The same was true of most other aspects of Alaskan life. A gold rush early in the twentieth century brought brief vitality to the area, but soon the bubble burst and prospectors led the withdrawal. Nome, which had a population of over 12,000 in 1900, was down to 2,600 in 1910 and 852 in 1920. Fairbanks had 3,541 inhabitants in 1910 but only 1,155 in 1920. From the beginning of the twentieth century to 1930, when the entire continental United States was taking great numerical strides, Alaska's population slipped from over 63,000 to less than 60,000. On the eve of World War II the largest town in the Territory, Juneau, could boast a population of only 5,700. With so unpromising a future, it is no surprise that America's denominations found the demand for missionary monies and personnel more pressing elsewhere. Even the native population failed to show much growth in this period: the number of Indians inched forward from 11,000 in 1882 to 12,000 in 1950; the Eskimos dropped back from 17,000 to 16,000 in the same period.

World War II radically altered the gloomy prospects for "Walrussia" and eradicated the last suggestion of folly on the part of William Seward. The strategic location led to an invasion of money, men and matériel related to the American war effort, all of which snatched the empire from oblivion and neglect. The airplane made political

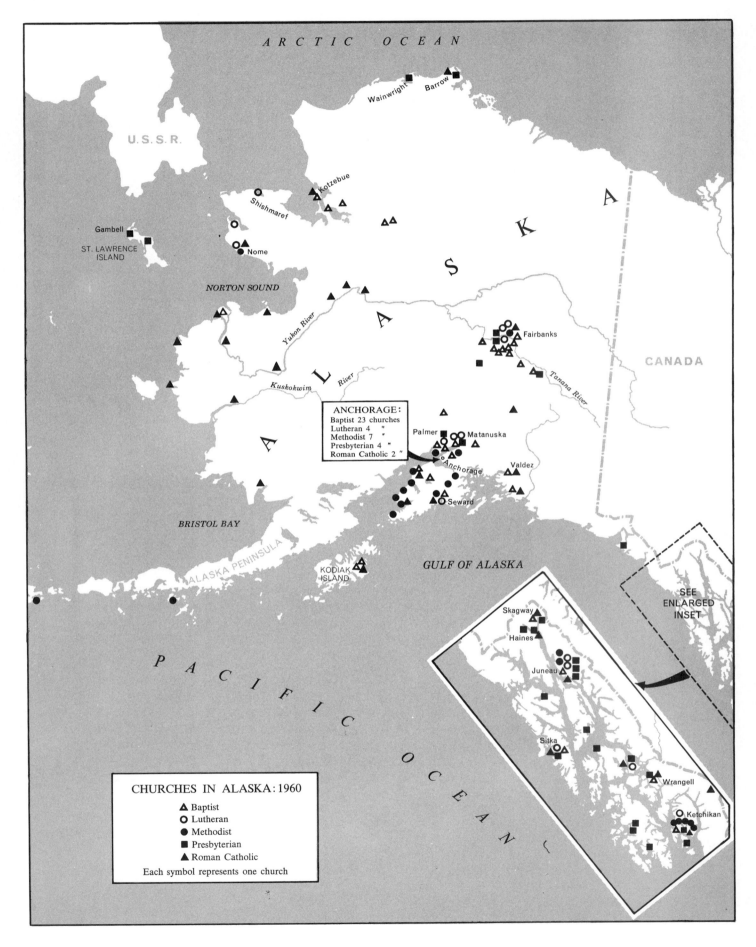

ANCHORAGE:
Baptist 23 churches
Lutheran 4   "
Methodist 7   "
Presbyterian 4 "
Roman Catholic 2 "

CHURCHES IN ALASKA: 1960
△ Baptist
○ Lutheran
● Methodist
■ Presbyterian
▲ Roman Catholic
Each symbol represents one church

Figure 125

and economic unity a fact where only a decade or two earlier it had been a wild fancy. Population, which had been stagnant for more than a generation, virtually doubled in a single decade. With a population of nearly 250,000 in 1960, Alaska at last presented a mission field of unmistakable challenge.

And the churches, even before statehood came in 1958, moved to meet that challenge (see Fig. 125). By 1960 the Baptists had over 60 churches in the new state, most of these resulting from the efforts of the Southern Baptist Convention. The Roman Catholics, operating out of the Diocese of Juneau and the Vicariate of Alaska, supervised 36 churches and missions. The United Presbyterian Church, U.S.A., was responsible for 32 churches; the Methodists for 23; and the Lutherans for 18. The Methodists, moreover, began at mid-century to lay careful plans for a fully accredited, four-year college to be erected at Anchorage; a decade later, the program was ready to be launched.

Alaska was indeed moving abruptly, as a Lutheran missionary suggested, from the stone age to the atomic age. Shaman séances grew increasingly rare and totem poles became less the objects of veneration for the Indians than for the annual visitors to Totem Pole Park near Ketchikan. Any doubt that Alaska had entered the mainstream of American life was erased in the fall of 1960 when both candidates for the presidency of the United States deemed it wise and proper to call at this last frontier—no longer considered a barren, worthless region.

SOURCES. Thomas A. Bailey, *A Diplomatic History of the American People* (New York, [second edition] 1945). Henry W. Clark, *History of Alaska* (New York, 1930). Ernest Gruening, *The State of Alaska* (New York, 1954). Kenneth Scott Latourette, *A History of the Expansion of Christianity*, IV (New York, 1941). J. Arthur Lazell, *Alaskan Apostle: The Life Story of Sheldon Jackson* (New York, 1960). *Mid-Century Alaska* [publication of the Department of the Interior] (Washington, 1951). *Report on Population and Resources of Alaska at the Eleventh Census: 1890* [also issued by the Department of the Interior; thoroughly and lavishly done] (Washington, 1893). See color map showing distribution of Alaska's Indians by linguistic stock (1920) in *Fourteenth Census of the United States . . .* III [following p. 1158] (Washington, 1922); see maps #156 and #157 showing location of Aleut, Athapaskan, Eskimo and Tlingit villages (1950) in *Report with respect to The House Resolution Authorizing the Committee on Interior and Insular Affairs to Conduct an Investigation of the Bureau of Indian Affairs* [House Report #2503] (Washington, 1953).

6. HAWAII

America nowhere else presents a more intriguing picture of religious diversity than she does in her fiftieth state. Until a century and a half ago, the Hawaiian Islands shared with other Polynesian lands the polytheism of a primitive nature worship built upon an elaborate system of taboos, led by a caste of powerful priests, and centered in hundreds of fixed places of worship. By the middle of the nineteenth century, the backbone of the native religion was broken, and the strength of the "higher" religions was on the rise.

The first religion of a more advanced civilization to reach the Islands was Christianity. Following the voyages of Captain James Cook in the 1770's which brought the "Sandwich Islands" to the attention of Europe and America, an organized effort to Christianize the natives began with the Congregationalists of New England. Whaling vessels and fur-trading ships, using the excellent island harbors, developed friendly commercial contacts among the Hawaiians. As a result, some of the natives were employed on the visiting ships, and one such seaman, Henry Obookiah, found his way from ship to a Connecticut shore where he discovered and entered Yale College. There, converted to Christianity by Samuel J. Mills, he impressed the missionary-minded with the needs and opportunities presented by the pagan Pacific isles, and the year following his death in 1818 saw a party of missionaries, teachers, physicians and their families embarking for Hawaii.

Arriving on March 30, 1820, the Congregationalists found the Islands in the throes of political and religious turmoil. The great King Kamehameha I, who had unified the area under his rule in 1809, had just died. At that time, 1819, there had already been sufficient contact with the white man's culture to bring about a weakening of the taboo structure and a questioning of the traditional beliefs. When in August of 1819 Kamehameha's successor publicly ate at the same table with women, thus violating a major taboo, the dissolution of the old ways was unmistakably at hand. It was, then, a propitious moment when the New England contingent set foot on the Island of Hawaii, at the village of Kailua. Instructed "to aim at nothing short of covering those Islands with fruitful fields and pleasant dwellings and schools and churches; of raising up the whole people to an elevated state of Christian civilization," the missionaries immediately set about their task (Bradley, 124). They learned Hawaiian, they ingratiated themselves with the royalty, they established churches and schools. Within a decade, a Puritan revolution had taken place: Sabbath observance was enforced, Watts' catechism was taught, a Hawaiian alphabet was created, and moral reform was undertaken. With reinforcements from New England, the mission work was able to reach more than half of the native population within two decades. In 1837 there were 87 missionaries appointed, 17 churches established, and approximately 10,000 converts won.

In 1838 an intensification of religious concern swept over the Islands, and for the next two or three years Hawaii had its own Great Awakening. Over 20,000 persons, or about one-sixth of the population, came into the churches in this period (Latourette, V, 250). In a single year, 1843, there were more than 5,000 conversions, but the pace decelerated sharply thereafter and the rate was less than 2,000 a year for the remainder of the century.

Utilizing some of the tested techniques of mainland revivalism, Protestant Christianity made its mightiest strides in the decades prior to 1850.

Roman Catholicism came to Hawaii in the first instance not from the United States but from France. In 1820 the chaplain of a French ship harbored in the Islands baptized two Hawaiian chiefs. Eight years later the first Catholic missionaries reached Hawaii. However, opposition from Protestantism, coupled with the still recent iconoclasm of the natives, led to the expulsion of these missionaries in 1831. Near the end of the decade, the tables were again turned when, in 1839, a French frigate captain forced the Hawaiian king to permit the propagation of Catholicism within his realm. With the doors opened once more, missionaries and teachers came from Europe, instructing the natives and making ready, unconsciously, for the influx of Catholic Europeans (notably Portuguese) which was to come before the end of the nineteenth century. By 1900, the number of Roman Catholics in the Islands virtually equaled the number of Protestants. Of the former, none was more widely known or more dearly loved than Father Damien, who in 1873 began a ministry to the leper colony on Molokai, his work continuing until leprosy brought his life to a courageous end.

Shortly after the middle of the nineteenth century, "higher religion" from the Far East made its appearance as Chinese plantation laborers began to arrive. About 300 Chinese were imported in 1852 by the Royal Hawaiian Agricultural Society, and for a generation this source of cheap labor supply (chiefly, the Canton delta of China) was continuously tapped. After working the required number of years on the plantation, the Chinese immigrant or his descendant frequently set up shop in the towns. The resulting economic competition led to the curtailment of Chinese immigration in 1883 and to its cessation three years later. At this time there were about 20,000 Chinese in Hawaii; in 1900 there were 25,000, a number that remained fairly constant for the next half century. Both Chinese Buddhism and Taoism accompanied these immigrants, but the latter religion remained largely a private exercise, while the former was to be overshadowed by its neighbor: Japanese Buddhism.

In 1868 the importation of Japanese laborers began, though organized religious activities did not commence until nearly a generation later. After a delay in this importation imposed by Japan, the immigration was renewed in 1884 and soon exceeded that from all other sources. By 1890 over 65,000 Japanese had entered the Islands, and by 1900 the Japanese had become the largest ethnic group of Hawaii. As with the Chinese, so with the Japanese, growth in numbers led to increased uneasiness and opposition on the part of non-Asians. The annexation of Hawaii to the United States in 1898 was accomplished at that time partly to forestall the threat (real or rumored) of an annexation by Japan. In 1907 Japanese immigration was restricted on a basis agreed upon by Japan and the United States; in 1924 the Immigration Act ("Japanese Exclusion Act") was passed, ending the flow of citizens of Japan to the Hawaiian Islands.

In 1894 Japanese Buddhism had its official beginnings in the mission work of the Jodo sect, and five years later Jodo Shin or True Jodo—the most active form of Buddhism in Hawaii at the present time—began its work. Both of these "churches" stressed the way of faith rather than the way of works or of study, Jodo Shin even permitting its priests to marry and to eat meat. And both sects showed themselves alert, in the Orient as well as in Hawaii, to the recruiting tactics and techniques of the Christian missionaries, imitating them and often improving on them. Other forms of Japanese Buddhism came into Hawaii: Nichiren (1898), Zen (1913) and Shingon (1917). None of these, however, proved as powerful or as attractive as the Jodo and particularly the Jodo Shin sects.

Shinto, the native religion of Japan, had in this period a national character which made it much less exportable than Buddhism; this was, of course, pre-eminently true of State Shinto. Even so, as early as 1898 a Shinto shrine was erected in Hilo on the Island of Hawaii. Fifteen years later, a second Shinto sect built its temple in Honolulu, and the next year a third representative of Sectarian Shinto entered Hawaii. Shinto, however, existed largely as a private religion within the home and was often confined to the first-generation immigrant. Second-generation Shinto was so rare that Japanese children or young people often found themselves in greater accord with contemporaries of another race, religion, and culture than with their own parents.

Hawaii was and is the racial and religious melting pot of the Pacific. Of the more than 600,000 inhabitants in the Islands at the present time, approximately 60% are from east and southeast Asia. The Japanese, who have come from Okinawa as well as from Japan, account for more than one-third of the entire population. The next largest Asiatic group, the Filipinos, arrived en masse in the twentieth century, constituting by mid-century more than 10% of the population. Chiefly, though by no means exclusively Roman Catholic, the Filipinos have lately responded to the newer Pentecostal sects which have crossed the Pacific from America. The Chinese, while not as numerous as the Filipinos, occupy a position of great social and economic prestige in the life of the Islands. Among the whites the diversity is hardly less, with Germans, Russians, and Spaniards being present in addition to the increasing "Yankee" influx. Hawaiians—pure and part—Negroes, Puerto Ricans, Koreans, and others contribute to the ethnic maze (see Walter Kolarz, "The Melting Pot in the Pacific," *Social Process in Hawaii*, XIX).

Religiously, the situation was comparatively simple prior to World War II. As noted above, Congregationalism, Catholicism, and Japanese Buddhism were the leading forces in the development of Hawaii's modern religious life. Other forces, however, were at work. The Mormons

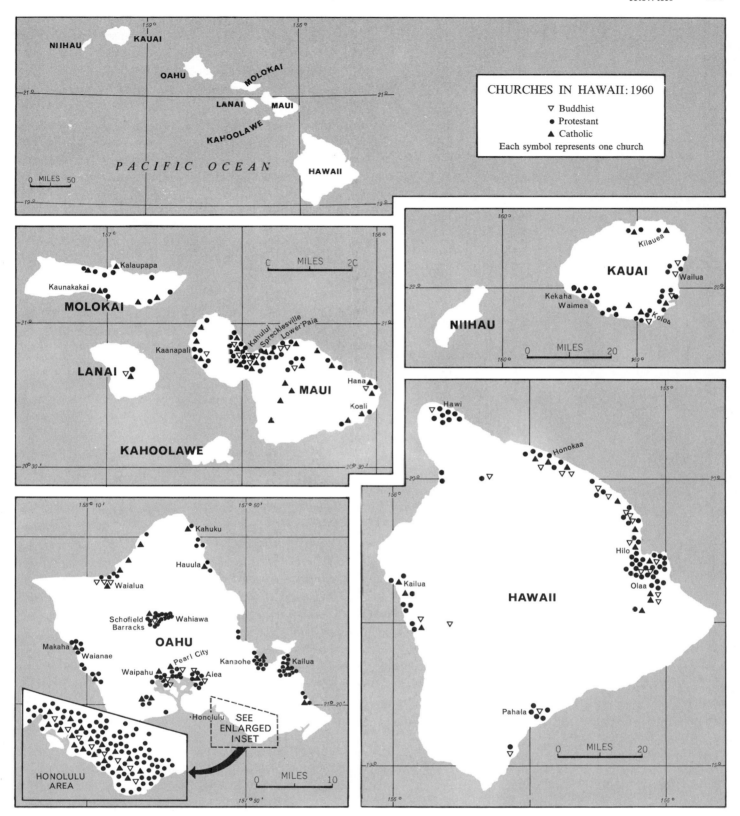

Figure 126

began their mission in Hawaii in 1850, only three years after their expulsion from Illinois (see Part II, 8). An Anglican Bishop of Honolulu, consecrated in England in 1861, arrived in his diocese the following year. Gaining much influence among the royalty, the Anglican Church grew steadily though slowly, but withdrew in favor of the Protestant Episcopal Church after Hawaii became a Territory of the United States. Methodists made a start in 1854 but remained only a few years; in 1888, however, the challenge of evangelizing the Japanese was accepted by the Methodists who returned, this time to stay. Lutheranism established itself on the Island of Kauai in 1883, and two years later the first Seventh-day Adventists arrived on Oahu. Before the turn of the century, the Disciples and the Salvation Army had launched their program in The Islands; and in the second quarter of the twentieth century

Baptists, Quakers, and Jehovah's Witnesses planted seeds in the wonderfully receptive soil.

Most of these later religious bodies enjoyed a modest increase up to the time of World War II. After that war, not only did these bodies experience a sudden growth but also many new groups came to early flower. Pentecostal sects, Bible centers, Full Gospel Churches, Grace Chapels, Dancing Goddesses, liberal and eclectic movements made a pattern of heterogeneity hardly to be matched. Figure 126, though showing this diversity in broadest outline, cannot represent graphically all of the religious bodies. The leading Buddhist religion, as stated above, is still Jodo Shin. The leading Protestant religion throughout the several islands is Congregationalism, though many churches founded by the Congregationalists no longer bear that explicit designation. On Oahu, the major island in the group, the Congregationalists early in 1960 had 34 churches, followed by the Baptists with 21, the Episcopalians with 20, the Mormons with 19, the Methodists with 16, the Lutherans with 12, and the Seventh-day Adventists and Jehovah's Witnesses with 11 each. The Roman Catholics had 34 churches on Oahu, one-half of which were in Honolulu itself. There were also at least 18 Buddhist temples on Oahu. On the Island of Kauai, Congregationalism and Catholicism each had 10 places of worship and Jodo Shin had 6. On Molokai the two Christian groups had 5 churches apiece; on Maui, Catholicism led Congregationalism, and on Hawaii the reverse was true.

The racial and religious variety of the Hawaiian Islands is reflected in the architecture of the houses of worship, in the language of the worshipers, in the ceremonies attending birth, marriage, and death. In the midst of such divergent and potentially antagonistic sociological and theological forces, the unity of Hawaii seems something of a wonder. That unity may be explained in part by (1) the prevalence of intermarriage (nearly 1 out of every 3 marriages is across racial lines); (2) a joyfully, perhaps even jocularly acquired loyalty to "old" Hawaii—its monarchy, its customs, its festivals, its words; and, more recently, (3) a growing identification with the interests of the United States and of its Stars and Stripes—especially those fifty stars.

SOURCES. Rufus Anderson, *The Hawaiian Islands: Their Progress and Condition under Missionary Labors* (Boston, 1864). H. W. Bradley, *The American Frontier in Hawaii: The Pioneers 1789-1843* (Stanford University, 1942). Edwin G. Burrows, *Hawaiian Americans: An Account of the Mingling of Japanese, Chinese, Polynesian, and American Cultures* (New Haven, 1947). Bernhard L. Hormann, "The Problem of the Religion of Hawaii's Japanese," *Social Process in Hawaii,* XXII. Walter Kolarz, "The Melting Pot in the Pacific," *Social Process in Hawaii,* XIX. Ralph S. Kuykendall, *The Hawaiian Kingdom 1778-1854* (Honolulu, reprint 1947). Kenneth Scott Latourette, *A History of the Expansion of Christianity,* V (New York, 1943). Henry Bond Restarick, *Hawaii 1778-1920 from the Viewpoint of a Bishop* (Honolulu, 1924). A useful year book of history and statistics, now called *All About Hawaii,* is published annually by the Star-Bulletin Printing Company of Honolulu.

CONCLUSION: THREE HUNDRED YEARS OF RELIGION IN AMERICA

Comparisons between one denomination and another, both of the same period, have their dangers, as observed above (pp. x-xi). For religious bodies do not count membership in the same way, and to count a "church" which serves 20 as the equivalent of a "church" which serves 2,000 is, obviously, to leave a very great deal to be desired. When both membership figures and the number of churches have been available, some balancing effect has here been sought by indicating strength in these two ways. In 1950, for example, the large color map is based upon membership, while the series of maps showing the distribution of each denomination by states has been based on number of churches (Figs. 46, 51, 53, 56, 60, 67, 76, 82, 85, 87, 92).

Comparisons are at least as risky when made between one century and another, even though the denominations be the same. For method of membership enumeration may change and conditions of that membership—environmental or doctrinal—certainly do change. In the twentieth century, for example, it is usually the case that more persons "belong" to a church than actually attend that particular church. In other words, the pastor may know that there are 2,000 members on his parish lists; he is reasonably content with a Sunday morning congregation half that size. In the colonial period, on the other hand, the size of the congregation generally exceeded that of the membership—church membership being regarded as a high privilege and often restricted by the severe demands in personal piety and moral purity. Trials for breach of discipline or eccentricity of faith were frequent; excommunication was commonplace. Regarding the size of congregations vis-à-vis membership, John Asplund noted in 1791 of the Baptists that "a large number attend the meetings, at least three times as many as have joined the church." And among the Anglicans, there were repeated references to an "auditory" of 200 or more persons, where there were only 30 or 40 communicants.

One must therefore temper the great gain in percentage of church membership from the end of the colonial period (about 10%) to the present (over 60%) with the knowledge that the churches' witness and watchfulness have not been multiplied 6 times over. And, as Figure 128 indicates, the actual ratio between number of citizens and number of churches in 1950 does not greatly differ from the proportion in 1650. From that point of view (and this, of course, is only one among many pertinent factors), the twentieth-century church is neither weaker nor stronger than its seventeenth-century predecessor.

Concerning the growth of the denominations themselves,

as charted in Figure 127, the most rapid multiplication of churches has occurred, clearly, among the Methodists and the Baptists. Although the Baptists had much the earlier start, they were behind the Methodists in 1850; their resumption of leadership by 1950 was due in some measure to the startling growth of the Negro Baptists. Presbyterians who were next in number of churches in 1850 had, a century later, dropped behind the Lutherans as well as the Roman Catholics. (For comparisons of *membership,* however, see Figs. 40 and 41; 95 and 96). Universalists declined, as did the Quakers, in the period from 1850 to 1950. The unchallenged numerical leadership of the Congregationalists and Anglicans in 1650 was still held in 1750, though threatened particularly by Presbyterian and Quaker growth. By 1850 the Presbyterians had moved far ahead of the two colonial leaders, but the Quakers had dropped further behind. Only two colonial bodies failed by mid-twentieth century to have at least 1,000 churches: the Quakers and the Dutch Reformed.

In 1650 American religion displayed a high degree of geographical unity (see Fig. 2), with Congregationalists in New England, Baptists in Rhode Island, Dutch Reformed in New York, Presbyterians on Long Island, Lutherans in Delaware, Roman Catholics in Maryland, and Anglicans in Virginia. It was not to be expected that this geographic pattern of religion could maintain itself as evangelists persuaded, colonies united, immigrants invaded, frontiers expanded, and people in general did an incredible amount of moving around. Yet even in 1950, clear geographic patterns of ecclesiastical regionalism could be discerned. Those patterns, however, differed sharply from the ones evident in 1650 and 1750 (see Figs. 2, 8, 10, 12, 14, 16, 20 and 23).

The following comments on religious distribution in the middle of the twentieth century all have direct reference to the color map, "Religion in America: 1950," *to which the reader's attention is now directed.*

Across the country as a whole, there were in 1950 amazingly few counties that were not dominated by one or another ecclesiastical body. "Domination" here means that at least one-fourth of all those affiliated with any church or synagogue are affiliated with one particular denominational family. And in approximately one-half of the counties of the nation, a single religious body accounts for at least 50% of all the membership in the county. The least homogeneity is to be found in the Pacific Northwest, notably in Oregon, where 19 of its 36 counties are so mixed that no religious group has even 25% of the membership in its ranks. And in the state of Oregon as a whole, there is not a single county in which any denomination enjoys a plurality of the membership. Of no other state in the nation is this true. (Oregon, incidentally, has the smallest percentage of its citizens as church members; Louisiana has the largest.)

The areas of greatest homogeneity are those dominated by four religious families, no one of which was a leader in the colonial period. The four territorial leaders are the Mormons, the Baptists, the Lutherans and the Roman Catholics. For geographical "control," the Mormons are without peer. In every single county in the state of Utah, the Church of the Latter-day Saints accounts for at least 60% of the total religious membership of the county. In only 3 counties is the percentage less than 90! And in 6 counties the percentage is 100! There is nothing comparable to this elsewhere in the nation. In adjoining Idaho, 21 of the state's 44 counties are predominantly Mormon. The same is true of 4 counties in Nevada and Wyoming, of 2 counties in Oregon. But that is virtually the full sweep. Except for Decatur County, Iowa, the Church of the Latter-day Saints does not lead in any other county in the country. The Church which began in Fayette, New York, migrated to Kirtland, Ohio, thence to Independence, Missouri, and environs, and in 1839 to Nauvoo, Illinois, was in 1950 a phenomenon primarily of the western basins and plateaus.

In the southeastern portion of the United States the Baptists far outnumber all other religious groups. And while it is true that 4 out of every 5 Negro church members are Baptists, this dominance in the southeast obtains even apart from the preponderance of Negro Baptists. In Virginia, for example, Baptists lead in almost one-half of the counties. In North Carolina, seven-eighths of the counties are "Baptist territory." Baptists lead in every county in South Carolina except 10, in every county in Georgia (and there are 159 of them) except 15. In Alabama, only 3 counties are not Baptist-dominated—only white Baptists being counted in each instance. In the border states of Kentucky and Tennessee, there is more heterogeneity, but the Baptists still lead in these areas. The same is true in Oklahoma, Texas, Arkansas, and Missouri.

The Lutheran leadership in the Midwestern farm belt is well known. Two-thirds of North Dakota's counties are in the hands of the Lutherans. In Minnesota, every county is either Lutheran or Catholic, with the Lutherans far in the lead, whereas in Wisconsin the two groups are more evenly matched. Lutherans lead in Nebraska and South Dakota, and have strong representation in Iowa and Montana. Far from the Midwest, Lutheranism dominates such counties as Lexington and Newberry in South Carolina, Lee and Lavaca in Texas; Page and Shenandoah in Virginia. While there are differences of territorial emphasis in the several synods of Lutheranism (e.g., Augustana strong in New England, United in Pennsylvania, Missouri Synod in the South and West, Evangelical in Minnesota and the Dakotas; see Fig. 62), the dominance here described is of the Lutheran family as a whole.

Roman Catholic territories are both ancient and recent in conquest. One of the clearest contemporary testimonies to the French and Spanish periods in American history is the Catholic majority in many areas of the Mississippi Valley and the Southwest. Alone among the southeastern states, Louisiana has a heavy Catholic population, harking back to the days of Jesuit operations out of New Orleans

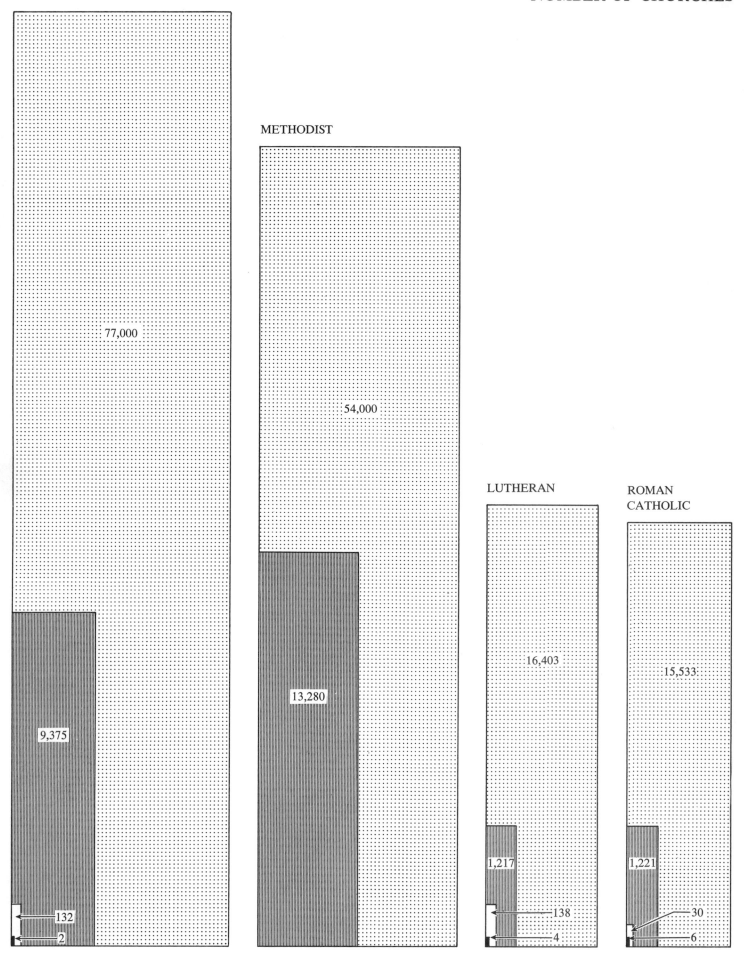

BAPTIST

METHODIST

LUTHERAN

ROMAN CATHOLIC

77,000

54,000

16,403

15,533

13,280

9,375

1,217

1,221

132

2

138

4

30

6

Figure 127

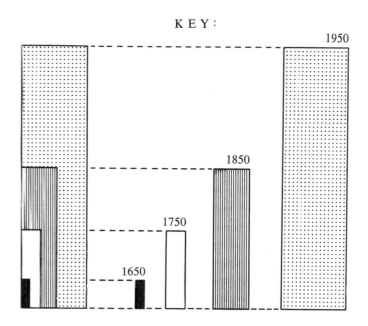

KEY:

1950
1850
1750
1650

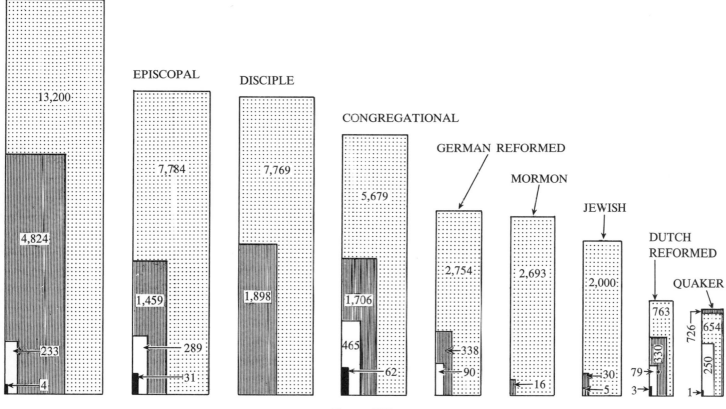

PRESBYTERIAN

13,200

4,824

233

4

EPISCOPAL

7,784

1,459

289

31

DISCIPLE

7,769

1,898

CONGREGATIONAL

5,679

1,706

465

62

GERMAN REFORMED

2,754

338

90

MORMON

2,693

16

JEWISH

2,000

30

5

DUTCH REFORMED

763

330

79

3

QUAKER

726

654

250

1

Figure 127

(see above, p. 33). Almost one-half of that state's parishes have a Catholic coloration, and in some of that number (e.g., Assumption, Lafourche, Saint James, St. John the Baptist, and Vermillion) Catholics account for more than 90% of the religious membership of the parish. In Texas, New Mexico, Arizona, and California, the impact of the Spanish conquest and the Mexican control is sharply focused. In Texas, the "valley" counties of Hidalgo, Wil-

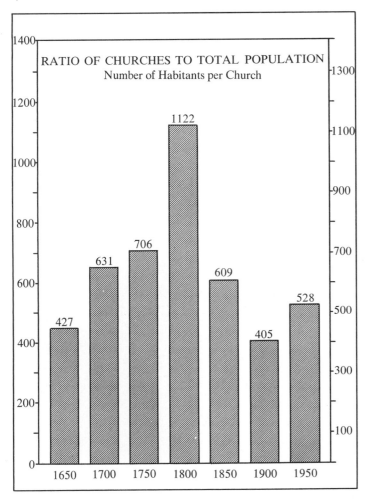

Figure 128

lacy, Starr, Kenedy, Zapata, Jim Hogg, and many others are from 90% to 100% Catholic. In New Mexico all counties but 5 are predominantly Roman Catholic; and in Arizona, all counties but 2. California, while somewhat more heterogeneous than these last two, is nonetheless Catholic territory, with the Roman Church being the principal religious body in every county of the state. In the north, French Catholicism still leaves its mark in the Upper Mississippi Valley, notably in Wisconsin, though nineteenth-century German migrations are a greater factor here. Farther to the east, the state of Maine also exhibits the influence of its northern neighbor. The nineteenth-century Irish immigration is most evident, of course, along the Atlantic seaboard. Except for Nantucket Island, every county of Massachusetts has a heavy majority of Roman Catholics. The same is true in New Hampshire and Ver-

mont, again with one exception each. In Connecticut and Rhode Island, there are no exceptions, Catholics having more than 50% of the religious affiliation in every county in these states.

These, then, are the four church groups which to the greatest extent determine the ecclesiastical cartography of the nation in 1950. There are some surprising omissions. What, for example, of The Methodist Church, the largest single Protestant denomination (though not the largest Protestant "family")? Methodism is simply national rather than regional. With the exceptions of Maryland and Delaware, no states are dominated by Methodism. Several counties in Ohio (e.g., Fayette, Gallia, Harrison, Morgan, Morrow, Noble, and Pike) and Kansas (e.g., Chase, Elk, Haskell, Lane, Linn, Morton, Stanton, and Wallace) are predominantly Methodist, but on the whole the church of Francis Asbury and Peter Cartwright is diffused throughout the whole country. The same is true, though to a lesser extent, of the three leaders in the colonial period: Congregational, Episcopal, and Presbyterian. Where Congregationalism accounts for 50% or more of the membership of a county, it is no longer in the once private preserve of New England, but in Nebraska (Hayes County), Colorado (San Juan) and Wyoming (Sublette). The Episcopal Church does not lead in a single county in the former Anglican colony of Virginia, but in far-removed South Dakota this Church has priority in 4 counties (Bennett, Dewey, Shannon, and Washabaugh). Presbyterianism maintains small islands of territory in such places as Forest County, Pennsylvania; Bath County, Virginia; Hoke County, North Carolina; and Hinsdale County, Colorado (the latter having a church affiliation that is 100% Presbyterian).

On the other hand, some of the smaller denominations which tend to congregate rather than scatter, show up on America's ecclesiastical map as well as the three larger groups mentioned above. The Evangelical United Brethren are predominant in 2 counties in West Virginia (Grant and Morgan), 2 in Indiana (Harrison and Orange) and 1 in Nebraska (Loup). The Dutch Reformed family prevails in 3 counties in Michigan (Missaukee, Newaygo, and Ottawa) and 3 in Iowa (Mahaska, Marion, and Sioux). In Sullivan, Kings, and Bronx Counties in New York, the dominant religious group is Jewish. Mennonite fellowships hold sway in Lagrange County, Indiana; Oscoda County, Michigan; and Holmes County, Ohio. The Unitarians are foremost in 1 county, not in Massachusetts, however, but in North Dakota: Billings County (total population in 1950, 218). And the Assemblies of God have an edge over the Congregationalists in Thomas County, Nebraska. The Disciples of Christ, staying fairly close to the areas of their early strength, show significant concentration in Kentucky, North Carolina, Virginia, Indiana, Illinois, Iowa, Missouri, and Oklahoma.

[*Note: An important limitation in the study upon which the color map is based should be called to the reader's at-*

tention. The Bureau of Research and Survey of the National Council of Churches indicates that "Figures were not available from two large Negro Baptist bodies nor from three Negro Methodist bodies, the Church of Christ Scientist, Jehovah's Witnesses, Churches of Christ, nor from most of the Eastern Orthodox groups."]

What will the ecclesiastical map of America look like in the middle of the twenty-first century? Will the kind of heterogeneity which Oregon now typifies be normative for most of the nation? Will the increased mobility, a mobility that is social as well as physical, result in greater ecclesiastical mobility? Will the rate of growth of the newer groups continue to accelerate, thereby bringing into being a whole new complex of religious dominance in the next century? Or, on the other hand, will the number of map colors necessary a hundred years from now be fewer rather than greater? The answer to the last question lies largely in the fortunes of the drive for unity—a drive which in the twentieth century has gathered considerable momentum.

As acerbity has given way to charity, as feud has yielded to fellowship, and arrogance has surrendered to tolerance, the ecumenical movement has grown in strength and sweep. America has contributed to the ecumenical movement—if in no other way—by starkly revealing the absurd lengths to which sectarian division could and did go. And while much of that diversity was transplanted rather than indigenous, the anomalies, embarrassments, harassments, and incongruities of partisanship were nonetheless awkward and debilitating. Yet, happily, it is the sick who most earnestly seek the physician's cure.

Attempts were made, even in the colonial period, to scale sectarian walls: John Eliot, Cotton Mather, Jonathan Edwards, Henry Antes and Zinzendorf were among those seeking to enlarge the circle of fellowship. Not until the nineteenth century, however, were interdenominational agencies and societies formally established. Beginning with the Congregational-Presbyterian Plan of Union in 1801 (see above, p. 62), evangelistic monies and energies flower through the American Board of Commissioners of Foreign Missions (founded in 1810), the American Education Society (1815), the American Bible Society (1816), the American Sunday-School Union (1824), the American Tract Society (1825) and the American Home Mission Society (1826). Major social concerns, moreover, found cooperative expression in such groups as the American Society for the Promotion of Temperance (1826), the American Peace Society (1828), and the American Anti-Slavery Society (1833). While clearly an entering wedge in the separating walls, these several societies represented primarily the cooperative efforts of individuals rather than of churches. And rather than seeking ecclesiastical union as such, the focus was on the task to be done, the mission to be accomplished.

In 1838, however, a Society for the Promotion of Christian Union was formed, in response to Samuel Schmucker's *Fraternal Appeal* "affectionately addressed to the American churches of every denomination" and published the previous year. Lutheran Schmucker's imaginative and vigorous proposal for an "Apostolic Protestant Church of America" fell far short of realization, though it had a pronounced influence on the German-American churches in general and on the Swiss Reformed leader, Philip Schaff, in particular. In 1846 the Evangelical Alliance was formed

RELIGIOUS PREFERENCES IN AMERICA: 1957

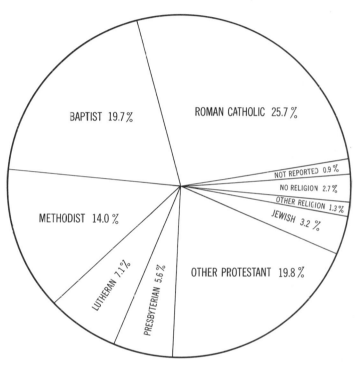

Figure 129

in England to promote organic union. Because of the North-South tensions in the United States at that time, an American branch of the Alliance was not organized until 1867. But this too raised hopes that could not be met, and the Alliance became virtually dormant after 1900. An American Congress of Churches gathered in New Haven in 1885, flourished briefly, then withered away.

Again, the drive for unity seemed to be more successful not in the agencies working *for* unity but in those working *in* unity. The Young Men's Christian Association, introduced into Boston from England in 1851, was shortly followed by the Young Women's Christian Association, organized in 1866. Both of these imports broadly and boldly interpreted the demands of Christian love so as to cross not only denominational lines but also racial, social, and national boundaries. The International Sunday School Association (1872), the Convention of Christian Workers (1886), the Student Volunteer Movement (1886), and the Open and Institutional Church League (1894) were other instances where Christians agreed to "share our mutual woes/our mutual burdens bear." It appeared that, for a truly ecumenical harvest, there was no better preparation than a laboring together in love.

The ingathering began in the first decade of the twentieth century. Near the end of 1908, in the city of Philadelphia, the Federal Council of Churches was organized. Unlike most of the previous associations or societies, this Council was composed of official representatives of the denominations and their established agencies. The 31 organizing denominations (major nonmembers: Roman Catholics, Southern Baptists, Episcopalians, and certain Lutheran groups) not only continued the social emphasis of many of the societies mentioned above but also purposed to seek a greater Christian unity, both in the local communities and on the national scene.

In 1950 the Federal Council of Churches merged with such interdenominational boards as the United Council of Church Women and the International Council of Religious Education to form the National Council of Churches of Christ in the United States of America. The greatly strengthened and more effectively organized National Council represented in 1960 the apex of a structured ecumenicity in America, with a total constituent membership of approximately 40 million. Other interdenominational alliances such as the National Association of Evangelicals (1942) and the American Council of Christian Churches (1944) enjoy memberships which are considerably smaller. The former, with headquarters in Wheaton, Illionis, had over 2 million members in 1960, some of its member churches also cooperating with the National Council. The American Council of Churches may be fairly regarded as more a reaction to the ecumenical movement than an evidence of it. Its voting membership in 1960 was slightly over 250,000.

Broader than the National Council, though not so deep in its penetration, is the National Conference of Christians and Jews. Organized in 1928, this group of Protestants, Catholics, and Jews has raised its voice repeatedly in opposition to bigotry and hatred no matter in whose back yard—or living room—these were to be found. With the inauguration of Brotherhood Week in 1933 and of the Religious News Service in the same year, the N.C.C.J. has, within its means, contributed much to the dissolution of those curious barriers that keep only friends apart and let only the enemy in.

While the Roman Catholic Church has not joined in any movements involving union or federation, it has in several ways registered its own concern about a splintered Christendom. Prayers offered by such orders as the Franciscan Friars of Atonement, books written by such persons as Karl Adam (e.g., *One and Holy*, New York, 1951) and Gustave Weigel (e.g., *A Catholic Primer on the Ecumenical Movement*, Westminster [Md.], 1959), and interfaith meetings encouraged by a variety of organizations within Catholicism—these raise hopes of a new approach to ecumenical conversation. More recently, Pope John XXIII has focused new attention on Christian unity, not only by calling for an ecumenical council in October,

1962, but also by establishing a high-level secretariat to maintain official contact with the World Council of Churches (organized in 1948 but largely boycotted by the Vatican). And in December of 1960, the Pope shattered a four hundred-year-old precedent by receiving the Archbishop of Canterbury for a courtesy call.

Meanwhile, among Protestants, mergers continue to occur, new proposals continue to be made. [For a full listing of twentieth-century mergers in America, see Ruth Rouse and Stephen Charles Neill, *A History of the Ecumenical Movement 1517–1948* (Philadelphia, 1954), appendix to Chapter 10.] In San Francisco, late in 1960, Dr. Eugene Carson Blake of the United Presbyterian Church in the U. S. A. (itself newly created, see Fig. 77) offered a dramatic plan for the union of his own denomination with The Methodist Church, the Protestant Episcopal Church and the United Church of Christ (the latter also newly created, see Fig. 52). The resulting body, "both Catholic and Reformed," would then open its doors for any other denomination which might wish to unite with that broad fellowship. Successful or not, the proposal is but one of many efforts designed, as the World Council's General Secretary W. A. Visser 't Hooft put it, to move from "the Church as men have conceived it toward the Church as God intended it."

In March of 1957, the Bureau of the Census of the United States Department of Commerce conducted a nationwide sample survey of civilian population in order to determine religious preference (see Fig. 129). The question, "What is your religion?" was asked only of persons 14 years of age or older. The response did not necessarily imply church membership or even attendance, but only "preference." The person responding "Lutheran" regarded Lutheranism as his religion, whether or not he was actively involved in any synod or parish. If a person had no religion or responded that he was either an atheist or agnostic, he was reported in the "No Religion" category. All answers to this question were obtained on a voluntary basis.

Considering only the population over 14 years of age, an astounding 96% indicated some religious preference. Of these, 70 million persons regarded themselves as Protestants, over 30 million as Roman Catholics and almost 4 million as Jewish. A little over 4 million either indicated that they had no religion or declined to report any preference. Of the Protestants, 23.5 million reported a Baptist preference; 16.7 million, a Methodist; 8.4 million, a Lutheran, and 6.7 million, a Presbyterian. The total adult population of the country in 1957 was placed at 119,333,000. Of this number, then, approximately 115,000,000 indicated a preference for some recognizable form of institutional religion in America.

These figures, though clearly not comparable to reports of church membership, of attendance, of contribution—or much of anything else—do indicate a broad basis of friendly interest in, and perhaps sympathy with, the tasks to which America's churches and synagogues have set themselves. The figures also suggest that most Americans, even in 1960, would have little difficulty understanding

Thornton Wilder's Stage Manager: "I don't care what they say with their mouths—everybody knows that *something* is eternal. And it ain't houses and it ain't names, and it ain't earth, and it ain't even the stars. . . ."

A NOTE ON THE SOURCES

Two steps have been taken in this *Atlas* in an effort to make the bibliographical data more readily accessible and thereby more useful. First, at the conclusion of each section of the text, the principal sources pertinent to that section have been listed alphabetically, by author. Second, an Index to Authors and Titles has been compiled, showing what authorities have been quoted or cited and where. To these two places the reader is referred for most of the bibliographical material. The comments below will be confined to the broader works in the field.

Bibliographical

For any study of American life, the excellent *Harvard Guide to American History* (Cambridge, 1954), edited by Oscar Handlin *et al.*, should be used. The older bibliographies in America's religious history, all severely dated, are Samuel M. Jackson, *A Bibliography of American Church History* (American Church History Series, XII) (New York, 1894); G. F. Bowerman, *A Selected Bibliography of the Religious Denominations of the United States . . .* (New York, 1896); and, Peter G. Mode, *Source-book and Bibliographical Guide for American Church History* (Menasha [Wis.], 1921). More specialized, more recent and generally more useful are W. H. Allison, *Inventory of Unpublished Material for American Religious History in Protestant Church Archives and Other Depositories* (Washington, 1910); John Tracy Ellis, *A Guide to American Catholic History* (Milwaukee, 1959); and Moses Rischin, *An Inventory of American Jewish History* (Cambridge, 1954). An outstanding two-volume *Critical Bibliography of Religion in America* has recently been issued by Princeton University Press (1961). This remarkable work by Nelson R. Burr may be consulted repeatedly—and never without rich reward—by the student seeking additional aid in the broad compass of America's religious history.

Statistical

After compiling denominational statistics for a time, John Asplund, weary in well-doing, wrote in 1790: "We have often been obliged to wade through an immense accumulation of rubbish before we could find the necessary materials; and many documents which we have received are sadly deficient, indefinite, or badly arranged." This has not been Mr. Asplund's experience alone. Since the days of this Swede's *Triennial Baptist Register*, however, certain labors have somewhat reduced the extent of rubbish-wading found necessary.

First among these, the patient compilations of the Reverend Frederick Lewis Weis should be noted. His volumes, all published in Massachusetts by the Society for the Descendants of the Colonial Clergy, have proved to be enormous timesavers, and his results have been relied on heavily in Part I. The volumes are *The Colonial Clergy and the Colonial Churches of New England* (1936); *The Colonial Churches and the Colonial Clergy of the Middle and Southern Colonies 1607–1776* (1938); *The Colonial Clergy of Maryland, Delaware & Georgia* (1950); and, *The Colonial Clergy of Virginia, North Carolina and South Carolina* (1955). Otherwise, for the colonial period, one is largely dependent upon regional studies, denominational histories, travel literature, almanacs and gazetteers.

In the latter, there is occasionally a happy unearthing of some reliable religious data, though one must often be content with learning that in New-Ipswich, N. H., there were in 1812 exactly 176 horses over 4 years of age, without discovering whether 1 or 1,000 Lutherans had settled anywhere nearby (E. Merrill, *Gazetteer of the State of New-Hampshire . . .* [Exeter, 1817]).

After 1800 the availability and reliability of religious statistics shows marked improvement. A spate of books reviewing the progress of religion in the United States began to appear, some of them dipping back into the colonial period for a quick generalization or two. Among the most useful for statistics, the following may be mentioned: Robert Baird, *Religion in America; Or, An Account of the Origin, Progress, Relation to the State, and present Condition of the Evangelical Churches in the United States* (New York, 1844; revised, 1856); also by Baird, *The Christian Retrospect and Register . . .* (New York, 1851); Joseph Belcher, *The Religious Denominations in the United States: their History, Doctrine, Government and Statistics . . .* (Philadelphia, 1855); H. K. Carroll, *The Religious Forces of the United States* (New York, 1893); Daniel Dorchester, *Christianity in the United States from the first settlement down to the present time* (New York, 1888); and by the same author, *The Problem of Religious Progress* (New York, 1881; revised, 1895; further revision, 1900); P. Douglass Gorrie, *The Churches and Sects of the United States* (Auburn, 1852); John Hayward, *The Religious Creeds and Statistics of every Christian Denomination in the United States and British Provinces . . .* (Boston, 1836); and I. Daniel Rupp (ed.), *An Original History of the Religious Denominations at Present Existing in the United States* (Philadelphia, 1844).

These works can be supplemented (1) by the reports on proceedings of missionary and educational societies or the denominational assemblies (annual or otherwise) themselves; (2) by the abundant religious periodical literature; and (3) by the reports, after 1850, made by the United States government. Although the federal census began in 1790, compilation of religious data did not begin until 1850. From 1850 through 1880, the government gathered facts concerning the number of churches, their location, their seating accommodations. In 1890 data on membership was first compiled, and in the years 1906, 1916, 1926, and 1936, elaborate tables were devised and separate volumes were published dealing with all phases of church life that gave themselves to statistical representation. Since 1936, no federal census of religious bodies has been taken, largely on the grounds of its alleged compromising of civil liberty and of church-state separation.

Denominational historians have occasionally taken up the task of statistical history, as seen, for example, in C. C. Goss's *Statistical History of the First Century of American Methodism* (New York, 1866) and Herman C. Weber's *Presbyterian Statistics Through One Hundred Years 1826–1926* (n. p., 1927), both of which volumes are exceedingly useful. But reliance in the modern period has rested chiefly on the "yearbooks" or annual summaries of each denomination, or upon the convenient and carefully edited *Yearbook of American Churches*, which—under varying titles—has been issued by the Federal (now National) Council of Churches since 1916. Dr. Benson Y.

Landis, current editor of the *Yearbook,* has graciously granted permission for use of the data contained therein. Concerning the denominational yearbooks and the federal censuses, no attempt has been made to list these repeatedly under each "Sources" paragraph in the text; where relevant, they have been regularly used.

Geographical

A history of ecclesiastical cartography in America would, if written, be quite short, for little has been done in the way of mapping the country's religious expansion and diversity. The most systematic effort in this direction has been Charles O. Paullin's *Atlas of the Historical Geography of the United States* (Washington and New York, 1932), where Marcus Jernegan directed the cartographic representation of America's churches in 1775, 1860, and 1890. (His maps thus complement those presented here for the years 1650, 1750, 1850, and 1950.) The reprint of Paullin's *Atlas* by the Antiquarian Press of New York is under way. Publications of the United States government, based upon official census reports, have also on occasion summarized the religious situation in cartographic form. The most notable examples of this are the following: Francis A. Walker, *Statistical Atlas of the United States . . . 1870* (Washington, 1874), Plate 31; Henry Gannett, *Statistical Atlas of the United States . . . [1890]* (Washington, 1898), Plates 35-40; and *Religious Bodies: 1906,* I (Washington, 1910), Diagrams 2 and 5, redrawn for the present work as Figures 34-39. C. Luther Fry, under the auspices of the Institute of Social and Religious Research, presented maps, charts, and tables based on the results of the federal census of 1926 in a volume entitled *The U. S. Looks at its Churches* (New York, 1930); see particularly Chapter IV. Quite recently, a geographer, Wilbur Zelinsky, has discussed "An Approach to the Religious Geography of the United States: Patterns of Church Membership in 1952," in the *Annals of the Association of American Geographers,* LI:2 (June, 1961), pp. 139-193 [26 maps]. Efforts other than these have been limited in scope and widely scattered in location. Some of the latter have been reproduced in this volume, while attention has been called to others in the "Sources" paragraphs.

A great many regional studies of American religion or of specific denominations are now being published, many of them as carefully researched doctoral dissertations. These offer opportunities for cartographic expression not often exploited. And there are certain counties in the United States whose careful religious history would—in intricate microcosm—tell the religious history of the nation. Such counties as the following deserve precise historical and cartographical examination from the vantage point of religion: Bristol (Mass.), Newport (R. I.), Schoharie (N. Y.), Lancaster (Pa.), New Castle (Del.), Frederick (Md.), James City (Va.), Charleston (S. C.), Glynn (Ga.,), Hamilton (Ohio), Lenawee (Mich.), Marion (Ind.), Jefferson (Ky.), Mobile (Ala.), Orleans (La.) and Sante Fe (N. M.).

General

Three general introductions to religion in America have been issued quite recently—too recently, unfortunately, to be exploited for this study. *History of Religion in the United States* (Englewod Cliffs, 1960) by Clifton E. Olmstead is a more comprehensive treatment of the broad field than is to be found in any previous single-volume study. *American Christianity: An Historical Interpretation with Representative Documents,* a two-volume work (New York, 1960, 1962) by H. Shelton Smith, Robert T. Handy, and Lefferts A. Loetscher, not only presents the major revealing documents but also provides discriminating interpretations and informative bibliographies. *Religion in American Life* (Princeton, 1961) is a significant and provocative four-volume study edited by James Ward Smith and A. Leland Jamison; Volume IV of this series is the Burr bibliography mentioned above.

The University of Chicago's History of American Civilization series, edited by Daniel J. Boorstin, includes three volumes on religion: *American Catholicism* by John Tracy Ellis (1956); *American Judaism* by Nathan Glazer (1957); and *American Protestantism* by Winthrop S. Hudson (1961). Among the many works of the late William Warren Sweet, pioneer in the study of American church history, the following may be noted: *The Story of Religion in America,* first published in 1930 and revised in 1939 and 1950; *Religion in Colonial America* (New York, 1947); *The American Churches: An Interpretation* (New York, 1947); and, *Religion in the Development of American Culture, 1765–1840* (New York, 1952). The monumental labors of Kenneth Scott Latourette are particularly relevant to the present work in Volumes III and IV of his *History of the Expansion of Christianity* (New York, 1939, 1941) and in Volume III of his *Christianity in a Revolutionary Age* (New York, 1961). From 1893 to 1906, the American Society of Church History published thirteen volumes dealing with the Church in America; with the exception of the first and last, all volumes in this series were denominational treatments and have been cited in Part II of this *Atlas.*

Older introductions to American religion which deserve mention include the following: L. W. Bacon, *A History of American Christianity* (American Church History Series, XIII) (New York, 1897); Henry K. Rowe, *The History of Religion in the United States* (New York, 1924); Luther A. Weigle, *American Idealism* (Pageant of America Series, X) (New Haven, 1928); W. E. Garrison, *The March of Faith* (New York, 1933); H. Richard Niebuhr, *The Kingdom of God in America* (New York, 1937; reprinted, 1959); and Willard L. Sperry, *Religion in America* (Cambridge and New York, 1947). In addition to those more recent surveys already cited, the following volumes published in the 1950's should be called to the reader's attention: J. C. Brauer, *Protestantism in America* (Philadelphia, 1953); John Cogley (ed.), *Religion in America* (New York, 1958); Will Herberg, *Protestant-Catholic-Jew* (New York, 1955; revised, 1960); Winthrop S. Hudson, *The Great Tradition of the American Churches* (New York, 1953); Martin E. Marty, *The New Shape of American Religion* (New York, 1959); F. E. Mayer, *The Religious Bodies of America* (St. Louis, 1954); Ronald E. Osborn, *The Spirit of American Christianity* (New York, 1958); Leo Pfeffer, *Creeds in Competition: A Creative Force in American Culture* (New York, 1958); Leo Rosten (ed.), *A Guide to the Religions of America* (New York, 1955); and Herbert W. Schneider, *Religion in 20th Century America* (Cambridge, 1952). Volume 256 (March, 1948) and Volume 332 (November, 1960) of *The Annals of the American Academy of Political and Social Science* were devoted entirely to a discussion of religion in American society.

Appendix A*

LOCATION AND DATE OF CHURCHES FOUNDED BY 1650

ANGLICAN

Virginia: James City, 1607; Kecoughtan (Elizabeth City), 1610; Henrico City, 1611; Harrop (James City), 1614/15; Martin's Hundred (James City), 1619; Elizabeth City, 1624; Charles City, 1634; Mulberry Island (Warwick), 1635; Hungar's (Northampton), 1635; Denbigh (Warwick), 1635, Isle of Wight, 1635; Lynnhaven (Princess Anne), 1639, Hampton (York), 1639/40; Lawn's Creek (Surrey), 1640; Nassawadox (Northampton), 1642; Newport (Isle of Wight), 1642; Wallingford (Charles City), 1642; Warwisqueake (Isle of Wight), 1642; Martin's Brandon (Prince George), 1642; Jordan (Charles City), 1642; Weyanoke (Charles City), 1642; West (Nansemond), 1643; Elizabeth River (Norfolk), 1643; York, 1645; New Pocoson (York), 1645; Southwark (Surrey), 1647; Fairfield (Northumberland), 1648.
Maryland: Christ Church (Queen Anne's), 1629; King & Queen (St. Mary's), 1650; St. Mary's, 1650; William & Mary (St. Mary's), 1650.

BAPTIST

Rhode Island: Providence, 1639; Newport, c. 1644.

CONGREGATIONAL

Massachusetts: Plymouth, 1620; Salem, 1629; Boston, 1630; Dorchester, 1630; Watertown, 1630; Roxbury, 1631/2; Charlestown, 1632; Duxbury, 1632; Lynn, 1632; Marshfield, 1632; Cambridge, 1633; Ipswich, 1634; Scituate, 1634; Hingham, 1635; Newbury, 1635; Weymouth, 1635; Concord, 1636; Springfield, 1637; Taunton, 1637; Dedham, 1638; Sandwich, 1638; Barnstable (West), 1639; Barnstable (East), 1639; Quincy, 1639; Rowley, 1639; Salisbury, 1639; Yarmouth, 1639; Wayland, 1640; Edgartown, 1641; Haverhill, 1641; Gloucester, 1642; Norwell, 1642; Woburn, 1642; Martha's Vineyard, 1642; Eastham, 1643/4; Wenham, 1644; North Andover, 1645; Wakefield, 1645; Malden, 1649.
Connecticut: Windsor, 1635; Hartford, 1636; Milford, 1639; New Haven, 1639; Stratford, 1640; Stamford, 1641; Wethersfield, 1641; New London, 1642; Fairfield, 1643; Guilford, 1643; Old Saybrook, 1646; Branford, 1647; East Hampton, 1650.
New Hampshire: Dover, 1638; Exeter, 1638; Hampton, 1638.
Maine: Saco, 1640; Wells, 1643.
Rhode Island: Newport, 1640; East Providence, 1643.
New York: Southold (L. I.), 1640.
Maryland: Annapolis, 1649.

DUTCH REFORMED

New York: New York, 1628; Albany, 1642.
Delaware: Newcastle, c. 1650.

LUTHERAN (Swedish)

Delaware: Wilmington, 1638; Newcastle, 1642.
Pennsylvania: Chester, 1648.

LUTHERAN (German).

New York: New York, 1648.

PRESBYTERIAN

New York: Southampton, 1640; Newtown, 1642; Hempstead, 1643; East Hampton, 1648.

ROMAN CATHOLIC (For location of missions outside the thirteen colonies, see Fig. 116).
Maine: Abenaki mission.
Maryland: St. Mary's City, 1634; St. Inigoes (St. Mary's), 1638; Kent Island (Queen Anne's), 1639; Port Tobacco (Charles), 1641; Patuxent (Prince George), 1647.

* These data are based chiefly on the compilations of F. L. Weis; for full bibliographical information, see p. 165.

Appendix B

NUMBER OF CHURCHES IN 1750: DENOMINATIONAL DISTRIBUTION

COLONIES	Anglican	Baptist	Congregational	Lutheran	Presbyterian	Dutch Reformed	French Reformed	German Reformed	Roman Catholic
Maine			16	1	5				
New Hampshire	1		40		5				
Massachusetts	17	16	231		8				
Connecticut	19	12	155		1				
Rhode Island	7	30	12						
New York	20	4	5	26	35	48	4	7	1
New Jersey	18	14	2	19	51	24		4	2
Pennsylvania	19	29		73	56	7		64	11
Maryland	50	4		3	18			4	15
Delaware	14	2		3	27				1
Virginia	96	3		5	17			5	
North Carolina	9	13		1				2	
South Carolina	16	5	4	5	9		2	4	
Georgia	3			2	1				
TOTAL	289	132	465	138	233	79	6	90	30

Appendix C*

NUMBER OF CHURCHES IN 1850:
DENOMINATIONAL DISTRIBUTION BY STATES AND TERRITORIES

States and Territories	Baptist	Congre-gational	Episcopal	Lutheran	Methodist	Presby-terian	Quaker	Dutch Re-formed	German Re-formed	Roman Catholic
STATES										
Maine	326	180	9		199	7	26			12
New Hampshire	193	176	11		103	13	15			2
Vermont	102	175	26		140	11	7			8
Massachusetts	266	448	54	1	262	15	39			41
Rhode Island	106	21	26		23		18			7
Connecticut	114	252	101		185	17	5			12
New York	781	215	279	81	1,231	671	133	233	1	176
New Jersey	108	8	52	7	312	149	52	66		22
Pennsylvania	320		136	498	889	775	149	7	209	139
Delaware	12		21		106	26	9			3
Maryland	45		133	40	497	56	26		22	65
District of Columbia	6		8	2	16	6	1			6
Virginia	649		173	50	1,025	240	14		9	17
North Carolina	615		50	49	784	151	31		16	4
South Carolina	413	1	72	41	484	136	1			14
Georgia	879	1	20	8	795	97	2			8
Florida	56		10		87	16				5
Alabama	579		17	1	577	162				5
Mississippi	385		13		454	143				9
Louisiana	77		14		125	18			1	55
Texas	82		5		176	45				13
Arkansas	114		2		168	52				7
Tennessee	646		17	12	861	363	4			3
Kentucky	803		19	5	530	224				48
Missouri	300		11	21	250	125				65
Illinois	282	46	27	42	405	206	6	2	3	59
Indiana	428	2	24	63	778	282	89	5	5	63
Ohio	551	100	79	260	1,529	663	94	5	71	130
Michigan	66	29	25	12	119	72	7	10		44
Wisconsin	49	37	19	20	110	40		2		64
Iowa	20	14	5	4	71	38	5		1	18
California	1		1		5	3				18
TERRITORIES										
Minnesota					1	1				1
New Mexico										73
Oregon	1	1			1	1				5
Utah (9 churches—unclassified)										
TOTAL	9,375	1,706	1,459	1,217	13,280	4,824	726	330	338	1,221

* These figures are based on *The Seventh Census of the United States: 1850* (Washington, 1853).

Appendix D*

NUMBER OF CHURCHES IN 1950: DENOMINATIONAL DISTRIBUTION BY STATES

STATES	Baptist (American & Southern Conventions only)	Congregational–Christian	Disciples of Christ	Episcopal	Lutheran	Methodist (The Methodist Church only)	Presbyterian (U.S. and U.S.A. only)	Quaker	Dutch Reformed	German Reformed (Evangelical and Reformed)	Roman Catholic	Mormon (membership) Salt Lake City Branch
Alabama	2,688	74	69	99	32	1,240	251	1	0	2	93	
Arizona	132	13	31	33	26	79	69	2	1	0	89	33,000
Arkansas	1,105	2	122	46	29	1,057	200	2	0	3	103	
California	875	220	237	263	480	603	426	29	20	39	767	110,000
Colorado	124	68	72	83	125	194	125	13	23	9	157	8,000
Connecticut	135	307	1	184	86	156	11	5	0	10	279	
Delaware	10	2	1	35	7	302	31	2	0	0	28	
District of Columbia	81	7	9	39	21	79	34	3	0	2	38	5,000
Florida	1,033	42	85	180	82	678	218	0	0	5	112	3,000
Georgia	2,736	44	163	87	39	1,566	299	0	0	0	40	
Idaho	44	26	34	42	57	71	50	0	0	2	56	140,000
Illinois	1,034	312	623	198	941	1,433	524	20	20	235	977	2,000
Indiana	458	163	693	56	338	1,298	307	152	7	128	427	
Iowa	192	194	322	67	720	931	339	50	65	92	563	
Kansas	372	86	335	103	291	817	226	2	1	34	376	
Kentucky	2,200	8	700	61	35	1,129	278	0	3	28	189	
Louisiana	1,141	20	33	77	33	623	125	0	0	10	365	
Maine	331	251	4	55	4	257	2	10	0	0	132	
Maryland	134	8	40	217	213	1,042	110	9	0	80	192	
Massachusetts	307	574	6	255	67	326	25	8	0	2	714	
Michigan	234	223	107	203	516	1,008	252	3	116	73	670	
Minnesota	63	150	48	83	1,626	336	253	0	13	58	746	
Mississippi	1,714	2	89	73	21	1,211	298	0	0	2	63	
Missouri	1,754	35	793	83	290	1,283	397	1	0	158	453	
Montana	38	51	24	58	205	135	74	0	1	2	112	3,000
Nebraska	87	125	131	72	520	404	168	8	5	42	284	
Nevada	17	2	2	36	10	20	10	0	0	0	27	16,000
New Hampshire	127	185	0	43	6	110	8	1	0	0	106	
New Jersey	230	54	8	300	222	649	399	26	154	14	561	
New Mexico	205	8	23	35	25	83	67	1	0	0	120	
New York	624	317	68	804	622	1,677	794	55	277	89	1,580	2,000
North Carolina	3,141	260	368	256	207	1,572	821	76	0	63	125	
North Dakota	28	113	2	31	775	149	106	0	5	21	301	
Ohio	376	335	511	178	745	1,882	584	57	3	342	872	
Oklahoma	1,258	24	338	51	84	624	186	0	0	5	113	
Oregon	87	49	167	80	124	190	125	17	0	10	117	21,000
Pennsylvania	637	105	172	460	1,644	2,008	1,115	72	10	888	1,403	
Rhode Island	95	40	0	75	13	33	7	3	0	0	142	
South Carolina	1,385	2	52	118	132	974	391	0	0	0	76	
South Dakota	57	136	18	61	429	184	124	2	26	35	194	
Tennessee	2,478	14	173	95	57	1,852	401	8	0	2	63	
Texas	3,563	15	524	286	506	2,242	606	0	0	54	526	10,000
Utah	19	8	2	16	9	18	17	0	0	0	20	451,000
Vermont	89	195	2	51	5	156	6	2	0	0	136	
Virginia	1,256	105	334	371	170	1,796	507	9	0	26	92	
Washington	178	111	106	97	254	257	173	13	4	8	172	19,000
West Virginia	784	2	155	76	61	1,545	254	0	0	10	85	
Wisconsin	142	185	34	131	1,057	414	188	4	19	168	839	
Wyoming	34	15	9	54	34	37	31	0	0	5	31	19,000
Total	35,252	5,287	7,559	6,467	14,014	36,722	12,012	674	773	2,718	15,726	842,000

* These figures are taken from the distribution study issued by the Bureau of Research and Survey of the National Council of Churches of Christ in the U.S.A., copyright in 1956. They are here used by permission of the National Council. For purposes of precise comparison, it should be noted that the survey drew most but not all of its data from denominational reports for the year 1952. In the selection given, three factors are called to the reader's attention: (1) the appendix is limited to those bodies treated in Part II; for statistical data concerning those discussed in Part III, see the text of that section; (2) in the case of the Baptists, Methodists, and Presbyterians, the figures do not include the entire denominational family (note the headings); (3) in the case of the Mormons, membership figures rather than number of churches are given, as the latter was not available by states.

Index to Authors and Titles

Works by a single author or editor are listed by his name only, not by title; all others are listed by title. Boldface type indicates the number of a Figure based on the work cited.

Index to Places

Boldface type indicates the number of a Figure.

Index to Religious Bodies

Boldface type indicates the number of a Figure.

Index to Names and Subjects

Boldface type indicates the number of a Figure.

Format by Stanley Wheatman
Set in Linotype Baskerville
Composed and bound by The Haddon Craftsmen, Inc.
Printed by Murray Printing Company
HARPER & ROW, PUBLISHERS, INCORPORATED